KU-325-529

DISPOSED OF
BY LIBRARY
HOUSE OF LORDS

Complaints Against the Police

Complaints Against the Police

The Trend to External Review

edited by

ANDREW J. GOLDSMITH

CLARENDON PRESS · OXFORD
1991

Oxford University Press, Walton Street, Oxford OX2 6DP

Oxford New York Toronto
Delhi Bombay Calcutta Madras Karachi
Petaling Jaya Singapore Hong Kong Tokyo
Nairobi Dar es Salaam Cape Town
Melbourne Auckland
and associated companies in
Berlin Ibadan

Oxford is a trade mark of Oxford University Press

Published in the United States
by Oxford University Press, New York

© The Contributors 1991

All rights reserved. No part of this publication may be reproduced,
stored in a retrieval system, or transmitted, in any form or by any means,
electronic, mechanical, photocopying, recording, or otherwise, without
the prior permission of Oxford University Press

This book is sold subject to the condition that it shall not, by way
of trade or otherwise, be lent, re-sold, hired out or otherwise circulated
without the publisher's prior consent in any form of binding or cover
other than that in which it is published and without a similar condition
including this condition being imposed on the subsequent purchaser

British Library Cataloguing in Publication Data
Complaints against the police: the trend to external review
1. Society. Role of police
I. Goldsmith, Andrew
363.2
ISBN 0–19–825257–9

Library of Congress Cataloging in Publication Data
Complaints against the policee: the trend to external review/edited
by Andrew J. Goldsmith.
Includes bibliographical references and index.
1. Police—Complaints against. 2. Police administration—Citizen
participation. I. Goldsmith, Andrew John.
HV7936.C56C66   1991   363.2'3—dc20   90–22060

Typeset by Cambrian Typesetters, Frimley, Surrey
Printed in and bound in
Great Britain by Bookcraft (Bath) Ltd,
Midsomer Norton, Avon

Preface

DAVID H. BAYLEY

The issue of police accountability is alive and well again. The decade of the 1980s has seen a spate of new writing and research about the handling of complaints against the police. This marks a return to a major theme of the 1960s when the modern period in scholarship about the police may be said to have begun (President's Commission on Law Enforcement and the Administration of Justice 1967.) Research attention on the police shifted in the 1970s to an almost exclusive concern with improving the strategic performance of the police. Now the carousel has revolved once again; but the new scholarship does more than rediscover the importance of making the police accountable. Operating in a new data-rich environment, it examines concrete experience with various complaints-processing systems, especially those that involve civilian review, and arrives at a new set of understandings about the problem.

In the 1960s, when systematic scientific attention was turned on the police for the first time, scholars discovered that police officers were not law-enforcement automata but exercised wide-ranging and often unstructured judgement about what laws to enforce, against whom, under what circumstances, and in what manner (Davis 1969; Skolnick 1966). This was called 'police discretion'. Impelled in the United States during the 1960s by the civil rights movement, attention centered on whether there were discriminatory patterns in the judgements police made. As abuses of police power became painfully evident during televised coverage of anti-Vietnam War as well as civil rights protests, many cities established civilian complaints tribunals (Chevigny 1969; Goldstein 1977). There was a great deal of heady discussion in minority communities about creating neighbourhood police forces. This was seen as a device for achieving accountability through decentralization, thereby transferring power from white-dominated governmental structures to local ethnic communities. The same idea surfaced in Great Britain in the early 1980s after the violent confrontations between police and minorities in Notting Hill, Brixton, and Toxteth. The development of civilian review of police actions in the United States was short-lived, however, as the police flexed their formidable political muscle and dismantled the civilian review boards one by one. As the Vietnam War wound down and race relations improved, interest in making the police accountable waned.

Concern with the propriety of police action, as opposed to its strategic efficacy, did not entirely die in the 1970s, but it shifted from individual to organizational behaviour, especially to the role of the police in monitoring and suppressing political dissent. Legislative bodies at many levels of government undertook investigations of the scope and character of police undercover surveillance, the creation of detailed files on the political actions of individuals, and charges of covert intimidation (Halperin 1976; American Friends Service Committee 1977; International Association of Chiefs of Police 1976). The same issues convulsed Canada at the end of the 1970s and led to the creation of the MacDonald Commission (1981).

In the 1980s interest in the handling of individual complaints against the police during routine operations quickened in most of the English-speaking democracies, notably Australia, Britain, Canada, and the United States. The British interest is easy to understand, representing the predictable aftermath of violent confrontations between police and public (Reiner 1983, 1985). Accountability in Britain became a matter of high politics with the issue of the Scarman Report (Scarman 1981). Interest in complaints against the police is less easy to understand in Australia, Canada, and the United States. It was not prompted by dramatic public events, nor by vigorous scholarly writing. Although abuses occurred and were publicized, there was not a great public outcry about an unbridled police force. None the less, governments quietly created mechanisms external to the police for receiving and investigating complaints or, alternatively, expanded the powers of existing supervisory agencies, such as ombudspersons, to include the police. My guess is that apart from a small group of scholars and police, few people are aware of how general this movement has been.

The new mechanisms for receiving and investigating complaints against the police have been created, I would argue, without a high level of political mobilization in the community. They are the products of routine rather than confrontational politics. Interestingly, more seems to have been achieved toward making the police accountable to civilian oversight in the calm 1980s than in the turbulent 1960s. This generalization applies particularly to the United States.

Why? I think that part of the explanation lies in an important and unappreciated change in the climate of opinion among the police. I am not suggesting that the police have undergone a magical character transformation. As the essays in this book demonstrate, the police continue to resent bitterly any form of civilian review. But the hostility has been less intense in the 1980s and it has been concentrated mostly among the rank-and-file. It finds voice especially through the unions and associations. Senior officers, on the other hand, have begun to recognize that civilian participation in the complaints-handling process is essential to their image of being community conscious. 'Community policing', which became the most popular slogan of the police during the 1980s, requires sympathetic and generous treatment of community input. Civilian oversight may have increased in the 1980s, therefore, because senior police officers thought it served their new strategic vision. It has gone further than it had before because the police felt they were developing it under their own auspices and for their own reasons rather than having it crammed down their throats. Obviously there is both opportunity and danger in this.

If my analysis is correct, there may be an important lesson to be learned: namely, if the issue of accountability becomes a matter of high politics, the police will destroy civilian review. I believe experience in Australia and Britain as well as the United States supports this proposition. And there is an important corollary. The tactics of reform should stress mobilizing senior officers, so that they bear the burden of convincing the lower ranks. A political confrontation with the police drives both these groups together. In effect, making accountability a matter of high politics ensures that enlightened leadership becomes hostage to reflexive rank-and-file hostility.

The way people outside the police think increased accountability may be achieved often contains a fine irony. Though reformers frequently criticize the police for having a military command system, they rather naïvely expect it to work for them if only appropriate legislation can be enacted. They are then surprised and angered when police establishments organize political counter-attacks or more cunningly sabotage implementation efforts. But the police are not as monolithic in opinion as they used to be. Enlistment must be part of the tactic of reform. Not only is this necessary politically, but, as I have argued elsewhere, the police know much more about what is wrong than outsiders and they are the only ones in a position to take effective preventive action (Bayley 1983).

My argument should not be misunderstood. The point is not that the police can be trusted to police themselves. They cannot. But there are new agendas within policing that provide opportunities for reformers who are concerned with breaking the police monopolization of the complaints process. In effect, reformers must become as clever and politically savvy as the police have been.

Police forces in all the developed democracies are talking about a new kind of professionalism that may both help and also retard the development of greater accountability. On the one hand, it involves paying attention to community opinion, not just political directives, because the law no longer seems to provide sufficient legitimacy for police action. 'Consumer satisfaction' is being discussed as an appropriate goal of policing. The new professionalism, unlike the old, stresses connection with communities rather than autonomy, civilian feedback rather than contempt for lay opinion. On the other hand, it involves granting new and undefined responsibilities to officers at the lowest ranks for devising new modes of policing in order to address persistent problems of public order. 'Community policing' and 'problem-oriented policing' both require personnel to do more than respond to successive calls for police assistance. They are supposed to diagnose underlying problems, solicit public input, formulate practical plans of action, and assist in mobilizing resources (Goldstein 1977, 1987; Eck and Spelman 1988). In doing all this, their discretion will increase. Command responsibility will no longer be concentrated among a few senior officers, but will be spread among all front-line personnel, especially among patrol and general-duties officers. Such a development will make supervision of policing much more difficult, both for people inside and outside the police. Front-line officers will be responsible for avoiding errors but also for determining priorities and the character of operations. They will be liable both for rectitude and efficacy.

The new professionalism, then, if it becomes meaningful in practice, requires accountability to be assessed along new dimensions and at more disaggregate levels in police organizations. This will expose individual police officers to more searching scrutiny. Will they be willing to accept this? Are police forces capable of doing it?

Are civilian complaints authorities prepared to expand the scope of their oversight? Indeed, should they do so?

The developments of the 1980s have transformed the scholarship about accountability by creating a data-rich environment. Most of the essays in this volume couldn't have been written a decade ago. Research has moved from demonstrating the need for enhanced accountability to evaluating the success of a host of concrete experiments. It has moved beyond horror stories. Moreover, the new scholarship contains an entirely new set of understandings about the search for accountability, that is, conclusions that are accepted as proven without the need for further discussion.

First, police cannot be trusted to police themselves. Exclusive reliance on internal investigations and discipline is foolhardy. Civilian review is essential.

Second, civilian review is critical to the legitimacy of the police. Its purpose is not simply to punish erring individuals but to demonstrate to communities that the police are responsible as an institution. Civilian review serves a demonstrative political function that is crucial to police in multi-ethnic democracies.

Third, the complaints-handling process must be separated into different catagories of problems and solutions. Specifically, many complaints can be handled satisfactorily to all concerned through conciliation. Such complaints are more misunderstandings than abuses of power. Even genuine mistakes of judgement are often not so serious that dismissal of police officers is required. In these cases expedited disciplinary hearings are sufficient to determine facts and recommend penalties, with the standard of proof being civil rather than criminal. That is, it is not necessary to establish guilt beyond a reasonable doubt, with all the procedural safeguards commonly associated. Very serious abuses of power, however, where career-threatening penalties are appropriate, may require more court-like processes and a higher standard of proof. Automatic referral of such cases to outside authority may be necessary for justice to be done and to be seen to be done. Finally, complaints should also be examined to determine recurrent problems in police operations that might lead to changes in policy, tactics, training, and supervision. Complaints can lead to preventive actions as well as specific punishments.

Fourth, because the process of ensuring accountability is complex, so too is the role of the police in it. It is not a case of either the police or not the police. For minor complaints the police might be responsible for the entire hearing process with civilian oversight directed at guaranteeing sympathetic listening and wholehearted commitment to reconciliation. Civilian review would focus here on the spirit of the enterprise, not on piecemeal investigation. In serious cases the instrumental role of civilian review would increase, although it seems likely that police would still play an important role in investigation. They would probably not, however, play an exclusive role. With respect to analysing patterns of complaints, police and civilian researchers would work together, their findings going to senior police managers for comment and solution, with civilian authorities stepping in if the police failed to take corrective action.

Fifth, police resistance to civilian oversight is more emotional than reasoned. The police have much to gain and little to lose as long as reasonable intelligence is employed in designing civilian review processes. In particular, discipline is unlikely to be undermined, as is often argued, because it is largely ineffective now. The control police fancy they will lose in enforcing the law in problematic situations will more than be made up by avoiding mistakes that jeopardize officers, members of the public, and the organization as a whole. Civilians are as capable of making judgements about the propriety of police action as they are about the guilt of defendants in criminal trials. And they have the right to do so. Police morale may actually increase under civilian review because the burden of defending the generally high quality of police performance, if this in fact is the case, will be borne by civilians.

Sixth, civilian review deflects unfounded criticism, isolates the persistently erring officer, strengthens the hands of police middle-managers, and attests to the good faith of the police. Civilian review is an important tool for managing the risks of dispersed police actions.

In conclusion, I make a prediction. This is a time of unprecedented change in policing within the developed democracies. There are many factors impelling change—strategic rethinking, more highly educated police officers, specialized career development for senior managers, technological change, and competition with the private security industry (Bayley 1989). A critical element in this mix is the growing attention to the problem of accountability, both inside and outside the police. I believe the movement toward civilian review now has institutional momentum. The question is not whether there

will be civilian review of complaints, but how soon? In the 1980s the
die was cast.

REFERENCES

American Friends Service Committee (1979) *The Police Threat to Political
Liberty* (Philadelphia: American Friends Service Committee).
Bayley, D. H. (1983) 'Accountability and Control of the Police: Some
Lessons for Britain', in T. Gennett (ed.), *The Future of Policing*
(Cambridge: Institute of Criminology, Cropwood Papers 15).
—— (1989) 'The Future of Police in the Industrial Democracies', *Bulletin of
the International House of Japan*, July 1989.
Chevigny, P. (1969) *Police Power: Police Abuses in New York City* (New
York: Random House).
Davis, K. C. (1969) *Discretionary Justice* (Urbana, Ill.: University of
Illinois).
Eck, J., and Spelman, W. (1988) *Problem-Solving: Problem-Oriented
Policing in Newport News* (Washington, DC: Police Executive Research
Forum).
Goldstein, H. (1977) *Policing a Free Society* (Cambridge, Mass.: Ballinger
Publishing Co.).
—— (1987) 'Toward Community-Oriented Policing: Potential, Basic
Requirements, and Threshold Questions', *Crime and Delinquency* 33:
6–30.
Halperin, M. *et al.* (1976) *The Lawless State: The Crimes of the US
Intelligence Agencies* (New York: Penguin Books).
International Association of Chiefs of Police (1976) *History of Police
Intelligence Operations, 1880–1975* (Gaithersburg, MD: International
Association of Chiefs of Police).
MacDonald, D. C. (1981) *Commission of Inquiry Concerning Certain Activities
of the Royal Canadian Mounted Police* (Government of Canada).
President's Commission on Law Enforcement and the Administration of
Justice (1967) *Challenge of Crime in a Free Society* (Washington, DC:
United States Government Printing Office).
Reiner, R. (1983) 'The Politicisation of the Police in Britain', in M. Punch
(ed.), *Control in the Police Organisation* (Cambridge, Mass.: MIT Press).
Reiner, R. (1985) *The Politics of the Police* (Sussex: Wheatsheaf Books).
Scarman, Lord (1981) *The Scarman Report: The Brixton Disorders* (London:
HMSO, Cmnd. 8427).
Skolnick, Jerome H. (1966) *Justice Without Trial* (New York: Wiley).

Acknowledgements

As a postgraduate student in law and criminology at the University of Toronto in the early to mid-1980s, I was able to pursue and develop an interest in police accountability. For my Masters degree, I examined the so-called doctrine of 'police independence', while my doctoral research focused upon the legal and administrative controls operating, at least in a formal sense, over rank-and-file police officers in Canadian municipal police forces. This led me to consider a series of contemporary developments in Toronto to do with external review of complaints against the police. Three scholars in particular, at the Centre of Criminology, University of Toronto, inspired and supported my intellectual pursuit of these dimensions of police accountability. These were (and are!) Richard Ericson, Clifford Shearing, and Philip Stenning.

Subsequently, while teaching in the UK, I received some travel moneys from the Nuffield Foundation to visit Canada and Australia to begin the comparative research on police complaints procedures which has become a series of articles and now this book. In addition to the Nuffield Foundation, I was encouraged in this venture by Martin Partington and Robert Reiner. Since returning to Australia, I have benefited from discussions with a wide range of people interested or involved in police complaints, but especially Ian Freckelton and Hugh Selby.

Finally, I would like to thank the contributors to this volume, and its publishers. Several of the contributors agreed to participate in this venture without ever having made the personal acquaintance of the editor, while the others agreed to contribute despite knowing him. Richard Hart of OUP has patiently tolerated a number of delays in the organization of this volume. Jan Jay of Monash University has helped with the typing and preparation. To all of these people, my thanks.

Contents

Notes on Contributors   xv

Introduction   1
Andrew J. Goldsmith

1. External Review and Self-Regulation: Police
   Accountability and the Dialectic of Complaints Procedures   13
   Andrew J. Goldsmith

2. Shooting the Messenger: The Trial and Execution of
   the Victorian Police Complaints Authority   63
   Ian Freckelton

3. Complaints against the Police in Australia: Where we
   are Now, and What we Might Learn about the
   Process of Law Reform, with Some Comments about the
   Process of Legal Change   115
   Matthew Goode

4. Police Complaints in Metropolitan Toronto:
   Perspectives of the Public Complaints Commissioner   153
   Clare E. Lewis

5. Complaints against the Police: The British Experience   177
   Mike Maguire

6. Multiple Realities, Divided Worlds: Chief Constables'
   Perspectives on the Police Complaints System   211
   Robert Reiner

7. The Police Complaints System in Northern Ireland   233
   Ivan Topping

8. Police Accountability and Civilian Oversight of
   Policing: An American Perspective   259
   Werner E. Petterson

9. Civilian Oversight of the Police Complaints Process
   in the United States: Concerns, Developments,
   and More Concerns   291
   Richard J. Terrill

   Index   323

Notes on Contributors

David H. Bayley is a professor in the School of Criminal Justice, State University of New York at Albany. He is a specialist in international criminal justice, with a particular interest in policing. His recent publications include *The New Blue Line: Police Innovation in Six American Cities* (The Free Press, 1986), with Jerome H. Skolnick, and *Community Policing: Issues and Practices Around the World* (National Institute of Justice, 1989) with Jerome H. Skolnick and a new revised edition of his book *Forces of Order: Police Behavior in Japan and the United States* will be published by University of California Press in 1991. Professor Bayley is married and has two daughters. He earned a BA degree at Denison University (1955), an MA at Oxford University (1957), and a Ph.D. at Princeton University (1960).

Ian Freckelton is a barrister practising in Melbourne, and a member of the Social Security Appeals Tribunal. Between 1986 and 1988 he was Manager of the Counsel Assisting the Police Complaints Authority of Victoria. Previously he was a Senior Legal Officer at the Australian Law Reform Commission. He has published widely in the fields of policing, criminal law, and criminology. His recent works include *The Trial of the Expert* (OUP, 1987), *Police in Our Society* (Butterworths, 1988), and *Expert Evidence: Practice and Advocacy* (Law Book Co., 1990 forthcoming).

Andrew J. Goldsmith is currently Senior Lecturer in Law in the Faculty of Law, Monash University, Melbourne, where he teaches law and social theory, criminology, and clinical legal practice. His research interests are in social and organizational theory and law, with particular focus on legal and administrative means of controlling police conduct and providing accountability of police actions. He has published several articles on these subjects as well as on criminological theory, law reform, and labour law. He is a graduate of Adelaide University, London School of Economics, and the University of Toronto, and has previously taught law and criminology in universities in England and Canada. He is a member of the editorial board of *Policing and Society*.

Matthew Goode is a Senior Lecturer in Law at the University of Adelaide. He is currently on leave advising the Attorney-General of South Australia on matters pertaining to law reform and criminal justice. When an academic, he lectures in criminal law, criminal procedure, and the conflict of laws. He is a member of the Society for the Reform of the Criminal Law, and the Australia and New Zealand Society of Criminology. He is also Mayor of the Corporation of St Peters, and is writing a book on local-government-meeting law and procedure. He is married with one child.

Clare E. Lewis, QC, is the Public Complaints Commissioner for Metropolitan Toronto, appointed in October 1985 for a five-year term. He received a BA in 1960 and an LL B. in 1963 from the University of Toronto. He has an LL M. degree from Osgoode Hall, Toronto, which he received in 1986. He is a lawyer whose practice was primarily restricted to criminal law. He was appointed Queen's Counsel in 1978 and Judge of the Provincial Court (Criminal Division) in 1979, serving until October 1985, when he resigned to become Public Complaints Commissioner. He served as President of the International Association for Civilian Oversight of Law Enforcement (IACOLE) from October 1987 to October 1989. In December 1988, Lewis was appointed Chair of the Race Relations and Policing Task Force, which reported to the Ontario Solicitor General in April 1989.

Mike Maguire is a lecturer in criminology and penology at the University of Wales, Cardiff, having recently moved from the Oxford University Centre for Criminological Research, where he was the senior research fellow for some years. His main publications include *Burglary in a Dwelling* (Heinemann, 1982), *Accountability and Prisons* (Tavistock, 1985), *The Effects of Crime and the Work of Victims Support Schemes* (Gower, 1987), and *Victims of Crime: A New Deal?* (Open University Press, 1988). He has recently completed a two-year study of police complaints procedures, and is currently working on a study of detective investigations. He is also, with two other writers, preparing a general textbook on criminology and penology. The author is particularly grateful to Claire Corbett, his collaborator on the project on which this article is based, for her assistance.

Werner E. Petterson began his career with the Community Relations Service, US Department of Justice, in 1969, specializing in police–community relations as a third-party intervenor. From its inception, Mr Petterson has been a member of IACOLE's Board of Directors, and was elected President in 1989. He has advised USA municipalities who initiated or revised citizens' complaints systems. He received a BA (1961) from Emory and Henry College in Virginia and an MA (1965) from Boston University in Massachusetts.

Robert Reiner is in the Law Department of the London School of Economics. He was formerly Reader in Criminology at the University of Bristol and at Brunel University. He is author of *The Blue-Coated Worker* (CUP, 1978), *The Politics of the Police* (Wheatsheaf Books, 1985), and numerous articles and chapters in books. He is currently completing a study of contemporary chief constables. He is review editor of *British Journal of Criminology*, co-editor of *Policing and Society*, and in 1987 edited (with Joanna Shapland) a special issue on policing of *British Journal of Criminology*. His edited volume (with Malcolm Cross), *Beyond Law and Order*, will shortly be published by Macmillan.

Richard J. Terrill teaches in the Department of Criminal Justice, Georgia State University, Atlanta, Georgia. He holds a BA in history from Wayne State University and an MA in history, an MS in criminal justice, and a Ph.D. in history from Michigan State University. In addition to an interest in civilian involvement in police complaints procedures, Dr Terrill has also been involved in publishing articles on comparative criminal justice and the history of criminal justice.

Ivan Topping is a Senior Lecturer in Law in the Department of Public Administration and Legal Studies at the University of Ulster at Jordanstown, Northern Ireland. His main interest is in policing matters and the law, especially legal constraints on police powers and activities, both locally and in the wider UK and international context. The Royal Ulster Constabulary and its operations in the troubled situation in Northern Ireland have occupied much of his attention. He teaches, writes, and researches on these and related matters for a diversity of courses and groups. He holds the degrees of LL B (Hons.) and LL M.

Introduction

ANDREW J. GOLDSMITH

THEMES OF THE COLLECTION

In its recently concluded Report, the Ontario Race Relations and Policing Task Force referred to what it saw as a widely felt need for changes in the handling of complaints against police officers in that Canadian province, commenting, 'It is patently obvious that a publicly credible, accountable and independent civilian mechanism for public complaints is basic to responding to allegations of racial intolerance or other misconduct by all police.' (1989: 184.) In the Report on London's Brixton disorders in 1981, Lord Scarman criticized the system then in place for dealing with complaints against Metropolitan police officers for its absence of a 'sufficiently convincing independent element, particularly in the consideration of the more serious complaints'. Later in his Report, Lord Scarman wrote, 'My own view is that if public confidence in the complaints procedure is to be achieved any solution falling short of a system of independent investigation available for all complaints (other than the frivolous) which are not withdrawn, is unlikely to be successful.' (1982: 182–3.) Commissioner Fitzgerald in 1989, after concluding his inquiry into police corruption and misconduct in the Australian state of Queensland, in commenting upon the complaints procedures then in place in that state, said, 'generally, the interrogation of police officers by the Internal Investigations Section has been pleasant, ineffectual and feeble . . . statements have not been closely tested and suspected police officers generally have not been subjected to any searching or subtle interrogation.' He continued: 'The policy of the Internal Investigations Section is a good indicator of the inability of police without external independent supervision to act objectively and effectively when investigating each other.' (Queensland 1989: 289.)

These statements raise a number of themes which link the essays in this volume. The overarching theme, as the subtitle indicates, is the trend in a number of countries (for the purposes of this book; Australia, Canada, Northern Ireland, England and Wales, and the United States of America) towards new forms of handling complaints by citizens against the police, forms which replace (at least to some degree) by external means the traditional internal methods by which the police have dealt with complaints against their own officers. It is possible to construe this trend in a number of ways. One might be to see it as symptomatic of the 'fall of professionalism' generally. Not just police, but also doctors, lawyers, and other occupational groups have increasingly had their 'professional' autonomy questioned and challenged in recent times. There would seem to be few events more likely to focus critical scrutiny upon the occupational practices of a particular group than allegations of misconduct by members of that group. The police, whose claims to professional status have frequently been questioned, and whose role and image have always been highly public, not surprisingly have fallen particular victim to these iconoclastic tendencies. This is hardly to say that police have acceded to this criticism or indeed that they have graciously acquiesced to any outside involvement in their affairs whatsoever; as the contributions to this book will indicate all too clearly, the extent of police defensiveness to external challenge has been remarkable, and particularly in the context of attempted reforms to the traditional ways by which police have dealt with public complaints. As the opening remarks suggest however, this defensiveness has not been without a significant price in terms of public confidence in the police and their overall legitimacy.

Another way of analysing the concerns of these essays collectively is in terms of political philosophy, and particularly in terms of changing conceptions of the democratic governance of public institutions such as the police. For many years there was a prevalent notion in most of the systems under consideration in this volume, if not all, that the police were 'above politics' and therefore immune from the usual channels of accountability. Certainly in the United Kingdom, Australia, and at least parts of Canada, there has been for some time a doctrine of constabulary independence, supported by a number of higher court decisions, in which it has been recognized that the individual police officer's primary allegiance to the law imposes certain restrictions upon the form and degree of responsibility of the police to the elected representatives (Lustgarten 1986; Jefferson and Grimshaw 1984). While having some basis in common law, this has been widely construed by senior police administrators as providing grounds for deflecting attempts from outside the police to make the police, as an organization, more accountable in terms of force policies and procedures (Lustgarten 1986). Against this background, it is possible to appreciate the extent of the threat posed by attempts to secure more independent (i.e. non-police) channels for handling public complaints against police. While more recently, police resistance to outside incursions upon their operating autonomy has tended to be justified in pragmatic terms (operational efficiency etc.) as well as legal principle (constabulary independence), community attitudes have increasingly reflected a demand for greater participation in 'public services', such as the police, which so vitally affect the lives of ordinary citizens. 'Police' and 'politics' are no longer seen by many as unrelated. Policing generally has become 'politicized' (Reiner 1985). It is therefore quite predictable that complaints about the 'sharp end of the state', and specifically proposals for more externally scrutinized or run systems for handling citizens' complaints, and the grounds upon which police resistance to changes of this nature is founded, should raise important questions of accountability and democratic participation in public bureaucracies.

Related to issues of community politics and democratic control are the problems of the legitimacy of the police institution itself and the potential role of complaints mechanisms, established at least partially independently of the police, in helping to restore public confidence in what periodically appears to many in the community to be a largely unaccountable organization. As well as notions of 'effectiveness', Scarman, Fitzgerald, and others have recognized the close relationship between complaints systems and public confidence in the police. None of the contributors to this book would see any particular version of external review of complaints as a complete antidote to the public legitimacy problems faced by many police forces, as it is too clear that difficulties in police–community relations stem from far broader questions than simply the appropriate form or degree of external involvement in complaints-handling procedures. These questions pertain to such matters as the structural location of the police in maintaining public order and the absence of anything approaching unanimity in public conceptions of the police role. Nevertheless, a fairly consistent picture to emerge from the essays in this volume is the failure by many police administrators to recognize the public confidence-building potential of working constructively with external complaints agencies. Given the scale of proved police malpractice and the demonstrable failure of the police to deal thoroughly with public complaints in some jurisdictions, senior police officers who presume that these developments can be avoided or given mere lip-service confirm the degree of isolation, and absence of *realpolitik*, in many police circles. As the essays make clear, this lack of vision is hardly confined to the senior ranks of police forces.

Last of the linking concerns of these essays, but by no means the least, is the relationship between social and legal change. Each essay charts, to some extent, the emergence of a new set of arrangements for dealing with public complaints against police, reforms which shifted control over complaints to some tangible degree from 'inside' the police to 'outside' agencies. To varying extents, the contributors document not only the processes of change, but also the processes of resistance to innovation in their jurisdictions. The collective picture from these essays of police conservatism in response to changes of this nature is not only surprising in its extent and effectiveness, but is also suggestive of some universal 'truths' about policing and the limits upon reform in this area. In terms of societal responses to legal changes generally, Watson has suggested:

The forces of inertia are so great that each time a legal change is made society reveals something important about itself. The changes should be examined from the perspective both of the rule or principle or proposition which is created and of that which is abrogated. The latter viewpoint . . . is at times especially significant since it not infrequently happens that the concern is more to abolish an existing rule than to introduce a particular reform. (1977: 135.)

Certainly in a number of the systems considered in this book, the forces of inertia described by the contributors do point to the difficulties of bringing about real change in the police. While the importance of understanding the dynamics of the law reform process in the area of police complaints has been identified previously (Goldsmith 1988), there is still an enormous amount that remains to be learned. Several essays attempt to understand these dynamics in the context of the case studies presented, not simply in terms of *what* happened in each case but also trying to assess *why* events took the form that they did and hence why certain external review 'experiments' failed.

In seeking to understand law reform, an obvious function served by a collection such as this lies in its purpose as an example of comparative scholarship. It seeks to describe and understand a variety of legal and administrative arrangements for the external handling of complaints against police. Simply through the collation and exhibition in this way of essays about different complaints systems, it is arguable that from the perspective of those involved in the operation or evaluation of particular systems, comparative scholarship encourages a 'greater degree of detachment, a greater scepticism about taking the assumptions and values underlying the. . . system for granted' (Wilson 1987: 833). If the collection achieves this goal to any appreciable extent on the question of external review, the value of the collection will have been realized. It is also fair to point out that overall, in most if not all essays, this book is not fundamentally concerned with providing 'better solutions' in any particular jurisdiction or with discovering the universally 'perfect' complaints system. Contributors will undoubtedly have their express or implicit preferences, but the principal concerns of the volume as a whole have already been outlined. It is indisputably true that 'at most times, in most places, borrowing from a different jurisdiction has been the principal way in which the law has been developed' (Watson 1977: 98). And if this collection contributes to a wider, more critical awareness of the range of potential models for handling complaints against the police, then its contribution to 'better solutions' law reform will have been sufficient (cf. Goldsmith 1988).

SOME TERMINOLOGICAL MATTERS

1. 'External', 'Independent', and 'Civilian'

The complaints procedures under consideration in this collection reflect a move away from the previous approaches to citizens' complaints in which the police assumed total responsibility for the receipt, investigation, and determination of all complaints. In essence, these approaches were adjuncts of the internal police disciplinary system, which historically has been the exclusive preserve of senior police officers, except where charges of a criminal nature had been laid. As the essays in the book make clear, the emergence of demands for forms of external review has generally occurred in the context of a perceived long-standing failure by police to respond adequately to citizens' complaints. This has resulted in reform proposals and implementation of new procedures which seek to ensure that complaints handling is not the exclusive responsibility of the police. It is specifically the ways in which this responsibility is shared with others that concern the contributors to this book. Thus the terms 'external', 'independent', and 'civilian' have been used by different writers to describe essentially similar systems. In each system so described, the following elements are material: the complaints handling occurs to some degree outside the physical and organizational confines of the police force (that is, it is external), it is accountable to an autonomous official or body (that is, it is independent), and the staff of the complaint agency is in some measure comprised of non-police personnel (that is, it is civilian). The term 'external' is intended to refer to those complaints systems in which some, if not in fact all, of these elements are present.

2. 'Review' and 'Oversight'

The term 'oversight' is commonly used in North America to encompass the sorts of external review systems considered in this book. It is defined and used, for example, by Petterson in his essay. The term 'review' however was chosen in preference because of its broader scope, implying not only the supervision by an external body of the actions of the police in handling complaints ('oversight'), but also referring, in a more active sense, to the duties of these agencies in carrying out aspects of the complaints-handling processes themselves. In this sense, what is being indicated is a more interventionist approach to the tasks of review in recent times than was practised by many of the earlier American review agencies (Littlejohn 1981; Brown 1985). In choosing one term over the other, therefore, it was simply thought that 'review' represented the better generic term to try to embrace the considerable variety of procedural approaches to the idea of outside participation in handling complaints against the police. It is not however intended to call into question the appropriateness of 'oversight' to describe, in particular, American forms of external review.

AN OVERVIEW OF THE BOOK

As indicated earlier, the essays cover recent developments in, or within, Australia, Canada, the United Kingdom (including Northern Ireland), and the United States of America. Despite the unifying themes outlined, the contributions represent a variety of approaches to, and perspectives on, the subject. Most importantly, the contributors represent a mix of academics, researchers, policy analysts, and practitioners who bring an interesting array of insights to the subject matter. The essays by Freckelton (Australia) and Lewis (Canada) provide the perspectives of persons intimately involved in the running of external review agencies; in other words, they are insiders' perspectives on the issue. From a policy perspective, Goode (Australia) and Petterson (United States of America) bring the vantage point of persons engaged over a considerable number of years in the formulation of legislative and executive policies on behalf of government, concerned with the range of possible external review models and with the evaluation of previous experiences with these models. The chapters by Maguire and Reiner (United Kingdom) contain discussions of the findings from two empirical research projects which examined the operation of the complaints scheme in England and Wales. The more 'detached' perspectives upon the subject are provided by the editor (Australia), Terrill (United States of America), and Topping (Northern Ireland), whose viewpoints derive from their academic interest in issues of police accountability and control of police misconduct.

The first essay, by the editor, is an attempt to contextualize the principal theme of the book. This is done through an examination of the socio-legal literature covering disputes and complaining behaviour and the literature which has addressed the reasons for the perceived failure of police self-regulation in the past. It thus considers the (largely unsuccessful) early experiments with external review, before discussing more recent attempts to introduce stronger forms of external review, utilizing the ombudsman model. The argument is made that external review agencies need to go beyond their present, predominantly *ex post*, individual complainant focus, to provide a range of information and policy analyses which will enable the police to adjust, at an organizational level, to the aggregated picture of policing provided by citizens' complaints. The role of these agencies is not to supplant police involvement in self-regulation, it is argued, but rather to enhance this self-regulatory potential through what the author calls an 'interpolable balance' approach.

The essay by Freckelton charts the writer's experiences as Deputy to the ill-fated and short-lived Police Complaints Authority (PCA) in Victoria. The PCA was legislatively abolished in 1988 in the face of strong police opposition in that state. The essay chronicles the rise and fall of the PCA, at the same time attempting to analyse 'what went wrong' and the forces which ensured its only fleeting existence. In the context of the law reform theme of this collection, Freckelton's account represents a detailed analysis of the forces of conservatism and inertia at work in the Australian state of Victoria, on an issue which continues to remain controversial in that state, and proffers some views on how things might have been different. Similarly, Goode's essay is primarily concerned with the emergence of the external review issue as one of the earliest, and also most persistent, law reform issues in the relatively short history of institutionalized law reform in Australia. He argues that the concern of law reformers with overhauling the complaints systems bears some relationship to wider currents of intellectual thought and social change evident not only in Australia but in other Western countries in the 1960s and 1970s. The success of the specialist law reform bodies in influencing changes to police complaint procedures is also explained in terms of the (in)capacity and (dis)inclination of the more traditional law reform channels (Parliament and the courts) to act on such issues. Goode suggests that some of the more recent techniques employed by law reform agencies in Australia, such as public hearings and widely distributed discussion papers, have played their part in influencing the state of public opinion on this question.

Lewis's contribution, to use his own words, is a review of 'the first successful Canadian effort at "civilianization" of police complaint procedures'. His perspective is that of the second Public Complaints Commissioner in Toronto. The Toronto scheme described by Lewis has survived, unlike the Victorian PCA, though not through any absence of police opposition in that city, which opposition is described and analysed by Lewis. Toronto's scheme (to be extended to the rest of the province of Ontario) is extremely interesting, not the least because of its overt attempt to balance external and internal investigation elements in the processing of complaints, and this is an issue which Lewis puts into context. He also makes some suggestions for dealing with the delicate problem confronting all external complaint review bodies—persuading the police of the benefits for them in such arrangements, without becoming co-opted by them.

The next three essays deal with recent experiences with external review in the United Kingdom. Maguire presents some of the results from a Home Office sponsored study of the operation of the latest external review scheme in England and Wales, established under the Police and Criminal Evidence Act 1985. This scheme provides for external supervision of more serious complaints, with the police continuing to investigate the vast bulk of complaints. As part of the study, the researchers interviewed police officers, complainants, and members of the Police Complaints Authority, so that Maguire's essay contains the perspectives of participants. In addition to this element, he offers an analysis of the effectiveness of the present system. Reiner's essay stems from his recent study of English chief constables, and in this contribution Reiner outlines the attitudes of the chief constables he interviewed to the PCA scheme and to problems of controlling police misconduct generally. Among the various matters to emerge from these interviews is the degree of apparent realization among senior police officers that one of the key issues in the trend towards external review of complaints is the legitimacy problems facing the police, and that it is no longer adequate to recycle well-worn police claims about the comparative 'ruthlessness' of police investigating their own, as the public is no longer so readily convinced. This, however, stands somewhat at odds with another of Reiner's findings, namely the persistence among chief constables of the 'rotten apple' theory of police misconduct. The survival of this theory certainly poses conceptual difficulties in the way of achieving the sort of external review agencies envisaged in several of the contributions to this book.

Northern Ireland's policing problems are difficult to compare with those of perhaps any other Western, English-speaking, 'democratic' regime. This makes its inclusion in this collection of particular importance. As Topping notes, the local political culture has been described as one of 'distrust and despair', of which the legitimacy problems of the Royal Ulster Constabulary play only a part, albeit an important one. Despite this however, there is an external review agency in place and it seems that the residents of Northern Ireland are much more likely to complain than residents in the rest of the United Kingdom, a fact which points to a residual legitimacy in this agency of the Northern Ireland administration, in spite of the deeply divided nature of public attitudes to many other aspects of the administration of that province. Topping's essay highlights the curious tension in which justice agencies (such as police complaints bodies) are caught, between the constraints associated with the unusual public order problems in the Province, and the constitutional and legal legacy derived from Britain and increasingly from Europe, which inclines these agencies towards some semblance of 'normal' operation.

The final two essays of the collection, by Petterson and Terrill, look at the trend to external review (or 'civilian oversight' as it tends to be called by them) in the United States of America. External review can really be traced almost exclusively to developments in American cities in the 1950s and 1960s, which despite the lack of success that these experiments had, acted as forerunners to many of the more recent ventures in external review. Petterson's concerns with a wide range of problems facing external review bodies in the United States in part reflects his involvement in IACOLE, the International Association for Civilian Oversight of Law Enforcement. Petterson locates his discussion in the context of the need for clearer police accountability, and in a similar vein to the essay by the editor, argues that complaints mechanisms should be structured to encourage a more self-conscious and critical awareness by police as to their role and tasks. Terrill examines the history of external review in the United States in order to extract lessons for the viability of present and future external review agencies. Despite the chequered nature of that history, Terrill argues that there have been ascertainable improvements in the accountability of the police in at least some cities where external review 'experiments' have been tried. He points also to the seeming paradox that in the 1980s, an otherwise highly conservative decade, the notion of external review has persisted and even grown in American cities and states. This survival is considered in terms of the changing face of minority politics, including in more recent times the public exposure of police abuses of certain minority groups. He also draws attention to the need in the United States to give greater thought to ways of formally entrenching external review mechanisms if their independence is to be preserved in future. Their traditional susceptibility to local politics in this regard stands in contrast to the usual legislative footing upon which these schemes operate in Australia, Canada, and the United Kingdom, although Freckelton's essay serves to remind us of the limits to the protection provided by legislative enactments in this area.

By concentrating on the trend to external review from a comparative viewpoint, inevitably certain aspects of police complaints procedures and the operation of external review agencies have not received detailed consideration. For example, issues such as the sorts of complaints that are made, the availability of and resort to informal conciliation procedures, problems of proof in substantiating complaints, the exact relationship between complaints and discipline, and the powers of external review agencies to investigate complaints, have tended to be addressed, in those essays in which they have been raised, only as aspects of the overall phenomenon under consideration. Nevertheless, these issues and many others are inevitably raised by the contributors in their varying approaches to this theme of external review. It is hoped that readers will be provoked to reach further into the array of issues in this field which requires much more careful consideration than is possible in one volume of essays.

REFERENCES

Brown, D. (1985) 'Civilian Review of Complaints Against the Police: A Survey of the United States Literature', in K. Heal, R. Tarling, and J. Burrows (eds.), *Policing Today* (London: HMSO).

Goldsmith, A. (1988) 'New Directions in Police Complaints Procedures: Some Conceptual and Comparative Departures', *Police Studies* 11: 60–71.

Jefferson, T., and Grimshaw, R. (1984) *Controlling the Constable: Police Accountability in England and Wales* (London: Muller).

Littlejohn, E. (1981) 'The Civilian Police Commission: A Deterrent of Police Misconduct', *University of Detroit Journal of Urban Law* 59: 5–59.

Lustgarten, L. (1986) *The Governance of Police* (London: Sweet and Maxwell).

Ontario (1989) *Report of the Race Relations and Policing Task Force* (Toronto: Ontario Solicitor General).

Queensland (1989) *Report of a Commission of Inquiry Pursuant to Orders in Council* (Brisbane: Queensland Government Printer).

Reiner, R. (1985) *The Politics of the Police* (Brighton: Wheatsheaf Books).

Scarman, L. (1982) *The Scarman Report: The Brixton Disorders 10–12 April 1981* (Harmondsworth: Penguin).

Watson, A. (1977) *Society and Legal Change* (Edinburgh: Scottish Academic).

Wilson, G. (1987) 'English Legal Scholarship', *Modern Law Review* 50: 818.

External Review and Self-Regulation:

Police Accountability and the Dialectic of Complaints Procedures

ANDREW J. GOLDSMITH

The saddest aspect of police abuses is that they defeat their avowed purposes. The rationalization for street abuses is that they create or at least maintain respect for authority. Punishment for the 'wise guy' is supposed to 'teach him a lesson', but the system of police abuses creates only contempt for authority . . . The system within which the police work is evil, for the simplest reasons: because it injures people and destroys their respect for the legal process.

Chevigny 1969: 283

INTRODUCTION

Recent events have identified a range of attempts to strike a balance in police accountability between citizens' demands for effective, external police accountability mechanisms and a police preference for internal forms of accountability, in other words, for self-regulation. The quest for this balance has emerged from the failure of the police in recent years to convince many segments of the community of their ability to investigate and prevent misconduct and corruption within their own ranks (cf. Scarman 1982; Queensland 1989). Demands for 'independent' or 'external' elements in the investigation and review of citizens' complaints against the police, while discernible over the last thirty years, have increased in recent times and show few signs of abatement. Some measure of co-existence between external and internal complaints mechanisms for the foreseeable future therefore seems inevitable.

In this Chapter, I propose to examine the relationship between external and internal mechanisms for handling complaints against the police as an aspect of changing expectations in the public culture concerning the accountability of the police. It is proposed to examine some of the reasons behind the apparent inescapability of a balance between external and internal complaints mechanisms, and to review several specific institutional responses to this perceived need.[1] A principal theme of this Chapter is the advocacy of a systemic and *ex ante* approach to the handling and analysis of complaints. This argument is consistent with the comparatively recent recognition that the causes of police misconduct are quite complex and often organizationally located (cf. Punch 1985; Shearing 1981; Skolnick 1966). Most current internal and external complaints-handling mechanisms are primarily concerned with dealing with a wide variety of complaints against police in an individualized, *ex post* way. However, given that much police work occurs within a complex setting consisting partly of formally prescribed procedures and objectives, complaints against police inevitably raise issues and problems of an *ex ante*, systemic kind requiring analysis which looks to the organizational dimensions and reform implications of police conduct subject to complaint.

The capacity and inclination of these complaints mechanisms to serve as bureaucratic monitoring systems (Hill 1981) or negative feedback systems (Dunsire 1986) in this way have been insufficiently considered in the police complaints literature. This reflects a failure to view citizens' feedback in the form of complaints as a necessary and valuable resource. 'Street-level bureaucrats' such as the police actually develop public policy while engaged in street-level inter-actions with citizens (Lipski 1980). Not only do street-level police officers frequently encounter areas of 'policy vacuum' in which there are no clear policies or procedures defined (Smith and Gray 1983; Goldsmith 1990), but also 'many of the complaints arise in areas in which there is no consensus about proper police practice' (Barton 1970: 462). It is contended in this Chapter that the relationship between citizens' complaints and the organizational needs of police

---

[1] While general considerations of police accountability are relevant, I intend essentially to ignore the respective roles played by other particular forms of police accountability, such as the courts (Clayton and Tomlinson 1987; Goode 1974; Williams 1984), the media (Freckelton 1988*a*; Skolnick and McCoy 1984), and the legislatures (Walker 1986), in order to focus upon the role of complaints-handling procedures in dealing with police misconduct. This is because these scholars and others have already dealt with them in some detail while internal and external mechanisms for handling complaints against police have received less attention.

forces is therefore as logical as it is inevitable and desirable, and that external review mechanisms for dealing with complaints against police need to take the initiative in this direction, given the failure of internal mechanisms to do so. The goal of external complaints-handling mechanisms in pursuing this approach should not be to supplant internal accountability mechanisms, but to contribute to the development of responsive police forces:

A responsive institution retains a grasp on what is essential to its integrity while taking account of new forces in its environment. To do so, it builds upon the ways integrity and openness sustain each other even as they conflict. It perceives social pressures as sources of knowledge and opportunities for self-correction. (Nonet and Selznick 1978: 77.)

It is the role of external review mechanisms in the analysis of complaints as 'sources of knowledge' and 'opportunities for self-correction' which forms a principal theme of this Chapter.

The next section explores the inevitability, and indeed desirability, of complaints against the police within the wider context of the socio-legal literature on disputes. In this way, a number of characteristics of police complaints will be revealed as not unique to policing, but rather as in many respects symptomatic of wider human relations problems arising in organizational settings. Thirdly there is an examination of the problems encountered historically by complaints mechanisms run by the police themselves, drawing upon the disputes literature and the evidence from a number of different jurisdictions concerning the difficulties emerging from the reporting, recording, investigating, and substantiating of complaints. In the fourth section, the trend towards greater external handling of police complaints is analysed, focusing upon the different forms by which demands for 'independent' and 'external' elements have been operationalized, using examples drawn from recent developments in Australia. The extent to which systemic considerations have been provided for in the complaints mechanisms examined is considered.

Finally, an argument is made for the inseparability of the police, the public, and external complaints bodies as components of the complaints process in the foreseeable future. The argument addresses two key difficulties; first, persuading the police that continued involvement by external bodies is both inevitable and beneficial and that citizens' complaints are an important source of organizationally relevant information, and secondly, determining an appropriate balance between internal and external responsibility for dealing with complaints.

WHY DO CITIZENS COMPLAIN?

In any society in which there are police, some level of complaints against police will be unavoidable. Firstly, there is the inevitability of police discretion. Many areas of police work are not subject to official rules or regulations intended to guide and limit the exercise of police discretionary authority, areas that Smith and Gray (1983) have described as 'policy vacuums'. When rules do exist, they tend to be general in character and to exhibit the problems of ambiguity and uncertainty of meaning inherent in language use, and are often accidentally or deliberately vague (Hart 1961). This problematizes the exercise of police discretion, making conflicting perceptions of 'appropriate' police work possible and even likely between police and citizens. Secondly, the often confrontational nature of police work adds to the risk of complaints:

The aggressively interventionist character of much of our criminal law thrusts the police into the role of snoopers and harassers. There is simply no way for the police to provide so much as a semblance of enforcement of laws against prostitution, sexual deviance, gambling, narcotics, and the like without widespread and visible intrusion into what people regard as their private lives. (Packer 1968: 283.)

Much of the policing described by Packer is of the 'order maintenance' kind. Such operational decisions are rarely clear-cut and often require the exercise of personal judgement by individual street-level officers as to what to do.[2] As Schuck points out, the

---

[2] Best (1981) describes a parallel situation between sellers and buyers of goods and services, drawing a distinction between 'manifest deficiencies' and 'deficiencies that are a matter of judgment'. The former usually do not involve differences of judgement—the goods were or were not delivered, the stereo does or does not work etc.—so that the issue of redress is relatively straightforward. In contrast deficiencies involving judgement will often result in differing opinions—whether or not an item is poorly designed or the result of bad workmanship, or whether the problem was caused by the buyer—resulting in greater problems of obtaining redress: 'For judgment problems, then, a disappointed buyer might reasonably anticipate that mere presentation of the facts may not establish the right to redress.' (p. 121). Police complaints are undoubtedly often vexed in nature and resisted by police because of the high number of 'judgement problems' arising in police work.

decision-making milieu of street-level officers is fraught with risks and constraints of various kinds:

Street-level officials are exposed to litigation-related risks that flow from systematic features of their work. These features include: the character of their interactions with the public; their ambiguous and conflicting goals; their duty to act; the risk of harm from official decisions; their risk of error; the scope of their discretion; and the external constraints upon their decisions. (1983: 60.)

While the appropriateness of police responses to particular situations is open to different interpretations, their significance is exacerbated by disparities of power which typically characterize many relations between police officers and citizens. The police officer has at her disposal the ability to embarrass, humiliate, and even harm the citizen. In addition, a police tendency to use stereotypes in carrying out their duties naturally inclines police patrols to focus their attention upon those groups within the community which are the subject of negative stereotypes. Unfortunately, stereotypes inevitably result in a significant number of 'false positive' interactions, that is, police-initiated contacts with citizens in which the police officer's reason for initiating the contact proves groundless. Even if groundless, the fact of the contact itself may provoke an outburst, giving rise to a more 'account-able' response by the officer. In either event, the risks to police–community relations from wide-scale negative stereotyping have been amply demonstrated in recent times by the Brixton riots in London (cf. Scarman 1982).

The circumstances just outlined are only explanations as to why dissatisfaction with police action can arise. Such grievances may or may not result in formal complaints (Felstiner, Abel, and Sarat 1981; Nader 1984), an issue which will be addressed shortly. It is, however, clear that a failure to complain does not indicate an absence of resentment or dissatisfaction. It seems at least likely that our tendency to be dissatisfied is quite fundamental. Hirschman has suggested that 'disappointment is a central element of the human experience' (1982: 11). If this is even partly true, it is quite unfair and pointless to blame the police for all citizen dissatisfaction with their behaviour. Human nature itself, and the problems associated with the use of bureaucracies for the delivery of services, are important considerations in any explanation of, and adequate response to, the problems of human dissatisfaction and grievance:

'No matter how well a society's basic institutions are devised, failures of some actors to live up to the behaviour which is expected of them are bound to occur, if only for all kinds of accidental reasons.' (Hirschman 1970: 1.)

It is also useful to realize, in response to dissatisfaction or complaint, that there are few, if any, easy solutions. As several dispute-resolution scholars have shown, 'relief from trouble is uncertain, contingent and costly' (Felstiner, Abel, and Sarat 1981: 653). Externally imposed pressures frequently only compound the potential for dissatisfaction with official responses to public problems: 'Generalized ignorance and uncertainty about what one is after exist typically when motivation to solve a problem is outrunning understanding and this situation arises in turn, when there are pressing public demands to "do something" about a poorly understood problem.' (Hirschman 1981: 221.) These dimensions to the issues raised by complaints against the police are too frequently ignored, as a result of which unrealistic expectations can be placed not only upon complaints-handling mechanisms but also upon the ability of the police to respond to complaints. There is a real need generally to understand better the limits of official agencies' abilities to identify sources of dissatisfaction and to respond effectively to them.

Another relevant consideration concerns an apparent assumption in some quarters that complaints are in some way *pathological* and that the ideal system would generate no complaints. This assumption inclines agencies to respond in a 'fire-brigade' manner, dealing punitively with complaints as isolated, individualized problems. In the light of what has been said about the inevitability, and organizational aspects, of complaints, there would seem to be a need to acknowledge that complaints in many instances will be *symptomatic* of more pervasive human relations and organizational problems which require careful systemic responses by the police forces concerned. In the next section, a failure in many instances by police administrators and relevant public officials to appreciate these aspects of citizens' complaints will be implicated in the discussion of the reasons for the widely perceived failure of internally run complaints procedures.

It is also possible, of course, to view complaints as profoundly *normal* and *democratic*. The expression of dissent and dissatisfaction in the form of complaints may be seen as a form of 'micro-politics', the expression by citizens of preferences for one outcome or state of affairs over another. On this analysis, 'disappointment is the natural counterpart of man's [sic] propensity to entertain magnificent vistas and aspirations' (Hirschman 1982: 23). Given that policing is likely to remain a contentious topic, complaints need to be seen not simply as *threats* to existing policies and procedures or individual officers but more importantly, as *opportunities* for re-examination of organizational policies and practices, particularly in terms of their community-relations dimension, of immense potential benefit to the police as well as to the public. The issue then is not whether or not complaints should be discouraged or tolerated, but whether there are adequate mechanisms and resources to ensure that citizens' complaints are articulated fully and that the information provided by complaints is systematically collected and analysed for the administrative lessons it provides for the future organization and practice of police work. The next section examines the reasons for the widespread failure of internal complaints-handling mechanisms to deal adequately with complaints, in particular to render police forces 'responsive institutions' (Nonet and Selznick 1969).

WHY HAS INTERNAL REVIEW FAILED SO FAR?

The widely attributed failure of internal complaints mechanisms reflects a loss of public confidence in the way in which the police have responded previously (or more to the point, not responded) to expressions of citizen dissatisfaction and to evidence of misconduct more generally within their own ranks. As the Fitzgerald commission of inquiry into official corruption and police misconduct in the Australian state of Queensland observed recently, this phenomenon has taken on global proportions:

To a large extent, attempts all over the world to combat police misconduct locally [i.e. internally] have revealed similar and recurrent problems: police culture, lack of effective control of internal investigative procedures, lack of investigative resources, organizations and procedures which inhibit honest police, and lack of public confidence in the Police Force's ability to investigate complaints against its members. (Queensland 1989: 285.)

Citizen attitudes towards police self-regulation have been compared with the situation of a chicken obliged to complain to 'one fox about the treatment he has received in the chicken coop from another fox' (Victoria 1978: 102). Public scepticism is amply justified by the findings of numerous official commissions of inquiry into police misconduct and related matters (e.g. Queensland 1989; Canada: Maloney 1975; UK: Scarman 1982; US: Task Force 1967). That lack of public confidence in police self-regulation is observable and significant at each of the four principal stages of processing a complaint against the police: (1) the *making* of a complaint by a citizen; (2) the *recording* of the complaint by police; (3) the *investigation* of the complaint by police; (4) the *response* by the police or other authorities in the case of a substantiated complaint.

(1) Why are Complaints not Made?

The decision not to voice dissatisfaction is one which has interested a range of scholars, including economists (e.g. Hirschman 1970) and legal anthropologists (e.g. Nader and Shugart 1980; Nader 1984; Felstiner, Abel, and Sarat 1981), while criminologists have been concerned for many years with the underreporting of crimes, a phenomenon known as the 'dark figure' of crime (cf. Hood and Sparks 1970). While undoubtedly some people consciously *decide* not to report certain negative experiences to authorities, it is also the case that objective grounds for grievance will not always be perceived by their 'victims' as cause for complaint. Perhaps due to ignorance, limited intelligence, or fraud, 'victims' will not interpret their experiences negatively so as to activate a 'sense of entitlement' (Felstiner, Abel, and Sarat 1981: 643). Others will make a conscious choice not to complain, instead deciding to 'lump' it, for reasons of cost (Best 1981: 39; Galanter 1974), convenience, embarrassment, frustration with the system, or fear of recriminations (Felstiner, Abel, and Sarat 1981; Hood and Sparks 1970).

Systematic evidence of the scale of non-reporting and the associated reasons is, not surprisingly, difficult to obtain. However in a recent public survey in London, in which evidence of widespread underreporting of complaints about police use of stop-and-search powers emerged, the 'most common reason given for not complaining . . . was a lack of faith in the police complaints system' (London Policing Strategy Unit 1987). What has to be remembered is that in many, if not even most, instances these perceptions held by citizens are based on personal experience or local knowledge and cannot simply be dismissed as the misperceptions of isolated crackpots and 'anti-police' elements (cf. Freckelton 1988*b*). This interpretation has been borne out by the findings of numerous official inquiries into police misconduct (e.g. Victoria 1978: 103; Queensland 1989: 289; Scarman 1982).

Failure to complain should raise obvious concerns. For one thing, as Nader put it, 'it takes skill to complain' (1980: 39). Complaints handlers need to be alert to the disincentives, barriers, and difficulties associated with lodging complaints if their function is to be anything more than window-dressing. Moreover, they cannot pretend that by failing to do so, they will avoid the 'costs' of citizen dissatisfaction, otherwise described by Felstiner as the 'long shadow of avoidance' (1974: 79–80).

These costs can be assessed in terms of loss of public co-operation, trust, and confidence. The scale of unreported grievances is therefore highly significant. As suggested earlier, evidence can be difficult to find, except when entire police forces are indicted for having a 'culture of misconduct', as recently happened in the case of the Queensland police force (Queensland 1989: 200). The evidence from the area of consumer behaviour (Best 1981) and the anthropology of disputes (Nader and Shugart 1980) points to underreporting as a pervasive phenomenon. Given the legal and quasi-legal 'resources' available to police officers to deter would-be complainants from filing complaints (threats and use of 'verballing', 'fit-ups', etc.), it seems likely that underreporting of police-related grievances is significantly greater than in the case of consumer grievances (Best 1981). A failure by complaints-handling mechanisms to address these issues will not only affect the mechanism's ability to deal with citizen dissatisfaction and collate information of systemic significance, but also do little or nothing to address the public legitimacy problems faced by the police or the issue of accountability. Ironically, it seems probable that citizens least often complain directly to the police when public confidence in the police is low; in other words when there is most *need* for complaints to be gathered and analysed systematically. In such circumstances, external agencies seem a necessary alternative means for receiving complaints for the purposes of remedying complainant injustices and addressing issues of systemic reform.

(2) Why are Complaints not Recorded?

Police forces have long exhibited a degree of laxity towards the recording of complaints, including the provision of adequate procedures and resources for keeping such records (e.g. Littlejohn

1981: 24). Part of the explanation almost certainly is that police probably make better law enforcers than desk clerks. But the causes of this laxity are much more entrenched and it would seem to reside largely in the organizational practices and culture of police forces (Shearing 1981; Punch 1983). It is difficult otherwise to account for either the persistence or the pervasiveness of police resistance to recording complaints.

An example is provided by events in the Australian state of Victoria. A Report on the state of the Victoria Police in 1971 by a visiting English police inspector, Sir Eric St Johnston, revealed that at that time systematic records of complaints were not compiled by the police, and that at the district level, superintendents exercised wide discretion in reporting complaints to headquarters, and many so-called minor ones were routinely not notified (Victoria 1971: 170). A tightening up of recording and reporting procedures was recommended, including the keeping of a complaints record book at each district office. Yet in 1976, only five years later, recording procedures were again attacked in the Report of the Beach Board of Inquiry (Victoria 1978), which found that prior to mid-1975 (when a new internal investigation section was set up), 'there was no satisfactory avenue through which a citizen could lodge a complaint against police misbehaviour' (106). Damningly, the Report stated: 'The Board's inquiries revealed that Police not only fail to record complaints when complaints are made, but go further and insert a direct "No" in the column appropriate to the recording of a complaint when one has been made; further, false entries are made in the Register.' (101.) Despite various administrative and legal changes since 1975 affecting the recording of complaints, police responses to persons wishing to make complaints have again been the subject of official criticism (Victoria 1987) and, more recently, a team of investigative journalists anonymously polling suburban police stations in Melbourne found that very few police officers approached indicated any familiarity with complaint-recording procedures (Melbourne *Age* 1989).

The explanation for this organizational reticence towards would-be complainants is widely attributed to the effects of the 'police culture', particularly the group loyalty police officers show towards other officers (Reiner 1985), and a consequent reluctance to assist citizens in the filing of complaints against fellow officers (e.g. Queensland 1989). The Fitzgerald Inquiry found that this attitude would sometimes take the form of actually obstructing persons who wished to report a police officer (Queensland 1989: 200). Similarly the Beach Inquiry discovered evidence of a 'them against us' syndrome, 'an attitude of police mind, which is affronted by the impertinence of the civilian in making a complaint at all and which then in a defensive reflex classifies him as a trouble-maker, or as being anti-Police, or motivated by malice or ill-will' (Victoria 1978: 106–7). Evidence from the United Kingdom points to the existence of a similar phenomenon there (Box and Russell 1975; Russell 1976).

Significant here is the systemic nature of police attitudes and responses to would-be complainants and what they indicate about relationships with the public. As discussed earlier, the nature of police work undoubtedly does cause police officers to be more exposed to the risk of complaints, perhaps more than any other occupation, and defensiveness in these circumstances is scarcely surprising and even natural. Moreover cynicism and resentment among those subject to complaint are not confined to the police ranks as the literature on disputes shows (e.g. Nader and Shugart 1980: 10). But what is regrettable specifically about the police response is its consequences for police–community relations. It has been noted in a number of jurisdictions that in such circumstances the police are prone to being excessively defensive. The challenge is to break this pattern of response: 'if, . . . [the police] cease thinking of themselves as a brotherly band beleaguered by citizens (and, of course, other hostile forces) and start thinking of themselves as public servants within a specialized law-administration organization— the gap between them and the community they serve should begin to close' (Gelhorn 1966: 205).

While police are probably correct when they accuse some would-be and actual complainants facing criminal charges of seeking to complain simply for revenge or tactical reasons, it is surely even less contentious that the police offend in some way far more citizens than those they justifiably investigate and charge. While the complaints of the latter should never be ignored, the police certainly ignore the complaints of the former (i.e. law-abiding citizens) at their peril. If police officers fail to record complaints, there is no other obvious capacity within the police organization itself to account through its administrative structure or to external review bodies for actions the subject of grievance by citizens. Moreover, it arguably indicates a serious lack of commitment to police–community relations. Where this is the situation, alternative recording arrangements outside the police organizational structure become inevitable.

(3) What is Wrong with Internal Investigations?

While in theory the case for police self-regulation seems overwhelming (cf. Bayley 1983, Goldstein 1967), the tide of recent experience, and expert and public opinion has been strongly against exclusive reliance upon self-regulation. Not surprisingly, both senior and junior police officers have tended to prefer self-regulation, for reasons not the least of which is the alleged superiority in access and investigative expertise in dealing with infractions internally (Rippon 1984: 9; Doyle 1976: 73; Kirby 1976: 18; Terrill 1982). Such an approach to discipline correlates closely with the aspirations of those officers who regard policing as a profession, in which regulatory autonomy is accorded as a measure of public trust and esteem (Hudson 1971: 518). Unfortunately, this preference has also come to be identified less nobly with the 'police culture' in those police forces in which institutionalized corruption and misconduct have been found (e.g. Queensland 1989). In these situations, self-regulation has served to obscure the amount and significance of misconduct. It is specifically public lack of confidence in the ability of the police to investigate themselves in the context of complaints on which recent evidence in a number of jurisdictions has been overwhelming and indicative of a serious malaise in police accountability. As one scholar has noted, 'this fact has been cited by every commission in every country that had examined complaint procedures' (Terrill 1980: 44). While the explanation for public distrust must be traced at least in part to the 'police culture' and its associated norms of 'loyalty' and secrecy, two particularly disturbing indicators of this malaise in complaints investigation have been the level of misconduct discovered by official commissions of inquiry, rather than through internal disciplinary and complaints mechanisms, and the low substantiation rates for complaints investigated by internal investigation units. Both pose questions concerning the quality of internal investigations of complaints.

Disturbingly, evidence of wide-scale police misconduct, challenging directly and indirectly the credibility of police internal investigations, is obtainable for virtually any jurisdiction one chooses. In London, Smith and Gray startlingly concluded on the basis of an extensive observational study of police work, 'we believe that police officers will normally tell lies to prevent another officer from being disciplined or prosecuted, and this is the belief of senior officers who handle complaints and discipline cases' (1983: 581). In Queensland, the Fitzgerald Inquiry found that the state police force was 'debilitated by misconduct, inefficiency, incompetence, and deficient leadership' (Queensland 1989) and that 'both honest police and citizens who report police misconduct risk serious detriment with little prospect of appropriate action' (p. 204). At times, the evidence has been overwhelming and even unsolicited. In his Report for the Royal Commission of Inquiry into Drug Trafficking, Mr Justice Stewart commented, 'this Commission, while conducting limited inquiries on specific terms of reference, are faced with a substantial amount of material indicating malpractice by police ranging from infractions of the disciplinary code to gross examples of premeditated criminal conduct' (Australia 1983: 571). In view of the media publicity that these sorts of revelation almost always receive,[3] the integrity of the internal investigation process in the eyes of many citizens is inevitably impugned either directly or as part of a general distrust of police conduct stemming from such revelations.[4]

While the inadequacies surrounding police complaint-recording practices have already been noted, police ability to substantiate complaints has scarcely inspired greater public confidence in police internal investigations (e.g. Littlejohn 1981: 15). Lustgarten examined the substantiation figures for the London Metropolitan Police: 'In 1984, 8 per cent of all complaints were substantiated. *Not one* complaint involving harassment, racial discrimination, false evidence or perjury was found substantiated; the same was true in 1983. Only 20 of 1410 complaints of assault—1.5 per cent—were substantiated.' (1986: 154.) As he goes on to suggest, 'Either those who do bother to complain are all liars, or there is something wrong with the system.' Similarly, in an official inquiry by a former federal ombudsman into internal investigations in the state of Victoria, the substantiation

---

[3] The public hearings of the Fitzgerald Commission into official corruption and police misconduct in the Australian state of Queensland (Queensland 1989) received widespread publicity by the media for a period of well over a year. At times, events resembled a soap opera, as allegations concerning prominent public figures and senior police officers became public knowledge. Although not televised, daily re-enactments of parts of the Commission's proceedings would appear on national and local news and current affairs programmes.

[4] For the results of UK public surveys dealing with confidence in police self-regulation, see Brown (1987) and Smith and Gray (1983). The latter also deals with public perceptions of police conduct generally.

figures were considered and the following analysis offered: 'From a complainant's stand point I have not heard of a lower success rate anywhere [2.3%]. Were the results to be understood publicly, it would add fuel to the argument that it is a waste of time to make a complaint of assault against the police in the absence of substantial, independent, corroborative evidence. (Victoria 1987: 22.)

Low substantiation rates can be explained in a number of ways. The overall system of criminal procedure in common-law countries is partly responsible, premised as it is upon police-controlled investigations of crimes, and even police-controlled prosecutions in some countries (e.g. Australia).[5] The fact that police–citizen contacts outside the police station environment are frequently 'low visibility' encounters (Goldstein 1960), presents many complainants with insuperable evidential difficulties if they file a complaint. The pressures at this stage either to withdraw the complaint or to accept the inevitability of an 'insufficient evidence' determination to the investigation, are very strong, and are reinforced by the situational ability of police to 'set up' or in other ways 'neutralize' the complainant. It has to be remembered that very often, the complainants are 'one-shot players' (Galanter 1974), while inevitably the police are 'repeat players' in systems in which they have tended to be prosecutor, judge, and jury.

Other relevant factors identified have included the inadequate provision of resources and the lack of investigative zeal within internal investigation units. For example, in Queensland the Internal Investigation Section of the Queensland police force was described by Commissioner Fitzgerald as 'an artifice' with 'no capacity to carry out surveillance of other police' (Queensland 1989: 288). The section was found to be carrying high case-loads, with few facilities for the conduct of investigations and that it was only recently that any specific training had been given to the members of the section (p. 288).

A lack of investigative zeal might be expected given the resources situation just described and the unsympathetic nature of the 'police culture' in many police forces. Another possible explanation is the attributed reluctance of senior officers to investigate complaints

---

[5] It is not uncommon in Australian lower criminal courts (known generally as magistrates' courts) for the police to conduct the prosecution of charges before the court. Thus, police power over the earlier stages of the criminal process in these cases is considerable. More serious prosecutions in the higher courts are conducted by lawyers.

against their subordinates for fear of the prejudicial effects upon staff relations and force morale (Australia 1983: 570). However, Hugh Selby, former head of the Victorian Police Complaints Authority (PCA) saw the failure of internal investigations in Victoria as the result of an inadequately defined mandate: 'The fundamental causes of the failure may be found in the lack of any coherent, logical statement of principle by police as to the purposes of police internal inquiries, appropriate methods to achieve these purposes, and obligations owed to interested parties, which include complainant, police complained of, PCA and parliament.' (Selby 1988: 230.) The failure of the same internal investigation department to give sufficient attention to the needs of complainants was also the subject of rebuke by an independent inquiry, which observed that the existing internal administrative procedures 'emphasise too much the convenience of the Force' (Victoria 1987: 32).

In the absence then of adequate resources, investigatory zeal, or a clear mandate, what exactly are these internal investigation units engaged in doing? A former Assistant Ombudsman for New South Wales accused the Internal Affairs Branch of that state's police force of being 'more concerned with public relations than [with] finding the truth of things' (Nelson 1986: 233). The Fitzgerald Inquiry could find virtually nothing positive to say about the role played by the Queensland police Internal Investigations Section. Consequently, its conclusion was scathing:

The Internal Investigations Section has been woefully ineffective, hampered by a lack of staff and resources and crude techniques. It has lacked commitment and will and demonstrated no initiative to detect serious crime . . . The Section's efforts have been token, mere lip service to the need for the proper investigation of allegations of misconduct. The Internal Investigations Section has provided warm comfort to corrupt police. It has been a friendly, sympathetic, protective and inept overseer. It must be abolished. (Queensland 1989: 289.)

Internal investigations, therefore, have been the target of sustained criticism across a range of police forces in different jurisdictions. The evidence considered so far in this Chapter challenges the conventional wisdom of police administrators that internal investigators are 'necessary to preserve the morale, effectiveness, and efficiency of a law enforcement organization' (Hudson 1971: 521). It points to the difficult problems associated with setting up an internal investigation process which can be relied on to be fair and effective. Its resolution, however, is critical, as Terrill points out: 'The investigatory stage of any complaint procedure is central to reducing the criticism of the entire process, because it does influence both the integrity of the steps that precede it and those that follow.' (1983: 620).

The failure of the police in many instances to provide a credible internal complaints investigation process serves to underline the need for an external investigative body if the integrity of public complaints procedures is to be re-established. As any reform concerned with public legitimacy entails, what is at issue is not merely the question of *effective* complaint investigation, but that such investigations are *credible* precisely to those groups in which 'legitimacy levels' are low. That numbers of these groups may often find themselves the target of police attentions does not detract from, but rather underlines, the importance of adequate complaints investigations. As Hogg and Findlay argue: 'The real test of police accountability and responsiveness to the community must lie in their relationships with those with whom they have the most frequent contact, groups who, currently tend to be the least favoured by police stereotypes and working images.' (1988: 52.) Poor internal investigation of complaints does nothing to restore the police relationship with these groups; for them, such investigations are 'incredible'. Therefore if external review agencies equipped with investigative powers can go some way to restoring the credibility of police internal complaints procedures, this will bring about something which in many cases the police themselves have not achieved.

(4) What Follows a Substantiated Complaint?

For the very small percentage of citizens whose complaints are investigated and upheld, the 'game' is still not over. The following is a summary of what occurs in the Victorian police force:

Where a complaint against a member is substantiated and charges are recommended the file is referred to the Assistant Commissioner (IID [Internal Investigation Department]). *If* he considers the charges are made out and *it is appropriate* to proceed he will forward it with a recommendation to the Deputy Commissioner (Administration) who will decide *what action, if any*, should be taken (e.g. charges) and *whether* the member should be suspended or transferred in the interests of the efficiency of the Force. (Walsh-Buckley 1989: 122, my emphases.)

In other words, the substantiation of complaints of itself does not ensure that the relevant officer involved will be formally disciplined or punished. Nor does the individualistic focus of these procedures ensure that appropriate systemic changes will be forthcoming.

In most police forces where charges of some kind are being considered, internal disciplinary charges are preferred to criminal charges (Goldstein 1977: 215; Queensland 1989: 289). Yet analysis of available figures, in the case of the Victorian police, would suggest that the disciplinary process fails to deal firmly with charges of misconduct, even the more serious ones. For example in 1986–7, of the 174 charges dealt with by the Victoria Police Discipline Board (that is, the more serious charges), exactly half the charges (50 per cent) were either withdrawn or dismissed, while another 10 per cent of charges were 'adjourned' i.e. no substantive result was obtained. The equivalent figure in 1987–8 was 58 per cent, with another 8 per cent adjourned. In total then, in 1986–7, 60 per cent of all charges referred to the Board resulted in no prejudicial outcome for the police officers charged, while the equivalent figure for 1987–8 was 66 per cent. In 1986–7, of the remaining 69 charges for which some formal sanction was imposed, over half (37) resulted in fines, while nearly a quarter resulted in reprimands. In 1987–8, of the 46 charges which resulted in some form of negative outcome, 18 resulted in fines and 7 in reprimands. In that year 12 of the charges concerned one police officer, who was dismissed (Walsh-Buckley 1989: App. G).

The issue of sanctions raises indirectly a very basic question: what should the philosophy and objectives of the complaints system be? It is the case, certainly for internal investigations and reviews, that the complaints procedure is 'grafted' directly on to the disciplinary system. Whenever a citizen's complaint has resulted in an investigation leading to discipline, the question is whether the principal objective is to satisfy the individual complainant or to assist the police administration in monitoring the conduct of its officers (Hudson 1972: 431). Some observers have even doubted whether any such objectives have been clearly defined (Selby 1988), while the evidence considered points to an absence of a practical resolution, and if anything, to a failure by internal investigation on both counts. Given an uncertainty of objectives, the appropriateness of the sanctions imposed by internal disciplinary mechanisms is open to question. In particular, it may be asked whether individualistic, punitive (i.e. *ex post*) measures are justifiable or the most appropriate outcome in many cases, especially in the more minor complaints of incivility and failure to act (Barton 1970: 457). Furthermore some cases might warrant compensation as a supplementary remedy to punishment or systemic reform, if not as the only outcome (see Victoria 1988: chap. 3). These philosophical issues have received little express attention in the police complaints literature. Moreover there would seem to be little or no evidence of police administrators addressing themselves to these questions.

The failure of traditional approaches to police complaints procedures to concern themselves with systemic reform (i.e. *ex ante*) issues was the subject of comment by Lord Scarman in his inquiry into the Brixton riots. Scarman regretted the 'insufficient discussion of policy matters arising from complaints' (1982: 182). Commissioner Fitzgerald similarly pointed to the 'ad hoc and reactive' nature of the internal complaints investigation system in Queensland, and to its failure to examine trends and identify particular sources of complaints within the police force (Queensland 1989: 289). A leading American police scholar, Herman Goldstein, has also criticized the traditional approach:

the narrow concentration on wrongdoing commits the police to waiting for complaints to be filed. It commits them to focusing their attention on investigations, disciplinary procedures and sanctions. Both police and public become so preoccupied with identifying wrongdoing and taking disciplinary action against errant officers that they lose sight of the primary objective of control which is to achieve maximum conformity with legal requirements, established policies, and prevailing standards of propriety. This objective is far more likely to be attained by fostering an atmosphere in which the police conform because they want to conform, rather than out of fear of the consequences if they do not. (1977: 160.)

The challenge therefore, at the 'sanctions end' of the police complaints procedure, is to reorient the current, essentially exclusive, focus on the 'micro-justice' concerns of past wrongdoings by individual officers, to include a 'macro-justice' perspective in which issues of compensation and punishment are considered alongside the aggregated evidence of patterns of wrongdoing and undesirable behaviour, and the need for systemic and policy reforms is expressly addressed.

In the absence of police initiative on this issue, the evidence points to the need for an external agency to take up the challenge. Commissioner Fitzgerald concluded that 'it is apparent that the Queensland Police Force cannot, in general, be made responsible for the control of a system to address official misconduct' (Queensland 1989: 299–300). Similar findings, replicated in reports of official inquiries into police practices in other jurisdictions (e.g. UK: Scarman 1982; Ontario: Maloney 1975), point to the conclusion that in many jurisdictions in recent years, citizens have had no justifiable basis for trusting internal mechanisms for dealing with complaints. By elimination, at least for the foreseeable future, the primary repository for citizens' concerns about police malpractices and a major guarantor of public trust must lie substantially outside the organizational structure of police forces.

OMBUDSMEN AND OTHERS: MOVES TOWARDS 'INDEPENDENT' REVIEW

Inadequate internal complaints mechanisms not only undermine public trust and confidence in the police; arguably they are also socially inefficient. Nader has observed that grievance often 'feeds alienation, anomie, frustration, anxiety and kinship friction, and is an enormous waste of money, time and resources for individuals and the economy in general' (1980: 7). Felstiner, Abel, and Sarat have similarly observed: 'People never fully relegate disputes to the past, never completely let bygones be bygones . . . there is always a residuum of attitudes, learned techniques, and sensitivities that will, consciously or unconsciously, color conflict.' (1981: 639.) An inadequate complaints mechanism only compounds the social inefficiencies associated with citizens' grievances. Failing the provision of credible internal mechanisms by police, external mechanisms are required to deal with these unresolved feelings as much as possible.

Already it should be clear that the distinction between internal and external mechanisms for dealing with police complaints corresponds closely with that between organizationally dependent (i.e. upon police control and authority) and organizationally independent (i.e. from police control and authority) mechanisms. Ironically, while the latter type of agency is usually located outside a police force, nevertheless some level of co-operation from within the force is necessary if it is to operate effectively. In this sense, complete independence of investigation and review of complaints is a myth.[6] It is also possible to have a measure of independence in internal mechanisms for handling complaints, when for example, a specialist complaints investigation unit is established within a police force, but outside the main organizational hierarchy (Goldsmith 1988). Questions of degree are therefore significant when considering the range of independent mechanisms for handling complaints against police and their acceptability to different groups within the community.

While complete independence of investigations may be illusory, and entirely external scrutiny of complaints impossible, the symbolic significance of these approaches for police self-regulation has resulted in enormous resistance from police and other lobby groups to all forms of external review. The road to independent review of police misconduct is littered with the carcasses of civilian review boards (Hudson 1971, 1972) and specialist police ombudsmen (Victoria 1988), the victims of concerted oppositional alliances of politicians, police administrators, and police unions (Brown 1985; Littlejohn 1981). But of course corresponding with the 'success' of this form of police politics in a number of countries (including Australia, Canada, and the United States), is, ironically, the earlier described failure of the very same politicians and police to maintain public confidence in the impartial, effective investigation and correction of police misconduct by the police themselves. The trend to 'independent' review mechanisms in the police complaints field will be examined in order to focus upon the principal features of the attempts to bring about more independent handling of police complaints. In particular, the phenomena of citizen review boards and more recently, police ombudsmen, will be considered as these have been the two main approaches to external review of police complaints since the 1960s. The more recent examples will be taken from Australia, where a number of different approaches have been attempted. The provision made in these mechanisms for dealing with complaints from an *ex ante* as well as *ex post* perspective will be considered.

---

[6] Somewhat ironically, while the police have tended to be critical of 'independent' forms of outside scrutiny in the area of complaints, they have actively pursued and stressed the importance of their own independence from various forms of political control. The symbolic significance of 'independence', while often considerable, is also quite variable. For consideration of the police 'independence' phenomenon generally, see Lustgarten (1986).

Citizen Review Boards

The background to the most prominent civilian review board (CRB) 'experiments' lies in the urban disorders and political protest movements of the late 1950s and 1960s in America (Brown 1985). Given the wide variety of police forces and levels of political organization in America, it is not surprising that the forms taken by CRBs have also varied considerably, so that it is somewhat difficult to generalize. None the less a broad definition of CRBs is offered by Littlejohn: 'Civilian review boards are composed of citizens who examine complaints against police officers and determine whether such complaints have merit. After reviewing investigations, review boards usually have only the limited authority to recommend punishment, or further investigation by the police department. The commissioner or chief retains full control over internal discipline.' (1981: 8). Significant variations between CRBs have included whether there is an independent investigation unit within the police force, the nature of the relationship between the CRB and the police department (whether it is concerned with force policies as well as complaints), and whether it receives complaints directly from the public or instead has them passed to it by police. Despite these variations, it has been suggested that each CRB attempt sought in some way or other to 'inject greater fairness into the complaint process, provide redress for complainants, and maintain desired standards of police behaviour' (Brown 1985: 143).

Overall, the CRB 'experiments' of the 1960s were considered to be failures. No one could have anticipated the degree of animosity with which they would be regarded by the police unions. One Fraternal Order of Police pamphlet in the 1960s portrayed CRBs as 'anti-law and order' and even as a 'secret weapon of the Communist Party' (Gelhorn 1966: 172). The intense political lobbying that characterized the opponents of CRBs ultimately outclassed their supporters (Littlejohn 1981; Brown 1985), with the result that they declined by the late 1960s, leading Littlejohn to observe in 1981 that 'no independent civilian review board operates in any major American city' (p. 11).

The grounds for police union opposition to the concept, and the criticisms offered by various police scholars, are significant for together they point to the challenge of establishing a complaints mechanism which is legitimate in the eyes of police and public alike (Hudson 1972; Gelhorn 1966). Hudson argues that police opposition stemmed from the perceived threat to police professionalism, and in particular the view that 'jurisdiction over the discipline of members of a police force belongs exclusively with the command structure' (1972: 521). Even though the powers of the CRBs in the 1960s were overwhelmingly advisory only, nevertheless the idea of external scrutiny of any kind was deemed 'repugnant' by police officers (ibid.). To allow such scrutiny threatened police morale and effectiveness, police unions argued. Lay involvement would result in a lack of appreciation of police work and the problems police face, including the occupational hazard of vindictive and vexatious complainants (Terrill 1982: 399). The consequent lowering of police morale would result not only in increased resignations but also in a 'chilling effect' on police responsiveness to law enforcement tasks, whereby police officers would hold back in situations in which they feared complainant reaction bolstered by predominantly anti-police CRBs (Hudson 1972: 521). Procedurally, CRBs were criticized by police officers for being 'kangaroo courts', in which few basic constitutional rights of police officers under investigation were honoured (Hudson 1972: 522), while administratively, police unions alluded to a form of bureaucratic 'overkill', in which CRBs, by entertaining a variety of minor complaints, would divert precious police resources away from more important tasks (ibid.). While the merits of many of these assertions by opponents of CRBs have been effectively challenged by scholars (cf. Terrill 1982, Barton 1970), none the less the perceptions of these opponents remain significant in terms of defining the nature of the legitimacy problems faced by reformers concerned with establishing external review mechanisms in the police field.

Scholarly assessments of CRBs have identified a number of drawbacks. For example, there is considerable consensus concerning the role played by police unions in bringing down various CRB experiments (Brown 1985; Littlejohn 1981; Terrill 1982). Gelhorn noted the absence of independent investigators in the case of the Philadelphia CRB, which called its overall independence into question, while in the case of the Rochester CRB, the board's functions were narrowly defined so as to exclude consideration of a whole range of misbehaviour of concern to local citizens (1966: 180). He is also particularly critical of CRBs' *ex post* focus, and their tendency to polarize the parties involved and to individualize the nature of the problems:

What is needed . . . is not a further institutionalizing, through a civilian board, of the notion that a complaint signalizes a dispute between two individuals alone. What is needed, rather, is acceptance of the view that a citizen's complaint about a policeman, just like a citizen's complaint about any other public servant, deserved the attention of superior administrators who are intent upon redressing irritation and improving services. (p. 191.)

Gelhorn specifically draws attention to the responsibility of supervisors for complaints and to his view of the relative significance of an independent complaints mechanism:

If anyone believes that the responsible superiors have not given the desired degree of attention, an outsider's inquiry becomes desirable. The issue then presented is not the guilt or innocence of a particular public servant, but the probity, efficiency, and policies of those who have weighed citizen's allegations about shortcomings or misdeeds . . . Persons who wish to protest about police operations should indeed be able to bring their protests before a competent authority wholly outside the Police Department, but this should not operate to supplant the Police Department as the primary investigator and decider of charges against its members. (ibid.)

Brown (1985) has reiterated a number of these criticisms and views, in particular the failure of CRBs either to detect wider patterns of police misconduct or to have a remedial influence at the policy level. Brown also describes the consequences for an independent board which cannot *depend* on the community it is intended to assist:

Ultimately, even if there is power to affect police policy and practice, this cannot be used to best effect unless there is also adequate information from complainants about malpractice. One of the important shortcomings of civilian review boards in the 1960s was that they lacked this kind of feedback, because, for a number of reasons, they failed to command sufficiently widespread public support and use. (1985: 158.)

Therefore, while police resistance to CRBs has been seen to render their influence nugatory, equally an unsupportive public can undercut the very rationale behind these boards. Clearly, if such agencies are to work effectively, they cannot then be 'empty shells'.

After the failure of CRBs in the 1960s, the continued public lack of confidence in the ability of the police to police themselves made it inevitable that American communities in the 1970s would experiment further with some form of external review. Although these experiments appear to have been few in number and to have had relatively little evaluation (cf. Littlejohn 1981, Terrill 1982), it is worth considering briefly two of these developments, the Chicago Office of Professional Standards and the Detroit Board of Police Commissioners, because they provide examples of the sorts of compromise struck between citizens and police interests in more recent times.

Littlejohn (1981) has extensively reviewed the establishment and operation of a civilian police commission in Detroit, the Board of Police Commissioners (BPC), which commenced operation in 1974. In contrast to CRBs, the BPC, as its title would indicate, is part of the police department hierarchy. As an internal administrative body, it is responsible for establishing departmental policy, and therefore is able to influence police activity directly, including the investigation of complaints. The BPC has established for this purpose an Office of the Chief Investigator, which reports directly on complaints investigations to the BPC. This Office, in addition to receiving, screening, assigning, and monitoring citizens' complaints, also employs 'mixed' investigative teams of civilian and police investigators (p. 13).

The Chicago Office of Professional Standards, also established in 1974, is part of the Chicago Police Department. It is 'independent' only to the extent that its personnel are lawyers and civilian investigators with non-police backgrounds, who are on the Superintendent of Police's personal staff. Its functions include receiving complaints, allocating complaints for investigation between itself and the Department's Internal Affairs Division, conducting investigations, and keeping a watching brief on cases of excessive force and corruption, liaising where necessary with outside bodies. They do not include hearing complaints or imposing penalties, which is done by an internal Complaint Review Panel, composed solely of sworn police officers (Terrill 1982: 402).

According to Littlejohn, the Detroit scheme saw a 'spectacular turnabout by some opponents of civilian review' (1981: 35) due in part, he suggests, to the perceived inevitability of some form of civilian review, but also to the recognition that it 'would be to the department's advantage . . . to propose the least meddlesome form of civilian involvement' (ibid.). Both the recent Detroit and Chicago models, while incorporating an element of civilian participation and appearing to have something of a systemic, reform orientation, are scarcely 'independent' or 'external' in an employment or organizational sense. The fact that civilian investigators are not sworn officers does not detract from their status as salaried employees located within police departments, nor does the civilian composition of a police commission detract from the fact that it employs police officers and is integrally involved in the provision of policing services. The risks of bureaucratic co-optation of civilians by police in these circumstances must be considered strong, and indeed this is a charge which has already been levelled against the Chicago Office of Professional Standards (Brown 1985).

But while police interests may be mollified by the prospect of a 'least meddlesome form of civilian involvement', the question may be asked how satisfied will the public remain with such a limited and co-optable form of 'independent' review? While not providing an exact parallel with Detroit or Chicago, the recent experience in Queensland with its Police Complaints Tribunal points to the limited credibility of such models where there is evidence of sustained and widespread misconduct in the police force. The Police Complaints Tribunal, more akin to a CRB but with some police representation, was condemned as a measure of sheer political expediency established in the face of criticism of police misconduct, and also for its ineffectiveness in dealing with complaints, which had resulted in its deservedly poor reputation (Queensland 1989: 292). In this case, despite its notional 'independence', co-optation by the police was more or less complete. Extreme caution therefore is necessary in the establishment and evaluation of any complaints mechanisms which are granted other than a strong form of independence and external control, more along the lines of the systems to be discussed in the next section.

In sum, it seems that CRBs have generally been regarded as inadequate in terms of independence of investigations, their focus on individual grievances, their emphasis on penalties and their lack of credibility with both police and public. In addition to police objections, CRBs and similar bodies can face legitimacy problems with the general, basically 'pro-police' public:

It is . . . important for public confidence that a civilian element is not introduced purely in response to pressure from particular minority groups or political factions which are opposed to the police. When this happens the resulting identification of complaint procedures with such groups will occasion automatic opposition from those of differing persuasions, and restrict the use of procedures to specific minorities. (Brown 1985: 159.)

Since the CRB experiments, the quest for more 'independent' forms of investigation and review of complaints has sought to contend with the issues of institutional independence (what form, how much), the degree of intrusiveness (scope of intervention), the form of intervention (supervision, investigation, adjudication etc.), seeking to find a balance which adequately reflects public distrust of police self-regulation as well as the police case for self-regulation. The challenge has been to construct a complaints mechanism capable of commanding respect and exercising authority over police and public alike. A model which emerged to coincide with the demise of CRBs in the 1960s was that of the ombudsman, to which we now turn.

The Ombudsman Model

Definitions of the term 'ombudsman' vary, and it is a concept which is showing signs of expansion (cf. Monk, Kaye, and Litwin 1984). The International Bar Association in 1974 defined the term in the following way:

> An office provided for by the constitution or by action of the legislature or parliament and headed by an independent, high-level public official who is responsible to the legislature or parliament, who receives complaints from aggrieved persons against government agencies, officials, and employees or who acts on his own motion, and who has the power to investigate, recommend corrective action, and issue reports. (Caiden, MacDermot, and Sandler 1981: 12.)

Hill attributes the following ten characteristics to what he calls the *classical* ombudsman: (1) legally established, (2) functionally autonomous, (3) external to the administration, (4) operationally independent of both the legislature and the executive, (5) specialist, (6) expert, (7) nonpartisan, (8) normatively universalistic, (9) client-centred but not anti-administration, and (10) both popularly accessible and visible (1977: 12). Typically, the Ombudsman investigates or otherwise reviews administrative decisions which are the subject of complaint and then reports his findings and recommendations. The position usually possesses 'minimal coercive capabilities' (ibid.), pointing to the importance of the status of the ombudsman if the position is to be effective.

Commentators have drawn attention to the benefits of the ombudsman office for administrators as well as citizens, and to the respect for, and reliance placed upon, internal control mechanisms by the Ombudsman. Aside from addressing specific grievances lodged by citizens, Hill notes, the office 'bolsters administrative morale by demonstrating that civil servants often are unfairly accused' (p. 13). Gelhorn points to its primary concern for patterns of misconduct and procedural reform and its role as a check or audit upon internal control mechanisms:

The inquiry [into complaints] need not . . . be made in the first instance by a critic external to the administration. Responsibility for investigation belongs to the supervisory ranks of the administration itself. The external critic's [i.e. the ombudsman's] concern should be less with the merits of the particular grievance than with the adequacy of the steps taken to discover what merit it has. Numerous personalized complaints of the same general tenor may add up to a different story altogether. In the aggregate they may suggest possibly defective supervision, structure or method—assuredly a broad enough matter to claim the external critic's attention without his assuming to be a government-wide sleuth dedicated to ferreting out the rights and wrongs of every civilian–official disturbance. (1966: 224.)

In other words, the ombudsman was never intended to supplant entirely or even substantially the role of internal control mechanisms, but was designed to assist in the recognition of patterns of organizational misconduct and the recommendation of suitable reforms, in addition to assisting individual complainants. These functions are central to the idea of a responsive institution.

In a number of jurisdictions, starting in the mid-1970s, attempts were made to fashion external mechanisms for dealing with complaints against police which incorporated basic features of the ombudsman model (cf. Goldsmith 1988). In some cases, police misconduct was subsumed within a larger ombudsman role, while in others, specialist police ombudsmen were established. More recently, attempts have been made to go completely outside the internal police mechanisms, to fashion a wholly independent, external complaints mechanism with its own investigation powers. Developments in Australia provide examples of each of these approaches.

1. The ALRC Model   The first Australian proposals for ombudsman-style supervision, and in some instances, investigation, of complaints by citizens against the police, emerged from two reports of the Australian Law Reform Commission (ALRC), (Australia 1975, 1978). The justification by the ALRC for an independent element in the handling of complaints against police, at least initially, seems to have been overseas experience with internal investigations, and particularly the evidence from the United Kingdom and the United States. By the time of the Supplementary Report (Australia 1978), comparable negative local experience in Victoria and Queensland had added further weight to the ALRC proposals.

The model proposed by the ALRC in its Supplementary Report provides a reference point for two distinguishable independent approaches to handling complaints, one being the generalist ombudsman seen in New South Wales and Western Australia, and the other the specialist police ombudsman in South Australia (and until recently, in Victoria),[7] known as the Police Complaints Authority. The ALRC model took as its starting point the assumption that it was 'fundamental to the proper maintenance of discipline in a police force that each force should bear responsibility, as far as possible, for discovering and dealing with complaints against its members' (Australia 1978: 60–1). The model's principal features were:

(1) All complaints made by citizens to the police should be forwarded by the Commissioner of Police to the Ombudsman. Alternatively, complaints could be made direct to the Ombudsman.

(2) The creation of a specialist internal investigation unit within the police force.

(3) Complaints investigations would normally be performed by this internal unit.

(4) The Ombudsman would have a reserve power to conduct independent investigations where:

    (*a*) the complaint concerns a police officer senior to all members of the internal unit;

    (*b*) the complaint concerns a member of the unit;

    (*c*) the complaint relates to a matter the Ombudsman is already investigating;

    (*d*) The Ombudsman is of the opinion that it is in the public interest that the complaint should be investigated by him [*sic*].

(5) Internal investigation reports should be sent to the Commissioner, who should refer them on (with his own comments) to the Ombudsman.

(6) While the bringing of charges following reports should normally

---

[7] Until 1988, the state of Victoria also had a Police Complaints Authority. See the essay by Freckelton, Chapter 2 of this volume, which deals with the downfall of the Victorian PCA.

be a matter for police discretion, where a citizen's complaint is concerned and there is a difference of view between the Ombudsman and the Commissioner, the Ombudsman should be able to direct that charges be brought.

(7) Citizen complaints resulting in disciplinary charges should be heard by an independent Police Tribunal, presided over by a single judge.

The ALRC saw the ombudsman's role in the context of police complaints as an 'active' one, involving powers of investigation and preferment of charges (Australia 1978: 64). Because it was reluctant to see a further proliferation of agencies for dealing with citizens' grievances against the state, it sought to supplement the ombudsman's existing powers by attaching responsibilities for citizens' complaints against police to the existing generalist office (pp. 64–5), rather than establish a specialist agency: 'the *Ombudsman Act* is designed to correct and prevent bad administration, not to secure the punishment of individual officers. On the other hand the proposals of the Commission, though they may be concerned with bad administration in part, or in the ultimate, are principally concerned with redressing improper conduct by individual police officers.' (p. 65.) It was noted earlier that not all supporters of the ombudsman concept for handling complaints against police officers share the stress apparently placed by the ALRC in its proposals on redress of individual complaints, but rather see the ombudsman's proper focus as being organizational efficiency and systemic reform, directed to the longer-term goals of administrative improvement and that individual complaints, when they arise, are properly dealt with internally (Gelhorn 1966). That the ALRC saw these functions as distinct and supplementary, rather than interrelated and complementary, indicates the persistence to some degree of the 'rotten apple' theory of police misconduct[8] which until recently has dominated conventional analyses of police misconduct (cf. Shearing 1981; Australia 1983). Criticism of this approach has taken issue with the dominance of an individualized retributive response to complaints and misconduct,

---

[8] The 'rotten apple' theory was described by the Knapp Commission in its report on corruption in the New York Police Department in the following terms: 'According to this theory, which bordered on official Department doctrine, any policeman found to be corrupt must promptly be denounced as a rotten apple in an otherwise clean barrel. It must never be admitted that his individual corruption may be symptomatic of underlying disease.' (Quoted in Australia 1983: 579.)

one which marginalizes the significance of such conduct for systemic analysis and reform. The task therefore which the ALRC reports did not adequately confront was the system's ability to deal with complaints against police as indicators of organizational problems.

2. The New South Wales Ombudsman   Although New South Wales has had an ombudsman since 1974, it was not until 1978 that the office was involved in anything other than administrative actions by police officers (that is, non-operational matters). In 1978, legislative amendments permitted a limited involvement by the Ombudsman in the handling of citizens' complaints about police misconduct (that is, operational matters). However this essentially took the form of a paper review of the internal investigation reports prepared for the Police Commissioner. The Ombudsman was able to consider the reports, together with an outline of the course of action proposed by the Commissioner, and to recommend further action where it was considered appropriate. There was no capacity to interview police officers, and the sole measure available to the Ombudsman, when confronted with an unsatisfactory proposal by the Police Commissioner, was to make a special report to the state Parliament (Nelson 1986: 231). The Stewart Royal Commission into drug trafficking in 1983 expressed its disquiet at the police-dominated investigation of complaints against police in New South Wales and Victoria and recommended strengthening the relevant legislation by providing for independent investigations by the ombudsman (Australia 1983: 621). Towards the end of 1983, the New South Wales government introduced a set of legislative proposals intended to enhance the powers of the ombudsman and to give the public greater confidence in the investigation of complaints against police. These proposals became operational in March 1984 (New South Wales 1987: 1).

The (then) New South Wales Ombudsman, in his triennial review in August 1987, offered the view that the New South Wales system of investigating complaints about police was 'one of the best of its kind in Australia or, indeed, the world' (New South Wales 1987: 91). He described the operating philosophy of his office in the following terms:

It is the policy of the Ombudsman to treat the New South Wales Police Force in the same way as any other New South Wales public authority; that is, where the Police Department itself has been unable to resolve a complaint by a member of the police or investigate it to the satisfaction of the complainant, to reinvestigate complaints against the police force and produce detailed, well-reasoned and fair reports about the conduct of individual police officers and the practices of the Force as a whole. It is up to the Commissioner of Police to implement the Ombudsman's recommendations as a result of being convinced by the Ombudsman's report of the correctness of the course recommended. (p. 49.)

The actual legislative and administrative scheme in operation resembles the ALRC model in a number of respects, although there are some material differences, particularly in respect of intitial investigations. The following list gives an overview of the New South Wales model:

(1) All complaints made by citizens to the police must be forwarded by the Commissioner to the Ombudsman. Complaints may alternatively be made directly to the Ombudsman.

(2) The Ombudsman decides whether or not a complaint is investigated.

(3) There is an Internal Affairs Branch within the police department, under the direction of an Assistant Commissioner.

(4) Complaints are usually investigated by the Internal Affairs Branch except where:

  (*a*) the complaint concerns a police officer who is senior to all members of the Branch;

  (*b*) the complaint concerns a police officer who is or was at the material time a member of the Branch;

  (*c*) the Ombudsman and the Commissioner of Police have agreed that the 'class or kind' of conduct complained of should be investigated by police outside the Internal Affairs Branch.

(5) Since May 1986, as a matter of practice, the Ombudsman and Commissioner have agreed that Internal Affairs Branch need only investigate 'serious assaults'. The remaining 'less serious' cases are delegated by the Ombudsman to police investigators at the divisional levels.

(6) The Ombudsman monitors initial investigations by police and is able to direct the police to conduct further investigations where he perceives deficiencies in the initial investigations.

(7) The Ombudsman can conduct reinvestigations, using a team of investigators seconded from the police force, using the powers

granted under the Ombudsman Act, which includes the power of a Royal Commissioner to hold hearings.

(8) Following the investigation stage, the Ombudsman makes a report, which goes to the Commissioner for comments, and to the Minister responsible for policing.

(9) The Ombudsman's report may make recommendations *inter alia* that:

    (*a*) action be taken to rectify, mitigate, or change the conduct or its consequences;

    (*b*) reasons be given for the conduct;

    (*c*) any law or practice relating to the conduct be changed;

    (*d*) any other action be taken.

(10) The Ombudsman may request the Police Tribunal to direct the Commissioner to comply with these recommendations.

(11) Disciplinary charges arising from complaints are heard by the Police Tribunal which is presided over by a person of judicial rank.

In respect of the ombudsman's limited role in initial investigations, the Ombudsman has recommended to the New South Wales Parliament that the office of ombudsman be allowed to conduct investigations of police misconduct of its 'own motion' (New South Wales 1987: 93), a proposal yet to find acceptance. In keeping with the philosophy quoted earlier, the Ombudsman has indicated his extreme reluctance to bring proceedings in the Police Tribunal to enforce his recommendations, stating that this is 'because the Police Department, like any other public authority in New South Wales, should be able to regulate itself' (p. 49).

On the other side of the ledger is the power to hold reinvestigations, utilizing the inquiry powers of a Royal Commission. Obviously, at the individual complaint level, this power represents a significant symbolic departure from the narrow concept of 'review' practised by the ombudsman prior to 1984, as well as providing a very real inroad into police self-regulation. Because of limited resources, however, only 'serious matters or matters with widespread implications for police practices are reinvestigated' (p. 31). Then there is the ability of the ombudsman's office to monitor the initial investigations conducted by the police, and to request further investigation where the preliminary police investigation report is considered to be deficient in some way. The Ombudsman observed in 1987 that the 'use of the requirement to further investigate a complaint has been an important part of the Ombudsman's role in ensuring that police internal investigations are thorough and consistent in approach' (p. 24). As indicated earlier, in 1987 the Ombudsman considered himself largely satisfied with the set of powers open to him to deal with complaints against police.[9]

The ability of the ombudsman to make recommendations of a systemic kind is obviously envisaged by the powers referred to in paragraph (9) above. The extent to which actual use is made of these formal powers, and the level of implementation of recommended changes to practices and procedures, are issues on which there would seem to be little if any systemic evidence, a phenomenon hardly confined to the New South Wales example. What is evident overall, however, is an apparent emphasis in the formal provisions upon the individual complaint process rather than systemic issues. This raises the important question of how the systemic function should be provided for in complaints mechanisms? Leaving aside issues of legislative form, it is by no means clear that skills appropriate to complaints investigations in organizational settings equate to skills of information processing and organizational change required for the police to become a 'responsive institution' (Nonet and Selznick 1969). Yet it is these latter skills, vested in an appropriate agency, which are essential if complaints against police are going to be analysed adequately for the purposes of systemic evaluation and *ex post* reforms.

3. The South Australian Police Complaints Authority The Police Complaints Authority (PCA) commenced operation on 1 July 1985, South Australia being the last Australian state other than Western Australia to introduce an independent element into the receipt and investigation of complaints against police.[10] The establishment of the PCA followed a government-appointed committee (the Grieve Committee) some two years earlier, which had recommended a separate, specialist ombudsman-type authority, dealing exclusively with complaints against members of the South Australian police force (South Australia 1983). Prior to the PCA, investigations of citizens' complaints had been purely internal investigations,

[9] The Ombudsman until Sept. 1987 was Mr George Masterman QC. The views of his successor may well be different to those stated here.
[10] Western Australia extended its generalist ombudsman's jurisdiction on 1 July 1985 to include complaints about police misconduct. See Western Australia (1989).

conducted by the force's Complaints Investigation Section. Interestingly, although the Grieve Committee took the view that 'public confidence and fairness to members of the police force complained against are best served by an independent element in the evaluation and investigation of complaints', it expressed its 'complete confidence in the thoroughness of the present [that is, internal] procedure' (p. 9).

The committee's main recommendations were influenced by three assumptions: (1) the independent element should be provided for in separate legislation; (2) it should not however diminish the ability of the Commissioner of Police to maintain a discipline force; (3) the present Complaints Investigation Section should be 'retained as is and operate as the principal investigative arm of the new complaints procedure . . . subject to oversight by and cooperation with an independent authority' (p. 11).

Organizationally, the Grieve Committee's principal recommendation was the establishment of a separate police complaints authority, unconnected to the existing South Australian Ombudsman's office. Among the reasons offered for this preference, the committee noted an overseas tendency towards specialist agencies for dealing with citizens' complaints against police, the possibility of confusion for an ombudsman required to consider misconduct as well as maladministration in the case of police, and the 'serious possibility that the addition of the police complaints responsibility, involving perhaps three hundred additional complaints, would overbalance the entire Office' (p. 30). A subsequent consultant's report took express issue with the committee's reasoning, drawing attention to a number of reasons in favour of giving the responsibility to the ombudsman (Goode 1983). The ALRC's preference for the generalist ombudsman model was noted, including one of its specific grounds for doing so: 'The creation of a specialised Ombudsman would involve a most substantial specialised staff establishment. It might encourage an attitude out of line with the more general protection of citizens against harassment and damage the morale of the police.' (Australia 1975: 18, quoted in Goode 1983: 28.) However, it was the specialist ombudsman model which found legislative favour. Nevertheless, in some respects, the South Australian PCA more closely resembles the ALRC model than the New South Wales ombudsman, particularly in terms of its powers of initial investigation. The PCA model has the following features:

(1) There is a separate internal investigation branch within the police force which has primary responsibility for investigating complaints by citizens.

(2) Not only must the PCA be notified of all complaints made, but it is able to determine which of these complaints are investigated. Citizens may explain directly to the PCA.

(3) Although it must be in consultation with the Commissioner of Police, the PCA may conduct initial investigations when it is satisfied:

   (*a*) the complaint concerns an officer equal or senior to the officer in charge of the internal investigation branch;
   (*b*) the complaint concerns the conduct of a member of the internal investigations branch;
   (*c*) the complaint concerns the practices, procedures, or policies of the police force;
   (*d*) there are other reasons justifying his investigation.

(4) The PCA may supervise the investigation of the internal investigation branch, including directing the manner in which investigations are conducted and ordering reinvestigations.

(5) Following investigations and the receipt of any comments on investigations from the Commissioner, it shall provide the Commissioner with a report containing its assessment as to whether the police conduct amounted to an offence, was 'unreasonable, unjust, oppressive or improperly discriminatory', or was for any of a variety of specified reasons, wrong.

(6) The PCA report referred to in (5) also contains recommendations as to whether action should be taken to:

   (*a*) charge an officer with legal or disciplinary offences;
   (*b*) reconsider, vary, or reverse a decision or to provide reasons for a decision;
   (*c*) rectify, mitigate, or alter the effects of a decision, act, or omission;
   (*d*) alter a rule of law or a practice, procedure, or policy on which a decision, act, or omission was based;
   (*e*) make other appropriate changes.

(7) Unless the Commissioner objects and appeals to the Police Minister, he must give effect to the recommendations of the PCA, including the bringing of charges where recommended.

(8) Disciplinary charges arising from a complaint are heard by the

Police Disciplinary Tribunal, which is presided over by a single magistrate.

(9) Where the Tribunal finds an officer guilty of a disciplinary offence, the matter is handed over to the Commissioner for the imposition of punishment.

The specialist nature of the PCA obviously opens itself to the risk, and public perception, of co-optation by police and pro-police bias. In a relatively small state like South Australia, with only a small PCA staff,[11] these risks might be considered to be even greater. On the other hand a specialist body would seem likely to develop a sophisticated understanding of police problems and practices, which would inform recommendations for changes in policy and procedures and potentially be more plausible from the police perspective. As various police scholars such as Bayley (1983) and Reiner (1985) have observed, there is little point in simply railing punitively in response to police misconduct unless there are also systemically sensitive reform proposals capable of *persuading* police officers of the need to change existing practices. In so doing, the policy proposals should not ignore the capacity of street-level officers to contribute to those proposals (Goldsmith 1990). Certainly, the policy recommendatory function of the PCA appears to have been taken seriously by the present incumbent in South Australia, and it seems that the Police Commissioner of that state has yet to reject any PCA recommendation (South Australia 1989: 20). As for bias, protection against this outcome lies substantially in the degree of public satisfaction with the PCA, and in the evidence from the quantitative performance indicators. The PCA claims to be receiving more public complaints than before, is conducting more independent investigations than in the past, and of those matters investigated and assessed, has substantiated police misconduct or malpractice in 26 per cent of cases (p. 19). These results, together with the evidence of the PCA's involvement in policy recommendations, are certainly encouraging.

4. The Queensland Criminal Justice Commission In the state of Queensland, the government is presently setting up an omnibus body, known as the Criminal Justice Commission (CJC), to deal with a wide variety of criminal justice matters. The outcome of

---

[11] Aside from support staff, the PCA consists of the Authority (Andrew Cunningham), his deputy, and one investigator.

recommendations from the recent Fitzgerald Inquiry in that state (Queensland 1989), the CJC has as one of its divisions the Official Misconduct Division (OMD). This division is envisaged as having a totally autonomous existence from other government departments, including the police department, although some of its investigators will be seconded police officers, presumably because of their investigative skills (p. 311). The OMD's role is a broad one. Like the traditional ombudsman, it can investigate the activities of all public officials, and is not confined to police officers. Its Complaints Branch will receive complaints of misconduct from the public and police officers, and all complaints against police officers must be referred by the Police Commissioner to the Complaints Branch for determination of the appropriate action to be taken. The OMD may institute investigations into any suspected official misconduct on its own initiative, and is not simply to be reactive to dissatisfied citizens, like the customary ombudsman's function. Those investigations may either deal with individual cases or conduct more wide-ranging inquiries into the incidence of official misconduct. Reports of its investigations and inquiries may be forwarded to another division of the CJC, the Misconduct Tribunal, in order to determine whether an administrative response 'apart from any prosecution' is appropriate to the relevant misconduct (ibid.).

The CJC's Official Misconduct Division would appear to remove much of the responsibility for police regulation from the police themselves, particularly once a complaint is made, even when that complaint is made by a police officer against another officer. The strongly external character of this complaints mechanism distinguishes it from those systems in which primary investigatory responsibility lies with the police, and perhaps reflects the type of reforms possible during periods of monumental and sustained community moral outrage at police misconduct (cf. Sherman 1978; Goode, Chapter 3 below), as seen recently in Queensland (Queensland 1989). Certainly, when compared to the other 'independent/external' models canvassed in this Chapter, it is the most 'independent' and 'external' of those models. It is doubtful however whether many recent observers of events in Queensland would question the appropriateness for the time being of such a strong external mechanism for dealing with complaints, given the magnitude of recent public disquiet at previous attempts at self-regulation by Queensland police.

An overall impression of the OMD's projected operation indicates a definite resemblance to the ombudsman-type models already considered. This is the strongly punitive and retributive (i.e. *ex post*) emphasis of its provisions. While certain provisions seem to provide for *ex ante* considerations, the dominant thrust is nevertheless retrospective and retributive. The OMD's powers of investigation are closely analogous to those of any other criminal investigation agency which, while not surprising, suggests an organizational ethos rather removed from the concerns of a system designed to provide bureaucratic monitoring functions. When the staffing recommendations for the OMD and Misconduct Tribunal are examined, the strong influence of lawyers is noted. While the OMD envisages a 'wide variety of skilled staff and consultants' (Queensland 1989: 313), its director is to be legally qualified. The Misconduct Tribunal similarly, which is to consider administrative *as well as prosecutorial* implications of complaints, is to consist of three persons who are either retired senior judges or who are qualified for high judicial office (p. 315). My point is that while the *ex post*, retributive dimensions of the reforms are quite explicit and comprehensively addressed, the *ex ante*, systemic issues are dealt with in less detail and are less openly addressed. Aside from this relative inattention, there is an often implicit assumption running throughout these schemes, and indeed much of the ombudsman literature, that legally trained personnel are appropriate for both functions in ombudsman-type agencies. While it is relatively straightforward that legal investigative and forensic skills are appropriate in matters of assessing allegations of misconduct and the carriage of complaints prosecutions, it is not evident (at least to this writer) that lawyerly skills are most appropriate to the performance of the systemic *ex ante* role. Whether this function continues to be dealt with alongside the other in the same agency, or whether a separate agency is established, is a question which requires further consideration. However in either event, much would seem to be gained by the active deployment of public administration experts, organizational behaviourists, and labour-relations practitioners in such agencies.

EXTERNAL REVIEW AND THE QUEST FOR 'INTERPOLABLE BALANCE'

An 'interpolable balance' perspective takes as its starting point a need to identify 'self-policing' mechanisms which are already present in any system, and to build on those; may point to the need to redesign government in a way which will strengthen immanent control rather than taking the existing structure as given and seeking to strengthen formal oversight and does not assume that 'control' is necessarily to be exercised from any fixed place in an institutional system, but can contemplate a network of complementary and overlapping detectors and effectors (that is, 'redundant channels', in information-processing language) with mobility—even lability—in the seat of the checking mechanism. (Hood 1986: 772.)

Finally, I propose to examine two perennial difficulties emerging from any discussion of complaints against police and external review mechanisms. These are firstly, the long-standing reluctance by police to be persuaded of the merits and benefits offered by external review, and secondly, in the light of the external pressures for, and internal resistances to, forms of independent review, the idea that there is an objectively optimal balance to be achieved between the two. In pursuing these two questions, I shall attempt to draw together the principal arguments running through this chapter, so as to articulate more precisely their relationship to the goal of producing more 'responsive' police institutions. By arguing for the importance of external review agencies in assisting police forces towards reaching 'interpolable balance' in the area of complaints, I seek to advocate a more imaginative and systematically oriented approach to the development of police accountability mechanisms by all parties concerned, one which looks beyond the familiar conceptual 'reform' traps of 'more of the same' and the dichotomous 'either/or' response.

The examination in the previous section of different 'external' responses to public criticisms of internal complaints mechanisms should confirm the inevitability for the foreseeable future, in many jurisdictions, of a trend towards strong forms of external review. By 'strong', I refer mainly to the growing phenomenon of agencies with separate investigative resources, in some cases having powers of initial investigation, and even, like Queensland's Criminal Justice Commission, being able to act in the absence of specific complaints. This trend has occurred despite often widespread police opposition, and in some cases, interestingly, with police support (cf. Maguire and Reiner, Chapters 5 and 6 below). Those police elements who continue to deny a need for some outwardly convincing, effective external review agency, apart from ignoring the daunting record of police failure of self-regulation in the complaints area, overlook the serious legitimacy problems faced by the police in many communities and that for many members of the public, policing issues no longer retain any 'above politics' innocence they ever possessed. In this sense, some police elements seem intent on denying the inevitability of external involvement in citizens' complaints against police.

These same elements fail to see the desirability of complaints *per se*, and to recognize the potential benefits from third-party involvement in such matters. I have suggested throughout this Chapter that there has been a comparative neglect by many persons interested and/or involved in the question of complaints in the bureaucratic monitoring potential of complaints mechanisms, that is, in viewing complaints as data sources relevant to systemic issues. The intrinsic advantages of so doing have already been suggested, but it must be conceded that external agencies seem to overlook these advantages almost as much as do internal agencies. In this respect, I have suggested that the *ex post*, retributive philosophy has continued to excessively dominate complaints-handling mechanisms of both types.

Aside from the intrinsic advantages, there are issues of fundamental equity and logical consistency which need to be more clearly identified in making the case for a broader view of complaints and a continued role for external agencies. On the issue of equity, there are clearly limits to the amount of control that can be exerted over or within any organization. Any control mechanism, be it internal or external, faces real constraints so that there is nothing magical about 'self-regulation' or 'external accountability'. Control problems in policing not only challenge the would-be controllers, but can also frustrate those who find themselves the target of police attention. As one public-administration scholar has noted: 'In performance arrangements, where central aspects of encounters between staff and citizens . . . cannot be monitored sufficiently from above or outside, the necessity for supplementary evaluation and control from below, exercised by the institutionally weaker, directly affected clients becomes obvious.' (Wirth 1986: 752.) The consequences for policing therefore must be that a viable complaints procedure should be mandatory if citizens' interests are to receive some measure of protection against the 'control' problems facing external and internal police administrators and the administrative responses to these problems. In view of the recent evidence, an external agency seems more likely to be credible and effective in providing this kind of protection and ensuring that the police 'clientele' is given a voice in matters which directly affect them.

There is also a logical inconsistency in police attitudes to organizational efficiency and effectiveness and to the (potential) systemic role played by external agencies. The stock-in-trade of the police and the public in their dealings with each other, at least substantially, is information. Information of relevance to police work comes in two distinct forms: criminal intelligence, that is, information about wrongdoings and suspicious behaviour in the community; and organizational knowledge, that is, information about how the organization is functioning. Citizens are sources of both kinds of information. Yet, mysteriously, many police would appear to think that the public should provide the former but not the latter (Bayley 1989), probably because 'criminal intelligence' is critically important to the police for the purposes of their own performance indicators. The latter, one form of which comes from complaints, is not widely understood by police as holding any potential value for themselves. More mysteriously, there seems to be an assumption by police that the two categories are distinguishable for all practical purposes, that somehow one can be obtained without the other:

As a general rule, in a community where there are numerous complaints against the police and accompanying clamour for establishment of a civilian review board or some other external mechanism for control of police behaviour, there are police–community problems and usually other problems of a serious nature . . . *There is an inconsistency between lamenting, on the one hand, the apathy of the public regarding problems that loom large for the police, and on the other hand resisting the right and obligation of citizens to complain about what they perceive an improper police conduct.* (Radelet 1980: 304–5, my emphasis.)

As Radelet implies, public apathy is scarcely likely to result in an impressive information flow from the public concerning 'problems that loom large for the police'. A complaints procedure widely viewed as ineffective is scarcely likely to allay public apathy or, even worse, defuse public hostility towards police concerns. Absent in such procedures is any basis for trust in the form of shared information and expertise; in other words, important elements of a reciprocal, negotiated relationship between the parties are missing.

The case for responsive complaints procedures is even more

compelling in those police districts which have expressly adopted the 'community policing' approach to police–community relations. As Bayley notes, one of the key elements of 'community policing' is the creation of 'mechanisms for grassroots feedback from the community' (1989: 64). Neighbourhood Watch schemes are a widely implemented example of this; adequate complaints mechanisms surely *should* be another. The police must learn to take advice as well as give it; if 'the police invite the public to a party, they cannot do all the talking and expect it to be fun for everyone' (p. 75). This has never been easy for the police, and their demonstrated resistance to dealing responsively with citizens' complaints is merely symptomatic of this problem.

A strong, systemically oriented complaints system conducted by an external agency would seem to answer a number of the shortfalls identified by Bayley (1989) in existing community policing schemes, including an absence of strategic urgency about community policing inside police forces and a tendency for community policing initiatives to suffer from budgetary constraints, resulting in a marginalization of these initiatives and a corresponding absence of operational consequences. An *ex ante* complaints system would provide a formula currently 'lacking for incorporating community policing into the traditional activities of policing, especially the work of general duties officers' (p. 86), upon which, Bayley argues, public acceptance of community policing is dependent. From an organizational perspective, the complaints-handling procedures advocated in this Chapter would provide a focus for the receipt, investigation, and assessment of complaints. Individually and in the aggregate, these complaints would offer a rich source of information on a variety of police organizational and field practices. Approached in this way, 'community policing' could not be marginalized or isolated from police operations, and because complaints most commonly emanate from street-level contacts with police officers, the reform proposals generated will be particularly directed to police practices at this level (see Goldsmith 1990).

If an external agency is required to educate the police in the advantages of proper complaints collation and assessment, then so be it. The effectiveness of the complaints mechanism in doing so will not depend necessarily on whether it is internal or external. At any given time it would seem that the contribution of internal and external mechanisms to police accountability is chiefly determined by the level of public trust and confidence in internal investigations.

The latter is desirable and should be encouraged, while the other is at times inevitable; essentially a stand-by, pragmatic arrangement rather than something intrinsically preferable to self-regulation (Goldstein 1967; Bayley 1983). When supervisory attention comes from outside an organization, there will be risks to employee morale and the legitimacy of the internal control mechanisms (Bayley 1983: 154). Yet while the police administration *should* assess primary responsibility for the conduct and discipline of police officers, it would seem that very often the lines of supervisory responsibility for the actions of street-level patrol officers are inadequate and require attention. A systemically oriented complaints system could assist in identifying these shortfalls (see Doig, Phillips, and Manson 1984). Moreover the evidence considered in this Chapter indicates that the time for the police to exercise predominant, let alone exclusive, control in the area of citizens' complaints is in many jurisdictions still a good way off. Therefore the case for the continued co-existence of both external and internal complaints mechanisms seems beyond contention.

The precise nature of the relationship between external mechanisms and internal control will need to be carefully considered and evaluated, and the balance struck will probably require periodic readjustment. The notion of 'interpolable balance' suggests an approach to organizational control which contemplates both changes in the patterns of distribution of control over time, and a multiplicity of forms and sites of control. It further points to a fundamental dynamic component in such control relations, requiring the participants in this dynamic to learn about each other's needs, values, and practices and how to enhance and complement, rather than frustrate and supplant them. In particular, it requires that 'outside' control agencies take adequate notice of the self-regulatory potential of any organization being considered. Obviously, the ability of police forces to exercise this potential in a credible manner will vary from force to force. This view underlines the important role that external review agencies have to play in improving police accountability, not by claiming 'property' in citizens' complaints by displacing internal mechanisms but by acting as a communication channel and analytical resource for these mechanisms. In large measure, the role of external review agencies is inherently educative. To employ a medical metaphor, such agencies should not ignore the need for chronic care and compulsory hospitalization where necessary (the disciplinary aspect of complaints), but should place equal, if not greater, emphasis upon the rehabilitation and re-integration aspects (the systemic, *ex ante* approach). External review agencies should devote greater thought and resources to developing the capacities of police forces in these respects. The more 'success' the external review bodies have in this role, the more likely is a rekindling of public confidence in the police and the ability of police forces to monitor effectively their own organizational 'bill of health'. 'Interpolable balance' implies that there is no ideal trade-off to be struck between external review and forms of internal accountability; there are too many situational factors at work in any given case to justify a particular balance. Rather it behoves police forces and external review agencies alike to re-examine many traditional conceptions of organizational control and responsibility, helping to identify new approaches to these issues as well as bases for the coexistence of 'external' and 'internal' agencies.

CONCLUSION

A persistent reticence among police to embrace the complaints process in the way argued for in this Chapter will ensure a continuing demand and role for external review agencies in providing a voice for disgruntled 'clients' of the police. Indeed, to conceive of perfect self-regulation by police forces in the face of the historical evidence is simply utopian, so that the disappearance of a role for external review in the complaints process is for all intents and purposes inconceivable. In addition to the more passive auditing role (reminiscent of traditional ombudsmen) adopted by complaints mechanisms, there has been a distinct trend recently towards stronger forms of external review (Goldsmith 1988). The next step is for a more thoroughgoing systemic orientation by and/or on behalf of the police to the analysis of complaints. The challenge posed for external review bodies is to persuade the police of the wider implications of complaints and of their own legitimate involvement in the process, and of the mutual benefits and commonality of interests at stake in the handling of complaints. As in other areas of organizational change, induced compliance is almost always preferable to exacted deterrence. Therefore in order to protect the public interest, two conditions must be met; the external agencies should strive continually to persuade and induce police forces, and in order to do so, they require sufficient constitutional protection to withstand the vagaries of police politics (cf. Freckelton and Terrill, Chapters 2 and 9 below). The conservative nature of most police forces seems likely to ensure that this challenge will not easily be met.

REFERENCES

Australia (1975) *Law Reform Commission Report No. 1: Complaints Against Police* (Canberra: Australian Government Publishing Service).

—— (1978) *Law Reform Commission Report No. 9: Complaints Against Police: Supplementary Report* (Canberra: Australian Government Publishing Service).

—— (1983) *Report of the Royal Commission of Inquiry into Drug Trafficking (Commissioner: Hon. Mr Justice D. G. Stewart)* (Canberra: Australian Government Publishing Service).

Barton, P. (1970) 'Civilian Review Boards and the Handling of Complaints Against the Police', *University of Toronto Law Journal* 20: 448–69.

Bayley, D. (1983) 'Accountability and Control of Police: Lessons for Britain', in T. Bennett (ed.), *The Future of Policing* (Cambridge: Institute of Criminology).

—— (1989) 'Community Policing in Australia: An Appraisal', in D. T. Chappell and P. Wilson (eds.), *Australian Policing: Contemporary Issues* (Sydney: Butterworths).

Best, A. (1981) *When Consumers Complain* (New York: Columbia University Press).

Box, S., and Russell, K. (1975) 'The Politics of Discreditability: Disarming Complaints Against the Police', *Sociological Review* 23: 315–46.

Brown, D. (1985) 'Civilian Review of Complaints Against the Police: A Survey of the United States Literature', in K. Heal, R. Tarling, and J. Burrows (eds.), *Policing Today* (London: HMSO).

—— (1987) *The Police Complaints Procedure: A Survey of Complainants' Views* (London: HMSO).

Caiden, G., MacDermot, N., and Sandler, A. (1981) 'The Institution of Ombudsman', in G. Caiden (ed.), *International Handbook of the Ombudsman: Evolution and Present Function* (Westport, Conn.: Greenwood Press).

Chevigny, P. (1969) *Police Power: Police Abuses in New York City* (New York: Vintage Books).

Clayton, R., and Tomlinson, H. (1987) *Civil Actions Against the Police* (London: Sweet and Maxwell).

Doig, J., Phillips, D., and Manson, M. (1984) 'Deterring Illegal Behaviour by Officials of Complex Organizations', *Criminal Justice Ethics* 5: 27–56.

Doyle, B. (1976) 'A Police Viewpoint', in Sydney Institute of Criminology, *Proceedings of a Seminar on Complaints Against Police* (Sydney: Faculty of Law, University of Sydney).

Dunsire, A. (1986) 'A Cybernetic View of Guidance, Control and Evaluation in the Public Sector', in F. Kaufmann, G. Majone, and V. Ostrom (eds.), *Guidance, Control and Evaluation in the Public Sector: The Bielefeld Interdisciplinary Project* (Berlin: de Gruyter).

Felstiner, W. (1974) 'Influences of Social Organization on Dispute Processing', *Law and Society Review* 9: 63–94.

—— Abel, R., and Sarat, A. (1981) 'The Emergence and Transformation of Disputes: Naming, Blaming, Claiming . . .', *Law and Society Review* 15: 631–54.

Freckelton, I. (1988*a*) 'Sensation and Symbiosis' in I. Freckelton and H. Selby (eds.), *Police in Our Society* (Sydney: Butterworths).

—— (1988*b*) 'Querulent Paranoia and the Vexatious Complainant' *International Journal of Law and Psychiatry* 11: 127–43.

Galanter, M. (1974) 'Why the "Haves" Come Out Ahead: Speculations on the Limits of Legal Change', *Law and Society Review* 1: 95–160.

Gelhorn, W. (1966) *When Americans Complain: Governmental Grievance Procedures* (Cambridge, Mass.: Harvard University Press).

Goldsmith, A. (1988) 'New Directions in Police Complaints Procedures: Some Conceptual and Comparative Departures', *Police Studies* 11: 60–71.

—— (1990) 'Taking Police Culture Seriously: Police Discretion and the Limits of Law', *Policing and Society* 1: 91–114.

Goldstein, H. (1967) 'Administrative Problems in Controling the Exercise of Police Authority', *Journal of Criminal Law, Criminology and Police Science* 58: 160–72.

—— (1977) *Policing a Free Society* (Cambridge, Mass.: Bollinger).

Goldstein, J. (1960) 'Police Discretion Not to Invoke the Criminal Process: Low-Visibility Decisions in the Administration of Justice', *Yale Law Journal* 60: 543–94.

Goode, M. (1974) 'Administrative Systems for the Resolution of Complaints Against the Police: A Proposed Reform', *Adelaide Law Review* 5: 55–78.

—— (1983) 'Consultant's Report on the Grieve Report on Complaints Against the Police' (unpublished).

Hart, H. (1961) *The Concept of Law* (Oxford: Clarendon Press).

Hill, L. (1977) *The Model Ombudsman* (Princeton, NJ: Princeton University Press).

—— (1981) 'Bureaucratic Monitoring Systems', in C. Goodsell (ed.), *The Public Encounter: Where State and Citizen Meet* (Bloomington: Indiana University Press).

Hirschman, A. (1970) *Exit Voice and Loyalty: Responses to Decline in Firms, Organization and States* (Cambridge Mass.: Harvard University Press).

—— (1981) 'Exit, Voice and Loyalty: Further Reflections and a Survey of Recent Contributions', in *Essays in Trespassing: Economics to Politics and Beyond* (Cambridge: Cambridge University Press).

—— (1982) *Shifting Involvements: Private Interest and Public Action* (Oxford: Blackwells).

Hogg, R., and Findlay, M. (1985) 'Police and the Community: Some Issues Raised by Recent Overseas Research', in I. Freckelton and H. Selby (eds.), *Police in Our Society* (Sydney: Butterworths).

Hood, C. (1986) 'Concepts of Control Over Public Bureaucracies: "Comptrol" and "Interpolable Balance" ' in F. Kaufmann, G. Majone, and V. Ostrom (eds.), *Guidance, Control and Evaluation in the Public Sector* (Berlin: de Gruyter).

Hood, R., and Sparks, R. (1970), *Key Issues in Criminology* (London: Weidenfeld & Nicolson).

Hudson, J. (1971) 'Police Review Boards and Police Accountability', *Law and Contemporary Problems* 36: 515–38.

—— (1972) 'Organizational Aspects of Internal and External Review of the Police', *Journal of Criminal Law, Criminology and Police Science* 63: 427–33.

Kirby, M. (1976) 'New Light on Complaints Against Police', in Sydney Institute of Criminology, *Proceedings of a Seminar on Complaints Against Police* (Sydney: Faculty of Law, University of Sydney).

Lipski, M. (1980) *Street-Level Bureaucracy: Dilemmas of the Individual in Public Services* (New York: Russell Sage).

Littlejohn, E. (1981) 'The Civilian Police Commission: A Deterrent of Police Misconduct', *University of Detroit Journal of Urban Law* 59: 5–59.

London Strategy Policy Unit (1987) Police Accountability and a New Strategic Authority for London (Police Monitoring and Research Group Briefing Paper No. 2) (London: LSPU).

Lustgarten, L. (1986) *The Governance of Police* (London: Sweet and Maxwell).

Maloney, A. (1975) *Report: The Metropolitan Toronto Review of Citizen–Police Complaint Procedure* (Toronto: Metropolitan Toronto Board of Commissioners of Police).

Melbourne *Age* (1989) 'Policing the Police', 11 September 1989, p. 1.

Monk, A., Kaye, L., and Litwin, H. (1984) *Resolving Grievances in the Nursing Home: A Study of the Ombudsman Program* (New York: Columbia University Press).

Nader, L. (1984) 'From Disputing to Complaining', in D. Black (ed.) *Toward a General Theory of Social Control* (New York: Academic Press).

—— and Shugart, C. (1980) 'Old Solutions for Old Problems', in L. Nader (ed.), *No Access to Law: Alternatives to the American Judicial System* (New York: Academic Press).

Nelson, P. (1986) 'Beyond the Blue Curtain: The Ombudsman's Role in

60   *Andrew J. Goldsmith*

Investigating Complaints Against the Police in New South Wales', *Australian Journal of Public Administration* 45: 230–8.

New South Wales (1987) *Ombudsman of New South Wales: Special Report to Parliament: The First Three Years of the New Police Complaints System* (Sydney: Office of Ombudsman).

Nonet, P., and Selznick, P. (1978) *Law and Society in Transition: Towards Responsive Law* (New York: Harper Torchbooks).

—— (1978) *Law and Society in Transition* (New York: Harper Colophon).

Packer, H. (1968) The Limits of the Criminal Sanction (Stanford University Press).

Punch, M. (1985) *Conduct Unbecoming: The Social Construction of Deviance and Social Control* (London: Tavistock Publications).

—— (ed.) (1983) *Control in the Police Organization* (Cambridge, Mass.: MIT Press).

Queensland (1989) *Report of a Commission of Inquiry Pursuant to Orders in Council* (Brisbane: Queensland Government Printer).

Radelet, L. (1980) *The Police and the Community* (3rd edn.) (New York: Macmillan).

Reiner, R. (1985) *The Politics of the Police* (Brighton: Wheatsheaf Books).

Rippon, J. (1984) 'Complaints Against Police', *Victoria Police Association Journal* 49: 9.

Rubinstein, J. (1973) *City Police* (New York: Farrar, Straus, and Giroux).

Russell, K. (1976) *Complaints Against the Police: A Sociological View* (Leicester: Milltak).

Scarman, L. (1982) *The Scarman Report: The Brixton Disorders 10–12 April 1981* (Harmondsworth: Penguin).

Schuck, P. (1983) *Suing Government: Citizen Remedies for Official Wrongs* (New Haven: Yale University Press).

Selby, H. (1988) 'Internal Investigations: Too Little, Too Late', in I. Freckelton and H. Selby (eds.), *Police in Our Society* (Sydney: Butterworths).

Shearing, C. (ed.) (1981) *Organizational Police Deviance* (Toronto: Butterworths).

Sherman, L. (1978) *Scandal and Reform: Controlling Police Corruption* (Berkeley: University of California).

Skolnick, J. (1966) *Justice Without Trial* (New York: Wiley).

—— and McCoy, C. (1984) 'Police Accountability and the Media', *American Bar Foundation Research Journal* 521–57.

Smith, D., and Gray, J. (1983) *Police and People in London: The PSI Report* (Aldershot: Gower).

South Australia (1983) *Report of the Committee on Complaints Against the Police* (Chairman: I. Grieve) (Adelaide: Government Printer).

—— (1989) *Annual Report of the Police Complaints Authority, 30 June 1988* (Adelaide: Government Printer).

Terrill, R. (1980) 'Complaint Procedures Against Police: The Movement for Change in England, Canada and Australia', *Police Studies* 3: 37–46.

—— (1982) 'Complaint Procedures: Variations on the Theme of Civilian Participation', *Journal of Police Science and Administration* 10: 398–406.

—— (1983) 'Complaints Against Police in England', *American Journal of Comparative Law* 31: 599–626.

US (1967) *The Task Force Report: The Police* (Washington: President's Commission on Law Enforcement and Administration of Justice).

Victoria (1971) *A Report on the Victoria Police Force Following an Inspection by Colonel Sir Eric St Johnston* (Melbourne: Government Printer).

—— (1978) *Report of the Board of Inquiry into Allegations Against Members of the Victoria Police Force* (Melbourne: Government Printer).

—— (1987) *Review of the Investigation of Complaints by the Internal Investigation Department of the Victoria Police: Report to the Minister for Police and Emergency Services by Professor J. Richardson.*

—— (1988) *Police Complaints Authority Final Report.*

Walker, S. (1986) 'Controlling the Cops: A Legislative Approach to Police Rulemaking', *University of Detroit Law Review* 63: 361.

Walsh-Buckley, W. (1989) 'Police Discipline in Victoria', unpublished honours thesis (Faculty of Law, Monash University).

Western Australia (1989) *Report of the Parliamentary Commissioner for Administrative Investigations*, 30 June 1989 (Perth: Government Printer).

Williams G. (1984) *The Law and Politics of Police Discretion* (Westport, Conn.: Greenwood).

Wilson, J. (1968) *Varieties of Police Behaviour* (Cambridge, Mass.: Harvard University Press).

Wirth, W. (1986) 'Public Administration and Publics: Control of Bureaucratic Performance by Affected Citizens', in F. Kaufmann, G. Majone, and V. Ostrom (eds.), *Guidance, Control and Evaluation in the Public Sector* (Berlin: de Gruyter).

2

Shooting the Messenger:

The Trial and Execution of the Victorian Police Complaints Authority

IAN FRECKELTON

Counsel assisting the inquiry, Mr Douglas Drummond QC, suggested to Sir Joh[1] that by taking the police force's side in all matters, resisting calls for inquiries into alleged brutality and by using it as a political tool in such matters as street marches, he might also have helped create a climate in which corruption was likely to flourish.

Sir Joh said: 'I can't accept that at all. . . . When you have top men in the department and they say it's not true, naturally you believe it. You have to believe it or otherwise you get into a very confused position yourself.

(Simons 1988: 10)

INTRODUCTION

The Police Complaints Authority of Victoria was abolished by its State Government in May 1988 only twenty-two months after its creation was announced with fanfare and expectation by the Victorian Minister for Police and Emergency Services. The story of its fall from grace is a short one but illustrative of important truths about Australian politics in the late 1980s and also about the nature of administrative reform. It is an unfortunate fact that the Victorian experience is part of a larger problem existing throughout Australia in relation to the accountability of all its policing institutions.

The premature end of the Police Complaints Authority was

This chapter is dedicated to the Authority's staff whose commitment made the Authority the threat to corrupt police and poor police practices that it had become by the time of its demise.

[1] Sir Joh Bjelke-Petersen, former Premier of Queensland testifying before the Fitzgerald Royal Commission into Corruption.

described by Paul Wilson, the Assistant Director of the Australian Institute of Criminology as 'one of the greatest tragedies of contemporary policing' (Voumard 1988). By contrast, its untimely demise was greeted with a sense of relief by the Labor government of the day. It is probable that members of the general community, who were the onlookers to an extraordinary saga of developing confrontation between an independent statutory authority and its government, simply viewed events with a sense of incomprehension and confusion.

The writer of this Chapter was a player in the drama of the short life of the Police Complaints Authority as its Manager and Counsel Assisting. As such he cannot be regarded as entirely disinterested in the events of 1986 to 1988, or always objective. None the less, he believes that it would be preferable to err on the side of Dr Wilson's assessment and that it is important not to let the events that brought about the end of the Authority go unrecorded and unexplained. The abolition of the Authority just when it was becoming fully effective and fulfilling the functions given to it by its charter was of course disappointing to all concerned with the body. But it was also a matter of acute embarrassment to the government, which somehow had to explain why it had felt the need to constitute the Authority in July 1986 and then only twenty-two months later to abolish it, returning its functions to the ombudsman from whom it had earlier felt it necessary to withdraw them. Most of all, though, the unnatural death of the Police Complaints Authority was a tragedy for the accountability of members of the Victoria Police Force, an extraordinary number of whom communicated their regret and anger to their own command and also to members of the Authority and the government. Eighteen months after the events of 1988, Victoria's leading newspaper twice felt sufficiently concerned about the lack of police accountability after the abolition of the Police Complaints Authority to advocate via editorials its reconstitution (*Age*, 15 and 29 September 1989).

Looking back with all the benefits that hindsight provides, there is no doubt that the Authority made mistakes (it would be foolish to pretend otherwise) but, as so often occurs, its best quality, its willingness and capacity to orchestrate change to Victorian policing, proved also to be the chief cause of its downfall. It is to be hoped that the lessons to be learned from its short life will in time avail those who inevitably some years in the future will be given a similar mandate to that entrusted in 1986 to the short-lived Victorian watchdog.

THE BACKGROUND TO THE VICTORIAN AUTHORITY

There were experiments with a variety of watchdogs over the police in Australasia during the 1980s (Goldsmith, Chapter 1 above, and Goode Chapter 3 below). The realization that an external body was necessary to supervise investigations into police misconduct found its clearest form in the first and ninth reports of the Australian Law Reform Commission in 1975 and 1978 (Australian Law Reform Commission 1975, 1978).[2] Those reports recommended the creation of an investigatory watchdog system along ombudsman lines. They also proposed that the new ombudsman have jurisdiction to oversee and monitor the investigations done internally by police into allegations of misconduct. They suggested the establishment of internal investigation departments within Australian police forces to have the primary responsibility for the investigation of police misconduct. The reasons advanced by the Commission have since been influential in the creation of a reasonably uniform model for internal/external review throughout Australasia:

There are a large number of reasons why, in the normal course of events, the investigation of complaints, and particularly complaints which may potentially involve criminal charges, can best be carried out by experienced police personnel. Policemen suspected of a crime ought to be investigated, just as any other citizen would be, by the police. Normally, the necessary investigatory skill and expertise can be found only in the police service, or in former members of that service. Furthermore, investigation of apparently non-criminal complaints may, in the process, reveal criminal or possibly criminal offences. It has also been the experience of police that complaints, especially serious complaints, frequently involve possible offences by both police and civilians. Accordingly complete exclusion of police from the investigation could result in the circumvention or oversight of criminal charges. (Australian Law Reform Commission 1975: para. 71.)[3]

By the mid-1980s all police forces in Australia had established internal disciplinary units and each state had established an independent body responsible for monitoring the performance of the units. Politicians in a number of states basked in the complacency of

[2] See also Board of Inquiry 1976; Committee of Inquiry 1985: 50.
[3] See also St Johnston (1971).

having done 'the necessary' about corruption by supervising the establishment of formalized internal and external review of police misconduct. As late as May 1988 the new Liberal Minister of Police in New South Wales felt able to proclaim, 'If anyone thinks that they are being harassed by a police officer, all they do is complain and as far as I am concerned the harassment stops.' (*Sydney Morning Herald* 11 May 1988.)

Similar pronouncements were heard from senior members of the Queensland government until the exposures of the Fitzgerald Royal Commission into Corruption in 1989 (Fitzgerald 1989), from the Victorian government in face of the evidence of the Police Complaints Authority in 1987, and from the South Australian Government until the setting up of a National Crime Authority branch in 1988–9 after undeniable evidence of major police involvement in drug-dealing. By the late 1980s the efficacy of the existing external review bodies had been seriously called into question in many quarters and changes to the existing models were being implemented in a number of jurisdictions.

In 1985 and 1986 separate Police Complaints Authorities had been created in South Australia and Victoria, withdrawing the police jurisdiction from the ombudsmen. 1988 brought the demise of the Victorian Police Complaints Authority and the return of its functions to the ombudsman but, ironically, the creation of another Authority, this time in New Zealand.

In New South Wales, police dissatisfaction with the ombudsman's role became a political issue in the 1988 election which brought the state's conservative opposition, the Liberal Party, to power. Moves to reduce the ombudsman's functions in the police complaints area proved to be extremely controversial. In Queensland in July 1989 Commissioner Fitzgerald recommended the abandonment of both the internal investigation department of the Queensland Police Force and the Police Complaints Tribunal. In its place he proposed a wide-ranging Criminal Justice Commission with an Official Misconduct Division, one of whose tasks would be to investigate complaints against police (see Goldsmith, Chapter 1 above). It would be an entity independent of the police but staffed by civilians and police. By the beginning of 1990 the new Labor government in Queensland was setting up the Criminal Justice Commission.

The reasons for the creation in 1986 of the Victorian Police Complaints Authority and the removal of monitoring functions over the police from the ombudsman have never been clear. When announcing the establishment of the Police Complaints Authority, the State Labor government expressed the optimism that one would expect about the initiative of a new 'anti-corruption body' but stopped short of criticizing the performance of the Ombudsman or his office in monitoring the performance of the Internal Investigation Department of the Victoria Police.

The mystery is deepened by the fact that Premier Cain had been one of the Commissioners at the Australian Law Reform Commission a decade earlier when that body had argued against the creation of a police-specific watchdog. It is clear, however, that concern had been expressed for a time by senior members of the Victoria Police that the ombudsman's 'paper warfare', as they termed his oversight of their activities, was consuming significant amounts of police time with few readily identifiable results. In fact, police antipathy toward the ombudsman's role by 1985 was threatening to become a political embarrassment to the government.

Ironically, in a memorandum to the Minister for Police in 1985, the then highly respected Chief Commissioner of Police reacted to dissatisfaction with internal handling of complaints against police and recommended that the process be taken from police entirely and given over to the ombudsman (18 March 1985).[4] The Chief Commissioner argued that an arrangement whereby an external body oversaw the investigations conducted by police was 'likely to produce conflicts of interest and control within the police force'.

POLICE POLITICIZATION

Thus it is likely that the Police Complaints Authority was born out of political pressure exerted in good part by police command and the Victorian police union, the Police Association. That the Association should have been able to accomplish the removal of responsibility for

---

[4] In this sentiment, he was later echoed by his successor and by the Secretaries of the Police Association. Littlejohn (1981: 35) noted that such suggestions can flow from a recognition that it 'would be to the department's advantage . . . to propose the least meddlesome form of civilian involvement'. There would be significant benefits, of course, for police departments no longer to have to endure criticism of their internal investigations. From a propaganda point of view (see D. L. Altheide and J. M. Johnson 1980), the enemy could more easily be criticized as anti-police and having a vested, uninformed interest. For the corrupt, the threat may well also be diminished because of the grave difficulties of investigating entirely from the outside. The truth is that police fear internal investigations (see Brown 1989).

monitoring the police from the ombudsman is no surprise in the Australian context in the 1980s.[5] The vesting of jurisdiction to monitor internal investigations in external watchdogs proved to be a sensitive issue from the earliest attempts. In South Australia and Western Australia it took place aimed threats of police strikes (Freckelton and Selby 1989). Immediately after the abolition of the Victorian Police Complaints Authority, the Association's focus turned towards the disciplinary tribunals to which they were subject. The Association's calls for substantial change were accompanied by thinly veiled threats of strike action if they failed to secure acceptance of their demands.

The 1980s in Australia saw a growing politicization of policing issues and of police forces themselves to the point where in the 1988 Victorian elections police played an active role in the campaign itself (Bailey 1988). Also, in line with trends in many parts of the western world, 'law and order' emerged as an increasingly emotive and potentially important electoral issue. Police forces stepped up their campaigns for additional funding, staffing levels, and powers. They met with no small measure of success as political parties recognized the superficial attractiveness of being seen to be doing something tangible to reduce the rising rates of property crime and the incidence of crimes of violence. In Victoria within four years the police gained new powers to take fingerprints and intimate body samples, and to keep suspects in custody, as well as a superannuation package that was the envy of most other unions in Australia. By the end of the 1980s it was recognized throughout the country that for a political party with an election in the offing to antagonize a police union was tantamount to electoral suicide. The police union would immediately consolidate its allegiance with the opposing party, and the party not behaving in compliance with the wishes of the union would run the risk of being portrayed as 'soft on crime' and 'anti-law-and-order'.

In some states a particularly close relationship developed between the conservative Liberal Party (often in opposition) and the police union. An example that was especially evident was the bond between the Victoria Police Association and the Liberal shadow Attorney General and shadow Minister for Police and Emergency Services. One of the fruits of this was a private member's bill providing for

[5] It would be useful to compare the tactics of United States police forces to the creation of Citizen Review Boards in the 1960s (see Goldsmith, Chap. 1 above).

significantly increased powers for the police force. It was introduced into Parliament by the shadow Attorney General and enjoyed the unqualified support of the Victoria Police.[6]

EARLY EXPERIENCES OF THE AUTHORITY

The Victorian Police Complaints Authority began to function in July 1986 and soon discovered that the legislation that had constituted it, the Police Regulation (Amendment) Act 1985 (Vic.), bore all the signs of having been drafted by committee rather than in any systematic and coherent fashion. The Authority's powers were vague and capable of many different interpretations and its teeth, if it could be regarded as having any at all, were thoroughly blunted. Moreover, the government, having approved its creation, did nothing month after month to secure office space or appropriate resources for the young watchdog.[7]

An early incident served to demonstrate the problems. Members of the Authority received representations that a number of raids had been improperly carried out on hotels in the northern suburbs of Melbourne. It was alleged to the Authority that undue force had been used by police on members of the public and that serious injuries had been inflicted on drinkers. It was even suggested that one of those arrested had committed suicide in police custody. However, the allegations were oral, sometimes anonymous and in one outstanding instance were made by a local personality, a former federal politician, claiming to represent up to thirty of those in the hotels at the time of the raids.

The traditional approach of external monitoring bodies in Australia had been to allow the police to have first opportunity to investigate allegations of police misconduct and to intervene only where the internal investigation was not adequate. However, it was expressly provided for in the Authority's enabling legislation that it could conduct the first investigation if it was 'in the public interest'.[8] In the circumstances it was impossible to assess whether it would be in the public interest for the Authority to conduct the primary

[6] Police (Powers of Investigation) Bill 1987 (Vic.).

[7] Wilenski (1986) commented that 'allocation of resources . . . may be seen as the practical manifestation of political will'. In retrospect, this unwillingness of the government to set up the Authority promptly and properly takes on sinister overtones.

[8] See Police Regulation Act 1958 (Vic.) s. 86 (4) (b) (i).

investigation because the information that it had hitherto received was somewhat garbled and much of it was at second or third hand. It was determined that the best course of action was to attempt to obtain first-hand information from those who had witnessed or been privy to the actual incidents. It was hoped that after such initial inquiries it would be possible to assess whether an investigation should be undertaken by the Authority, using, if necessary, its powers to compel information from police members. However, there were difficulties. Because of months' delay by government officials, all the Authority's staff were housed in two small rooms in the back of a government department (ironically the Department of Police and Emergency Services) in the centre of Melbourne, some forty kilometres from the scene of the alleged incidents. It seemed incompatible with the idea of the Authority being a public-access body (see Hill 1977: 12; Goldsmith, Chapter 1 above) that it should sit in its offices and summon people far from their homes to provide information about a matter which, potentially at least, was of serious public concern. Thus, the Authority had a notice posted in two of the hotels stating that anyone with relevant, first-hand information could provide it on the next Saturday afternoon to members of the Authority who would be present to take their statements. Readers were reminded that it was a criminal offence to give false information to the Authority.

The response of the Police Association was instant. It proclaimed the Authority's action to be 'touting for business' and exceeding its charter. It sought an immediate injunction from the Supreme Court to prevent the Authority attending at the hotels and from initiating any inquiries in relation to the police conduct there. The application was heard as a matter of urgency by a single judge of the Supreme Court on Friday afternoon, and was granted. It was not until September of the next year that the Full Court of the Supreme Court of Victoria overruled the earlier interim decision and held that 'the Authority cannot be confined to the totally passive role of receiving complaints' (*Selby* v. *McCrohan* [1988] VR 460, 464). By this stage, of course, all point in determining whether or not the Authority should itself investigate had been lost. The only positive aspect in the exercise had been the demonstration that the Supreme Court was prepared to interpret the Authority's ambiguous legislation in such a way as to allow it to advertise 'in any appropriate way that it existed to receive complaints about members of the police force, where such

complaints might be made, between what hours and related matters.'
(ibid.).

The experience showed the hostility to the new style of watchdog
on the part of the Police Association. It also highlighted the
unpreparedness of the government to intervene to remedy problems
that were remediable, such as the enabling legislation which already
fettered the Authority's work and left doubt as to the propriety of its
conduct in the minds of those over whom it was to be a watchdog.

The Authority, though, had experienced subtler difficulties than
the frontal assault by the Police Association. An attempt had been
made by a very senior member of the Internal Investigation
Department to insinuate himself into the good graces of a member of
the Authority's staff. The attempt had been most successful and
chronic leaks developed in relation to the Authority's investigations
until the situation was remedied.

Crises continued with the relationship between the Authority and
police hierarchy who were discovering that the approach of the
Authority was quite different from that which had developed from
the ombudsman. The hierarchy had been irritated and dissatisfied
with the approach of the ombudsman, which had been to review
every file produced by the internal department and to oversee on
paper every investigation. Paper warfare had developed but few
useful results had been achieved by the ombudsman. The Authority
deliberately adopted a different tack. It would not examine every file
but chose to focus instead on random selections of internal
investigation department files and also on instances where complainants maintained that the internal investigation had been deficient. In
these circumstances the Authority would examine the materials
compiled by the internal department exhaustively and, if necessary,
by compelling the police involved to give once more an account of
their behaviour. On occasions it conducted a thorough reinvestigation
using its formal powers to assemble evidence.[9]

The Authority also attempted to circumvent a number of formal
procedures that it saw as clogging up police efficiency. This was its
response to the grievance that was so often articulated by police
officers that they spent an increasing amount of their time
completing bureaucratic exigencies and not doing 'police work'. The

---

[9] This was in contrast to the approach envisaged by the Police and Criminal
Evidence Act 1984 (Eng.), s. 87 and the Police (Complaints) (Mandatory Referrals,
etc.) Regulations [1985] SI 1985 No. 673. See also Nelson (1986).

decision was made to open up contact with the internal department and to use the advantages of the Authority's independence to short-circuit minor complaints, deal with them quickly in co-operation with the internal department, and thereby free police investigators so that they could expend their energies on the most serious matters (Freckelton 1988c). Thus, fewer formal letters were drafted and demanded of police by the Authority. When a telephone call would suffice, the pen was discarded. Attempts were made to extend an olive branch and work with police on sensitive investigations. To a police force that had had formalism thrust upon it and had become comfortable with long and unnecessary letter-writing and back-protecting procedures this was anathema (Selby 1989). A traditional defence of an organization perceiving itself under threat was adopted:

to publicly proclaim support of innovative goals, and while doing that to build in various controlling safeguards, such as special committees, thereby insuring that the work is always accomplished through power structure channels and thus effecting no real change. This tactic achieves the nullification of the innovator while at the same time giving the power structure the public semblance of progressiveness. (Graziano 1969: 12.)

For a time, every reduction in paper-flow attempted by the Authority was matched with further bureaucratism from senior police. Difficulties were only temporarily reduced, and legalist testing of the Authority's powers in the Supreme Court avoided, by the pronouncement by the Chief Commissioner of Police that the Authority, by the spirit of the legislation creating it, had a right to expect reasonable co-operation from the police force. For about two months passive obstructionism by senior officers was suspended.

THE PROBLEMS RECOGNIZED

From the beginning of 1987 the Authority devoted its energies to an attempt to understand why so many were dissatisfied with the operation of the Internal Investigation Department of the Victoria Police. Community centre lawyers, solicitors' firms specializing in criminal law, representatives of minority groups, and youth workers were vocal in their disparagement of even submitting grievances to the police because of the low record of successful resolution of complaints. They were similarly disillusioned with the ombudsman's ineffectiveness in improving the performance of the internal unit and were interested in the idea of abandoning the concept of an internal investigating mechanism (Federation of Community Legal Centres 1987; see Settle 1990: 119 ff). The figure of 3–4 per cent resolution of complaints in favour of the complainant was often cited in discussions with the Authority.[10]

The usual approach adopted by the Authority to select complaints for thorough reinvestigation was on the basis of the complainant's appeal for the Authority to follow up the Internal Investigation Department's investigations. The negative side of this policy was that it stressed the importance of the complainant demonstrating his or her bona fides by actively seeking redress through the newly established Authority. The positive side of the policy was that the Authority could focus its limited resources (the whole office only consisted of seven people) on those investigations where complainants maintained that something had gone wrong and the truth had not been arrived at.

Patterns soon began to emerge (Freckelton and Selby 1989; Selby 1988; Police Complaints Authority 1987, 1988*a*). It was discovered that the police internal unit in Victoria, which at that stage numbered some seventy people, lacked any real investigative energy (see also Fitzgerald 1989: 366.) The initial attitude to the complainant was one of suspicion and readiness to disbelieve. This meant that immediate attention was devoted to means of discrediting the complainant. Unfortunately, all too many complainants with grievances against a practice within the force, or who had suffered at the hands of a member's misconduct, were emotive in their language and lacked objectivity in the expression of their frustrations. Also many had criminal records and were known to members of the unit. They were ripe for being labelled as malicious, vexatious, or vindictive (Freckelton 1988*c*; Freckelton and Selby 1990). The internal unit obliged. Sometimes investigations into police misconduct turned into interrogations of the complainant and focused on the possible criminality of the complainant's behaviour. On other occasions, pressure was put on complainants or witnesses, subtly or even overtly, to think again about persevering with their

---

[10] Later that figure was to be specifically quantified at 2.3% by Prof. Richardson (1987), the former Commonwealth Ombudsman, in his review of the performance of the internal investigation department. However, Littlejohn (1981: 15) in the USA and Lustgarten (1986: 154) in England cite not dissimilar figures, particularly in relation to substantiation of assault allegations.

assertions against serving police members. They would accomplish little. The process was long. The assertions might harm them in court. They were distressing for the members' families. They might harm a member's promotion chances (Police Complaints Authority 1988*b*). Later, we were to learn of even more sinister attempts to intimidate complainants by preferring extra charges against them when they had the temerity to complain and even by contemplating the possibility of prosecuting them for contempt when they aired their grievances publicly (see Simons 1989*b*, 1989*c*; see also below).

This process translated into something even more pernicious for the effective investigation of complaints. Little effort was made to ask probing questions of police against whom allegations had been made. Their word was accepted at face value. Often there was no record of interview with questions and answers. Police officers were simply allowed to make a statement after having the full details of the complaint against them set out. Sometimes they were shown the statement of another member and simply asked if they had anything to add. Frequently, they were given the opportunity of saying nothing if they so desired. This was so even though the investigation was primarily disciplinary—it was only ever likely that the member would be charged in the disciplinary tribunal and not in the criminal courts.

Many of the problems came down to grossly deficient investigative technique.[11] Internal investigators permitted rampant opportunities for collaboration among suspects.[12] An extreme example illustrating this was where internal investigators broadcast details of an alleged incident of misconduct by members over radio in order to take a short cut to finding the police car involved (Freckelton and Selby 1989; Police Complaints Authority 1988*a*: 52 ff.). Investigations were terribly slow and there appeared little systematic decision-making about the order in which witnesses and suspects should be interviewed by the investigators. The only discernible consideration appeared to be the convenience of the investigator. Thus there were occasions on which the officers most directly the subject of complaint were interviewed last, by which time their colleagues had

---

[11] The PCA had on its agenda for 1989–90 a close analysis of investigative practice within the Victoria Police to determine the extent to which internal investigations differed from those of 'ordinary criminals'.

[12] See Punch (1985: 163) for 'sympathetic' attitudes in the Dutch Police Force to 'suspects' by other police officers.

had the opportunity to explain in detail to them the direction which the investigation was taking. If they were not by then able to fabricate a plausible, exculpatory version of events, they did not deserve to be in the police force because of lack of intelligence!

Another criticism which had frequently been made to the Authority about internal investigations was the time that they took. Serving police found lengthy inquiries untenable because they had a cloud of unresolved suspicion hanging over them for anything up to eighteen months (see also Chesshyre 1989: 215). The average period for resolution of a complaint varied during the life of the Authority but averaged between eight and ten months. This had the additional consequence that it was quite unlikely that complaints with a justifiable basis would be resolved in favour of the complainant. Time played into the hands of police malefactors. Memories faded, documents could be doctored, stories could be concocted, and alibis cemented. The hierarchy in the Internal Investigation Department would not acknowledge this. Instead, they stressed the importance of following procedures and interviewing all witnesses, however tangentially relevant (or irrelevant) their contribution to the investigation manifestly was.

The Authority also found that the absence of any clear charter for the Internal Investigation Department meant that its members were unclear on the fundamental policies that should have been guiding their investigations (Selby 1988: 242). In these circumstances, they were indecisive about whether in individual cases they should be conducting a criminal or a disciplinary inquiry. This had significant implications for the way in which they went about their investigations and the depth to which they pursued their inquiries. Ironically, too, this perception by the Police Complaints Authority drew attention to the absence of any clear charter for the Authority, a matter which it highlighted to the government in its 1987 Annual Report (Police Complaints Authority 1987). Also, the way in which the internal unit communicated with complainants was high-handed and terse, giving little information about the investigations which had been conducted but giving the impression (perhaps correctly) that police had automatically been believed rather than complainants. The vast majority of complaints were classified with the unsatisfactory description 'not substantiated' in the absence of independent evidence. This exacerbated the tendency of many of those who had dealings with the internal unit to believe that their investigations were no more than a whitewash. When matters came to court, an improperly close relationship between members of the internal department and police prosecutors was repeatedly described by practising barristers and litigation solicitors. This meant that internal investigators frequently focused upon possible criminality on the part of the complainant rather than upon his or her grievances about police treatment. They once again confused roles, lapsing into their more usual identities as detectives investigating reported criminal offences.

The Authority repeatedly drew the attention of police command to the methodological deficiencies which it had identified in internal investigation department practices. No response was forthcoming save that attention would be given to the matters raised by the Authority. No changes of any substance were implemented and during 1987 a hardening of attitude was noticeable from senior police towards day-to-day requests for co-operation from members of the Authority's staff.

The Authority responded by publishing its previously private critique in its 1987 Annual Report and addressing a series of seminars on policing which it had been a party to organizing.[13] These covered issues such as police accountability, police powers, police management, community policing, and police and the media. This prompted concern from police command and the Minister for Police and Emergency Services. The Chief Commissioner forbade his senior officers at the last minute to participate in the seminars (although the force had been officially engaged in organizing them until the last stages) on the basis that they would be 'contrary to the good order and discipline of the Victoria Police'. The Minister attempted to 'persuade' the Authority to renounce any involvement, stopping just short of giving orders to the supposedly independent body to forswear its self-proclaimed role as catalyst for informed discussion about the reform of policing in Victoria.

It was only in 1989, through obtaining documents under freedom of information legislation, that the role of the police during the seminars came to public light. Melbourne investigative journalist Margaret Simons discovered that members of the police special intelligence unit, which had taken over the functions of the special

---

[13] The proceedings of these seminars were published in Freckleton and Selby (1988*a*).

branch when it was disbanded in name in 1983, attended the seminars covertly. They reported directly to the Chief Commissioner about those who attended the seminars, the reception accorded to individual papers, and their views about 'anti-police' elements in the audience and in the programme (Simons 1989*a*). Early in 1990 (Simons 1990) the not unsurprising response to Ms Simons's journalism came from the Acting Chief Commissioner to the *Age*:

It is my view that despite the considerable effort which the force has expended to provide responses, your newspaper has failed to give a balanced version of the issues. I therefore advise that there will be no further comment made to assist you in what seems to me to be little short of a vendetta against the Victoria Police.

The game was no longer being played according to the rules the police wanted, so they kicked over the stumps and declared the umpire to be biased. By April, senior police stepped up their campaign of attrition against the *Age* by threatening to take Ms Simons to the Press Council and by reducing their level of contact with the paper wherever possible. Scoops went elsewhere to more co-operative journalists.

In spite of the withdrawal of formal police involvement, the 'Police in Our Society' seminars proved of great interest to the media, as did the revelations by senior members of the Authority that Victorian internal investigations and police management left much to be desired. Whenever a policing issue became news, it subsequently became the practice of members of the media to contact the Authority and ask for comment from its senior staff. This was provided whenever it was viewed as relevant to the role of the Authority to make recommendations for change to policing practices and procedures. It was one of the few times when an organization was routinely approached in Australia to give an informed alternative opinion to the views propounded by the police on policing issues (see also Grabosky and Wilson 1989). The high profile of Authority members also had the bonus of keeping the Authority visible to members of the community uncertain whether or not they should report their grievances about police behaviour so that they could be investigated (see Hill 1977: 12). It 'flushed out' many legitimate complainants who were either hesitant about whether to complain or did not know whom to approach.

THE LEGISLATIVE PROBLEMS

After the publication of the 1987 Annual Report, the Authority made a policy decision to concentrate its resources thenceforth on formal investigations. Its aim was to demonstrate how the internal unit could most effectively utilize its now waning resources and to correct individual injustices perpetrated by poor police investigative practice. However, this caused it to confront regularly a problem which it had already drawn to the attention of government.

The legislation which had created the Authority was poorly drafted and cryptic. On a practical level, this meant that when the Authority had to exercise those powers which had apparently been intended by the parliamentary drafters to be analogous to those of Royal Commissions, they were seriously in doubt. The Authority was hamstrung by its inability to compel police to obey its directives. Although it was supposed to be armed with the same powers of investigation as the Chief Commissioner,[14] there was no means other than police co-operation to enforce directives given to members of the police force.

The response of the government to the 1987 Annual Report of the Police Complaints Authority was to set up a working party to examine the feasibility of the Authority's proposals. This superficially sounded a reasonable reaction, but the import of the move was demonstrated by the constitution of the working party. It was to be chaired by a medium-level, non-lawyer bureaucrat from the Ministry of Police and Emergency Services. The others on the committee, aside from the two senior members of the Authority, were representatives of the Victoria Police and the Police Association. There were no lawyers, other than the Authority's own, to scrutinize the draft legislation, nor any representative from the Attorney-General's Department or any other part of government. From the beginning it was clear that setting up the working party was a gesture intended to secure the appearance of government responsiveness to the concerns of the Authority but guaranteed to torpedo any proposals advanced by the statutory body. After a series of utterly fruitless meetings the Authority withdrew its participation from the exercise.

In its 1987 Annual Report the Authority presented to the

[14] Police Regulation (Amendment) Act 1986 (Vic.) s. 86 Q.

government a draft bill to remedy the deficiencies which it had identified in its enabling legislation. It pointed out the absence of a clear charter for the Authority, as well as for the internal department of the police. It noted that the Authority could conduct investigations when that was 'in the public interest' but that no indication was given of when that would be. The result of this was that neither the Victoria Police nor the Authority knew when the Authority rather than the police should investigate. Members of the police force were also unable to complain directly to the Authority and were having to resort to ruses, through spouses and parents, to bring forward their concerns. There were occasions too when the Authority needed to be able to investigate matters on its own initiative, without having to wait for someone to lodge a formal complaint. This was easily remediable without allowing the Authority to behave unacceptably.

The Authority, although nominally independent, was linked to the Minister when it needed to exercise its powers to take evidence from a member of the public. His permission was required, as was his intervention when a disagreement existed between the Authority and the Chief Commissioner. This had the potential to place the Minister in an invidious position. Much more sensible from an investigative point of view was to give to the Authority standard Royal Commission powers, such as already possessed by the National Crime Authority,[15] and ensure that legal procedures existed for the courts to review any abuse of those powers.

The Authority also recommended that complainants be accorded the right to a statement of reasons for the decisions of the Internal Investigation Department or of the Authority and an explanation of what action had been taken on the basis of their complaints. It was also suggested that members of the Authority be obliged by legislation to disclose any conflicts of interest that they encountered (Police Complaints Authority 1987, 1988*a*). The Authority also drew attention to an anomaly in the legislation that allowed the ombudsman to act as a court of appeal when complainants were dissatisfied with the Authority's determinations, as well as those of the Internal Investigation Department. Apparently through oversight, the ombudsman had the power to review the decisions of the Police Complaints Authority. Such a mechanism would inevitably prove problematic as it involved one statutory watchdog monitoring

---

[15] The pre-eminent body in Australia for investigating organized crime, set up by the National Crime Authority Act 1984 (Cth).

another. It was an extraordinary duplication of resources. In this instance, though, it was all the more inappropriate because the legislature had seen fit to abandon the ombudsman system of reviewing complaints against the police and at significant cost had established a new body with expertise imported from interstate to do the job. The anomaly allowed the ombudsman repeatedly to undermine the new system for dealing with complaints against the police that the Authority was trying to establish. He apparently perceived his role as a court of appeal as a means of making the new police watchdog reluctantly 'accountable'—to him.

Finally, the Authority drafted legislation clarifying its powers and the rights of those whom it proposed to investigate. The need for such clarification was vividly instanced by ongoing police obstructionism in the course of the Authority's investigations. On one occasion five young men alleged that they had been seriously assaulted by inner-city Melbourne police. The two senior members of the Authority arranged to interview police officers who had allegedly been closely involved in the incident. The officers refused to be interviewed unless they could record all questions and answers and retain the tapes. The irony was that the Authority always permitted a senior policeman to be present at its interviews, as well as allowing all discussions to be tape-recorded. It did not permit the tapes to be removed from its premises immediately, however, because this permitted an intolerable degree of collaboration between suspect police.

The Authority was powerless to force the police to answer its questions without conditions. It had the option of initiating a Supreme Court challenge to its legislation but this would take a considerable amount of time during which it feared the police union could be expected to undermine its investigations on a systematic basis. The Authority decided to exercise its powers to compel all the police officers suspected of misconduct to come to its city offices at the same time and answer its questions in written form. This would avoid the possibility of collusion. It depended on the role of Authority personnel to act as schoolteachers watching for cheating among those answering their questionnaires. The police indeed did attempt to 'cheat' and had to be warned that by doing so they were disobeying a lawful directive of the Authority and so committing a statutory offence with which they could be charged. One of the officers then heightened the farce by refusing to answer his questions in writing, and instead answered them out loud, laconically and ludicrously. When cautioned he walked out in protest. The Authority was powerless to stop him. Police command did nothing to intervene.

QUIS CUSTODIET CUSTODES CUSTODIUM—WHO WILL GUARD THE GUARDS' GUARDS?

By mid-1987 the relationship between the Police Complaints Authority and the upper levels of the Victoria Police had deteriorated severely. Police command had reacted to the confidentially expressed concerns of the Authority with obstructionism and complete unwillingness to meet the problems demonstrated by the external monitoring body. The Authority had 'gone public' with its criticisms of policing procedures and internal review mechanisms and a stand-off had been reached. The response of police command was, as far as possible, to ignore the Authority, stonewall its proposals and recommendations, and promote its demise.

The irony that existed was that by this stage the relationship between the investigators of the Internal Department and the Authority had for the most part become very good (Freckelton 1988*a*). Joint work was being done and many minor matters were being effectively conciliated or resolved by co-operation between the two bodies. Moreover, many police members were covertly approaching the Authority to express their support for the independence of the statutory body. Others appreciated the attempts at expediting the process of investigation of serving police so as to remove the cloud of unfair suspicion that was hanging over many members. Myths about what the Authority was doing and the principles that it stood for were being dispelled by the Authority's participation in police training courses and by its policy of sending each of its members out with policing squads for at least one shift every month. Also the Police Association had undergone a leadership change with the result that channels for communication had reopened between the Authority and the industrial representatives of the Victoria Police.

However, the Minister for Police and Emergency Services bowed to the representations of police command and determined to create a mechanism for investigating the causes of the deteriorating relationship between the Authority and police command. He commissioned a report from the former Commonwealth Ombudsman, Professor Jack Richardson, into the workings of the Internal Investigation Department (Richardson 1987). This of necessity entailed some consideration of the relationship between the internal unit and the Authority. It appears that in fact this may well have been the hidden agenda of the brief given to Professor Richardson.

Professor Richardson's report, released in late October 1987, in general supported the Authority's assertions about the Internal Investigation Department's performance. In addition, though, he expressed concern about the relationship between the Authority and the police. He suggested that if the relationship did not improve within the next six months, consideration should be given to returning the Authority's jurisdiction to the ombudsman's office, where a Deputy Ombudsman should be appointed specifically to oversee review of police complaints. The Professor also voiced concerns about the public profile of the Authority and about the time spent by its members on developing conceptual critiques of current internal investigation and policing practices. Finally, he expressed doubt as to the suitability of the Authority's head and suggested that his talents might be better utilized elsewhere. The Richardson report was not presented to Parliament. It attracted no political comment and virtually no media coverage.

THE AUTHORITY'S RESPONSE

The Authority responded to the Richardson recommendations by making further efforts to communicate with police command, the Police Minister, and the Police Association. Meetings were held with the new Chief Commissioner and the head of the Association. In spite of repeated attempts by the Authority at convening meetings with the Minister and his senior bureaucrats, he and his Department head were obdurate in their unavailability. No progress was made on the Authority's legislation. This in particular presented increasingly difficult problems as the Authority embarked upon further investigations. Its resources were devoted more and more to reinvestigations (subsequent to initial internal investigations) and 'public interest investigation' of police misconduct. Work on major investigations regularly continued past midnight in the Authority's offices, and all members in turn carried a bleeper, allowing complainants to make urgent contact with the Authority twenty-four hours a day, seven days a week.

A series of Authority investigations found significant misconduct on the part of serving members of the police, and recommendations were made to the Chief Commissioner, in the form contemplated by the legislation, that disciplinary or criminal action be brought against the personnel involved. Police command refused on every occasion to bring such action. Letters were repeatedly received from senior police denouncing Authority investigations and asking for further and better documentation of the bases on which the Authority's reports were grounded. These requests were a smokescreen as extensive information was being given to police command to enable them to proceed with criminal and disciplinary charges, as well as with procedural reform. It became increasingly clear that police command was united in its determination not to respond positively to any proposals from the Authority.

The options for the Authority were limited indeed. The Director of Public Prosecutions (DPP) did not generally bring prosecutions against serving police unless the offences were very serious. This meant that the Internal Investigation Department, without a lawyer on its staff, was itself responsible for making the preliminary decision about whether a police member should be prosecuted in the criminal courts. If doubt was entertained about the advisability of such a course an opinion would be sought from the Legal Adviser's section within the Force. This took some considerable time and was rarely positive. No independent body, such as the DPP, was at any stage involved. In the case of actions before the Disciplinary Tribunal, it was the internal unit itself that made the decision to prosecute and then referred conduct of the matter to the police prosecutors who bring minor criminal charges in the criminal courts in Victoria. The only recourse for the Authority was to report its findings and concerns to Parliament and attempt to encourage the Minister to resolve the impasse reached between the watchdog and the Chief Commissioner. The Authority began to prepare for both courses.

THE LAST STRAWS

The Authority received complaints about a wide range of misconduct. Some of these could readily be categorized. Occasionally multiple complaints were received about one individual. Sometimes complaints about a certain locality or police station increased. More often the complaints could be classified into issues which presented particular difficulties to members and which gave rise to unsatisfactory interaction with the public.

During 1987 the Authority had received complaints about police procedures for dealing with victims of sexual assault. It had been suggested by complainants to the Authority that the Sexual Offences Squad, the group responsible for interviewing victims, was insensitive and inadequately trained to carry out its job effectively. It had also been argued that women were treated like criminal suspects in Victoria when they reported a rape and that they were cross-examined shortly after the time of the crime as though they themselves were in the witness box. Moreover, it was also put to the Authority that victims were not infrequently shuttled between one group in the police force and another before they came anywhere near a hospital for medical treatment or a counsellor for support. It was suggested that pressure was exerted upon victims by police to undergo a forensic medical examination by a police surgeon and that Sexual Offences Squad interviews often lasted over five hours, being conducted at quite inappropriate times.

The Authority also received a number of disturbing individual reports from sexual-assault victims and workers. One told of a woman who reported that after she had been savagely assaulted by four young men in inner-city Melbourne, she was prevailed upon to leave her hospital bed for a statement to be taken at Police Headquarters. The Sexual Offences Squad members did not believe her story and ran a check on her to see if she was known to the police. They found that warrants were outstanding against her for unpaid parking fines so she was conveyed to the cells to begin serving her time. With the assistance of lawyers from a legal centre and the Authority she was extricated from this appalling situation and conveyed back to hospital (Police Complaints Authority 1988*b*: 21 ff.).

In the light of these concerns the Authority conducted an investigation into the practices and procedures of the Victoria Police when dealing with sexual-assault victims. In February 1988 it released a 100-page Discussion Paper, *Sexual Assault Victims and the Police*, which made thirty-two recommendations for major reforms to police procedures (Police Complaints Authority 1988*b*). The Authority's Paper received extensive media coverage around

Australia. The police were criticized widely for their treatment of such victims and undertook to implement significant changes forthwith. Documents obtained under freedom of information legislation during 1989 disclosed that the senior officer (not a member of the police force) in the Victorian government department responsible for making recommendations to the Minister on policing matters dismissed the report as 'pro victim'. The *Age* newspaper once more pilloried the government for its 'deeply disturbing' response and commented in its editorial of 25 October 1989: 'The public is entitled to wonder whether the disbanding of the Police Complaints Authority a month after the report was released (even though there had been a number of problems with the Authority) was one way of preventing any further such reports.' As of February 1990 the reforms recommended by the Authority had not been forthcoming save that the Sexual Offences Squad had been disbanded. Its functions had simply been given to another group in the Force, the Community Policing Squads, whose members received no training and whose numbers were manifestly inadequate.

Ironically, during 1987 the Federation of Community Legal Centres had requested that the Authority investigate the use of excessive force by police, in particular focusing on the use of deadly force by police. This followed well-publicized injuries to, and deaths of, citizens when police entered their houses or confronted them in conflict situations.[16] In addition the Police Association asked the Authority to report to Parliament on the conditions of police cells. This arose out of concerns about the role of police acting as quasi-wardens in cells the conditions of which were frequently nineteenth century. The Authority also received many complaints from prisoners and relatives about cell conditions. At the time publicity was increasing about Australia's terrible record of deaths of Aborigines in custody and a Royal Commission was under way to

---

[16] The Deputy Ombudsman refused to pursue this issue on assumption of office and continued to refuse as police killings of unarmed citizens continued. A year after the Authority's abolition further police killings had taken place and public pressure on the government to declare a Royal Commission mounted in face of representations from legal groups, civil liberties organizations, and newspapers. In May 1989 the Deputy Ombudsman agreed to conduct an investigation into one of these incidents where it was claimed that a suspect had been executed by being shot by police in the back of his head. In July 1989 the Coroner began an unparalleled series of inquests into the police killings in the previous two years, together with an analysis of other recent shootings by police. At March 1990 it was expected to last until early 1991.

investigate over 100 such instances. Many of those deaths had occurred in police custody (see Hazlehurst 1988).

The Authority had begun work on these sensitive projects when it was terminated. It would have reported to Parliament on both issues during 1988.

THE FINAL PHASE

The antagonism of police command hardened in early 1988 with the Authority's succession of inquiries and reports recommending criminal and disciplinary action to be taken against various members. This came on top of its conceptual criticisms of 1987 of the functioning of the Internal Investigation Department. Finally, in February 1988 the media attention given to the criticisms of policing practices in *Sexual Assault Victims and the Police* compounded the anger felt by some senior police about the conduct of the Authority.

The Authority braced itself for making public, by report to Parliament, the continuing refusal of the government to remedy its legislation and allow it to do its job effectively. It also prepared to report publicly the results of its investigations and the refusal of the police to take any action against the members identified by the Authority as having breached the internal discipline code and the criminal law. The Minister was inevitably going to become embroiled in the conflict between the police command and the independent Authority as the confrontation threatened to become a political issue. To him this meant trouble as he had consistently endeavoured to distance himself from both the Authority and any conflict between police command and the Authority.

One of the Authority's investigations had become particularly notorious. Five young men had complained that they had been seriously beaten one after another at an inner-city police station and that evidence against them had been fabricated by police. The Internal Investigation Department had been unable to substantiate their claims. The Authority, by contrast, had come to the conclusion after extensive investigation that the complainants' claims were credible and should be tested by charges being brought against the police. The investigation had been the Authority's most difficult because of systematic obstruction by the police concerned and by their superiors. Police had refused to answer questions, be present when ordered by the Authority, reveal documents as requested, and comply with lawful directions of the Authority.

It was always clear that the case was going to prove a turning point for the Authority. By the beginning of 1990 charges had still not been brought against the police concerned but the complainants had been acquitted of all charges against them after utilizing evidence brought to light by the Authority's investigations. The magistrate hearing the charges preferred by police against the young men took the unusual step of awarding $A38,000 costs to them against three police officers who were the subject of their allegations of misconduct (Police Complaints Authority 1988*a*). (See *Latoudis* v. *Casey*, unreported, High Court of Australia, 20 December 1990.)

At the same time, the Authority investigated a complaint that a police officer already the subject of an investigation by the Authority had given to a court evidence which was totally inconsistent with what he had earlier told the Authority. The Assistant Commissioner heading the Internal Investigation Department accompanied the officer to his subsequent interview with the Authority and repeatedly interrupted the questioning of the officer. He acted as the officer's unofficial legal representative, intervening to query the Authority's policies and procedures and to advise the officer (Police Complaints Authority 1988*a*). By this stage it was evident that senior police had firmed in their antagonism to the Authority and determination to subvert its investigations. The situation had become untenable.

The first sign of the end for the Authority came in March 1988 when at the last moment the Minister retracted permission for a previously confirmed study trip to the United States for the chairman of the Authority. This prompted angry responses from the embarrassed head of the Authority who had no choice but to cancel all the arrangements that had been made with government approval over the previous months. Some days later the senior public servant in the Police Ministry unlawfully purported to overrule the decision by the head of the Authority to extend the tenure of the Authority's Manager and Counsel Assisting. That extension had been confirmed in writing some two months earlier. This was a sinister move as it represented a naked attempt by the Minister to intervene in the internal arrangements of a supposedly independent statutory authority. It seemed like a last desperate attempt by the government to silence an Authority that was becoming a political liability. The act was immediately denounced as such by the head of the body and so the last phase of the Authority's existence began.

By early April 1988 it was clear that the Victorian Labor government was biding its time and looking for a politically opportune moment to terminate the small body that had become a high-profile embarrassment. With every day that passed the stand-off between the doomed Authority and the waiting government deepened. In its editorial of 13 April, the *Age*, Melbourne's premier newspaper, called for the retention of the Authority:

Now, with so much accomplished after so much struggle, it would be unwise for the Government to abort the new system. Returning the watchdog function to the state ombudsman would mean less active monitoring of police complaints, a development the police themselves are reluctant to see.

More work needs to be done. In particular, the Government needs to amend the Authority's legislation, for it remains flawed, as we have pointed out in the past.

The government had asked confidentially in December 1987 and again in January 1988 (because it received such a poor response the first time) for views from a number of organizations which it expected would be willing to have an input to the Authority's future. The most significant was the Ombudsman, the man who two years before had had the jurisdiction to investigate complaints against police removed from him. As a result of poorly drawn legislation, as noted above, he had been in the bizarre position of having to respond to complaints from citizens displeased with the responses of the Police Complaints Authority. This in effect meant that he inquired *again* into the matters initially referred to the police and then relayed to the Authority. Of course, his methods and priorities had been different from the Authority's and inevitably fundamental differences of philosophy had surfaced. The Ombudsman was critical of the Authority's style, its allocation of resources, and its internal systems (Victorian Ombudsman 1988, letter to Police Ministry, 21 January 1988).

None the less, the Ombudsman endorsed many of the Authority's and Professor Richardson's criticisms of internal investigation practices, but he was far from backward in his offer to resume Authority functions:

My personal view is that the setting up of the Police Complaints Authority was a wrong decision resulting in the loss of many years' experience in the investigation of complaints against the police. . . . The option of integration of the Authority with the Ombudsman's Office could, perhaps, restore some of the lost ground and make for better relations between the complainants, the reviewing authorities and the police. (ibid.)

The Ministry for Police and Emergency Services was unwilling to release the responses of the various organizations to which copies of the Richardson Report were sent. This writer obtained copies of them through review processes pursuant to the Freedom of Information Act 1984 (Vic.). In the light of government pronouncements about the Authority, they make interesting reading. The Law Reform Commission expressed concern about the mooted amalgamation of the Authority into the office of ombudsman:

The recommendation appears to have some drawbacks. In the first place, it may encourage those in the police force who are resistant to external review and, according to Professor Richardson, have contributed to the impasse that has developed between the IID and the PCA. It could also provide fuel for those who might think that it was a retreat from previous policy and a device to mute an agency which has been a vocal critic of the police. (Law Reform Commission of Victoria, memorandum conveyed to Police Ministry, 2 February 1988)

However, the author noted the Authority's view (Freckelton and Selby 1989: 32–3) that ultimately the appropriate monitoring agency would be the ombudsman, agreed with that view, but drew attention to the need for amendments to the legislation governing complaints. The Legal Aid Commission maintained that the Authority had 'done an effective job of highlighting the inadequacies of the present IID procedures concerning the investigation of complaints'. Curiously the Commission also commented that, 'We agree with the views of both senior personnel of the PCA and Professor Richardson that the PCA has outlived its usefulness' (Legal Aid Commission of Victoria, letter to Police Ministry, 10 March 1988). It can only be assumed that the Authority's views about the ombudsman *in general* being the preferable vehicle for external review (Freckelton and Selby 1989: 32–3) had been misinterpreted by the Commission. The Victorian Council for Civil Liberties (memorandum sent to Police Ministry, 19 February 1988) and the Supporters of Law and Order (letter, 27 January 1988), an organization closely affiliated with the Victoria Police, predictably took opposing views. The Council 'endorsed the operations of the PCA' and recommended 'that further and more extensive powers be given to the PCA'. It commented: 'One of the few rays of light in the picture of our policing is the Police Complaints Authority and its fragile attempt to be independent and to show the public that it is not afraid to speak out when it sees something wrong.' In contrast, the Supporters of Law and Order described the Authority as 'an abject and costly failure'. The Society of Labor Lawyers expressed the view that 'the case has not yet been made out that [the Authority] should not continue as a separate statutory authority' (letter, 26 February 1988). The Federation of Community Legal Centres (letter, 21 December 1987) concentrated on criticizing the 'subjective bias' of the Internal Investigation Department and the absence of adequate powers in the Authority.

Perhaps most interestingly, the Victoria Police Internal Investigation Department was extremely hostile to the Richardson Report (memorandum, 25 November 1987). The memorandum prepared by a Chief Superintendent of that Department asserted that:

It is also obvious that the Professor, like the PCA, has very little conception of how to commence and then follow through an investigation. . . . It can be shown throughout this report that the bias against members is shown by advocating questioning without cautions, discipline before all else, questioning members before testing complainants' evidence and no consideration when arranging interviews. These and other reflections throughout this report tend to make one consider that the authority has police on a lower level than criminals and if one were to recommend treating an offender with such contempt as the Professor considers we should our own, a furore of huge proportions would erupt.

The Chief Superintendent remembered nostalgically the 'excellent relationship' which he declared had been enjoyed between his Department and the ombudsman and blamed the Authority for the deterioration in relations between the internal and external watchdogs.[17]

On 19 April 1988 the Minister for Police and Emergency Services announced that the Authority was to be abolished and replaced with a Deputy Ombudsman who would oversee police internal investigations into complaints. The Minister said that the establishment of the Authority had been a mistake and that the Authority's accusations of political interference and sabotage were 'bizarre' (see the *Australian, Age, Sun,* 19 April 1989). He maintained that no one had had a positive word to say about the Authority and that the

---

[17] See Police Complaints Authority of Victoria (1988c). Other responses were received, including from the Victorian Law Institute, and the Victorian Bar Association. All declined to express a view on the future of the Authority. None expressed negative views of the Authority's conduct.

government had consulted widely about its future. On the same day the Ombudsman announced that he was 'confident' that his office would competently oversee police investigations: 'We will be more involved in investigating complaints thoroughly than creating publicity.' (*Sun*, 19 April 1988.) The Chief Commissioner said: '[The PCA] was a sound idea which could have been of great benefit to both police and the public but which, unfortunately, never really yielded practical benefits to either.' (*Sun*, 19 April 1988.)

THE LEGACY

By May 1988 the functions of the Police Complaints Authority had been transferred to a Deputy Ombudsman working in the Ombudsman's office. The situation was as it had been in 1986 save that the unsatisfactory legislation that had thwarted the Police Complaints Authority now stood in the way of the effective functioning of the Deputy Ombudsman. The Authority existed under a different name with only one of its former staff *in situ*.

For almost a full year thereafter the media did not once have occasion to report an utterance of the Deputy Ombudsman or of the Ombudsman in relation to police complaints. Yet overt police abuses of power became more public during 1988–9 than at any time in recent years in Victoria. Clearly, the new appointee had learned some of the political lessons from the experience of the Authority and intended to assume a much less prominent media profile than had members of the Authority. He was finally disturbed from his quietude by allegations that a suspect was executed by police by being shot through the back of the head during a raid. He agreed to investigate this matter but refused to look into any other of the police shootings that had taken place in the previous months and years. In spite of grave community concern about the subject of his investigation, when finally he completed his report, it was not made available to Parliament—it was given solely to the family of the deceased and to the Chief Commissioner.

The staff of the Authority have been dispersed, the two senior members returning to legal practice, neither having been recompensed for the contracts which they had had with the government. The embarrassment caused by a body determined without fear or favour to investigate and report on inappropriate or corrupt police practices has been removed but widespread dissatisfaction remains

among legal-centre workers, youth workers, barristers, representatives of minority groups, civil libertarians, and the police themselves about the internal and external investigation bodies in
Victoria. The Authority's legacy is examined below.

WHAT BROUGHT ABOUT THE DEMISE?

The Authority's Independence

The Police Complaints Authority was an independent statutory
authority, responsible only to the Victorian Parliament. This aspect
of its existence was taken more seriously by the Authority than some
other such bodies take their separation from other organs of
government. Attempts were made by the government in power to
silence the two senior members of the Authority when they publicly
raised issues related to the functioning of the Victoria Police Force
when these had been brought to their attention by specific
complaints. These attempts were firmly rebuffed on each occasion.

Thus it was unmistakably apparent to the government of the day
that the Authority could not be relied upon to be 'tactful' or
'pragmatically mindful' of the nature of its public utterances as the
next election (during 1988) approached. Labor Party research
showed that 'law and order' was one of the most electorally sensitive
issues of the late 1980s. In the 1987 lead-up to the election a 'tough'
minister was moved into the portfolio of Police and Emergency
Services to replace the former incumbent who was perceived as
equivocating on too many issues and with whom the police were
dissatisfied.

In this writer's view it was inevitable that the Authority would
have to be 'neutralized' prior to the 1988 election if the political
feelers that were extended by senior ministers seeking for restraint
met with no satisfaction. The political price of the independence of
the police watchdog had become too high. There might have been a
few votes in creating the Authority but maintaining it threatened to
be a significant electoral liability. The alternative—that of standing
up to the police and attempting genuine reform of a poorly
performing and anachronistic upper structure of the Victoria Police—
was not a short-term option. The Police Association, the Force's
industrial arm, was powerful, easily mobilized, and militant. Its
rhetoric was well-honed and superficially attractive to a public
worried about the possibility of being 'mugged' on the way home or

robbed when it reached there (Grabosky and Wilson 1989; Freckelton 1987, 1988*b*). As it was, the Police Association threatened to enter candidates in the election and did in fact play a role in campaigning on specific issues (Bailey 1988).

If, with the wisdom of hindsight, one is to be critical of the political sophistication of members of the Authority, one might suggest that it would have been more pragmatic to have taken a longer-term view of the watchdog's objectives and to have been more moderate in confrontations with government and senior police during the pre-election period. This was an option that was canvassed within the Authority but the danger was that it involved to an unacceptable degree 'going quiet' on issues and particular grievances for the sake of longer-term survival. The decision to stand on principle was made in the context of dealings with the police force that demonstrated that every compromise made by the Authority was taken advantage of by senior police unwilling to make any changes to accepted practices unless forced to do so by the unwelcome light of media publicity.[18]

Almost every significant suggestion made confidentially by the Authority for change to practices or procedures was shelved or rebuffed by police command during the twenty-two-month existence of the Authority. The exception was the creation of an Inspectorate, staffed by two former members of the Internal Investigation Department, to address systemic problems within the Police Force. This had seemed a particularly heartening step because so often police mythology fails to accept the possibility of systemic problems within police forces and embraces the notion that police complaints can be remedied by the weeding out of a handful of bad apples (see Chesshyre 1989: 211). To this writer's knowledge, however, the Inspectorate never addressed any such problems.

Every recommendation for disciplinary or criminal action to be taken against serving police members was rejected by police command. No action had been taken by government to secure any

---

[18] Before the demise of the Authority, Wilenski (1986: 181) wrote that institutions set up for the purpose of reform 'should be concerned solely with the promotion of change and be staffed by persons who are both committed to the task and aware that their performance and that of their agency will be assessed solely on the basis of their success or failure. The agency will not then be tempted into other activities or into trading-off reform objectives against other priorities. This also suggests that those who staff the new agency will have different values from those predominating in the bureaucracy and conflict is likely to occur.'

measure of compliance with the watchdog's reports. For the Authority to acquiesce in current practices or to fail to pursue specific grievances to the full risked betraying the trust of its complainants and giving to senior police ammunition to use later against the Authority; for instance, alleging that the Authority's concerns were erratic and unpredictable. There was no easy option. That of principle was preferred.

Perceptions of the Authority

A corollary of the Authority's determination to assert its independence was that on occasions it rejected the representations of organizations or individuals who acted as champions of particular complainants. The nature of the Authority's role was misunderstood by some politicians and by some advocates of individuals who had been aggrieved. It was thought that the reaction of the Authority should have been assumption of the validity of the complainant's assertions and preparedness to attack the police on that basis.

The fact was that the Authority discovered that a significant percentage of complaints was made by disturbed, malicious, or vexatious people with an axe to grind (see also Fitzgerald 1989: 295; Chesshyre 1989: 214).[19] Some of them moved almost professionally from one grievance mechanism to another in a desperate attempt to gain an audience for their complaints. The reasons for this behaviour varied from the malicious to the psychiatrically disturbed. The Authority went to the extent of publishing a significant study on this phenomenon in Australia and overseas (Freckelton 1988c and d; see also Smith 1989). The consequence of the existence of a significant proportion of baseless allegations against serving police was that those members had to be protected. It was essential that the Authority function in a thoroughly neutral, non-partisan manner. One of the primary functions of the Authority's interviewing process for applicants for its positions was an attempt to sift out the pro-police and the anti-police from the remainder of the field.

---

[19] Some of these individuals were the most memorable with whom the Authority came into contact—those convinced the police helicopter was watching them in their houses, those who believed the police were stealing their underwear, those of the view that the police had trained insects to persecute them, the complainant objecting because the police had removed from him his petrol-can pyramid which he had erected to protest against nuclear weapons, and those who believed that the police were responsible for the foul smells emanating from their baths and toilets . . . see Freckelton 1988c and d.

Where necessary the Authority was prepared to make the difficult decision to classify a complainant as vexatious or without a legitimate grievance. It did so only on the basis of exposure to the complainant and the other information available to it. This preparedness to dismiss complaints where the circumstances demanded it had several consequences. It meant that suspicion could be removed from serving police who were innocent of the allegations made against them. This could only help morale and restore some integrity to the investigation processes. It also, however, antagonized some champions of specific complainants when they were not able to be in possession of all the facts. There were times when Authority staff had to be very firm with individuals dissatisfied with the decisions of the Authority. To those without full acquaintance with all the facts, such individuals could appear as just people pursuing a legitimate grievance against all odds. Some of these complainant advocates became convinced that the Authority was pro-police. Finally, some of the dissatisfied individuals pursued their grievances to the 'court of appeal' the ombudsman, who investigated their grievances against the Authority.

Many misunderstood the inherent difficulties of the police complaints process. At least a third of complaints made to the Authority asserted 'undue force'—that a police member had assaulted a member of the public. Invariably the incident had taken place without independent witnesses. One or more police officer had, however, been present. They almost always provided a plausible explanation for what had happened. All too often the complainants were at the time affected by drugs or alcohol or had already been involved in some form of violent altercation. A very high percentage of Internal Investigation Department findings in such complaints were 'not substantiated'. Generally this was the correct finding because, for whatever reason, there was not sufficient evidence to justify any other finding against the police officer who was the subject of the complaint (Brown 1989).

As with allegations of sexual assault, the inability of fact-finding bodies to determine what happened between two or more individuals in private is immensely frustrating to all concerned. Some critics of the Authority and of the Internal Investigation Department of the police did not adequately appreciate the impropriety and bias that would have been involved in a finding critical of police behaviour against the weight of the evidence—where there was no independent witness and where there were two plausible but completely conflicting versions of an incident. The frustration with this difficulty at times spilled over into an irritation with the determinedly neutral stance of the Authority. This is the inevitable concomitant of the job of non-partisan watchdog.

Reformist Approach

The Police Complaints Authority was an unusual phenomenon from many perspectives. It was dedicatedly and avowedly reformist in its approach to its task. Its two senior members were barristers who had no intention of embarking upon long public service careers in ombudsman work. Their oft-stated intention was to improve the quality of internal investigations within the Victoria Police to a point where within four years the jurisdiction could be returned to the ombudsman (Freckelton and Selby 1989). Their hope was that he would then need to exercise his Royal-Commission-like powers much less often than had the Authority and that his main task would be to ensure the continuing high quality of internal investigations. They were committed to the principle of self-regulation as the optimal form of monitoring of police conduct.

A consequence of their reformist approach, however, was a readiness to confront issues as well as particular cases. The head of the Authority, Hugh Selby, as well as being a former Senior Assistant Ombudsman and practising barrister, was qualified as a social worker and was particularly conscious of the danger of 'missing the wood for the trees', being so preoccupied with an avalanche of specific complaints that the problems giving rise to them were never confronted (Selby 1988). His Counsel Assisting had spent some years as a senior law reformer for the Australian Law Reform Commission and brought to the job at the Authority a readiness to tackle police practices and procedures identified as outmoded or inappropriate for current conditions.

The Police Complaints Authority legislation imposed a duty to make recommendations as to practices and procedures where it considered that an appropriate course of action. The Authority did this on many occasions and it is clear that senior police found this aspect of the Authority's functions particularly difficult to come to terms with. It was different to standard ombudsman practice which tended to focus on individual investigations and not to make considered and extensive evaluations of current work practices within police forces. It was said by senior police on a number of occasions that the conduct of such investigations and even the making of such recommendations was outside the proper purview of the Authority. It was said to be intruding into police internal management and it was resented. This was undoubtedly one of the factors that alienated police command.

Wilenski has suggested that 'the first prerequisite of which the reformer should be certain is *political will*'. He pointed out that the benefits of reform are often long-term and from an electoral point of view not particularly alluring. By contrast, the costs of reform 'are immediate and tangible and include the cost to the politician of antagonising senior officials' (Wilenski 1986: 176). When those officials are as politically powerful and perceptive as the police in Australia his words about reform in general might have been written about the Police Complaints Authority experience: 'It is little use embarking on reform without being at least certain that minimum interest is present and that there is a willingness on the part of government leaders to expend the political capital to give the initial backing to reform and then to intervene at critical points.' (Wilenski 1986; see also Caiden 1970.) If the Police Complaints Authority made a fatal mistake, it was in taking the government which created it at face value when it claimed to be supportive of the Authority and its enabling legislation. Both Ministers for Police, during the existence of the Authority, declined at critical times to intervene to facilitate the investigations being conducted by the Authority when the police expressed their opposition to the Authority's activities. The government at all times operated on the basis that it would lose more votes than it would gain by attempting serious reform of policing practices during the life of the Authority. Without executive support, the chances of success for the Authority were never more than minimal.

Anti-Bureaucratism

Added to this was the enthusiasm of the Authority to rationalize the way in which the police and the external monitoring agency related. The internal unit of the police was loath to do this for fear that it would later be criticized for failing to pay due heed to the niceties of a complainant's allegations. One of the hallmarks of the Authority was its readiness to break down formal bureaucratic procedures and deal with investigating police on an individual basis to achieve the goal of determining the substance or lack thereof of particular complaints.

Hindsight suggests that this process should at times have been tempered with more caution given the organizational ethos of Victoria's highly traditional police force. In Victoria it is still a fact in 1990 that induction procedures for police are minimal (a fourteen-week course, followed by a probationary period), training is non-existent for some of the most difficult areas (such as community policing), lateral recruitment is unknown, incentive for tertiary qualifications is not apparent, and management skills among senior officers to administer a $A500m budget and 10,000 police, such as they exist at all, are acquired solely through step-by-step promotion and the effluxion of time. Such an institution will necessarily be extremely formalistic and mistrustful of the attempt to orchestrate change from the outside.

LESSONS TO BE LEARNED

The Political Issue

In Australia recent experience has demonstrated that in many states there is not the political will or courage to confront the entrenched conservatism of police forces. This is because of the prevailing political conditions. Law and order is one of the most sensitive items on the political agenda. Police forces have the pre-eminent voice in Australia on this issue. Until the 1989 Report of the Fitzgerald Royal Commission in Queensland, Australian governments had not regarded themselves as commanding the necessary community support to take on police forces and reform them in the interest of the community. This meant that governments were locked into adoption of short-term, superficially attractive solutions to policing problems. Such solutions did not include real reform of police structures and procedures. Nor did they include creation or maintenance of genuinely independent grievance mechanisms for members of the public dissatisfied with police performance. In such circumstances, a watchdog intent on fulfilling its charter to monitor the effectiveness of internal police departments, and itself to investigate without fear or favour, was bound to run into trouble.

The Resistance Phenomenon

Reform always takes place against resistance (Wilenski 1986; Caiden 1970) but the depth of unpreparedness of police to modernize and become accountable has often been inadequately recognized. As Machiavelli pointed out:

It should be borne in mind that there is nothing more difficult to handle, more doubtful of success, and more dangerous to carry through than initiating changes . . . The innovator makes enemies of all those who prospered under the old order, and only lukewarm support is forthcoming from those who would prosper under the new. Their support is lukewarm partly from fear of their adversaries, who have the existing laws on their side, and partly because men are generally incredulous, never really trusting new things unless they have tested them by experience. (Machiavelli *c*.1514, ch. 6.)

Looking back, it is clear that the Victoria Police and their political arm, the Police Association, during the period of the Authority embraced many of the well-recognized forms of behaviour exhibited by organizations that perceive themselves under pressure from an outside entity attempting to facilitate change. Something useful for future attempts at policing reform might be gained from reflecting upon the strategies adopted successfully by the Victoria Police in response to the threat that they saw the Police Complaints Authority posing. As Zaltman and Duncan point out: 'The display of resistance is an opportunity for insight into the various conditions that should be considered in selecting and shaping intervention strategies.' (1977: 62–3.)

As long ago as 1967 Coe and Barnhill identified the fear of disruption of the social unit and loss of authority by management as potent factors inhibiting change in organizations (Coe and Barnhill 1967: 149; Blake and Mouton 1984: 53). But there is much more to the dynamics of the relationship between the reformer and the organization to be reformed. Conventional responses to the facilitation of reform included anxieties surrounding job security, change to informal relationships on the job, the possible requirement for additional education for remaining workers, misunderstanding of proposed reforms, fear of a loss of prestige and status for certain employees, mistrust of outsiders and a predilection among long-time workers for retention of the status quo (Champion 1975: 243–4). Many of these responses were encountered among police by the Authority's staff as they sought to initiate change in police practices and procedures.

Rejection of the Authority's role to audit police practices and procedures was a constant during the period of the Authority's existence. In many ways this was to be expected, as was a significant degree of mistrust about the capacity of the Authority to evaluate fairly the role of the police. Police forces had become accustomed during the last decade in Australia to ombudsmen criticizing particular instances of police misfeasance, but when a body with a high media profile drew public attention to the need for large-scale organizational and attitudinal changes, that was genuinely confronting. It was always going to be a long-term task to persuade police that a body of individuals, who had not joined the force as probationary constables and proceeded by gradations through the career structure, could contribute usefully to the future of policing.

It is well recognized that hostility towards outsiders is a source of resistance to change that is exacerbated by a high degree of in-group identification, a bonding that gives coherence to a group and emphasizes the differentness of that group from those not part of it (Watson 1971: 745). Police forces are notorious for their exclusivity, their brotherhood ethic, and their conservatism in face of proposals for reform (Reiner 1985: 97). These characteristics merge readily into a self-justifying homeostasis when confronted with the possibility of having weaknesses, inadequacies, and structural deficiencies highlighted to a non-sympathetic audience. Not surprising then that police should adopt a self-protective mechanism to ward off externally arising instruments of change.[20]

Commissioner Fitzgerald in his 1989 report into corruption expressed the view that the 'unwritten police code', developed over decades in Queensland, was responsible for much of the lack of accountability that by the later 1980s had become endemic in that state. He commented that the code:

effectively makes police immune from the law. In conflicts between the code and the law, the code prevails. Under the code:

—loyalty to fellow officers is paramount;
—it is impermissible to criticise fellow police, particularly to outsiders;
—critical activities of police, including contact with informants, are exempt from scrutiny;

---

[20] Lippitt and his co-writers, J. Watson and B. Wesley (1958: 180–1) as long ago as the 1950s recognized that the reluctance to avoid having weaknesses exposed, awkwardness and fear of failure associated with doing something new, bad experience with past efforts at change, and concern about loss of present satisfaction were all factors that militated towards organizational homeostasis. See also Hall 1977: 346; Klein 1976: 118; Zaltman and Duncan 1977: 83 ff.; Warren 1977: 190 ff.

—police do not enforce the law against, or carry out surveillance on other police; and

—those who breach the code can be punished and ostracised . . .

The operation of the code means that police reject criticism and external supervision. The Force then counters criticism with misinformation and deceit. Reforms are said to be bad for 'morale'. Those who make allegations against police often themselves become the subject of abuse, criticism or allegations. Problems are denied or minimized, which makes planning difficult and increases the cynicism of the community about the Force. (Fitzgerald 1989: 362–3; see also 202–5.)

In Australia, as elsewhere, a characteristic of the resistance phenomenon is rhetoric that incorporates the *ad hominem* attack against the outsider and concentrates on the incapacity of the agent for change to comprehend adequately the special conditions of the target organization.[21] This is precisely how the Victoria Police reacted to the reformist recommendations of the Police Complaints Authority. Attacks were made by Association activists suggesting that members of the Authority should return to the closeted world of government or academia (Freckelton 1988b: 59), and pejorative epithets that came to be regularly applied to its members included 'anti-police', 'anti-law-and-order', 'self-appointed management experts', 'armchair critics', and 'civil libertarians'. This was the public face of opposition to the Authority but it was matched by a range of other strategies, including passive obstructionism, and at times overt sabotage, that were calculated to push the Authority into a role that would appear anti-police.

Reasons for the resistance were consistent with those which are to be anticipated from a large, disciplined, and traditionally organized para-military body. Undoubtedly, those entrenched and experienced in their positions of responsibility found the preparedness of the Authority members to be confrontationist and direct in their criticism a threat to the status quo. In an organization that all too often perceives public discussion of its role and its functions as personal attack from the uninformed, the malicious, and the criminal, a challenge to the status quo would no doubt represent an affront of serious dimensions. Inevitably, too, some in senior positions reacted uncomfortably to university-trained non-police

[21] See Chesshyre (1989: 216; Pike 1985: 175) for recent examples of police reaction to criticism in England and Goldsmith's summary (Chap. 1 above) of the experience of CRBs in the United States.

addressing policing policy in a fashion that showed every sign of being ongoing until changes eventuated.[22] This was no short-term Royal Commission whose recommendations could be made the subject of continuing discussion and debate until they had been acceptably diluted long after the Royal Commission patent to inquire had expired.

Inevitably, some police felt threatened in the senior positions to which they had risen without relevant tertiary training (see Wilenski 1986: 173; Bradley and Cioccarelli 1989: 7). Talk of revision of induction procedures and training, introduction of lateral recruitment, provision of incentives for management training, and the creation of a police board were new concepts indeed for Victorian police in the 1980s. Such ideas could be very intimidating for men who would not adapt readily to modern policing of the kind to be found outside Victoria.

Management experts stress the advantages of development of acceptable models for change in organizations when the differing parties can work co-operatively (Blake and Mouton 1984: 18 ff.). However, this did not prove to be an option with the Victoria Police, senior members of which repeatedly would purport to be party to such co-operative arrangements but would not genuinely co-operate in any meaningful sense. This fundamental difficulty is a reflection of the reality that change cannot be *imposed* effectively from outside upon an organization. It can be facilitated, but even this is only possible when the organization can be brought to recognize the need in principle for change and some willingness exists to bring it about. This at no stage was evident among the upper echelons of the Victoria Police during the Police Complaints Authority period.

At another level, had the Authority opted for setting long-term objectives and refraining from all-out assault on specific areas of unacceptable police performance, it would have laid itself open to the charge of allowing itself to be manipulated by police propaganda. Given the government's failure to provide unequivocal support to the Authority, the approach adopted by the watchdog was one of strict adherence to principle. This meant fighting battles as they arose—with discernment but without approaching them on the basis that they were necessarily part of a thirty-years' war. The result of this was that police were antagonized, rumours of 'anti-police'

---

[22] See the comments of Chesshyre (1989: 219) on attitudes toward civilian commissioners and (*alibi*) civilian investigation of police misconduct.

sentiments allegedly harboured by members of the Authority's staff flourished, and resolve at senior ranks in the Force to resist moves for change to policing practices was galvanized. Without clear indication from the government of the day that it was committed to implementation of reforms advocated by the Authority and to removing from the Force those against whom complaints of significant misconduct were proved, the Authority's days were always going to be numbered. Resistance from police would succeed.

The Ramifications for Statutory Independence

The Victorian Government succeeded in divesting itself of an aggressively independent organization that had begun the process of uncovering embarrassing evidence of the police force's poor performance and of corruption, as well as of unsatisfactory training, promotion procedures, leadership, management skills, and procedures for policing its own abuses.

The government removed the Authority by sacking it through Parliament and by changing its name. After the government's intervention, the Authority to all intents and purposes still existed— it just had different personnel. In 1989 the significance of the government's removal of a statutory appointment by this means was beginning to be appreciated. What had happened was that the government had been unable to take advantage of the procedures enshrined in the Authority's legislation for removal.[23] There had been no grounds for the government to remove the Authority by demonstrating its misconduct. Instead it had had to use its numbers in the two houses of Parliament to rid itself of a dissentient statutory authority. This was recognized by a leading Melbourne Queen's Counsel as a serious attack on the independence of statutory officers: 'The concept of independent officers constituted under parliamentary authority to oversee various functions of executive government was diminished. So was Parliament. The police, the public servants and the politicians all felt good about it.' (Castan 1989: 21.) In essence, the Victoria government's actions make clear its readiness to intrude in any way politically pragmatic into the independence of a statutory authority. It serves notice on holders of statutory appointments (for example, judges, Royal Commissioners, and ombudsmen)

---

[23] Police Regulation (Amendment) Act 1985 (Vic.).

that if they do not perform in a politically expedient fashion, they may lose their mandate.[24]

The Toothless Watchdog

An outside facilitator of change that does not itself have the power to enforce reformed practices or, in the case of a Police Complaints Authority, to insist upon the charging of those against whom it finds that there exists a case to answer, operates in a difficult context. Its functioning must perforce revolve around its capacity to 'persuade'. This is a real problem when the subject organization is a police force, none too amenable to persuasion. By early 1988 the Authority found itself in a position where the Chief Commissioner was pointedly rejecting all its recommendations and the Minister for Police was forswearing any form of intervention. The Authority remained a body that could only make recommendations and could only report to Parliament as it saw fit. The operation of the Authority risked becoming entirely farcical. Something had to break.

In such circumstances, where powers beyond those to make recommendations do not exist, as is generally the case with ombudsmen or Police Complaints Authorities, the role of the media is critical. The Authority found that it had no option but to air its concerns about lack of follow-up of its recommendations for charges to be brought against serving police and for urgent change of practices and procedures through reports to Parliament and response to the subsequent media requests for comment. The Police Minister and the head of his public service department made themselves unavailable for consultation with the Authority and refused by determined inaction to commit themselves to the process of reform that the Authority felt obliged to recommend. Apart from anything else, the situation became a major news item. The Authority's readiness to be accountable through the media and to respond to journalists' requests for informed comment on the state of policing itself became a focus for criticism of the Authority (Richardson, 1987). Certainly, the Victorian Ombudsman's office had not availed itself of the opportunity to report to the public through Parliament

[24] Selby (1990) has since called for the formulation of a code with bi-partisan support to protect independent statutory appointees and, in particular, to ensure that removal of such individuals from office for purely political reasons cannot so easily be accomplished.

on matters of particular public concern as they arose; neither did it do so later. The Authority regarded such an exercise as a duty, not an option, given that it was a public-funded institution. None the less, it must be said that this view did not sit well with traditionalists in the public service and with the political advisers to the government, who undoubtedly saw the Authority as an increasing embarrassment, given the government's unpreparedness to support the Authority's calls for action.

In retrospect it is now clear that the Victorian Labor government was in no way committed to a genuinely independent watchdog on police misconduct. It found itself with legislation that had created an independent body and had given it a clear job to do. However, the government was not prepared to give it the powers or the support to do that job. If the holders of office in the Authority were to remain ethical and bona fide, the body was inevitably going to be disbanded. It was only a matter of time. It will only be when the media uncover clear evidence of widespread police misconduct and inept management, that governments in Australia will assume the political will to reform their police forces. Then they may give their watchdogs the powers to do the job.

This process has already begun. In Queensland, where the Fitzgerald Royal Commission into Corruption uncovered large-scale misconduct among police at all levels, it is likely that 'the Manitoba option' of wholly independent investigation of police complaints will be adopted (see Goldsmith 1988). This is particularly significant as the wide-ranging Fitzgerald Commission had the advantage of an opportunity to assimilate the many developments in relation to police complaints that have taken place in Australasia in recent years. Commissioner Fitzgerald's response was to recommend the abandonment of the internal investigation/external watchdog model. In its stead he proposed one-tier investigation by the Misconduct Division of a Criminal Justice Commission, a body independent of the police force and with the responsibility of 'monitoring, reviewing, co-ordinating and initiating reform of the administration of criminal justice in Queensland on an ongoing and permanent basis', and 'discharging the criminal justice functions not appropriately to be carried out by the Police Department or other agencies' (Fitzgerald 1989: 273). Commissioner Fitzgerald's answer to the police complaints problems experienced in Australia during the 1980s was to abandon the concept of self-regulation for police and regard them as a body inappropriate to police their own members. His comments could easily have been made in Victoria:

The Internal Investigations Section has been woefully ineffective, hampered by a lack of staff and resources and crude techniques. It has lacked commitment and will and demonstrated no initiative to detect serious crime . . . The Section's efforts have been token, mere lip service to the need for proper investigation of allegations of misconduct. The Internal Investigations Section has provided warm comfort to corrupt police. It has been a friendly, sympathetic, protective and inept overseer. It must be abolished. (Fitzgerald 1989: 289; see also Goldsmith, Chapter 1 above.)

It would not be surprising if other states follow his example and take away.from police the power to heal their own wounds.

A POSTSCRIPT TO THE AUTHORITY

Later in 1989, more than eighteen months after the abolition of the Victorian Police Complaints Authority, one of Australia's leading investigative journalists, Margaret Simons, wrote a series of prominent articles in the *Age* newspaper reflecting on the then procedures for handling complaints in Victoria. She highlighted very powerfully, by a myriad of case examples that procedures for investigating complaints of police misconduct had actually deteriorated since the demise of the PCA. If anything, public confidence and, in particular, confidence of the legal community, in the handling of complaints by the police internal unit and by the Deputy Ombudsman had reached an all-time low.

The case of one man, Trevor Hay, whose problems Ms Simons detailed, became front-page news in Victoria (Simons 1989*b*, 1989*c*, 1990). Hay, a university lecturer, claimed that he had been assaulted by police and that they had then unjustifiably charged him with assault. In due course he was convicted of the charges against him. Most interesting, though, was a series of measures taken against him by police. Hay had immediately complained to the Internal Investigation Department of the police. The officer from that unit assigned to investigate his complaints became actively involved in assembling evidence against him for the prosecution of the criminal charges (Deputy Ombudsman, 1989: 22). Immediately before the case reached court, Hay was told that the charges against him had been upgraded. A policeman testified that the magistrate directed that the more serious charges should be proceeded with. An investigation by the Acting Chief Magistrate found that there was 'nothing to substantiate' such an assertion.

Further material assembled by Margaret Simons disclosed that two years later, and subsequent to the *Age's* investigative work, the same officer who was the subject of Mr Hay's complaint served Mr Hay with more charges arising out of the same confrontation with police (this time traffic matters). In the light of the media coverage given to Mr Hay's situation, internal police documents obtained by Ms Simons showed that serious thought was then given by senior police to charging Mr Hay with contempt of court for his public utterances when he aired his grievances with the processes of internal investigation. Although in possession of all Mr Hay's complaints, the Deputy Ombudsman took twenty months to resolve them. In spite of the community concern about Mr Hay's case, he did not report to Parliament. However, Ms Simons obtained a copy of his report which was extremely mild in its criticism of police procedures, commenting, for example, that police 'response time was not as short as I would like to think it could be' (Deputy Ombudsman 1989, unreported; Simons 1990). The Deputy Ombudsman said that the police 'deficiencies' had been procedural and had not adversely affected Mr Hay. He did not recommend any action against police but said that he had drawn the 'deficiencies' to the attention of senior police. Not surprisingly the Victorian Council for Civil Liberties criticized the Ombudsman's response as 'limp' in face of the 'gross errors' committed by police (Simons 1990).

In a bizarre postscript, the *Age* commissioned Professor Richardson, the former Commonwealth Ombudsman and author of the 1987 report critical of the Internal Investigation Department and the Police Complaints Authority, now a lawyer in private practice, to review the Hay investigation. Professor Richardson was extremely critical of the time taken by police investigators before they interviewed the police on the subject of Mr Hay's allegations. He said that the delay 'combined with a sequence of unfortunate errors and further action taken against Mr Hay by police, when taken all together, adds up to a situation which is most unsatisfactory' (Simons 1990). He noted that the case was typical of many of the cases of assault which he had examined in 1987 in which the rate at which allegations were found sustained by the internal police investigative unit was 'negligible'. The response of the police was to advise that no further comment would be made to the *Age* newspaper which they maintained had failed to give a balanced version of the issues and which the Acting Chief Commissioner maintained was waging something 'little short of a vendetta against the Victoria Police' (Simons 1990).

After her articles on Mr Hay's predicament and a series on police complaints handling, Ms Simons was deluged by complaints from members of the public who saw her as an alternative Police Complaints Authority. Many had been too disillusioned with the system to make formal complaints, others were not even aware that the low profile Deputy Ombudsman existed, others had received no satisfaction through existing mechanisms. The response of the *Age* editorial column was to call twice for the reinstatement of the Police Complaints Authority. The government remained silent.

THE FUTURE

Victoria has now joined other states in Australia that do not have a credible system for investigating complaints against police. The passing of the Police Complaints Authority marked the conclusion of a short but extraordinary experiment that could have led to the modernization and procedural improvement of one of Australia's oldest police forces. The losers through this are the officers of an anachronistic police force but also members of the public who do not receive the quality of policing that their $A500m yearly investment deserves. The saddest legacy of the demise of the Police Complaints Authority is the guarantee that it has given that misconduct among Victorian police will go largely unchecked until it reaches the highest ranks, as has happened in other Australian states. It is only when that fact is brought ineluctably home to the politicians, when police corruption means that seats will be won and lost in elections, that a 1986–8-style Police Complaints Authority will become feasible.

For such a body to have a chance to be effective in facilitating reform to outmoded practices and procedures and in encouraging police to improve their commitment to internal investigation, it will need:

1. The dawning of understanding among senior police that they stand to benefit by becoming and being seen to be truly accountable;
2. the necessary powers to conduct investigations;
3. authoritative, talented and patient staff; and, most importantly,

4. genuine political commitment on the part of the government of the day.

The events of the 1980s in Australia have posed many difficult questions about the efficacy of ombudsman-style bodies that are only recommendatory in character. The 1990s promise to refocus the debate about how the police can most effectively be policed onto the role of external investigative bodies, and, in particular, onto whether such institutions should be empowered to do more than merely investigate, report, and make recommendations. Rather than how external units should supervise the performance of the internal police mechanisms, the issue is likely to be whether the 1970s' model, which is predicated on primacy of investigation by internal police departments, should be abandoned and the internal units scrapped in favour of external investigation of complaints.

It may be that one of the conclusions to be drawn from the short life of the Police Complaints Authority and the nature of the relationship between Australian governments and their police forces during the 1980s is that the option of wholly external investigation of complaints against government employees (including police) along the lines of the model proposed by Commissioner Fitzgerald is worth a try. If that is so, the opportunity for police to be self-regulatory and to police their own abuses will have been lost. However, the Fitzgerald model in the policing context is to a significant degree 'the option of despair', an acknowledgement that previous attempts to improve the quality of police self-regulation have failed. There has been little analysis of the consequences of such a transfer of responsibility for ills away from police control to an external 'Big Brother'. Inherent in a system which abrogates internal responsibility for abuses and poor procedures is licence for sub-standard and irresponsible management practices. Such a licence is something that the movement towards police professionalism during the 1980s has dedicated itself to fight against. To opt for the unprofessional in one important context but to pursue the professional in all others is not only anomalous but guaranteed to affect adversely the important reforms that have taken place thus far in police management.

In the light of the widespread problems experienced in so many jurisdictions with the internal/external model of police complaints handling, fundamental questions have to be posed afresh. How much of a value is there in having the police predominantly self-regulatory? Are they to be equated to 'other' professionals for whom such a notion is generally regarded as one to be favoured? Has the performance of internal police units been shown to be of such a low order that we would be foolish to accord primary responsibility to police to remedy their own abuses? And, importantly, would a wholly externally generated system of complaints investigation (presumably seconding some police) meet a united brick wall of brotherhood-inspired obstructionism, a wall of silence? (see Punch 1985, 155; Christianson 1973). It is to be hoped that those who frame recommendations in the 1990s will take more realistic account, when they assess the feasibility of their preferred investigative model, of traditional police subculture in which resistance to reform, especially that which is externally generated, is such a powerful conservative influence. This remains a very practical consideration.

It is this writer's view that it is not in the community's interest to create new super-investigatory bodies *if* existing institutions can be encouraged to cure their own ills. The experiences of the 1970s and 1980s have shown how demanding a task it is to mould modern, accountable police forces that reflect community values about dealing appropriately with unacceptable policing practices and the handling of police complaints. Undoubtedly, we have not as yet arrived at a satisfactory relationship between the external and internal bodies; nor have we settled the question of the powers that each should possess to accomplish their aims.

What can be said on the basis of the Victorian experience is that external watchdogs need to play a more active and at times a proactive role in investigating and facilitating the process of policing reform if useful change is to be wrought. This may mean that they should be given power to depart to some degree from the traditionally recommendatory character of ombudsman-style bodies. Indeed, they may need a variety of extra teeth. Fundamentally, however, the question is not so much one of preferred models of oversight or even of specific powers. It is a political one. Action to counteract poor policing practices and specific abuses will only take place when governments have the political courage to insist upon it. During the 1980s in Australia they did not.

REFERENCES

Altheide, D. L., and Johnson, J. M. (1980) *Bureaucratic Propaganda* (Boston: Allyn and Bacon Inc.).

Australian Law Reform Commission (1975) *Complaints Against the Police* (Canberra: Government Printer).
—— (1978) *Complaints Against the Police, Supplementary Report* (Canberra: Government Printer).
Bailey, S. (1988) 'Electioneering by Police', *Legal Service Bulletin* 13(6): 263.
Bennis, W. G., Benne, K. D., Chin, R., and Corey, K. E. (eds.) (1976) *The Planning of Change*, 3rd edn. (New York: Holt, Rinehart, and Winston).
Berah, E., and Greig, D. (eds.) (1988) *Community Issues in Psychiatry, Psychology and Law*, Proceedings of the 8th Annual Congress of the Australian and New Zealand Association of Psychiatry, Psychology and Law (Melbourne: ANZAPPL).
Blake, R. R., and Mouton, J. S. (1984) *Solving Costly Organizational Conflicts* (San Francisco: Jossey-Bass).
Board of Inquiry into Allegations Against Members of the Victoria Police Force (1976) *Report (Beach Report)* (Melbourne: Government Printer).
Bradley, D., and Cioccarelli, F. (1989) 'Chasing Vollmer's Fancy: Current Development in Police Education', in D. Chappell and P. Wilson (eds.) (1989) *Australian Policing* (Sydney: Butterworths).
Brown, G. (1989) 'Police Disciplinary Procedures in Australia', in D. Greig and I. Freckelton (eds.) (1989).
Caiden, E., (1970) *Administrative Reform* (Harmondsworth: Penguin).
Caplow, T. (1983) *Managing an Organization*, 2nd edn. (New York: Holt, Rinehart, and Winston).
Castan, R. (1989) 'Stapled to the Wall', *Victorian Bar News* 68: 20.
Champion, D. J. (1975) *The Sociology of Organizations* (New York: McGraw-Hill Book Co.).
Chappell, D., and Wilson, P. (eds.) (1989), *Australian Policing* (Sydney: Butterworths).
Chesshyre, R. (1989) *The Force: Inside the Police* (London: Sidgwick and Jackson).
Christianson, S. (1973) 'Albany's Finest Wriggle Free', *Nation*, December, p. 3.
Clayton, R., and Tomlinson, H. (1987) *Civil Actions Against the Police* London: (Sweet and Maxwell).
Coe, R. M., and Barnhill, E. A. (1967) 'Social Dimensions of Failure in Innovation', *Human Organization* 26(3): 149.
Cohen, S. (1985) *Visions of Social Control* (Wiltshire: Polity Press).
Committee of Inquiry (1977) *Enforcement of the Criminal Law in Queensland (Lucas Report)* (Brisbane: Government Printer).
Committee of Inquiry, Victoria Police Force (1985) *Report* (Melbourne: Government Printer).
Deputy Ombudsman (Police Complaints) Victoria, *Letter of Report* to T. T. Hay (33 pages), 18 December 1989.

112   *Ian Freckelton*

Federation of Community Legal Centres (Vic.) (1987) *The Investigation of Complaints Made about the Police*, (Melbourne: FCLC).

Findlay, M., and Hogg, R. (1988*a*) 'Police and the Community: Some Issues Raised by Recent Overseas Research', in I. Freckelton and H. Selby (eds.) (1988*a*).

—— (1988*b*) *Understanding Crime and Criminal Justice* (Sydney: Law Book Co.).

Fitzgerald (1989), see Queensland.

Freckelton, I. (1987) 'Police Statistics and the Media', *Legal Service Bulletin* 12: 242.

—— (1988*a*) 'Police Complaints Authority: Shooting the Messenger', *Legal Service Bulletin* 13(2): 58.

—— (1988*b*) 'Police and the Media: Sensation and Symbiosis', in I. Freckelton and H. Selby (eds.) (1988*a*).

—— (1988*c*) 'Querulent Paranoia and the Vexatious Complainant', *International Journal of Law and Psychiatry* 11: 127, and (1988*d*) in E. Berah and D. Greig (1988).

Freckelton, I., and Selby, H. (1987) 'Police Accountability: How Serious the Commitment?', *Legal Service Bulletin* 12(2): 66.

—— (eds.) (1988*a*), *Police in Our Society* (Sydney: Butterworths).

—— (1988*b*) *Police Accountability*, M. Findlay and R. Hogg. (1988*a*).

—— (1989) 'Piercing the Blue Veil: An Assessment of Internal and External Review of Police', in D. Chappell and P. Wilson (eds.) (1989).

—— (1990) 'Complaining about Government Employees', in T. Pagone and J. Wallace (1990).

Goldsmith, A. (1989) 'Police Misconduct and the Limits of Law', paper presented to the International Civil Liberties Conference, Sydney.

—— (1988) 'New Directions in Police Complaints Procedures: Some Conceptual and Comparative Departures', *Police Studies* 11(2): 60.

—— (ed.) (1990*a*) 'External Review and Self-Regulation: Police Accountability and the Dialectic of Complaint Procedures' in A. Goldsmith (1990*b*).

—— (ed.) (1990*b*) *Complaints Against the Police: The Trend to External Review* (Oxford: Oxford University Press).

Grabosky, P., and Wilson, P. (1989) *Journalism and Justice* (Sydney: Pluto Press).

Graziano, A. M. (1969) 'Clinical Innovation and the Mental Health Power Structure: A Social Case History', *American Psychologist* 24(1): 10.

Greig, D., and Freckelton, I. (eds.) (1989), *International Perspectives on Psychiatry, Psychology and Law*, Proceedings of Australian and New Zealand Association of Psychiatry, Psychology and Law and American Association of Psychiatry and Law, Joint Annual Congress 1988, (Melbourne: ANZAPPL).

Hall, R. (1977) *Organizations: Structure and Process* (New Jersey: Prentice-Hall).

Hazelhurst, K. (1988) 'Black Death in Custody', in I. Freckelton and H. Selby (1988*a*).

Hill, L. (1977) *The Model Ombudsman* (Princeton: Princeton University Press).

Kirby, M. (1983) *Reform the Law* (Melbourne: Oxford University Press).

Klein, D. (1976) 'Some Notes on the Dynamics of Resistance to Change: The Defender Role', in W. G. Bennis, K. D. Benne, R. Chin, and K. E. Corey (eds.) (1976).

Lippitt, R., Watson, J., and Wesley, B. (1958) *The Dynamics of Planned Change* (New York: Harcourt, Brace, and Jovanovich).

Littlejohn, E. (1981) 'The Civilian Police Commission: A Deterrent of Police Misconduct', *University of Detroit Journal of Urban Law* 59: 5.

Lustgarten, L. (1986) *The Governance of Police* (London: Sweet and Maxwell).

Machiavelli, N. (*c*.1514) *The Prince*, tr. G. Bull (Harmondsworth: Penguin).

Morgan, R., and Smith, D. J. (eds.) (1989) *Coming to Terms with Policing* (London: Routledge).

Nelson, P. (1986) 'Beyond the Blue Curtain: The Ombudsman's Role in Investigating Complaints Against the Police in New South Wales', *Australian Journal of Public Administration* 45: 230.

Pagone, T., and Wallace, J. (eds.) (1990), *Rights and Freedoms in Australia* (Melbourne: Federation Press).

Perry Report: see Deputy Ombudsman (Police Complaints), Victoria.

Pike, V. (1983) *The Principles of Policing* (Hampshire: MacMillan Press).

Police Complaints Authority of Victoria (1987) *Annual Report, 1986–7* (Melbourne: Government Printer).

—— (1988*a*) *Final Report* (Melbourne: Government Printer).

—— (1988*b*) *Sexual Assault Victims and the Police* (Melbourne: Government Printer).

—— (1988*c*) *Special Report* (Melbourne: Government Printer).

Police Complaints Tribunal (1987) 'Tribunal Internal Review' *Quarterly Newsletter* 2: 1.

Punch, M. (1985) *Conduct Unbecoming* (London: Tavistock Publications).

Queensland Commission of Inquiry into Possible Illegal Activities and Associated Police Misconduct (1989), Chairman: G. E. Fitzgerald (Brisbane: Government Printer).

Reiner, R. (1985) *The Politics of the Police* (Bristol: Harvester Press).

Richardson, J. (1987) Review of the Investigation of Complaints by the Internal Investigation Department of the Victoria Police: Report to the Minister for Police and Emergency Services, Melbourne (unpublished).

St Johnston, E. (1971), *Report on the Victorian Police* (Melbourne: Government Printer).

Selby, H. (1987) 'Ombudsman Inc.: A Bullish Stock with a Bare Performance', in Police Complaints Authority of Victoria (1987).

—— (1988) 'Internal Investigations: Too Little, Too Late', in I. Freckelton and H Selby. (1988*a*).

—— (1989) 'Police Discipline: A Strange Case of Bondage', in I. Freckelton and D. Greig (eds.) (1989) *International Perspectives on Psychiatry, Psychology and Law* (Melbourne: ANZAPPL).

—— (1990) 'Without Fear or Favour', paper delivered at ANU Seminar on 'The Role of the Public Service in the 1990s', Canberra, 16 February 1990.

Settle, R. (1990) Police Power Use and Abuse (Melbourne: Muxworthy Press).

Simons, M. (1988) 'The Fitzgerald Inquiry', *Age*, 3 December 1988.

—— (1989*a*) 'Police Spied on Guests at Complaints Seminar', *Age*, 29 September 1989.

—— (1989*b*) 'Inquiry into Upgrading of Hay Charges', *Age*, 26 October 1989.

—— (1989*c*) 'Hay: New Inquiry Move', *Age*, 3 November 1989.

—— (1990) 'Lawyer Finds that Hay Case was "Fatally Flawed" ', *Age*, 15 January 1990.

Smith, S. (1989) 'Vexatious Litigants and their Judicial Control: The Victorian Experience', *Monash University Law Review* 15(2): 48.

Victorian Ombudsman (1988) *Annual Report 1986/7* (Melbourne: Government Printer).

Voumard, S. (1988) 'Young People Think Police Discriminate Against Them, Says Criminologist', *Age*, April 1988.

Warren, R. L. (1977) *Social Change and Human Purpose: Toward Understanding and Action* (Chicago: Rand McNally College Publishing Co.).

Watson, G. (1971) 'Resistance to Change', *American Behavioral Scientist* 14: 745.

Wilenski, P. (1986) *Public Power and Public Administration* (Sydney: Hale and Iremonger).

Zaltman, G., and Duncan, R. (1977) *Strategies for Planned Change* (New York: John Wiley).

Zaltman, G., Duncan, R., and Holbeck, J. (1973) *Innovations and Organizations* (New York: John Wiley).

3

Complaints against the Police in Australia:

Where we are Now and What we Might Learn about the Process of Law Reform, with Some Comments about the Process of Legal Change

MATTHEW GOODE

What then explains why, at a particular moment, change takes place in the legal system while at other times no change takes place? It would be very helpful if some general theory could be developed to explain the phenomenon of change in this, or indeed, in any other, context. But I am sceptical whether this will happen—save at the level of trite generality. During the past fifteen years or so I have seen at close hand campaigns to achieve change in a variety of fields. If one looks for an overall theory to distinguish between the campaigns that prosper and those that do not I believe that one looks in vain. I am far from saying that there is no value in the study of individual case histories of such campaigns, but I do not believe that such study will throw up any very profound insights. Nevertheless there are, perhaps, certain observations one can make that throw some light on the process of achieving change.

(Zander 1979: 491)

What is needed is a theory that can be shown to be in harmony (or at least not out of harmony) with the observed phenomenon of legal growth in a range of societies. However attractive a theory of legal change and of law and society might be on a priori terms, it requires to be checked and rechecked against systematically collated historical experience.

(Watson 1981: 1473)

INTRODUCTION: WHAT IS THIS ALL ABOUT?

As a law student in 1971, I took a seminar course in Civil Liberties in which I was required to present a paper. My topic was 'Complaints Against the Police'. Doubtless neither the presentation nor the paper were massively insightful, but when I came to write an Honours thesis, I did so on the same topic, and parts of this thesis have been published (Goode 1974, 1975). In the years since then, I have been involved in the reference to the Australian Law Reform Commission on Complaints Against the Police (Australian Law Reform Commission 1975*a*, 1978), the controversy concerning the dismissal of the South Australian Police Commissioner, Harold Salisbury, for allegedly misleading the South Australian Government (Goode 1978), and advising the South Australian Government on the appropriate administrative arrangement for processing complaints against police. Somewhat against my will, I have been involved in the policy area of the police and, in particular, the control of police misconduct, as a result of an initial research decision. That may have been a good or a bad thing, but I have seen, over the years, not only the evolution of arguments on the merits of the appropriate policy in relation to the control of police misconduct, but also the way in which the institutions of legal change have reacted to the progress of that debate. I have been trying to extrapolate that experience to some kind of idea about the ways in which the formulation of legal policy and legal change work in this and other societies (Goode 1987).

This project is complex enough when thought of simply in relation to the formal legal controls of police misconduct, let alone when abstracted to the process of legal change in general. If a police officer misbehaves, the possible ways in which that misconduct may be addressed are (1) by way of criminal prosecution, for example an assault charge; (2) by way of civil suit, again, for example, for assault or false imprisonment; (3) by way of a variety of exclusionary rules, of greater or lesser significance, according to which evidence procured by police misconduct is excluded from criminal prosecutions, and (4) administrative or disciplinary controls which are directed to 'employer' regulation of 'employee' misconduct in the workplace. These methods of control have evolved over the years to a varying degree, but one of the features of the area is that, although these methods of control all interact, they have evolved in a variety of ways without reference to each other. They have not really been viewed holistically—rather, they have been seen as rather distinct issues and have been considered accordingly.

An introduction of this kind can make some preliminary assessment of where those methods of control were and where they are now. The use of the criminal sanction against police misconduct is about as useful now as it was in 1971, or, for that matter, 1961. Nothing has changed. It is a dead loss. The only significance of this area of control is by way of a bargaining chip in the political fight in other areas of control. It is difficult to interpret what this means, but that verdict must at least await an assessment of change in other areas.

I had some hope that the civil remedy might prove to be significant if Crown immunity for police torts was abolished. I thought that the vicarious liability of the Crown for police misconduct might prove to be the vehicle whereby a focus on the behaviour of the individual might be replaced, or augmented by, a litigation-derived emphasis on the organizational milieu in which the instances of police misconduct arose. I thought that the imposition of vicarious liability on the Crown for the torts of police officers would inspire the police policy makers to encourage and/or require the police to police themselves (Goode 1975). Some States in Australia legislated to allow for vicarious liability—but I was wrong. Nothing came of this. The process of legal civil liability was and remains too slow, expensive, complex, and simply draining for those who have real and sustainable complaints. The civil process was moving towards an exclusively compensatory mode. In short, the use of the civil process to achieve organizational or personal change was an idea which, in this area, has no relevance.

Real change, when it came, occurred in the area of exclusionary rules and administrative controls, and both reforms were an effort to increase independent oversight of police behaviour. That fact is, in itself, interesting, because one area of change is judicial and the other is executive/legislative. The former is, in my opinion, of some consequence, and requires discussion. The latter forms the subject of this essay. Neither authority paid any significant attention to the other. Despite all efforts at law reform co-ordination, the practice of legal change shows that the real drivers of legal change, that is the courts and the politicians, pay no attention to the efforts of each other. There are, therefore, two themes to this essay: the historical transformation of the debate over the appropriate mechanism for controlling police misconduct, and what lessons, if any, about the nature of law reform or legal change may be derived from the process.

SOME PRELIMINARY OBSERVATIONS ON THE NATURE OF LEGAL CHANGE

Analogous but different societies, such as Australia, Canada, the United States, and Great Britain, were compelled by some force to address the issue of controlling police misconduct in great detail, often more than once, at various times in the last twenty years; but in different ways, to different extents, for different reasons, and with different results. All of these differences appear to be insignificant when compared to less analogous societies (in the policing and legal system sense), but their existence suggests that legal reform is society-specific rather than topic-specific. That is, analogous social and political systems may and do produce the impetus for change at similar stages, but the differences between them dictate differences in reason, procedure, and result, despite the similarities in legal and political structure which dictate that change must be made. Sumner has pointed out:

> what is vital is the recognition that problems only appear in a certain manner depending on the social structural context in which they exist and are only perceived through the ideological grids of the people observing them. Thus the system may require legislative action, but it does not dictate to legislators (or law reformers) how they are to see the problem or how to deal with it. (Sumner 1979: 268.)[1]

It is tempting to conclude that, given the coincidence in analogous societies (Goldsmith 1982), the differences are due to what may be called 'random factors'; that is, events uncontrollable by any determined campaign for the alteration of social rules by legal change. In short, once the demand for change has arisen, its priority and result are random in the context of analogous societies. In this

---

[1] See also e.g. Watson (1977: 130, 134), 'in many cases legal rules are equally at home in many places. Even some of the most particular rules will equally suit a similar or different environment. Different reasons will favour the acceptance of the same rule in several jurisdictions. Legal rules tend to be general in the sense that they exist in and should operate for a community of people from different backgrounds living in different geographical, economic and social circumstances . . . there must be some relationship between the needs and desires of society and its legal rules. The rules must have a connection with the society in some way and to some extent. But this relationship seems impossible to define, perhaps because it varies from state to state and from one area of law to another.'

sense, law reform is akin to Gould's summary of the theory of natural selection:

The theory of natural selection is a creative transfer to biology of Adam Smith's basic argument for a rational economy: the balance and order of nature does not arise from a higher, external (divine) control, or from the existence of laws operating directly upon the whole, but from struggle among individuals for their own benefits (in modern terms, for the transmission of their genes [read 'ideas'] to future generations, through differential success in reproduction [read 'law reform']). (Gould 1980: 67.)[2]

In a formal sense, randomness is promoted by the diversity and numbers of the institutional agencies of legal change, which interact loosely when they interact at all[3] (Missen 1979). In a social sense, randomness is promoted by the centrality of the influence of public scandal or 'exposé criminology' (Taylor, Walton, and Young 1975) in demanding change. Accident is crucial to scandal: both are random and in that sense arbitrary. The disclosure of police misconduct, be it individual or organizational, the reaction of the public, the media, and the powerful, whether community tolerance, official tolerance, or the power balance in the given society is high or low for that kind of police deviance and the effects, if any, in and beyond the police organization are random and hence, to a significant degree, the law reform which may or may not result is random. This describes quite accurately the process currently under way in Queensland known as the Fitzgerald Inquiry, but Sallmann's account of the Victorian Beach Inquiry into police deviance provides an equally dramatic example of the random factor as a determinant of particular law reform processes. He notes:

The Beach Inquiry came about because of the activities of Dr Wainer. There was no public outcry, nor even a discernible level of consternation once the news of the allegations reached the media. Beach himself acknowledges in the Report that without Dr Wainer there would not have been an inquiry. What is interesting is that despite Dr Wainer's apparent sincerity and his alleged penchant for publicity it is by no means clear that he wanted the sort of public inquiry which the Beach Board turned out to be.[4] (Sallmann 1981: 252)

---

[2] Slogan: Ontogeny recapitulates phylogeny.

[3] For a concise summary of the 'randomness' of Australian law reform agencies and the non-utility of Parliament in this role in the period in question, see the Fifth Annual Report of the Australian Law Reform Commission (1979) para. 2. There is, of course, some effort at interagency consultation by the Australian Law Reform Agencies Conferences and the Standing Committee of Attorneys-General (SCAG), but the reinvention of the wheel was and is the order of the day.

[4] See also Ingber (1981: 334): 'Whether law develops by legislation or through the

It is of course the case that reliance upon scandal for reform is not only an indication of the disorganized and unprincipled way in which law reform proceeds; it may also challenge, as socially unsound, aspects of the societal status quo:

While . . . exposés may puncture the legitimacy of the powerful in the eyes of those other social groups who may previously have accepted such legitimacy, the approach hinges very problematically on the view that the legitimacy of the powerful over the powerless has been and is maintained on the basis of an exclusively moral appeal. The picture of power implied . . . is that the powerful rules by virtue of moral right rather than by the realities of ownership and distribution in a society of inequality. (Taylor, Walton, and Young 1975: 30).

THE SOCIAL IMPETUS FOR CHANGE

The general issue of the control of police misconduct became an important one on the social agenda of change in the analogous polities of Australia, Canada, the United States, and Great Britain between 1960 and 1980, and resulted in differing degrees of reform in each society. One of the most important factors which led to this commonality of interest was the remarkable degree of identity in the social and political forces at work in those countries in that period which produced relatively large and unprecedented demonstrations of public dissent. The differences between the polities in question led to differences in timing, but, with that caveat in mind, it is generally true to remark that towards the end of the 1960s, police forces in those countries were involved in conflict, often violent, with a substantial and potentially influential minority of citizens who, in simpler times, would have been regarded by police as being basically law-abiding (Rumbaut and Bittner 1979). A crucial factor was the then innovative use of the public demonstration and displays of public disobedience in support of such ideals as pacifism and equality, and, more recently, conservation and opposition to the mining and use of uranium (Grunis 1978).

The immediate effect of this was to place the police under high stress. It was nothing new for the police to face large public demonstrations of dissent (although their frequency may have been

common-law mechanism of case-by-case adjudication, the individual case must act as an instrument for carrying out the policy to be used by the institutions confronting human problems.'

new), but the causes of the dissent, the nature of the dissenters, and hence the reactions of the dissenters were and are less class-specific than had hitherto been the case. That in itself may reflect a postwar shift in Australian politics and class structure. Be that as it may, the involvement in public protest and disobedience by those who would earlier have been viewed as the law-abiding middle class was something new and may have proved centrally influential in the result.

Large public demonstrations of dissent placed the police in a difficult position. That is still the case, but, at first, the police were caught off guard, and were, it appeared, threatened by and frightened of the new phenomenon. Both statute and common law then reflected only two interests; the suppression at all costs of any sign of organized public dissent based on antiquated policies relevant to the suppression of trade unions, chartists, vagrants, and other social misfits, and the protection at all costs, of the 'right' of some users of the public highway to pass and repass at the fastest legal pace and manner from one place to another.[5] The police felt bound to enforce those laws, but were confronted by citizens who relied upon 'rights' to dissent, freely associate, freely speak, and to do all of those things in public places. These 'rights' were not recognized by Australian law, nor had Australia a Bill of Rights by which an appeal to the 'rights' of free citizenship could be arbited.[6] The result was polarization and alienation[7] between the warriors of ideological positions, or rather, between the proponents of the natural 'right' to public dissent, and the paid enforcers of those who would deny them (Sumner 1979).

[5] See also Whitaker (1979: 57). The latter quotes John Alderson, a high-ranking British police officer, as saying: 'There have been some disturbing signs recently that the very virtue of the police in ensuring freedom of process for all has rebounded on them. They are placed in a virtually impossible position by escorting extreme right-wing and orderly processions with offensive racial characteristics through hostile and violent crowds of coloured minorities and their activist supporters. The police are thus made to appear identified with racist groups and accordingly lose the confidence of some of the coloured people who at the best of times have somewhat uneasy relationships with them. It is one of the great challenges for the police at the present time to develop their own counters to this dilemma.'

[6] This should not be read as a blanket endorsement of Bills of Rights. Quite apart from the political dimension to that dispute, it is clear that some Bills of Rights do not perform as advertised. See e.g. *Engler and Latimer* [1978]. Moreover, of course, the American Bill of Rights did not prevent the same process of alienation in that country. Indeed, it may have exacerbated the process.

[7] One example of this phenomenon is to be found in the *Report of the South Australian Royal Commission into the September Moratorium Demonstration* (1970: 78), citing *Wright* v. *McQualter* (1970).

Ordered to remove or control a situation perceived to be threatening on a social, class, or individual level, the police often provoked the very violence which they were supposed to prevent.[8] It is also the case that some police welcomed that result, but the inevitable general consequence was substantial conflict over the appropriate procedures for the acceptable expression of social dissent. That debate raised and still raises vital issues of social policy, ranging from the theoretical issues of prior restraint to the practical problem of the best police operating procedure on the ground (Whitaker 1979: 56).

Police tactics which had been used in dealing with union marches and demonstrations before the Second World War were employed, but no longer enjoyed even the modicum of success which they may have had in the past. The demonstrators were different, the issues were different, and the social context was different. Moreover, the police made a major mistake. Individually and collectively, the police allowed themselves to become identified substantively with those interests they were protecting procedurally from the demonstrators (Sumner 1979; Whitaker 1979; Weiler 1969).[9] In short, it was one thing for police to say 'we have a duty to enforce the law'; it was quite another for the police to say that 'these demonstrators are deviants'.

So, for example, in Australia, not only did the police enforce the laws in relation to the prevention of public dissent about conscription and the Vietnam War, but they also made it clear that they regarded the objectors and dissenters as cowards, or traitors, or both. It may be conceded that, in coping with public dissent, the police are inevitably identified to some degree with one side of the substantive issue at stake (Campbell and Whitmore 1977) but the police went far beyond that at that time. Rumbaut and Bittner have found the same phenomenon in the United States:

in the 1960s, the minorities and the poor found 'the thin blue line' between themselves and their aims. Even though the police were not the real adversaries of civil rights activism, they were the adversaries' most exposed

---

[8] That was, of course, not new. An extremely interesting early example of the phenomenon is to be found in Engels, 'Postscript to "The Condition of the Working Class in England" ' in Cain and Hunt, *Marx and Engels on Law* (1979: 198 ff.).

[9] Rumbaut and Bittner comment (1979: 255): 'Skolnick also provided evidence of political conservatism among police, arguing that their social role . . . invites an emotional attachment to the status quo; the fact that a man is engaged in enforcing a set of rules implies that he also becomes implicated in affirming them.' (Referring to Skolnick 1966.) See also Grunis (1978).

element, a position the police seemed to accept without qualm. . . . given their normally conservative disposition, many police were unsympathetic to the aims of the civil rights struggle even before it started. From the typical police perspective, the Warren Court decisions created an obstacle course of procedural protections for defendants in the criminal process. . . . There was a general failure by the police to recognise that these apparent indulgences toward the black and the poor were more apparent than real, that they represented little more than a trail of broken promises. Instead of seeing the protests of the 1960s as an expression of anger by deceived people, they saw them as an impudent demand for the good life on the part of people who would not work to earn it. Indeed, many police officers dealt with the protest exclusively in terms of its outward form, without regard for its content. All that was seen was the breach of the peace; that was all that deserved attention. (1979: 246–8.)

The result was a significant alienation between the police and a section of the policed society usually in a state of social conformity. That alienation was not confined to the police; that was just a part of a deep and growing cynicism about institutions, particularly those of government, although it seemed that the police institution was particularly addressed. (Rumbaut and Bittner 1979; Scheerer 1978). The police lost substantial support amongst the public generally, the middle class in particular, and the young specifically.

THE CONTEXTUAL EFFECTS OF SOCIAL CHANGE

The crisis of legitimacy manifested itself in at least two socially significant ways. One was a theoretical movement in perspectives on social policy, which, for the purposes of discussion, will be called 'conflict theory'. It is also called 'critical sociology' and 'new criminology' (Taylor, Walton, and Young 1975). The theories may or may not have been 'new' but they were certainly 'critical'[10] and they affected the way in which the control of police misconduct was and is perceived. The second was what I shall call the 'overcriminalization argument'. This was a theoretical, yet more practical discourse, directed to the reach of the criminal law and spurred by the conviction that the overreach of the substantive criminal law was at the root of many social ills (Packer 1968; Morris and Hawkins 1970; Goldsmith 1982).

[10] 'This is not an age of acceptance but rather one of enquiry. There is little if anything taken as so fundamental as to be beyond critical examination' (Barwick 1980: 242).

Both notions are central to the development of social policy in relation to control of police. Both, twenty years later, are still matters of current controversy. For example, the Queensland Fitzgerald Inquiry quite clearly links the issues of police and public corruption to the criminalization of such activities as gambling and prostitution; and the public campaign of denigration directed at the Law School of MacQuarie University is directly linked to the teaching of conflict theory.[11] Both remain central to the law reform process, and both remain central to the issue of controlling police misconduct.

Conflict Theory

Those who, in the 1960s, became alienated by their personal or vicarious experiences of policing, began to develop ideas and theory to accommodate a new version of reality. As positivism was born as a reaction to the failure of classical theory, so critical theory was born as a reaction to the failure of positivism to account for the record of actual experience (Goode 1976). It proved in analogous societies that, despite some vigorous efforts by a radical and violent minority, revolution would not follow an escalation of demonstrations and other public expressions of disaffection. The hope of praxis turned to the construction of theory. Here it is not desirable or practical to attempt more than the most general account of the development of critical theory—and that development is still occurring.[12] This is a historical, not a definitive, account.

In the beginning, there were two important matters to note about the crisis of alienation and the new theoretical perspective. The first was that, as with any new theory, it takes a while for the whole thing to be worked out, if that happy state can ever be reached. There is an ebb and flow to creation. Sumner remarked of the European experience:

Since the middle 1960s, European culture and politics have undergone profound changes, inspired by radical students, innovative youth, militant

---

[11] For the benefit of those readers unacquainted with the problems at MacQuarie, that law school has been very publicly divided between those who believe in the teaching of law as a profession and who are conservative about social content in law courses on the one hand, and those who see legal education as rooted in social theory and critical social appraisal on the other. The results of the dispute have not been edifying.

[12] After twenty years, the mainstream of American legal theory is still discovering what it calls 'critical legal studies'.

workers and their suppression by, and frequent incorporation into, the dominant political and cultural institutions. . . . Doubt prevailed . . . Ripples of doubt, and sometimes tidal waves, passed through the academic world, notably the social sciences. Many classical orthodoxies were run aground, not the least in Marxist scholarship. (1979: 3.)

The second is that the dissenters, who had been through the whole practical experience of the reality of conservative policing strategy, began to come to power. The middle-class children of the 1960s started to come to positions of political power. They started to influence policy in a significant way, and that influence was not about preserving police power and police immunity to oversight (Duncan 1981). The theorists and the practical politicians were coming together. This had practical consequences for the control of police misconduct. One of the more important of these was the development of research which indicated that some forms of police deviance were organizational in nature (Shearing 1981). The crisis of legitimacy and the consequent re-examination of the nature of the police institution as an organization led to a review of the previous self-serving histories of police forces. This was done in the light of the view that not only are the powerful in society at least as deviant as the powerless, but also that the categories of exploitation and dominance may be a better explanation and definition of anti-social behaviour than the notion of deviance itself (Becker 1963; Braithwaite and Wilson 1978).

Where does the notion of a police establishment come from? What is its legitimacy? The policing structure of Australia, Canada, and the United States derives from the common English heritage of 'the Peelers'. What has been lost in the twentieth century is the fact that the creation of the essential elements of the modern police institution was bitterly fought at the time by the powerless, was designed by its founders to reinforce the legitimacy of the then regime, and was regarded by many as a defective and dangerous idea (Storch 1981; Cohen 1981).

The 1830s saw the replacement of policing by some degree of mutual security and informal policing arrangements by an incipient bureaucratic professional organization directly controlled by a ruling class. It is impossible to take an accurate view of the beginnings of modern policing without recognizing that the discussion took place in the context of a polarized political debate about the whole nature and function of the criminal process. The propertied classes felt the need for better protection from the 'dangerous classes', (Howe 1966; Silver 1967; Storch 1981) but were sufficiently aware of the social situation to realize, in the end, that they must achieve that aim by means which would minimize disruption and resentment.

England in the 1830s was in the middle of unprecedented social change. Industrialization was proceeding apace, modern capitalist production was emerging, increasingly visible inequalities and hardships were being created, and the cities were growing rapidly to accommodate, in gross poverty, those forced from local industry to the factory and the mill. There was a new and affluent middle class which owed its rise to this process, but their rise effected social conditions which produced the creation of a strong working-class movement, or series of movements. That led to unionism, and other, more radical movements, which reminded the powerful of the recent French revolution—which directly threatened the new urban élite.

The creation of the police apparatus had little to do with a more effective treatment of traditional crime; it had a great deal to do with Chartism, unionism, and the fear that the working class would revolt violently (Radzinowicz 1981). The design was to create an aspect of 'capitalism with a human face'; a deflector of working-class resentment, and an enforcer from but not of the working class. It worked beautifully. It still does.

These themes recurred later. Working-class movements threatened the avenues to the free pursuit of profit. As late as 1908, the FBI was founded specifically to deal with labour movements in the United States. Later empire builders transformed it. Then, as now, proponents of the new police propagated, very successfully, the myth that the police were just ordinary citizens who happened to be paid for doing what all ordinary citizens could and should do. That was never so, though the myth lives on in the common law.[13]

It is, of course, the case that the method of policing replaced by the new police was incapable of coping with the drastic changes wrought by the evolving society and its pressures and demands, and

---

[13] In the guise of the complete fiction that every constable is endowed with original, individual, and uncoordinated ministerial authority. The practical result of this was that the common law denied a master–servant relationship between the constable and the Crown and hence there could be no vicarious liability of the latter for the torts of the former. See *Enever* (1906); *Fisher* v. *Oldham Corp.*; A/G *NSW* v. *Perpetual Trustee Co. Ltd.* (1955). A recent example is *Lackersteen* v. *Jones and Others* (1988) 92 FLR 6. The doctrine is, of course, complete nonsense. See Lustgarten (1986).

that it was corrupt in modern terms. The old standard solution of calling in the troops did not work as it had; either the troops obeyed their orders and behaved as if dissenting citizens were the dreaded French, in which case resistance and resentment was maximized when they left for other tasks, or, even more feared, they failed to move at all.[14] In 1812, the government had 12,000 soldiers in the north of England—more than Wellington had in Europe—to control industrial unrest, and there was a justifiable fear that the troops might defect to the unionists (Whitaker 1979). One is foolish to dice with the loyalty of the army, and the professional police would be so unpopular in the north that there would be a minimal chance that the police and the unionists would form a common front. The development of the professional police can be seen as the creation of an almost private, almost public, almost army, to control the oppressed urban poor.

The creation of the new police had at least four important and interrelated results. First, the new policing function began, quite quickly, to move from simply seeking out and bringing to justice those who had committed crimes, to the notion of 'crime prevention' and hence the active seeking out of deviance. The reasons for this are not hard to understand. The new professionals sought reasons for employment, expansion, and preferment. Moreover, it is clearly easier to catch deviants before they do what they plan than when they do it—or later—because, when it happens, it happens as fast as possible and after that, the deviants will be engaged in the enterprise of evading capture. It is also more satisfying, interesting, and productive to seek out deviants in advance rather than waiting for them to strike. This new function created work, thus also creating an argument for expansion and increased status. This, and more, is common to the more sophisticated, bureaucratic organizations of the twentieth century.

The second result was that the new preventive approach produced a new direction in law enforcement: the old order had found it neither desirable nor necessary to watch the under-class all the time,

---

[14] See, for example, Storch (1981: 89): 'By 1830 the deficiencies of the army in order keeping were manifest. The inflexibility of the military, its inability to act with anything less than the maximum of force when compelled to intervene, and the consequent and frequent refusal of its commanders to act; but more important its inherent unsuitability to the task of providing the type of daily protection now demanded made its use increasingly inappropriate except in pressing emergencies.' So too in Australia. Consider the Eureka Stockade.

but the new approach created the mechanism and the desire to do so.[15] Third, the preventive push and the idea of constant surveillance 'creates' criminals. It is no coincidence that the new police grew up to enforce the growing legislative regulation of many aspects of working-class life, both by the enactment of new laws and the use of old laws for new purposes.[16]

Fourth, the nature of the new police was such that the institution was particularly immune to external control. Rumbaut and Bittner, for example, argue:

Among the main influences shaping the police conception of order is the police organisational model, with its paramilitary structure, its stress on hierarchy, command, routine and obedience to orders, all of which tend to discount the need for discretion and initiative in policing and to value crime control more than accountability to the rule of law. [Notable effects of this model are] its pressure toward goal displacement in the interests of efficiency, internal discipline, and 'production demands' and its effects on the work of members who are molded into soldier-bureaucrats (1979: 253).[17]

It is interesting that, by the late 1980s, this debate had resurfaced under the guise of 'community policing' and the Neighbourhood Watch movement. These ideas represent, however haltingly, an attempt at the decentralization and localization of policing, and consensual policing involving quite small communities and their residents in preventive policing strategies. While these general ideas are still in their infancy, and so outcomes are difficult to assess, some, Professor Norval Morris for example, believe that these developments have significant inbuilt accountability advantages (Morris 1989). Consideration of the history of policing—the real history—suggests that that result would not be surprising. Account-

[15] See e.g. Storch (1981: 86): 'By 1840 it came to be an axiom in police that you guard St James by watching St Giles. This was a novel attitude. Eighteenth century governments and the upper classes in general were surely apprehensive of the movements of the lower orders, but did not consider it either useful or necessary to watch St Giles *all the time*.' (Emphasis in the original.)

[16] The classic example is the law in relation to the status of vagrancy. Originally passed to protect the then existing feudal order of labour, these laws were used e.g. in the 1920s and 1930s to enforce anti-gambling laws, and in the 1960s and 1970s in order to persecute hippies and demonstrators.

[17] Citing: Skolnick (1966); Bordua and Reiss (1966: 68); Niederhoffer (1967); Bittner (1970); Rubinstein (1973); Manning (1977). See also Book Review (1980) *British Journal of Criminology* 2: 178.

ability should work best locally. This may be one of the principal themes of policing in the 1990s and beyond.

Whether any of this was appreciated in the middle of the nineteenth century, and to what extent, is a moot point, but it can be said that the idea of the new police generated a debate concerning the appropriate nature and form of the policing function and its role in the emerging capitalist state. Until the emergence of the conflict theorists, that debate remained an inarticulate major premise in late twentieth-century consideration of the appropriate level of control of police misconduct. For example, it is no coincidence that the advocates of civilian control boards as a strategy for control harked back to the old English police boards. But until relatively recently, there was little or no discussion of ideas such as that which argues that the centralization of the whole criminal justice process, from policing to policy formulation, is an extreme which is productive of damaging effects on, for example, accountability; or that the rhetoric of centralized crime prevention, professionalism, and organizational efficiency commonly obscures the protection and enlargement of budgetary allocation, an excuse for the barely discriminate regulation of private behaviour, the preservation of uncontrolled discretion, and the discriminatory penalization of social status.[18]

The conflict theorists may or may not have been right about all of this, but the debate was undoubtedly a healthy sign, and it opened up a new realism in the way in which participants in that debate saw where police accountability came from and where it might be expected to go. It set the accountability debate in a new context—a context in which accountability could not be viewed in isolation from reality or from the overall social context of policing of which it was a significant part.

The Overcriminalization Argument

If critical concentration on the effects of the new police revealed that there was an association between the political will for the new police and the increasing regulation and penalization of a variety of hitherto private behaviours, that merely reflected the fact that the crisis of legitimacy experienced in the 1960s focused, not only on the nature and function of policing, but also on other aspects of the criminal

---

[18] There are any number of examples of this. One of the more notorious is the criminalization of cannabis after the repeal of Prohibition in the United States. See e.g. King (1972). An interesting perspective on the problem is provided by Dickson (1968: 143).

justice system, notably the reach of the criminal sanction. Goldsmith has remarked:

The 1960s was a decade in which a liberal awakening occurred as to the 'overreach' of the criminal law. This was in part doubtless precipitated by the interest in legal academic circles in labelling theory, which drew attention to the fact that criminality was a status that could be arbitrarily applied, and that in fact certain groups were [more] likely to be labelled as criminals than others. (1982: 104–5.)

In 1989, this seems commonplace in an environment in which questions are commonly asked about the desirability of the role of the criminal law in regulating such as abortion, prostitution, gambling, homosexuality, and drug abuse in a way and tone unthinkable in the 1960s. The theoretical debate about the role of the criminal law had existed for some time (Mill 1859; Stephen 1872; Devlin 1959; Hart 1963); what was new was increasingly vigorous non-theoretical public dissent on very specific issues. Those who actually engaged in such illegal behaviour as homosexuality took to flaunting the fact and daring the authorities—such as the police—to use the criminal law against them. In other words, what was new was the public agitation for the withdrawal of the criminal sanction by publicly declared but unrepentant deviants. It was as if the burglars' co-operative had publicly demonstrated in favour of the repeal of the law against breaking and entering. In short, the mere existence of the law was no longer a sufficient condition for compliance or concealment (Weyrauch 1978). The law imprisoning those who refused to be conscripted into the army and shipped to Vietnam must have had a central role in the extension of the crisis of legitimacy from those who enforced the law—the police—to those who made it—the law-makers.

The original form of the debate focused on so-called 'victimless crimes', and that still is the case to a large extent.[19] As the debate developed, however, less obvious questions emerged. For example, if X fills in a bank withdrawal slip for $100 and the teller mistakenly pays out $200, under which circumstances should X be convicted of larceny, if at all (Potisk 1973)? If banks knowingly design a computer system so that a child could fool it, should the criminal law be used to collect the debt when X fools it and gains money to which

---

[19] The label 'victimless crimes' is not beyond reproach, but serves a sufficiently indicative if not definitional purpose. Thus Schur and Bedau (1974).

he or she is not entitled (*Kennison* v. *Daire* 1986)? And, even where it is conceded that the criminal law should become involved, what about issues such as overlapping offences and the perils of double jeopardy, both legal and non-legal? On another level, conflict theorists argued that the overcriminalization debate was an important indication of significant dysfunction in the relationship between the powerful and the rest of the political process, in particular demonstrating the use of the criminal sanction as a device for the repression of one social class in furtherance of the interests of another.[20]

The overcriminalization debate had important implications for police accountability. The most important of these was that, where the police seek to enforce a law, the existence or extent of which is significantly disputed by a substantial social or cultural grouping, the police organization is faced with a choice between failing to enforce to a satisfactory extent, or obtaining a level of enforcement by illegal or immoral practices such as the planting of evidence, 'verballing' (Lucas 1979; Fitzgerald 1989) or a variety of entrapment strategies. In short, the evidence that there is a causal relationship between police misconduct and overcriminalization is now over-whelming (Packer 1968; Morris and Hawkins 1970; Heydon 1973). So too the failure of the law-makers to appreciate that fact. It quickly became evident that the then existing mechanisms for the control of police misconduct were at best ineffective and at worst served as a vehicle for the concealment of abuses either individual or, worse, organizational.[21]

---

[20] This is a recurrent theme but the point is well made by Sumner (1979: 270): 'Some classes, some occupational groups, some pressure groups and some individuals have more power than others in the legislative process. It [law] is not as pluralistic as other ideological forms because it is subject to the political process and, hence, the relative ability of different classes and groups to establish their ideas as law. Political success requires money and power as well as potent ideas, even more so than other fields of superstructural practice. Thus law as an ideological form is less pluralistic, than, say, the novel and music. It is a much closer reflection of class inequality than other forms. It tends to express the ideologies of the dominant class and their political and cultural representatives . . . When the chips are down, the essential function of the legal system is revealed as itself: the reproduction of class power.' Whether this is right or not is not the point. The point is that it was said and said often.

[21] Outstanding examples of this phenomenon are to be found in Cox, Shirley, and Short (1977). A specific example concerned a police officer named Challenor. Whitaker (1979: 254) comments on the Challenor case: 'Challenor's earlier victims had all been working class people, often black, whose rights the police, the legal profession, and the courts had totally failed to safeguard: but for the accident of picking on one person who was able to exonerate himself by his own efforts, Challenor's methods might be

The connection between the many issues intertwined in this essay is neatly encapsulated by Kessler:

The creation of specialised law enforcement agencies may result in more efficient law enforcement, yet certain activities of such agencies raise important issues. While these activities are not necessarily confined to victimless crime control agencies, the activities of drug control agencies have been much criticised. Packer concludes that our over-reliance on the criminal sanction to deal with narcotic and other drug violations has led to the creation of a well entrenched bureaucracy which has a vested interest in the status quo and has thwarted major reform efforts. (1980: 142)

WHAT HAPPENED TO THE MECHANISMS OF LEGAL CHANGE

Discussion now turns to the impact of these social and political changes on the mechanisms of legal change. It is hardly surprising that the crisis of institutional legitimacy did not leave these institutions untouched. They were found to be inadequate as a matter of operational reality to cope with the new pressures for fundamental and relatively immediate reform in a host of areas, notably including police accountability. Inadequacy in fact promotes investigation of inadequacy in theory, and so this period saw renewed examination of the mechanisms of legal change in Parliaments, the media, scholarly and popular journals, academic and bureaucratic activity, and other more or less public forums (Missen 1979; Castles 1977).

The result was a reforming of law reform. This centrally involved the reform of controls of police behaviour. Reforming law reform was in part driven by the inability of the then existing mechanisms of legal change to cope with the manifest need to improve police accountability. It is by no means a coincidence that the first reference to the shiny new Australian Law Reform Commission was on public complaints about police behaviour, and the second, criminal investigation and police powers, despite the fact that both topics were of marginal relevance to Commonwealth jurisdiction (Australian Law Reform Commission 1975*a*, 1978).[22]

continuing to this day. A system of justice that cannot operate without good luck and a campaign by voluntary organisations . . . must be capable of improvement.'

[22] In the American context, Rambaut and Bittner (1979: 275) observe the same phenomenon: 'the 1960s saw a succession of presidential and other official

The Failure of the Legislature

The increasing pace of change in modern industrial democracies highlighted the incapacity of the reformation model of Parliament to cope. The industrialization of society required more and more intervention, and, as society developed, became post-industrial, more complex, and more interdependent, the demanded intervention became more and more complex and harder and harder to achieve. Parliament was enacting vastly more legislation, and achieving less and less. In short, parliamentary responsible government overloaded. Necessity dictated that the work be done none the less, and the solution employed was the rapid redevelopment of the administrative process. The result was that legislation tended to spell out the general principles, and leave the details to delegates, either expressly or by implication.[23]

The development of a large and powerful administrative process amounted to a recognition of the inability of the traditional agencies of change to cope with a social milieu dominated by an increasing desire and/or need (depending on the speaker's position) to regulate more and more human behaviour by the device of rule-making. The administrative process offered a more efficient preservation and enlargement of the rule structure by the growth and specialization of legal authority without threatening the centrality of the rule of rules itself. While the administrative process has significant inherent advantages *qua* process, it seems likely that its growth was a conservative response to the incipient strangulation of the legal system by a web of social and political demands and the difficulties of rule-based regulation. Thus the simple, expedient, and in a sense perverse transfer of power from the legislative to the executive branch of government accomplished much. Indeed, social, political, and systemic threats to the status quo are typically met, as in the collapse of feudalism, by the centralization of power. It is no

commissions which both focussed unprecedented public attention on the police institution and provided the rationale for a major mobilization of . . . resources'.

[23] Rumbaut and Bittner (ibid. 243) comment: 'Legal commentators were alarmed by the seeming paradox of the superior powers of the ministerial, as compared to the magisterial, functionaries of the state. And, not surprisingly, their minds turned to rule-making and policy formulation . . . There existed, it seemed clear, a wide area of decision making that should be brought under control, long before one reached the limits of necessary discretion.' The shifts in political power within the Westminster system are well beyond the range of this essay.

coincidence that the growth of the administrative process marked the increased political domination of the legislature by the executive in Westminster-based, constitutional systems of governance. The establishment of the new police can be seen in this context as part of that process.

Over time, the legislature simply ceased to be a law reform agency of first impression, acting in rare exceptions if at all, only in deliberation upon administrative/executive proposals generated externally. A good example of this process may be seen in the death of the private member's bill as an agency of reform.[24] The Missen Report noted that there is currently no realistic possibility of legislative consideration of measures neglected by the executive, and recommended that, at least, some time be guaranteed by Australian Parliaments for consideration of, if not enactment of, private members' bills. (Missen 1979: r. 2.45). That proposal has fallen on deaf ears. For similar reasons, there has been a call for an annual 'miscellaneous reform bill' to guarantee some consideration of neglected reform proposals or needs. All that has happened on this front is the increasing employment by the executive of general Statute Amendment Bills in which the substantive is so mixed with the cosmetic that the former escapes Parliamentary scrutiny.

Three general themes run through explanations of the decline of the legislature as a primary agency of law reform as distinct from the administrative/executive processes. First, the growth in the size, complexity, and interdependency of society strangled a legislative process designed and developed for simpler times. Part of this is the obstruction of Parliament simply for the sake of obstruction. Second, the legislature was overwhelmed by the executive in the development of modern party government. The reason for this 'tyranny of the executive' was neatly summarized by a Canadian legislator as follows:

Under British parliamentary theory, the executive serves at the pleasure and control of the legislature, and should they be rejected on any item of consequence, it is their duty to leave office. No one wants to leave office, and continuity in office has become more coveted as government itself has become more important. The Cabinet therefore made the logical move—it

[24] The Australian Law Reform Commission (1979: 1) commented: 'In Australia, the general position is that for a proposed law reform to be even debated, let alone enacted, the support of the Government or at least of the responsible Minister or Department must first be obtained.'

arranged to take control over the institution, which, in theory, controlled it since, under our system, the government has no security without complete control of Parliament.[25]

Third, and perhaps as a consequence of all this, the legislature proved at the crucial time to be incapable of acting in the interests of minorities and human values; it could not and did not act in areas of controversy yet productive of injustice unless there was obvious political profit immediately. There developed an atmosphere in which issues, such as the external control of police accountability, were so controversial as to prohibit any political party with a realistic chance at government (or staying there) from acting at all.

The legislature became inadequate as a generator of responses to demands for change. Something had to give, and the response was the 'new principle law reform agency'. That development will be examined. Before that, however, it is necessary to consider how the judiciary reacted to this situation.

The Evolving Judicial Role

A feature of the period in question has been the tension between the two extremist positions on the question of whether judges make law or merely apply it. It has become very clear that the courts can and do reform the law, engage in 'social engineering' (Dobie 1930; *Fahey and Lindsay* 1978: 582–3), sometimes with important social and political effect (Fox 1980). Any system of social control principally dependent upon the operation of rule-based compulsions necessarily implies the existence of a mechanism for deciding whether a given rule governs a given instance, and the existence of inflexible rules operating upon the infinite variety of human behaviour and endeavour implies the transference of flexibility required by notions of justice to the evaluator. Judges do make law: what remains most unclear is any set of criteria which will determine when, how, and to what extent. For example, Eskridge's recent study on the influence and employment of 'public values' in judicial statutory interpretation reveals that those values—defined as background norms that contribute to and result from the moral development of our political community—are inconsistently and arbitrarily applied (Eskridge 1989).

---

[25] The legislator was Sir Robert Stanfield. I am unable to find the source of the quotation.

This is not the place in which to add to the rivers of ink and forests of trees that have been devoted to all aspects of judicial reform and judicial law-making. Some introductory comments on the judicial process as an agency of legal change are, however, necessary.

The judicial process has some advantages as an agency of change. Castles cites the minimization of social disruption and enhanced political acceptability of judicial reform of controversial matters (Castles 1977; Jaffe 1969). Tay and Kamenka cite the ability of judges to produce controllable and predictable change, and their natural predilection to 'shun the pretensions of the universal legislator' (Tay and Kamenka 1980). However, the judicial process often places the considerable expense and burden of initiating change upon those who lack resources; a good example of this is the field of controlling police misconduct.[26] By comparison, the costs of the new principle law reform agency or executive process are more widely distributed, and the burden of initiating reform may be taken up by the process of change itself.

Moreover, legal change by judicial process depends, not merely upon the random accidents of litigation, but also upon the functioning of the appellate structure. Some rules of appeal are designed to catch the case requiring contemplation of reform, but many are not, in part because the judicial decision to change is so unpredictable (Fox 1980). In general, the judicial process is constrained by criteria of relevance imposed as part of a strategy to conserve expensive judicial resources by constraining inquiry, decision, and, of course reform. This conservation policy is unrelated to the merits of litigation—for example, the non-availability of the class action or the restriction on advisory opinions. In addition there exist what have been called 'the passive virtues' (Gunther 1964; Denvir 1980), criteria of relevance, standing, statutes of limitation, and so on. There are many such 'masks' (Weyrauch 1978); one for every dilemma. The judicial process is not constrained by its perception of the wider political or social reality, but is constrained by reference to the policies of change *qua* change—whether it is right, and in what circumstances, for the law to change its mind (Denvir 1980). The prime example of this is, of

[26] The point is made by a number of sources, but a ready example is to be found in Levine (1971: 206): 'The victims of police brutality are ordinarily lower-class men . . . who lack the initiative, fortitude and skills to fight the injustices inflicted upon them . . . These people are social expendables and are thus left largely on their own.'

course, the doctrine of precedent. In short, the judicial process serves other interests than justice on the merits, and these purposes sometimes conflict.

The judicial process did achieve change in the control of police misconduct in the period under discussion. It did so by, in effect, inventing an exclusionary rule of evidence. An exclusionary rule of evidence had been in place in relation to confessions and admissions for many years, and had had a discernible effect in controlling police misconduct in that area, yet the common law in Australia, until at least 1970, had steadfastly refused to extend the rule to real evidence unlawfully or illegally obtained (Australian Law Reform Commission 1975b). The principal reason given for this lay in the reliability differential between real and confessional evidence. Who could be sure that a confession obtained under duress was true? But a gun found under the bed was undoubtedly 'true', no matter how it was obtained. It was true that the real evidence would be excluded if its admission would be 'unfair' to the accused; but that notion was defined very narrowly, and in terms of probative value (Weinberg 1975). It is beyond the scope of this paper to canvass the very vexed question of whether exclusionary rules are a good idea, or whether or not they work effectively to control police behaviour. It is also beyond the scope of this paper to canvass the reasons for or against the reliability criterion. The fact is that the Australian judiciary changed the rule. The question is, why? Why then? Why that case?

The case was *Bunning* v. *Cross*.[27] It was, in many respects, a very odd case by which to achieve so fundamental a change. It was a prosecution for 'driving under the influence'. A police officer observed a car, driven by the accused, behaving erratically. He stopped the car, and observed symptoms of liquor consumption in the driver. He formed the opinion that the accused was under the influence of alcohol and asked him to undergo a breathalyser test. The reading was positive. At trial, the magistrate acquitted the accused on the 'driving under the influence' charge on the basis that the breathalyser reading was inadmissible. This was so, the magistrate held, because the police officer had no reasonable grounds to suspect that the accused was so under the influence of alcohol as to be incapable of controlling the motor vehicle. The prosecutor obtained an order to review. A judge of the Supreme

---

[27] (1978) 141 CLR 54. The High Court appears to be of the view that it signalled the change in *Ireland* (1970) 126 CLR 321. This is, in my opinion, a precedent 'mask'.

Court found the magistrate to be in error and remitted the case. The magistrate then excluded the breathalyser reading on the basis that its admission would be unfair. There was another application for an order to review. It went to the Full Court of the Supreme Court of Western Australia. The Court found that the magistrate had erred. It remitted the case. This all went to the High Court. Those were the facts on which the High Court decided to change the law.

There is, of course, no answer to the questions 'why this case?' and 'why at this time?' Perhaps personal memoirs published in the future will provide a clue. But the facts were most unsympathetic. There could be no doubt on the agreed facts as to the cogency of the evidence. It was not as if the police officer had committed some egregious crime in order to obtain the impugned evidence. It was hardly a *cause célèbre*. Indeed, the majority of the High Court held that the court below was in error in not remitting the case to the magistrate *with a direction to convict*. And yet the High Court chose this case.

There is no answer to the questions posed in the influential joint judgment of Stephen and Aickin JJ. Nor would one be expected. Judges do not commonly supply the answers to questions like that. They do not give *process* reasons. They do give policy reasons. And the reasons given by Stephen and Aickin JJ. contain no clue as to the answer to 'why this case?' But they do provide a clue to the answer to the more general question 'why about now?' Here it is:

The relevance of the competing policy considerations to which we have referred becomes of especial importance in an age of sophisticated crime and crime detection when law enforcement increasingly depends upon electronic surveillance and eavesdropping, the unannounced search of premises or of the person and upon scientific methods, whether of identification, by fingerprints or voiceprints, or of ascertainment of bodily states, as by blood alcohol tests and the like. In many such cases the question of fairness does not play any part. . . . It is not fair play that is called in question in such cases but rather society's right to insist that those who enforce the law themselves respect it, so that a citizen's precious right to immunity from arbitrary and unlawful intrusion into the daily affairs of private life may remain unimpaired. (*Bunning* v. *Cross* 1978: 75.)

It seems that their Honours were motivated by the view that there was insufficient control of police investigative behaviour in an age in which technological sophistication equipped investigators with increasingly intrusive techniques of uncovering real evidence and at the same time trespass on the civil rights of the innocent. One can only speculate as to what caused their Honours to form that view, but they were, of course, absolutely right, as subsequent events such as the '*Age* Tapes' saga revealed. There Australian society was faced with just that which their Honours feared: widespread, unauthorized, police electronic surveillance. Of course, the fact that there was an exclusionary rule in place had no effect on the police behaviour concerned. The limited utility of the judicial process as an agency of desired legal change is evident.

ONE PRACTICAL RESULT: THE CREATION OF THE NEW PRINCIPLE LAW REFORM AGENCY

The mechanisms of legal change were clearly inadequate as a matter of operational reality to cope with the new pressures for relatively immediate and fundamental reform. The 1960s saw renewed examination of the mechanisms of legal change, the core of the constitutional power structure, in Parliaments, the media, scholarly and popular journals, and other more or less public forums. The result was a reforming of law reform. Reform of the processes of legal change and reform of the controls over police misconduct are subtly interrelated. While it is obvious that the outcome of attempts to reform controls over police misconduct will depend on the adequacy and responsiveness of the mechanisms of legal change that are in place, in practice reform of the mechanisms of legal change was fundamentally affected by attempts to reform controls over police misconduct.

With some exceptions, but in general, the judiciary retreated from as much law-making function as possible—while recognizing that judges could and did make law, the judiciary as an institution retreated in the face of the legislature, activist by reputation. But the legislature found itself strangled by the dominance of the executive and the complexity of post-war society. If it could act at all, it acted only on the political will of the government of the day. In the area of policing, that was very slowly. Kirby has remarked: 'Into the vacuum left by the retreating judiciary, diminished Parliaments and distracted and sometimes hostile Executive Government, has come the law reform agency.' (1980: 62.)

What occurred was an increased advocation and establishment of variations on the permanent law reform agency model of legal change, the creation of an administrative structure devoted to the consideration of reforming the law, a body upon which difficult problems could be devolved with comfort; the 'new principle' of law reform, described by Castles as: 'a principle qualitatively different from past practice in which the *whole* body of law stands potentially in need of reform and there should be standing bodies of professional experts to consider reforms continuously.' (1977: 4.) It is important to note that permanent law reform bodies imply not only experts in the area of law to be reformed, but experts in the business of law reform itself.

Sackville (1985) defined the 'new principle' agency in more detail. He described five characteristics.

(1) permanence; by which is meant an expectation of continuity of establishment;
(2) democratic legitimacy; by which is meant a continuing relationship with the government of the day in such matters as appointment, reference, and implementation;
(3) the consultative function; by which is meant the practice or obligation of extensive community consultation on reform ideas, either through the holding of seminars or public meetings and/or the dissemination of discussion papers;
(4) the public function; by which is meant that the agency operate and recommend in the public domain;
(5) a measure of independence; by which is meant a freedom from the constraints of government policy.

Acceptance of the 'new principle' was widespread and relatively rapid. The 'law reform commission' sprang up all over the place. Reform of law reform also turned out to be 'society-specific'—in comparable societies, for similar reasons, the inadequacy of alternative, systematically comparable agencies of legal change combined with the political necessity of delegating difficult questions from government (without delegating political power) in the face of a crisis of institutional legitimacy led to a recognition of the utility of the 'new principle'. The agency was new and untried, and so it could not be caught up in institutional cynicism. The agency was semi-independent and expert, so there was a ready answer to questions about what was being done. A potentially new dimension to masterly inactivity arose.

However, it became clear that what have been described in this text as 'random factors' maintained a powerful role. In the context of the reform of law reform, there were significant differences between the various 'new principle' models. There were differences in involvement and implementation. Randomness was, in a sense, built into the new principle agencies.

First, no new principle agency has exclusive jurisdiction over law reform. That is not surprising, but it means that the new principle may be overridden at will by the use of alternative agencies of legal change, for example, the Royal Commission. The selection of the agency to which the question at issue is referred may be dictated by the old adage of choosing the result by choosing the inquiry.

Second, most new principle agencies are not self-activating. Hence, whether or not a matter is referred for reform proposals is as random as ever it was. So too the terms of reference. Nothing can prevent the new principle agency requesting a reference—but that may or may not matter according to the views of the government of the day.

Third, the 'new principle' does not, as a principle of law reform, address the all-important issue of implementation. Whether or not the recommendations generated by the new process are implemented in whole, in part, or not at all, is left to the old randomly influenced processes.

The significance of random factors in the 'new principle' system is vividly portrayed in Hodgson's appraisal of his experience with the English Law Commission:

A survey of the way in which the report of the Law Reform Commission on Conspiracy and Criminal Law Reform came to have the form it did vividly illustrates the influence of these different factors. Its subject matter and the form in which some only of its recommendations were included in a government Bill, also owe a great deal to *purely fortuitous events*, the interaction of which influenced a political climate which proved fruitful for some part at least of the law reform project. Two elementary mistakes in drafting Acts of Parliament, the one in 1875, the other in 1959, the criminal activities of some pickets in the course of a trade dispute, the intemperate behaviour of some students from Sierra Leone and the efforts of Mr Blackburn to rid the country of pornography have all had their part to play in the timing of the report and its implementation (1978: 245.)

The goals of the 'new principle' of law reform were uniform, systematic, comprehensive, expert reform. But the 'new principle' agency turned out to have similar constraints as the traditional avenues of change, albeit in different ways.[28] In the Australian context, these goals were inevitably compromised by the Federal system of government. Castles integrated the systemic factors with the federalism factors when he wrote:

law reform in Australia is obviously still very much the sum of many parts. The structure and methodology adopted for law reform vary from jurisdiction to jurisdiction and sometimes even within a political unit. Political considerations, particularly as they relate to moves concerned with uniformity, can and do play at times, a significant and perhaps a decisive role in determining the direction of law reform activities. Not surprisingly, too, population size, the relative affluence and other factors like this affecting one political unit, compared to another, have influenced the way in which law reform agencies have evolved. (1977: 8.)

Castles concentrates on the randomizing influence of federalism upon the form of the 'new principle' agency which may be established. He regards this as a 'valuable feature' of the present situation, for variety will ensure wider experimentation in forms or options within the new principle model, which variation is to be seen as desirable in its formative years, not only to provide a 'gathering store' of experience, but also to ensure that the principle itself is adequately assessed in the light of experience. Twelve years later it is possible to say that not only were the differences between law reform agencies not motivated by decisions of principle about the 'new principle' idea, but also that no one seems to be studying the issues in any systematic way.

There are some forces for some kind of co-ordination and interaction between law reform agencies at work in different jurisdictions. There is the regular Australian Law Reform Agencies Conference, the Standing Committee of Attorneys-General, the publication by the Australian Law Reform Commission of the journal *Reform* which valuably lists the ongoing programmes of all Australian law reform agencies. And of course law reform agencies talk to each other either institutionally or individually on an informal or a formal basis. Discussion now turns to the impact of this new law reform framework and movement on the issues surrounding police accountability.

[28] See also Zander (1979: 494): 'What one may loosely term the Spirit of the Times may, therefore, have a powerful effect in promoting change, but it is right to notice that much may turn, also, on the fortuitous conjunction of events and individuals.'

LAW REFORM AND POLICE ACCOUNTABILITY:
THE ADMINISTRATIVE SYSTEMS FOR HANDLING
COMPLAINTS AGAINST THE POLICE

How, then, did all this ferment affect the administrative systems set up to control police accountability? A logical starting place is the Second Report of the Criminal Law and Penal Methods Reform Committee of South Australia released in July 1974. This committee, popularly known as the 'Mitchell Committee' after its Chair,[29] was established in 1971 by the government of South Australia as a special-purpose committee to investigate and report on reform of the criminal justice system. The committee looked at the processing of complaints against the police, and concluded that the then current, entirely secret, and internal system was unsatisfactory because, *inter alia*, it involved the system being a judge in its own cause, and recommended very conservative and minimal reforms to correct the worst features of the internal system (Mitchell 1974).

However, in May 1975, the Commonwealth Attorney-General, Kep Enderby, gave a comprehensive reference on law enforcement to the new Australian Law Reform Commission (ALRC), the first 'new principle' law reform agency in Australia. The Commission had been established by legislation in 1973, but its members were not appointed until 1975. Its first Chair was the formidable Justice Michael Kirby, who, ever a controversial figure, is on every hand regarded as a dedicated, hard-working, and inspiring law reformer. The Commission reported on 'Complaints Against Police' in August 1975. In a concise, well-focused report, the Commission recommended a system of administrative accountability for the proposed Australia Police which differed markedly from the old internal disciplinary structure models. It also held that the police should not be seen as judges in their own cause, and, in brief, recommended the formation of a separate police internal investigation division, and the involvement of the Australian Ombudsman as an alternative recipient of complaints, and an overseer of the results of investigation, with a power of independent investigation in certain cases, including those in which internal investigation has not, or is apprehended not to have, produced a defensible result. This went

[29] Then Mitchell J. of the Supreme Court of South Australia, now Dame Roma Mitchell.

much further than Mitchell, and the recommendations in that report were discussed and rejected (Australian Law Reform Commission 1975*a*: 82).

This was the 'new principle' agency working at its best. It produced a concise and readable report which, none the less, canvassed opinions from home and overseas, undertook wide consultation, examined alternative models, and consulted with the public; it proposed a compromise solution which attempted to address the concerns of many sides in the context of an ethos of policing in transition. As a result, it was crucially influential. The basic model proposed in 1975 is now in place in almost all Australian jurisdictions. That did not happen, however, without significant and informative hiccups.

For a variety of reasons, notably the change in government in 1975, the ALRC proposals did not go ahead. In 1977 the government asked ALRC to reconsider its original report. It did so. The result was a supplementary report issued in 1978 (Australian Law Reform Commission 1978).

Meanwhile, the Premier of New South Wales announced in October 1976 that he favoured the ALRC recommendations. That announcement was followed by legislation: the Police Regulation (Allegations of Misconduct) Act 1978. The difficulty was that this legislation differed from the ALRC recommendations in one highly material respect. The ombudsman was given an oversight function only. He or she had no power of reinvestigation in a case in which he was unsatisfied with the initial police internal investigation. The balance—the compromise—was significantly affected. The result was disaster.

The Ombudsman received internal investigation reports which he regarded as opaque. Acrimonious correspondence ensued (Masterman 1988). In the event, the Ombudsman decided to take the course of reporting in such cases that he had been unable to decide whether or not the complaint had been sustained. The police union took the issue to court. It argued that the Ombudsman had to decide one way or the other. The Ombudsman won (*Ombudsman* v. *Moroney* 1983). Also taken to court was the issue of whether the Ombudsman, having made a report, could require the police to reopen the investigation. The Ombudsman won that one too (*Boyd* v. *Ombudsman and Others* 1983)—but the basic point is that alteration to the compromise proposed by the ALRC led to the investigation of complaints against police being litigated in the Court of Appeal. The government of New South Wales remedied the defect in 1983.[30] While it appears that the office of the ombudsman is satisfied that the resulting system suffices, it is also clear that the system could not cope with significant levels of corruption in the force, and that New South Wales police continue to oppose it on the basis that external investigation is anathema (Masterman 1988).

In Victoria, events took a slightly different course. In 1975 the Victorian Ombudsman took the view that he was entitled to investigate police complaints which fell within his general remit of investigating matters 'relating to administration' (Australian Law Reform Commission 1978: para. 23). That would cover a percentage of citizen complaints against police (but not all) and was a mirror of similar positions taken by ombudsmen in other jurisdictions. Again there was acrimonious correspondence, and again the Ombudsman was taken to court, this time in relation to correctional services. This time the result was inconclusive, but tended against the Ombudsman (*Booth* v. *Dillon 1 and 2* 1976).

In 1976 the Beach Committee reported that it favoured the ALRC recommendations (Beach 1976). The position of the Victoria Police was that they had created an independent internal investigations branch and that was enough. Later, and significantly, they espoused the idea of a separate Police Commissioner of Complaints. The Beach recommendations were referred to yet another committee, with the inevitable result that everything died for some time.

There was a major review of policing which reported in 1985. In that year, Parliament passed the Police Regulation (Amendment) Act which set up a body to be known as the Police Complaints Authority. The legislation was based on the ALRC model, but with this significant difference—the complaints jurisdiction was given, not to the ombudsman, but to a separate 'quasi-ombudsman' created for the purpose. Trouble came quickly. In late 1986 the police conducted raids on a number of hotels and arrested a number of people. The PCA publicized the fact that it would attend one of those hotels so that any person who wished to make a complaint about those actions could do so at that time and place. A number of police officers sought an injunction in the Supreme Court of Victoria

---

[30] But there were still problems: see the Annual Report of the NSW ombudsman for the year ending 30 June 1986, p. 160.

to prevent that action. The Full Court held that the PCA could do so (*Selby* v. *McCrohan* 1988). But by that time a year had passed.

The relationship between the PCA and the police was awful. In mid-1987 the PCA 'publicly pointed out that the investigations of the Victoria Police . . . (IID) were seriously lacking in professionalism and effectiveness' (Freckelton 1988: 58). A report by the former Commonwealth Ombudsman noted the appalling relationship between the PCA and the police and recommended that, if it did not improve, the PCA should be abolished and the jurisdiction given to the ombudsman. Despite attempts by the PCA to preserve its position, the final straw appears to have been a PCA Report on the operations of the Sexual Offences Squad. That report was highly critical and recommended that the squad be disbanded. Within weeks, legislation was introduced and passed which disbanded the PCA and transferred the function to the ombudsman's office. This was done amidst a great deal of public *angst* and recrimination. It is too soon to tell whether reversion to the structure advocated by the Australian Law Reform Commission will be both effective and non-controversial.

It may have been that the PCA variation on the ALRC recommendations failed because the creation of a specialist authority distinct from the ombudsman's generalist authority gave those who oppose the external review of police behaviour a highly visible, one-issue target at which to throw half-bricks.[31] It is clear that governments perceive police accountability to be an unproductive issue except in special circumstances. The 'law and order' vote is still perceived to be a winner (and it may well be), and the external review of police behaviour is not an issue which provides a counterbalancing political will.

While it is not proposed to survey all Australian jurisdictions, any failure to comment on the Queensland situation would be remiss. The police accountability disaster in that State is well known. It is noteworthy that Queensland did not adopt the ALRC model at all. In 1982, the Queensland Government enacted the Police Complaints Tribunal Act, which constituted a tribunal consisting of a judge as Chair, a magistrate as Deputy Chair, a nominee of the police union, and another. A pamphlet issued by the PCT described this system as the envy of other jurisdictions. This was wrong. It was a catastrophe.

---

[31] On the other hand that has not occurred in South Australia, which also has a specialist PCA.

There is not the space here to analyse the reasons for that, but any reading of the Eighth Report of the Police Complaints Tribunal (5 April 1989) will show that there was a disaster. The Tribunal emphasizes again and again that the lack of resources was crucial. Yet it is clear from the Report that, for example, in 1982 the Tribunal was hosted by the Ministry of Lands and that for some months, the Tribunal could not achieve a quorum. In any event, the results speak for themselves. Again, significant variation from the ALRC model simply did not work.

LESSONS

(1) Reform of administrative control of police behaviour in Australia has been dominated by the ombudsman-based model recommended by the Australian Law Reform Commission. Where that model has varied, the variation has proved to be productive of litigation, acrimony, and disaster.

(2) By and large, the ombudsman-based bodies have worked well. There are two caveats to this. The first is that current evidence indicates that the system deals well with individual misconduct, but has failed to cope with organizational misconduct. Hence the perceived need to set up such bodies as the National Crime Authority and independent commissions against corruption of various kinds Second, and perhaps relatedly, the ombudsman-based model is characterized by an emphasis on internal police investigation with limited ombudsman investigation. That balance is a difficult issue, but if the system does come under stress, it is there that the stress will tell. Should the 1990s see further proved revelations of either individual or organizational misconduct in an ombudsman system, the pressure for entirely external investigation of the police will become irresistible.

(3) In the period in question, change has been slow but fundamental. Structures are now in place which would have been unthinkable twenty years ago. If the idea that police misconduct is no business of the public and the exclusive business of the police still exists, it is well underground.

(4) Scandal is central to the promotion of legal change. But there is a relationship between legal change and the evolution of societal values as a whole which sets the scene for scandal to work. Central

influences in the re-evaluation of the policing pole in Australia were the debate about the appropriate reach of the criminal sanction and the crisis of institutional legitimacy which led to a new scepticism about the function and history of policing in society.

(5) The reforming of law reform and the creation of the 'new principle' law reform agency interacted closely with the reform of the law in relation to complaints about police. This factor is also referable to the base relationship between social and legal change. They occurred together and for similar reasons. Whether we are now in a situation in which the new principle agency will wither and be replaced by some other mode of promoting legal change is a moot point. It is still too early to tell.

REFERENCES

A/G NSW v. *Perpetual Trustee Co. Ltd.* (1955) 92 CLR 113 [1955] AC 457.
Australian Law Reform Commission (1975*a*) Report No. 1, *Complaints Against Police* (Sydney: Australian Government Publication Service).
—— (1975*b*) Report No. 2, *Criminal Investigation* (Sydney: Australian Government Publication Service).
—— (1978) Report No. 9, *Complaints Against Police: Supplementary Report* (Sydney: Australian Government Publication Service).
—— (1979) *5th Annual Report* (Sydney: Australian Government Publication Service).
Beach, B. (1976) *Addenda to the Report of the Board of Inquiry into Allegations Against Members of the Victoria Police Force* (Melbourne: Government Printer).
Becker, H. (1963) *The Outsiders* (New York: Free Press).
Bittner, E. (1970) *The Functions of Police in Modern Society* (Chevy Chase, Md.: National Institute of Mental Health).
Booth v. *Dillon No. 1* [1976] VR 291.
Booth v. *Dillon No. 2* [1976] VR 434.
Bordua, D., and Reiss, A. (1966) 'Command, Control and Charisma: Reflections on Police Bureaucracy', *American Journal of Sociology* 72: 68.
Boyd v. *Ombudsman and Others* [1983] 1 NSWLR 620.
Braithwaite, J., and Wilson, P. (1978) 'Pervs, Pimps and Powerbrokers', in J. Braithwaite and P. Wilson (eds.) *Two Faces of Deviance: Crimes of the Powerless and the Powerful* (Brisbane: University of Queensland Press).
Bunning v. *Cross* (1978) 141 CLR 54.
Campbell, E., and Whitmore, H. (1977) *Freedom in Australia* (Sydney: Sydney University Press).

Castles, A. (1977) 'The New Principle of Law Reform in Australia', *Dalhousie Law Journal* 4: 3.

Cohen, P. (1981) 'Policing the Working Class City', in M. Fitzgerald, G. McLennan, and J. Pawson (eds.) *Crime and Society: Readings in History and Theory* (Milton Keynes: Open University Press).

Cox, B., Shirley, J., and Short, M. (1977) *The Fall of Scotland Yard* (Harmondsworth: Penguin).

Devlin, P. (1965) *The Enforcement of Morals* (Oxford: Oxford University Press).

Denvir, J. (1980) 'Professor Dworkin and an Activist Theory of Constitutional Adjudication', *Albany Law Review* 45: 13.

Dickson, D. (1968) 'Bureaucracy and Morality: An Organizational Perspective on a Moral Crusade', *Social Problems* 16. 143.

Dobie, A. (1930) 'Seven Implications of *Swift* v. *Tyson*'. *Virginia Law Review* 16: 225.

Duncan, P. (1981) 'Achieving Law Reform' in J. Basten, M. Richardson, C. Ronalds, and G. Zdenkowski (eds.) *The Criminal Injustice System* (Sydney: Australian Legal Workers Group).

Enever (1906) 3 CLR 969.

Engler v. *Latimer* [1978] 6 WWR 230 (Alta CA).

Eskridge, W. (1989) 'Public Values in Statutory Interpretation', *University of Pennsylvania Law Review* 137: 1007.

Fahey v. *Lindsay* (1978) 19 SASR 577.

Fisher v. *Oldham Corp.* [1930] 2 KB 364.

Fisse, W., and Jones, J. (1973) 'Demonstrations: The 1972 South Australian Legislation', *Australian Law Journal* 47: 603.

—— (1971) 'Demonstrations: Some Proposals for Law Reform', *Australian Law Journal* 45: 593.

Fitzgerald, T. (1989) *Report of a Commission of Inquiry Pursuant to Orders in Council* (Brisbane: Queensland Government).

Fox, R. (1980) 'The Judicial Contribution', in A. Tay and E. Kamenka, *Lawmaking in Australia* (Melbourne: E. Arnold).

Freckelton, I. (1988) 'The Police Complaints Authority: Shooting the Messenger', *Legal Service Bulletin* 13: 58.

Goldsmith, A. (1982) 'The Ontario Provincial Offences Act: A Political History of Reform', *University of Toronto Faculty of Law Review* 40: 88.

Goode, M. (1974) 'Administrative Systems for the Resolution of Complaints Against Police', *Adelaide Law Review* 5: 55.

—— (1975) 'The Imposition of Vicarious Liability to the Torts of Police Officers', *Melbourne University Law Review* 10: 47.

—— (1976) 'Law Reform Commission of Canada: Political Ideology of Criminal Process Reform', *Canadian Bar Review* 54: 653.

—— (1978) 'The Sacking of Salisbury', *Legal Service Bulletin* 3: 49.

—— (1987) 'Controlling Police Misconduct, Complaints Against the Police and the Process of Law Reform: As It Happens', *Proceedings of the Australian Institute of Criminology* No. 17 (Canberra: Australian Institute of Criminology).

Gould, S. (1980) *The Panda's Thumb: More Reflections in Natural History* (New York: Norton).

Grunis, A. (1978) 'Police Control of Demonstrations', *Canadian Bar Review* 56: 393.

Gunther, G. (1964) 'The Subtle Vices of the "Passive Virtues": A Comment on Principle and Expediency in Judicial Review', *Columbia Law Review* 64: 1.

Hart, H. (1963) *The Concept of Law* (Oxford: Clarendon Press).

Heydon, J. (1973) 'Illegally Obtained Evidence (2)', *Criminal Law Review* 1973: 690.

Hodgson, D. (1978) 'Law Commission No. 76: A Case-Study in Criminal Law', in P. Glazebrook (ed.), *Reshaping the Criminal Law: Essays in Honour of Glanville Williams* (London: Stevens).

Howe, R. (1966) *The Story of Scotland Yard* (London: Barker).

Ingber, S. (1981) 'The Interface of Myth and Practice in Law', *Vanderbilt Law Review* 34: 309.

Jaffe, L. (1969) *English and American Judges as Lawmakers* (Oxford: Clarendon Press).

Kennison v. *Daire* (1986) 64 *Australian Law Reports* 17.

King, R. (1972) *The Drug Hang-up: America's Fifty-Year Folly* (New York: Norton).

Kirby, M. (1980) 'The Limits of Institutional Law Reform', in A. Tay and E. Kamenka (eds.) *Lawmaking in Australia* (London: Arnold).

Kessler, R. (1980) 'Enforcement Problems of Gun Control: A Victimless Crime Analysis', *Criminal Law Bulletin* 16: 131.

Lackersteen v. *Jones and Others* (1988) 92 FLR 6.

Levine, J. (1971) 'Implementing Legal Policies through Operant Conditioning: The Case of Police Practices', *Law and Society Review* 6: 195.

Lucas, J. (1979) *Final Report of the Committee of Inquiry Into the Enforcement of Criminal Law in Queensland* (Brisbane: Government Printer).

Lustgarten, L. (1986) *The Governance of Police* (London: Sweet and Maxwell).

Manning, P. (1977) *Police Work: The Social Organisation of Policing* (Cambridge Mass.: MIT).

Masterman, G. (1988) 'External Review: The New South Wales Experience', in I. Freckelton and H. Selby (eds.) *Police in Our Society* (Sydney: Butterworths).

Mill, J. S. (1859) *On Liberty* (London).

Missen, A. (1979) *Reforming the Law: A Report from the Senate-Standing Committee on Constitutional and Legal Affairs on the Processing of Law*

Reform Proposals in Australia: Parliamentary Paper No. 90/1979 (Canberra: Government Printer).

Mitchell, R. (1974) *Criminal Law and Penal Methods Reform Committee of South Australia, Second Report, Criminal Investigation* (Adelaide: Government Printer).

Morris, N. (1989) 'Police and the Community', paper presented to the Conference of the Society for the Reform of the Criminal Law, 'Investigating Crime and Apprehending Suspects: Police Powers and Citizens' Rights', Sydney.

Morris, N., and Hawkins, G. (1971) *The Honest Politician's Guide to Crime Control* (Chicago: University of Chicago).

Niederhoffer, A. (1967) *Behind the Shield: The Police in Urban Society* (New York: Doubleday).

Ombudsman v. *Moroney* (1983) 1 NSWLR 317.

Packer, H. (1968) *The Limits of the Criminal Sanction* (Stanford: Stanford University Press).

Potisk (1973) 6 SASR 389.

Radzinowicz, L. (1981) 'Towards a National Standard of Police', in M. Fitzgerald, G. McLennan, and J. Pawson (eds.), *Crime and Society: Readings in History and Theory*.

Rubinstein, J. (1973) *City Police* (New York: Farrer, Straus, and Giroux).

Rumbaut, R., and Bittner, E. (1979) 'Changing Conceptions of the Police Role: A Sociological Review', in N. Morris and M. Tonry (eds.), *Crime and Justice: An Annual Review of Research*, i (Chicago: University of Chicago Press).

Sackville, R. (1985) 'The Role of Law Reform Agencies in Australia', *Australian Law Journal* 59: 151.

Sallmann, P. (1981) 'The Beach Report Resurrected: Reason for Hope or Despair', in J. Basten, M. Richardson, C. Ronalds, and G. Zdenkowski (eds.), *The Criminal Injustice System* (Sydney: Australian Legal Workers Group).

Scheerer, S. (1978) 'The New Dutch and German Drug Laws: Social and Political Conditions for Criminalization and Decriminalization', *Law and Society Review* 12: 585.

Schur, E., and Bedau, H. (1974) *Victimless Crimes* (Englewood Cliffs NJ: Prentice Hall).

Selby v. *McCrohan and Others* [1988] VR 460.

Shearing, C. (ed.) (1981) *Organizational Police Deviance: Its Structure and Control* (Toronto: Butterworths).

Silver, D. (1967) 'The Demand for Order in Civil Society', in D. Bordua (ed.), *The Police: Six Sociological Essays* (New York: Wiley).

Skolnick, J. (1966) *Justice Without Trial: Law Enforcement in Democratic Society* (New York: Wiley).

Stephen, J. F. (1872) *Liberty, Equality, Fraternity* (Cambridge: Cambridge University Press).

Storch, R. (1981) 'The Plague of Blue Locusts: Police Reform and Popular Resistance in Northern England 1840–1857', in Fitzgerald *et al.* (eds.) *Crime and Society: Readings in History and Theory* (Milton Keynes: Open University Press).

Sumner, C. (1979) *Reading Ideologies: An Investigation into the Marxist Theory of Ideology and Law* (New York: Academic Press).

Tay, A., and Kamenka, E. (1980) 'Editors' Introduction', in A. Tay and E. Kamenka (eds.), *Lawmaking in Australia* (London: Arnold).

Taylor, I., Walton, P., and Young, J. (1975) 'Critical Criminology in Britain: Review and Prospects', in *Critical Criminology* (London: Routledge and Kegan Paul).

Watson, A. (1977) *Society and Legal Change* (Edinburgh: Scottish Academic).

—— (1981) 'Society's Choice and Legal Change', *Hofstra Law Review* 9: 1473.

Weiler, P. (1969) 'Who Shall Watch the Watchmen? Reflections on Some Recent Literature about the Police', *Criminal Law Quarterly* 11: 420.

Weinberg, M. (1975) 'The Judicial Discretion to Exclude Relevant Evidence', *McGill Law Journal* 21: 1.

Weyrauch, W. (1978) 'Law as Mask: Legal Ritual and Relevance', *California Law Review* 66: 699.

Whitaker, B. (1979) *The Police in Society* (London: Eyre Methven).

Wright v. *McQualter* (1970) 17 FLR 305.

Zander, M. (1979) 'Promoting Change in the Legal System', *Modern Law Review* 42: 489.

4

Police Complaints in Metropolitan Toronto:

Perspectives of the Public Complaints Commissioner

CLARE E. LEWIS QC

The Office of the Public Complaints Commissioner represents the first successful Canadian effort at 'civilianization' of police complaints procedures. The public complaints commissioner administers the statute of the province of Ontario which regulates the receipt, investigation, and disposition of public complaints involving officers of the Metropolitan Toronto Police Force.

As our democratic institutions have matured, it has become increasingly apparent that no individual or organization perform- ing important public services can maintain widespread respect and support without public accountability. The more significant and public the function, the more insistent is community need and demand for accountability to balance the responsibility and trust granted to the individual or organization. The purpose of the Toronto police force complaints legislation is to provide for such accountability and to ensure that an individual who has a complaint about the conduct of an officer of the Metropolitan Toronto police will receive fair treatment in its disposition, while preserving appropriate protection for subject officers.

Since 1981 the members of the Metropolitan Toronto Police Force have been subject to an employment disciplinary system which

Portions of the text have been excerpted from an article entitled 'Public Complaints Against Police in Metropolitan Toronto: The History of Operation of the Office of the Public Complaints Commissioner' published by Canada Law Book Company and co- authored by the present author, Clare Lewis QC, Sidney Linden QC, first Public Complaints Commissioner, 1981–5, and Judith Keene, previous Executive Assistant to both Commissioners. The consent to the use of these excerpts so generously and graciously granted by Canada Law Book, Mr Linden and Ms Keene is sincerely appreciated.

differs radically from that applicable to police in the rest of the province.[1] The innovative Toronto police disciplinary scheme operated initially as a pilot project under the Metropolitan Police Force Complaints Project Act, 1981 (being chapter 43 of the Statutes of Ontario 1981), and operates currently under the Metropolitan Toronto Police Force Complaints Act, 1984 (being chapter 63 of the Statutes of Ontario 1984).

A BRIEF HISTORY OF THE LEGISLATION

The legislative history of the police complaints system in Metropolitan Toronto reflects the complexity of the issues and the diverse interests at stake. While citizens' complaints about police have long been a part of the justice system, they began to be seen as a matter of broad community concern in Ontario in the 1970s. Although well-publicized allegations of police misconduct aroused public concern throughout the province, it was predictably within Metropolitan Toronto, an aggregate of several cities with a population at that time of 2.5 million and a police force of 5,000 officers, that public debate was the most frequent and wide ranging.

The critical focus was the perceived nature of the complaints process as a closed, secretive system. Concerns centred on the lack of documentation regarding complaints, and on the lack of information available to a complainant or the public about the investigation and any disciplinary action taken as a result of the complaint. Increasingly, there was a public belief that the police attitude towards citizens' complaints was self-protective. In 1974, after a series of highly publicized complaints involving the actions and activities of officers of the Metropolitan Toronto Police Force, the late Arthur Maloney QC was appointed by the Municipality of Metropolitan Toronto to study police complaints procedures. Among other initiatives, he recommended the appointment of an independent civilian commissioner of complaints (Maloney 1975).

Public and media concerns continued unabated. Three further major studies examined Metropolitan Toronto police conduct, their resolution of public complaints, and the nature of their relations with visible minorities (Morand 1976; Pitman 1977; Carter 1979).

---

[1] The disciplinary system applicable to other Ontario police forces operates under the authority of the Police Act RSO 1980, c. 381 as amended, and is outlined in RRO 1980, Reg. 791.

Each concluded that there was need for an independent civilian review agency to ensure fairness in the disposition of public complaints against Toronto police. There was particular concern about a continuing erosion of the confidence of visible minority communities in the force. Independent civilian review was recommended as one means of restoring general public confidence. In 1977, the Solicitor-General of Ontario introduced in the Legislature a Bill which represented the first legislative attempt to incorporate civilian involvement in the police complaints procedure. That Bill, which advocated a province-wide complaints system with a civilian component, came under attack from both police and community and did not receive a third reading.

In 1978, the Solicitor-General asked the Ontario Police Commission to make inquiries of Ontario police forces for the purpose of revising procedures for dealing with public complaints against the police. A recommended procedure was developed in consultation with police forces and many local boards of commissioners of police adopted it, or much of it, by by-law. That procedure currently governs the disposition of civilian complaints in most communities in the province outside Metropolitan Toronto. However, while it provides some regularity through more formal documentation and response, it does not include any independent civilian review. This initiative did not satisfy the concerns of some community groups in Metropolitan Toronto. In June 1979 the government of Ontario appointed Sidney Linden QC to study possible methods of injecting a civilian component into the handling of police complaints. That study was wide ranging and included an assessment of police complaints procedures in many other jurisdictions.

Events in Ontario between 1978 and 1981 clearly demonstrated a clash between the views of the police and a large number of community groups, many of whom were dissatisfied with the existing system of handling complaints. Equally clearly, there was discontent among police officers with their own internal complaints system. In Metropolitan Toronto, the Police Association made statements to the media to the effect that internal Police Act trials were a 'kangaroo court' (Kashmeri 1983). However, a large proportion of the police force was opposed to participation by civilians in any aspect of the complaints system. Some officers expressed concern that such participation would lower the morale of the police force.

A threshold question, and one about which polarized opinions were most evident, was whether the police, civilians, or a combination of the two, should do initial investigation into the complaints. The Linden research into the structure and function of police complaints systems throughout North America, Great Britain, and other countries had revealed that an attempt to substitute civilian for police participation in investigation and disciplinary action could cause serious difficulties. In Philadelphia, a city in which this type of system had been tried in the late 1960s, the police force mobilized public opinion in its favour, with the result that the system was overturned. New York had a similar experience. In other jurisdictions initial civilian investigation of complaints was seen to be the exception rather than the rule, and, when there was civilian participation in initial investigation, there appeared to be an effort to 'balance' the system in a number of ways. In some, such as Chicago, civilian investigators were hired by, and reported indirectly to, the chief of police. In others, such as Detroit, the investigative powers of civilian investigators were extremely limited. Further, the research uncovered no jurisdiction in which civilian investigation was combined with the power to make disciplinary decisions at the end of the process. In those jurisdictions in which civilian investigation at the outset was a part of the system, the process led ultimately to empowering a civilian commissioner or board to recommend disciplinary action to the chief of police. Whether disciplinary action would be carried out was solely at his discretion.

With these considerations in mind, the Linden model for importing civilian participation into the police complaints process recommended initial investigation of complaints by the police, subject to monitoring by a civilian review agency which could, in certain exceptional circumstances, conduct initial investigation. The model required the civilian agency to review the police investigation and disposition of the complaint when requested by the complainant. It further provided for the creation of an independent civilian adjudicative body which could impose discipline directly.

The then Solicitor-General and the mayors of the municipalities comprising Metropolitan Toronto decided that provincial legislation was necessary to establish an independent review of public complaints against members of the Metropolitan Toronto Police Force. Although the province-wide legislation introduced in 1979 had failed to win the support of the Legislature, in 1980 Metropolitan Toronto

Council asked the province to endorse the concept of a public complaints commissioner and to appoint such a person immediately. In 1981, Sidney Linden QC was appointed as commissioner with a mandate to receive complaints on an informal basis prior to the enactment of legislation. The appointment was made with the co-operation of the Metropolitan Board of Commissioners of Police, the police force, and the Police Association.

On 20 December 1981, the Office of the Public Complaints Commissioner was established as a three-year pilot project. The basic scheme of the Act provided that the Office would:

1. monitor the handling of complaints by the police;
2. perform initial investigation in unusual circumstances;
3. reinvestigate and review findings when the complainant was dissatisfied with the action taken by the police;
4. when the public interest required a hearing, refer cases to a civilian adjudicative tribunal with direct disciplinary power; and,
5. perform a preventive function, making recommendations to the chief of police, the board of commissioners of police, the Attorney-General, and the Solicitor-General, with respect to policing issues arising out of complaints.

The project nature of the legislation was an acknowledgement that new ground was being broken and that trial and experimentation was to be the order of the day. In 1984 the new Act, embodying basically the same system with some housekeeping amendments, was passed to establish the system on a permanent basis.

OVERVIEW: THE FUNCTION OF THE OFFICE AND THE
GENERAL SCHEME OF THE ACT

The Office of the Public Complaints Commissioner, and the complaints system under the Metropolitan Toronto Police Force Complaints Act, 1984, are not intended to remove the discipline of police officers from police management. Indeed, one of the purposes of the legislation is to encourage police management to be responsive to citizens' complaints, and to exercise disciplinary authority to that end. To the degree that police management is itself prepared to initiate and effect discipline and avoid the intervention of the Public Complaints Commissioner, the process serves to promote harmony between the police and the community. To the degree that the intervention of the Commissioner is necessary, the process serves to provide checks and balances to a system that was once perceived to be closed and partial.

The legislation incorporates the existing Code of Offences under the Police Act. No new offences are created. However, public complaints are not restricted, as in some jurisdictions, to limited forms of police misconduct such as excessive use of force or exercise of racial bias. They can encompass minor discourtesy, racist slurs, failure to provide assistance, excessive force, and a wide range of other conduct. As is the case with other professional disciplinary systems, it is the prevailing view in Ontario that a police complaints system must be flexible enough to accommodate both minor matters and allegations as to conduct which could also be the subject of criminal charges. Complainants consider any occasion of police misconduct, however minor, as significant. Members of the public, used to holding their police in high regard, are quite troubled by, and take considerable exception to, any police conduct which distorts their positive image of the police. Police managers can gain needed insight into public expectations of police through ready receipt, analysis, and proper resolution of all public complaints, however minor. The Toronto complaints system is a recognition of these realities. By permitting broad civilian jurisdiction in all instances which can constitute misconduct against the public, effort is made to maintain public respect for the police by ensuring that police maintain appropriate regard for the public they serve.

The actual investigation of a complaint is normally initially conducted by the Public Complaints Investigation Bureau, which is a separate unit of the police force created by the legislation and dealing only with public complaints. In certain limited circumstances, the public complaints commissioner's staff of civilian investigators undertakes initial investigations. Every complaint lodged by a citizen against the police is received by the commissioner forthwith, whether the complaint is registered at a police station, at the Public Complaints Investigation Bureau, or at the Office of the Public Complaints Commissioner. The commissioner monitors the police investigation and the decision of the chief of police in the matter. A complainant who is dissatisfied with the decision of the chief of police can request a review by the commissioner. The commissioner then reinvestigates and reconsiders the matter. If, upon reviewing a complaint, the commissioner decides that it is required in the public interest, a public hearing by a board of inquiry composed of a panel of civilians may be ordered. These boards of inquiry, which are established by the legislation, are administrative tribunals independent of the police and of the Office of the Public Complaints Commissioner. The boards, which may be composed of one or three persons, hear and decide upon allegations of misconduct. When misconduct is proved beyond a reasonable doubt, the board imposes discipline directly upon police officers. Penalty in major cases can range from a reprimand to dismissal from the force.

Police officers themselves have recourse to boards of inquiry in circumstances in which the chief of police has ordered an internal trial arising from a citizen's complaint. The subject officer has a right of appeal from a finding of misconduct by the internal tribunal to a civilian board of inquiry. Any party can appeal a decision of a board of inquiry to the Divisional Court, a branch of the Supreme Court of Ontario.

There are three features of the legislation which have received rather widespread and persistent public criticism. The first is that the scheme only applies to the Metropolitan Toronto police. The public complaints commissioner has no jurisdiction over the remaining 120 police forces in Ontario, including the Ontario Provincial Police. There are approximately 13,000 police officers in the province who are not subject to independent civilian review of public complaints against them. The provincial government is now considering means by which other Ontario police would have some form of civilian review of their public complaints. The extent and mechanics of such a system have not yet been determined.

Secondly, critics of the Toronto system consistently deplore the ability of the police to perform the initial investigation of a complaint. This feature is seen by many as a fundamental weakness in the process, permitting police the opportunity to manipulate the process to the detriment of the complainant. While this concern was considered by the legislators, initial police investigation of a complaint was intended as a means of giving the police a stake in the system, thereby encouraging their acceptance of it and preserving an important management role. The monitoring and review power of the public complaints commissioner, together with the commissioner's extraordinary right of initial investigation, was intended to ensure that initial investigation and adjudication by police would be thorough and impartial. There can be no doubt, however, that the initial police involvement can have considerable impact in shaping the ultimate result. On occasion there are legitimate concerns as to the advice given to complainants, the effect of the time taken to investigate and the diligence employed in those investigations. Some critics contend that events give little reason to believe, to date, that granting such important concessions to the police has encouraged police acceptance of the system. Nevertheless, it is submitted that permitting initial police investigation and decision authority remains a rational and acceptable compromise in a scheme which also grants to civilians ultimate authority to impose discipline upon police at the request of, or on appeal from, the decision of the chief of police.

Thirdly, no allegation of misconduct, however minor, can be sustained unless it is proved beyond a reasonable doubt. Critics have correctly stated that this is an employment discipline system, not a criminal trial process, and that no other employee or professional group has the protection of the criminal burden of proof in employment or professional disciplinary hearings. This criminal burden of proof results in few findings of misconduct against officers, and has an inevitable impact on the decisions of the commissioner as to whether, in a given case, a hearing by a civilian board of inquiry is required in the public interest.

An anomaly in the process is illustrated by the fact that an officer appearing before a police tribunal charged by a superior officer with, for instance, neglect of duty, may be found guilty of misconduct on the civil standard of proof normally applicable to employment discipline. However, an officer appearing before the same police tribunal, or before a civilian board of inquiry, on the complaint of a member of the public regarding the same neglect of duty, may only be found guilty of misconduct on the criminal burden of proof beyond a reasonable doubt.

Those members of the public who criticize these features of the Toronto system raise important issues which deserve consideration. They properly evince scepticism about the degree of impartiality inherent in the process. They do not, however, generally recognize that the legislation is, at least potentially, the most intrusive and far-reaching public complaints scheme in existence. The powers granted to the independent civilian public complaints commissioner are extensive. They include powers of search; right of entry into police establishments and seizure of documents and other evidence; the authority to obtain evidence under the Public Inquiries Act (being chapter 411 of the Revised Statutes of Ontario 1980); the right to take over initial investigation from the police in the case of delay or in extraordinary circumstances; the right to monitor and reinvestigate; and the right to order a public hearing by a civilian board of inquiry when such is required in the public interest.

Those critics also do not take account of the considerable turmoil involved in creating and maintaining a non-traditional complaints structure. Police organizations are very hostile to efforts to increase their public accountability through civilian incursion into their discipline systems. While police in democratic societies are subject to the rule of law and state allegiance both to legal constraints on their authority and to their obligation to account to civilian masters, they also operate organizationally by much more informal rules understood within the institution as more reflective and supportive of police attitudes and values. Attempts to create or operate civilian review of police complaints systems which ignore this police subculture or which determine to defeat it will have little impact on police and may be vulnerable to police counter-attack.

The Toronto complaints system was the result of protracted negotiation with police management and the Police Association. Its creation was a timely response to a true crisis in police–community relations in the city during the 1970s. There was much in its creation to benefit police. Management saw the value of reducing persistent, debilitating criticism through sharing authority with the community and through increased openness and regularity in complaint resolution. The Police Association saw that the proposed system offered greater protection of officers than was afforded by the internal discipline system. The Association also saw an opportunity to defuse considerable public hostility and, through enhanced community support, to improve officer morale.

The negotiation process resulted in a reasonable system of checks and balances. Police officers gained several real protections in the matter of public complaints. No officer can be compelled to testify before a police tribunal or civilian board of inquiry convened under the Act. No statement of an officer, required to be given in response to a complaint, can be introduced at a hearing without the officer's consent. There is provision for the chief of police, subject to review by the public complaints commissioner, to declare a complaint to the frivolous, vexatious, or made in bad faith. There are extensive provisions for disclosure of the case to the officer. The officer is entitled to periodic reports on the progress of the investigation. Complaints can be informally resolved, with the officer's consent, without detriment to the officer. Minor penalties of counsel and caution must be removed from the officer's record within two years if no further discipline is imposed within that period. No record, report, writing, or document arising out of a complaint is admissible or may be used in evidence in any civil suit or proceeding. Police generally retain initial authority to investigate the complaint and always retain the initial authority to decide whether or not discipline should occur. The police commission and the Police Association are entitled to nominate one-third of the civilians who sit on the boards of inquiry. No misconduct can be found unless proved beyond a reasonable doubt. There is a right of appeal to the Divisional Court.

Conversely, the community achieved a complaints system which at a minimum compelled police to open the books on their handling of complaints. The legislation creates a paper trail which can be examined at any stage by the complainant, the subject officer, and the civilian public complaints commissioner whose role is to maintain the integrity of the process. At no time before this legislation was enacted was there access to what, if anything, police were doing in respect of a public complaint. There was no means by which the police could be compelled to investigate and resolve a complaint or to reveal whether or not they had done so.

Dr Andrew Goldsmith has characterized the Toronto public complaints scheme as representing a Civilian External Investigatory/ Adjudicative model with three significant features distinguishing it from other models (Goldsmith 1988). The three distinguishing features of the Toronto system as seen by him are the extensive civilian investigation of complaints, the substantial rights of complainants, and, paramount, civilian board of inquiry hearings. Civilian critics of the process tend to have little regard for the significant impact of these factors. Dr Goldsmith describes the Toronto complaints scheme as a 'product[s] of dynamic, ongoing reform processes which have merged and been shaped within a set of important structural constraints'. He states further, 'an adequate appreciation of these constraints and the volatility of the reform process is critical if scholars and policy makers are to make significant contributions to law reform in the area of police complaints procedures' (1988: 69).

The Toronto scheme uses the potential for active civilian oversight to encourage the police to exercise their authority and obligation of self-regulation. The Act recognizes and promotes police entitlement to self-discipline and self-management while also recognizing and guarding against internal impediments to their fulfilment.

Although complaints investigations are normally undertaken by the police through the special bureau established for that purpose, the commissioner can take over that initial investigation at any time after thirty days from the filing of the complaint, at the request of the chief of police, or whenever the commissioner has reasonable grounds to believe that there has been undue delay or other exceptional circumstances in the conduct of the investigation. The commissioner maintains a staff of civilian investigators to conduct both these initial investigations and to conduct reinvestigations if the complainant is dissatisfied with the decision of the chief of police.

The complainant enjoys meaningful rights and protections in the Toronto scheme. Complaints must be received by the police and investigative reports must be provided to the complainant every thirty days. A final investigative report must be provided to the complainant. The chief of police must deliver a written decision. The complainant has a right to demand that the commissioner review that decision. The commissioner's conclusions must be provided in writing. If a board of inquiry is convened, counsel on behalf of the Attorney-General has carriage of the case and the complainant is routinely named as a party and entitled to appear with counsel. If named as a party, the complainant has a right of appeal to the Divisional Court. It ought to be recognized that the complainant's right to demand a review by the commissioner is a powerful limiting factor on the police handling and disposition of the complaint.

Finally, the Toronto system is distinguished by the civilian boards of inquiry which may be convened at the discretion of the chief of police, the commissioner, or any officer who appeals a finding of misconduct arising from a complaint and imposed by a police tribunal. The panel of persons from which boards of inquiry are drawn is appointed by the government of Ontario on nomination by three discrete groups. One-third, all of whom must be lawyers, are nominated by the Attorney-General and Solicitor-General of Ontario jointly. These persons always chair proceedings. One-third, who must not be serving police officers, are nominated by the police commission and the Police Association jointly. One-third are nominated by the council of the Municipality of Metropolitan Toronto.

The boards of inquiry have considerable authority. They may dismiss a complaint or find misconduct if proved beyond a reasonable doubt. If misconduct is found, the civilian board imposes the penalty it deems appropriate, from mere reprimand to dismissal from the force. No other system, except that in the Province of Manitoba, and another proposed in the Province of Quebec, vests such power external to the police. All other systems, at most, permit civilian agencies or boards to recommend discipline to the chief of police. In none of those systems is the chief of police bound to respect the recommendation. Indeed, in the Toronto system, the board's penalty decision can supplant that of the chief of police. Under the legislation, the disciplinary authority of the chief of police is not final, although the process fosters and protects appropriate decision-making on the part of the chief. Predictably, this extraordinary aspect of the system has drawn the greatest police resistance and has been the focus of a significant police attack on the legislation.

POLICE CHALLENGES TO THE LEGISLATION AND TO THE OPERATION OF THE PROCESS

The nature of the attack and the position of the police in its conduct were telling indicators of the degree of police commitment to the new complaints process. The circumstances which gave rise to the police challenge were suggestive of a belief on the part of the police that the complaints process, which they assisted in creating and to which they consented, would never succeed in seriously disciplining an officer for misconduct against a member of the public if the police themselves did not believe that serious discipline was appropriate.

In 1985, a board of inquiry heard an allegation against an officer of excessive use of force upon a prisoner. The chief of police had dismissed the complaint and the public complaints commissioner ordered the hearing. The civilian board of inquiry found that there had been particularly egregious misconduct resulting in serious and permanent injury to the complainant. The board ordered the officer to resign or be dismissed. An appeal was taken to the Divisional Court. Concurrently, the Police Association announced its intention to devote energy and considerable resources to the destruction of the public complaints system. In furtherance of its end the Association devised a series of strategies designed to obstruct, delay, and defeat the legislative process. The impartiality of civilian boards of inquiry was denounced, and their competence maligned, although one member of those boards of inquiry has since been appointed to the Supreme Court of Canada. The boards were given the mantle 'kangaroo court' earlier reserved by the Association for internal police tribunals. Officers were advised not to submit obligatory duty statements to superior officers in response to complaints. Service of documents was evaded. Despite disruption, the system continued to operate with little public awareness of the fundamentally serious nature of the conflict. Police management was reserved in its response to this revolt by the Police Association against the law of Ontario as it applied to police discipline in Toronto.

The particular case, on appeal to the Divisional Court, became the Police Association's vehicle for the legal challenge to the validity of the Metropolitan Toronto Police Force Complaints Act, 1984 and to the jurisdiction of the civilian boards of inquiry. The challenge alleged that the legislative framework offended the provisions of the Canadian Charter of Rights and Freedoms.[2] The principal complaints were that the legislation contravened the equality provisions of the Charter in that all Ontario police officers were not subject to its strictures, and further, that the boards of inquiry were not independent and impartial tribunals. An appeal against the penalty of enforced resignation of the officer was included.

In a decision of 29 September 1987 the Divisional Court delivered its judgment.[3] The constitutional challenge to the process was dismissed and the penalty of enforced resignation was upheld. On the issue of independence and impartiality, the court stated that: 'In our view, the Legislature has in this way provided for a three panel board that is *prima facie* impartial . . . There is then no apprehension of bias on the part of the Board that tried the appellant.' (1987: 2.)

With respect to the argument that the legislation offended the equality provisions of the Charter and had an adverse impact on Metropolitan police officers the Court concluded:

If it is proper to look at the overall effect of the legislation, and to set off the advantages gained from it by Metro police officers against whatever

[2] Part 1 of the Constitution Act 1982 being Schedule B of the Canada Act 1982 (UK), c. 11.
[3] *Re: Metropolitan Toronto Police Complaints Board and Weller*, 27 September 1987, Ontario Divisional Court (unreported).

disadvantages to the officers may be contained therein, we conclude that the overall effect of the legislation causes no prejudice to the Metropolitan Police and certainly none that can be viewed as undue.

The evidence is clear that the Metropolitan Police Association supported the new legislation in briefs submitted to the Legislature, both as to the new rights it gave to police officers, such as more independent investigation and adjudication of complaints, and better procedural protections, as well as the other changes, some of which are attacked in this case. That is, on balance, and taking an overall view of the legislation, the Metropolitan Police Association supported it. While that does not bind the court's hands, it is a helpful guide to how the legislation was viewed in totality before anyone's ox had been gored. (p. 4.)

In upholding the penalty of enforced resignation the Court said: 'when we consider the extent to which the special trust placed in police officers was abused by this unprovoked assault, together with the serious and permanent injuries which resulted from it, and in spite of the officer's prior good record and strong possibility of rehabilitation, the penalty imposed was the proper one.' (p. 6.)

The decision of the Divisional Court was appealed to the Ontario Court of Appeal, which denied leave to appeal in an unreported decision on 11 January 1988. The officer was required to resign. The response of the Police Association was swift. Confronted now with both the statute of the Legislature of Ontario and with adverse decisions of the highest courts of the province, the Association immediately called a mass meeting of its member officers. A decision was taken to conduct a partial withdrawal of services until the legislation was repealed, the officer was reinstated, and the Office of the Public Complaints Commissioner dismantled.

For a period of two weeks officers wore baseball caps with emblems symbolizing their demand for the destruction of the Office of the Public Complaints Commissioner. Further, they refused to summons any drivers of motor vehicles for traffic infractions. Government coffers were to be denied traffic fines and the public was to be made fully aware of police frustration that one of their members had lost his job at the hands of civilians, and in response to a civilian complaint. This strike, for it was no less, received neither management condemnation nor discipline. There was a precedent for this behaviour in that in 1985 the Police Association had ordered its members to wear baseball caps and to refuse to give traffic tickets to offenders as a wage-bargaining tactic. Management response at that time was similar.

A furious media campaign occurred and the public complaints commissioner was required to take a firm public position in defence of the statute, the decisions of the courts, and the integrity of, and need for, the public complaints process. The Toronto police, in the end, did not receive judicial, media, or public support for their demands.

As a prelude to actual confrontation, the Police Association position had been clearly stated in 1987 by its then president who wrote, 'The Association fervently believes that the only good external complaints system is a dead complaints system.' (Walter 1987.) To achieve that goal, two further strategies were undertaken. The first was to have the Association representative from the dismissed constable's division charge the dismissed officer with the criminal offence of assault causing bodily harm upon the complainant. The intention was to prosecute the former officer criminally with his full co-operation, and with the clear expectation that now, four years or more after the event, he would be acquitted. The criminal process was to be used to impugn the complaints process. Since the officer laying the charge had previously publicly stated his belief in the officer's innocence, this instance can be fairly said to have been a unique situation in which a person was charged with a criminal offence with the express intent of exoneration. This use of the criminal process as a collateral attack upon the complaints legislation was eventually ended by the Attorney-General who stayed the criminal proceedings.

The Police Association and police management then both approached government in early 1988 with recommendations for changes to the legislation. Their proposals, some of which were common to both, were wide-ranging and included: replacing board of inquiry members with criminal court judges; removing the power of boards of inquiry to impose discipline, leaving them only with authority to recommend discipline to the chief of police; and limiting the complaints process whereby boards of inquiry would be unable to hear complaints which contained allegations which could amount to those of criminal misconduct. The Office of the Public Complaints Commissioner opposed most police recommendations.

The police challenge and its several tactics, including representations to government, did, in time, attract public attention and public response. Many community organizations, some of which had been early advocates for the creation of the complaints process, made submissions to government in its defence. They touched upon some issues which are important in this community. The Council on Race Relations and Policing said: 'However, legislative changes to the Public Complaints Act that are being proposed by the Police Association, appear to be designed to undermine the important work that the PCC does in bringing confidence to police–community relations in Metropolitan Toronto . . .'[4]

The President of the Criminal Lawyers' Association wrote:

In my opinion this city's public complaints system is a very good one which has served to act as a deterrent (with some exceptions) to those officers who might otherwise have crossed the line of proper police conduct; it has brought the City of Toronto additional respect for its civilized way of life, particularly from a number of minority groups who had become so disturbed by police treatment; and it gave to the Metropolitan Toronto Force a new-found respect which it was losing through the media.[5]

The Canadian Bar Association urged:

that the Office of the Public Complaints Commissioner be expanded . . . that this legislation be amended to create municipal or regional police complaints commissions modelled upon that in Metropolitan Toronto and which would include the Ontario Provincial Police . . .[6]

The Urban Alliance on Race Relations submitted:

While the record of the Public Complaints Commission is not as effective as many would wish, it apparently has had some positive results. And, even more important, the fact that a Public Complaints Commission exists has an important symbolic effect. Ordinary individuals can expect a sympathetic rather than a hostile hearing from officers attempting to protect their colleagues.[7]

The matter has received serious and positive government consideration. On 20 December 1989, the Solicitor-General of Ontario introduced the Police Services Act 1989.[8] The Act will be the controlling statute for all police forces in Ontario. It will, when proclaimed, expand the jurisdiction of the Office of the Public Complaints Commissioner on a mandatory basis throughout the province. All 117 Ontario police forces will be subject to a consistent

---

[4] Submission to AG of Ontario, 28 Jan. 1988, p. 1.
[5] Submission to AG of Ontario, 28 Jan. 1988, p. 3.
[6] Submission to AG of Ontario, 31 Dec. 1987, p. 5.
[7] Submission to AG of Ontario, 26 Jan. 1988, p. 2.
[8] 2nd Session, 34 Legislature, 38 Elizabeth II, 1989.

public complaints system based on that now in effect in Toronto. The Metropolitan Toronto Police Force Complaints Act 1984 will be repealed. Its provisions, with some modifications, are adapted in the new Act to the province-wide mandate.

THOUGHTS ON THE FUTURE

The Toronto complaints system has been a catalyst for interest in the 'civilianization' of police complaints procedures elsewhere in Canada. The government of Canada, which is responsible for the national Royal Canadian Mounted Police, has amended the governing Act of that force to create a Public Complaints Commission.[9] That Commission began its duties in September of 1988. Dr Goldsmith has characterized the RCMP complaints system as the Civilian External Supervisory model (1988: 65). That process grants the civilian agency an active monitoring and inquiry role, while maintaining the major investigative and disciplinary decision-making within the police structure. While not as intrusive as the Toronto model, many provisions of the Toronto system's enabling legislation were incorporated in the federal amendments.

The Province of Quebec has recently passed a far-reaching police complaints statute which has yet to take effect.[10] It proposes to place all municipal forces in the province and the Quebec Provincial Police under a standardized complaints scheme which bears striking, but not total, similarity to that in Toronto. Boards of inquiry will be permitted to impose discipline directly. The standard of proof is that applicable to employment discipline, not the criminal standard. Police opposition to the implementation of the legislation has begun.

The Province of Manitoba has a legislative complaints framework under the supervision of the Law Enforcement Review Agency.[11] That scheme is described by Dr Goldsmith as following the same Civilian External Investigation/Adjudicative model as the Toronto system (1988: 64–5, 68–9). It is restricted by limited funding and staffing, and by reliance on government investigative support.

---

[9] An Act to Amend the Royal Canadian Mounted Police Act, RSC 1985, c. R–10, as amended by RSC 1985, c. 8 (2nd Supp.).

[10] Police Act RSQ, c. P–13 as amended by An Act Respecting Police Organization and Amending the Police Act and Various Legislation, SQ 1988, c. 75, parts of which have come into force.

[11] Law Enforcement Review Act, SM 1982–83–84 c. 21—Cap L 75.

However, in theory at least, all complaints which are not resolved must be heard by a civilian board of inquiry.

The Province of British Columbia has recently passed a new Police Act (being chapter 53 of the Statutes of British Columbia 1988). It has a revised public complaints scheme which, while still largely internal, borrows extensively from the Toronto system's enabling legislation. There is a complaints chair who functions under the aegis of the British Columbia Police Commission.

As the Toronto controversy has abated, it is clear that, nationally, the interest in improved public complaints procedures has continued and heightened. While the intensity and apparent rancour of the Toronto dispute gave pause to interested policy-makers, its present state of resolution has shown that such mechanisms serve important public needs and can survive if properly mandated. Dr Goldsmith rather neatly described the challenge for the Toronto system:

At the moment, both in terms of investigations and boards of inquiry, the PCC would appear to be steering a difficult course between the Scylla of complete non-involvement and the Charybdis of total usurpation of police self-regulation. Given the volatility of the various factors operating in this area, the future of civilian boards of inquiry, and indeed of the whole new statutory scheme, seems assured of controversy. (1988: 68.)

The view of this commissioner is that the described tension is both inevitable and ought not to be avoided in any worthwhile system of civilian review of public complaints against police. Police have not generally shown themselves vigilant in response to public complaints of police misconduct. Police organizational factors and resistant police attitudes may lead to attempts to undermine externally imposed civilian review mechanisms. In a recent judgment of the Divisional Court of Ontario compelling the Toronto chief of police to make a long-delayed decision in a complaint which was also the subject of a civil suit against the police, the judge said: 'It is apparent to me that the police force is strongly opposed to the legislation. What service it has performed in ostensible obedience to it amounts to little more than lip service.'[12] While one need not be supportive of such police reaction to publicly legislated obligations upon them, one can recognize the response as an expression of the very problem which creates the need for civilian review. Proper administration of

---

[12] *Ramsay* v. *The Chief of Police for Metropolitan Toronto et al.* (1988), 66 OR (2d) 99, p. 11.

an effective civilian review system requires a certain stoic resolve if police resistance is to be met and countered.

It is this author's opinion that, in the early stages of the quest for useful civilian review, police statements and actions in support may be largely illusory. While police want the public relations advantage which an ostensibly publicly accountable civilian review system of complaints affords them, they do not naturally embrace its goals. Police forces, which may well be vigilant in avoiding or punishing force corruption or breaches of internal discipline, nevertheless do not necessarily view much of what the public considers excessive use of force or incivility as requiring discipline. Given the conflict-ridden nature of some police functions, police may tend to apply rather elastic standards to their judgement of their officers' use of physical and verbal force. There is, at times, a distinction between what is lawfully or publicly permissible and what police deem necessary to get the job done. Police have long taken some comfort in their view that the justice system and its professionals tend implicitly to acknowledge this distinction as legitimate, despite legal proscriptions. This assessment is not to ascribe necessarily evil intent to police but to recognize their different milieu, and the organizational and value base from which they approach these issues.

Public complaints systems, which tend to reflect community attitudes and not those of justice system professionals, are not seen as being protective of police values. They are, on that ground alone, threatening to police. Further, civilian involvement in complaints review is seen as threatening to necessary police management control of the force. Such fear, of course, presupposes that police management exercise some form of effective control over dealings with the public in the first place. The minimal response often attendant in the matter of public complaints does not always suggest a high degree of either actual or desired control over officers in their physical and verbal interaction with the public. However, public complaints systems incorporating civilian review can assist interested police managers in asserting worthwhile authority over officer conduct and reduce unnecessary and debilitating conflict with the community.

Perhaps the more important concern for police managers is fear that any external disciplinary authority may subvert the whole of their managerial legitimacy. The potential for such undermining is a matter for consideration. Police associations, with their elected leaders, may seek political advantage in opposing effective civilian review. Police management, which has shown indifference to public complaints legislation or which has been seen to attempt to thwart civilian review, is vulnerable to loss of general disciplinary authority through co-option by police associations on this serious matter of management rights.

Despite the unsettling nature of recent conflict over the Toronto complaints system, its prognosis is quite optimistic. The hallmark of the Toronto system is its fairness. That fact of fairness has preserved it during attack. That essential fairness is becoming evident to rank-and-file officers and to the public who have witnessed the dispute and have now had some opportunity for independent evaluation. It is becoming clear that the process affords the force itself both the opportunity and the authority to require appropriate conduct and to penalize its absence. There is now potential for police to be accepting of the values of the system, and for the public to view the process as limiting police excess.

A clear trend has developed in the nature of complaint allegations in Toronto. At the time of the creation of the Office in 1981, extremely serious allegations of police brutality were common and the subject of intensive media and government scrutiny. While the absolute number and type of complaints made annually remains fairly consistent, the gravity of the allegations is generally much reduced. Granted that there are significant exceptions, there is evidence of increased professionalism on the part of the Toronto police in their conduct with the public. Police managers merit consideration for such improvement. The public complaints legislation and its administration have contributed to this improved awareness and professionalism by police. More emphasis by police managers and the Office is required in the matter of police race relations. That need was starkly illustrated in the latter part of 1988 when two black men were killed, in separate incidents, by on-duty members of different police forces, one of which was the Metropolitan Toronto force. A crisis quickly developed in relations between police and visible minority communities in the province. Demonstrations occurred, and angry words were expressed by some community members and some police. Criminal charges of manslaughter were eventually laid in each case against involved officers.

The Solicitor-General of Ontario appointed the author to chair a six-member task force which became known as the Ontario Task Force on Race Relations and Policing. Public hearings were held in Toronto, Ottawa, Windsor, and Thunder Bay. There were 118 oral presentations and over seventy briefs submitted to the Task Force. Most Ontario police forces participated either through public presentation, briefs, or response to a questionnaire prepared and distributed by the Task Force. The Task Force submitted an extensive report in April 1989, with fifty-seven recommendations related to police interaction with visible minority communities (Lewis *et al.* 1989: 198). The recommendations dealt with police race-relations training, use of force, community liaison, employment and promotion, and ongoing monitoring of relations. While the terms of reference of the Task Force did not include a consideration of public complaints mechanisms, there were over fifty public presentations urging province-wide civilian review of public complaints against the police. Many urged the mandatory expansion of the Office of the Public Complaints Commissioner throughout the province. The Task Force did recommend that the government take a consistent approach to the issue. Through the introduction of the new Police Services Act, the government has done so.

CONCLUSION

One lesson which has been clear to the civilian administration of the Toronto complaints system is that restraint must be mixed with resolve. Resolve is necessary to confront inevitable police resistance and to match both police power and police perception of their power. Restraint is necessary to take account of the tumultuous effect of the imposition of significant civilian review upon police institutions. Persuasion and guidance are essential tools in the achievement of oversight goals. A long-term view of the evolution of the process is required. Police need considerable time, education, and even consideration, in adapting to civilian review. The challenge is to recognize and meet these police needs while maintaining a process which can have actual influence upon police. There is a real danger of undue caution, of conceding police demands to the degree that the complaints process is merely another means of legitimizing in-appropriate police conduct. This criticism has been made of the operation of the Office of the Public Complaints Commissioner (McMahon 1988). Some tension between police and civilian administrators of review systems is appropriate. Co-option of the civilians by the police is as certain a defeat as loss of mandate. The tension is necessary as a sign of civilian effort to expand gradually the impact of the process upon the police.

The Toronto office serves the public and the police not only through occasional discipline of errant officers. The legislation and its administration have an actual deterrent effect on police misconduct. The statute permits the commissioner to make useful recommendations to the police as to changes in police policies and procedures which might help avoid future complaints. The Office has influence on some important police decisions, performs an educational function, and has been able to act as a mediator between the police and community groups.

The recent creation of the International Association For Civilian Oversight Of Law Enforcement (IACOLE), has highlighted civilian review as an idea for which the time has arrived. Representative of civilian review agencies and practitioners internationally, it has also attracted considerable police and governmental interest.[13]

As Maxwell Yalden, Chief Commissioner of the Canadian Human Rights Commission, said in his presentation to the Ontario Task Force on Race Relations and Policing: 'The greatest enemy of effective policing is loss of public confidence.' Civilian oversight, through review of public complaints, assists police to achieve congruence with the values and expectations of the broad community and has the potential for generating high police morale through that increased public support necessary for police and community harmony.

The Toronto experience should give confidence to those interested in complaints reform. Its history illustrates that a carefully structured civilian review system, founded in fairness and administered with caution, can survive to influence another day.

REFERENCES

Carter, G. E., Cardinal (1979) Report to the Civic Authorities of Metropolitan Toronto and its Citizens (Toronto: Office of the Cardinal).
Goldsmith, A. J. (1988) 'New Directions in Police Complaints Procedure: Some Conceptual and Comparative Departures', Police Studies 11: 60–71.

[13] The author has served as President of IACOLE from October 1987 to October 1989, and as a member of its Board of Directors from its inception in October 1985.

Kashmeri, Z. (1983) 'Police Group Seeks Probe—Disciplinary Committee is Described as Illegal', *Globe and Mail* 8 February 1983: 4.

Lewis, C. E., Linden, S. B., and Keene, J. (1986) 'Public Complaints Against Police in Metropolitan Toronto: The History and Operation of the Office of the Public Complaints Commissioner', *Criminal Law Quarterly* 29: 115–44.

Lewis, C. (Chair), Agard, Dr R., Gopie, K., Harding, Chief J., Singh, T. Sher, and Williams, R. (1989) *Report of the Task Force on Race Relations and Policing* (Ontario: Queen's Printer).

McMahon, M. (1988) 'Police Accountability: The Situation of Complaints in Toronto', *Contemporary Crises* 12: 301–27.

Maloney, A. (1975) 'The Metropolitan Toronto Review of Citizen–Police Complaint Procedure' (Toronto: unpublished).

Metropolitan Toronto Police Board and Weller

Pitman, W. (Chair) (1977) Metropolitan Toronto Task Force on Human Relations *Now is Not Too Late* (City of Metropolitan Toronto).

Morand, J. (1976) Royal Commission Inquiry into Metropolitan Toronto Police Practices (Ontario: Queen's Printer).

Walter, P. (1987) President's Message, *News and Views* 5 November 1987.

5

Complaints against the Police:

The British Experience

MIKE MAGUIRE

INTRODUCTION

The need for a more effective system for dealing with complaints against the police has been a 'live issue' in Britain since the late 1950s. Recurrent demands for reform in this area are only one manifestation of a sustained period of instability—some would say, crisis—in public confidence in the police. Over this period, the positive image of the 'British bobby' so successfully projected to the world during the early post-war years has been seriously, perhaps irreparably, dented by numerous highly publicized cases of violence or malpractice, compounded especially by the revelation of wide-spread corruption among London detectives in the 1970s and by the insensitive policing of inner-city areas which led to rioting in the early 1980s (see, for example, Reiner 1985; Hobbs 1988; Scarman 1981). Such events have generated a continuing debate about police powers and accountability, and have prompted a number of major legislative changes and policy initiatives. These have included several alterations to the complaints system, although it will be argued that reform in this area has not been sufficiently radical to meet the key objections raised.

Broad constitutional questions about accountability were first addressed by the 1962 Royal Commission on the Police, whose recommendations led to the passing of the Police Act 1964. This established the current 'tripartite' system of control, carving out separate areas of responsibility for chief constables, local authorities, and the Home Secretary. Two major criticisms have been made of

The research project described in this article was carried out at the Centre for Criminological Research, University of Oxford, and was funded by the Home Office, whose generosity and assistance are gratefully acknowledged.

the outcome of the Committee's deliberations. First, the constitutional arrangements have failed to allow adequate democratic control over police policy-making and the setting of objectives and priorities (cf. Lustgarten 1986). Secondly, although one of the main reasons for the setting-up of the Commission was concern about the behaviour of individual officers 'on the street',[1] it side-stepped the crucial problem of 'controlling the constable' (Jefferson and Grimshaw 1984).

It is the latter problem which forms the background to this paper, and which exercised the minds of many of the official committees and working parties which sat during the twenty years after the Police Act, culminating in the 'solutions' legislated in the Police and Criminal Evidence Act (PACE) of 1984. It had long been accepted that, in order to do their jobs effectively, even the most junior officers require a considerable amount of autonomy and discretionary power in their day-to-day dealings with the public. When confidence in the police was high, few challenges were made to this principle or to the extent of its application. However, when serious doubts arose about the use—or misuse—of individual officers' powers, deeper questions began to surface about the very 'legitimacy' of the police (Reiner 1985). Clearly, if constables were to be permitted to keep their autonomy, more effective ways of preventing abuses would have to be found.

The three strategies most often advocated—and to varying degrees implemented—in recent years have been to improve training and supervision, to draw up more specific codes of conduct, and to create a more effective complaints and discipline system. We are principally concerned with the last of these. However, it should be noted that all three are interlinked and it is unlikely that any one will be effective if the others are inadequate: complaints and discipline procedures may act as a deterrent and provide the 'long stop' of punishment when more positive measures for promoting good conduct fail, but *post hoc* sanctions cannot be expected to bear the full burden alone. It is further emphasized that the complaints system has other vital functions beyond that of keeping misconduct in check. It should also satisfy complainants that their case has been appropriately handled

---

[1] e.g. the Rix case of 1958–9, a relatively minor incident which attracted public interest because it involved a popular actor. The suspicious death of a man called Woolf in police custody in 1962, shortly followed by the notorious 'Sheffield rhino whip affair' and the Challenor case of 1963 (involving the planting of evidence), also coloured the debate leading to the Police Act 1964.

and, above all, convince the general public that inquiries are thorough and unbiased.

In the following pages, I shall discuss these and related issues in the light of a two-year study of the complaints system which I conducted with a colleague, Claire Corbett, in 1986–8. The field-work included a period spent in the offices of the Police Complaints Authority (PCA), an independent 'watchdog' body created in 1985 under PACE. We were given full access to PCA files and received co-operation from all members and staff. We also conducted research into the handling of complaints in three police-force areas, based upon file analysis, observation, and interviews with investigating officers, complainants, and subject officers. In addition, we were permitted space in the 1988 British Crime Survey for some questions about people's experiences of police misconduct and their opinions and experiences of the complaints system.

I shall begin by outlining the recent history of the complaints system, its general shape, and the principles upon which it is founded. It will be shown that the system has adapted to some degree to its greater public profile, including a slow integration of mechanisms for independent scrutiny, but that it remains in essence largely unchanged. This will be followed by a summary of the findings of our study, leading to some broad conclusions about the degree to which the current arrangements achieve a number of definable objectives.

THE COMPLAINTS SYSTEM: RECENT HISTORY

1. A Tale of Compromise

Despite the incorporation of an independent element, which will be discussed further, the basic shape of the complaints system retains much in common with that first conceived by the Metropolitan Police in the 1830s and honed over the next 100 years into a set of principle and procedures gradually adopted by other forces (see, for example, Select Committee 1834; Royal Commissions 1908, 1929).[2]

---

[2] Arrangements outside London varied widely in the 19th c., but external control was initially quite common; e.g. the County and Borough Police Force Act 1859 authorized the Watch Committees of city and borough forces to suspend or fine any officer 'remiss or negligent in the discharge of his duty', and in some forces disciplinary committees consisted of Justices of the Peace. However, by the end of the century, Chief Constables had largely assumed these powers (see e.g. Critchley 1978;

Official complaints can be made only against misconduct by individual officers, not against the force, force policy, or operational decisions; complaints are inextricably bound up with the internal police disciplinary system, being recorded and investigated as alleged breaches of a specified section of the disciplinary code;[3] investigations are carried out by senior police officers, in most cases from the same force; another senior officer (usually the Deputy Chief Constable) scrutinizes their reports to determine whether there is sufficient evidence to substantiate a charge at a disciplinary hearing and, if so, whether to hold such a hearing or to deal with the matter by a warning; in the case of a hearing, he or she also frames the charges; and guilt or innocence and the level of punishment are then determined in most cases by the Chief Constable of the force concerned. All these practices are long established, and the majority of complaints continue to be processed in a manner which would not be unfamiliar to generations of police officers.

This is not to say that the system has remained unaffected by events over the past twenty-five years. On the contrary, while the changes I shall describe may be regarded as essentially 'tinkering' rather than fundamental, it is indisputable that one consequence of all the attention has been the elevation of complaints handling from a fairly marginal area of police activity to an important and highly organized specialism within every force. Let us now chart the main developments since 1964.

It has already been noted that the 1962 Royal Commission largely ducked the issue of controlling individual police misconduct. In particular, it failed to accede to demands for the introduction of an independent element into the complaints system. It contented itself instead with measures to tighten up internal police procedures. Under the 1964 Act, chief officers were required to ensure that all complaints were recorded and investigated, to appoint investigators from outside forces for serious cases, and to refer all cases in which a criminal offence may have been committed to the Director of Public Prosecutions (DPP). All these were practices already espoused in theory by most forces, although by no means regularly carried out.

West Midlands Police 1984). The 1929 Royal Commission found that only one force, Birmingham, retained the practice of leaving disciplinary decisions to the Watch Committee.

[3] The disciplinary code was made uniform in 1919, following police strikes and the recommendations of the Desborough Committee on police pay and conditions.

One obvious effect of the legislation was to bring about a dramatic improvement in recording practices. A previous Royal Commission set up in 1928[4] had found only 149 complaints officially recorded in the whole of England and Wales over a twenty-two-month period. The 1962 Commission discovered that the annual total had risen to over 4,000, but the extent of under-recording was highlighted by a doubling of this number in the year after their report emerged, and even more so by further sharp rises after the Act. By the mid-1970s annual totals were close to their present level of around 30,000.

A secondary effect of the growth in recorded cases, combined with the legal obligation to investigate every case and to notify the complainant of the outcome, has been a huge increase in the time, money, and manpower expended in dealing with complaints. Investigations were traditionally carried out by divisional Superintendents in their 'spare time', but as the workload has grown, there has been a country-wide trend for forces to expand headquarters-based Complaints and Discipline Departments, seconding superintendents and chief inspectors to work full-time on investigations. Within a few years of the Police Act, these developments had led to new kinds of concern about the complaints system: excessive bureaucracy, long delays, and the waste of highly paid senior officers' time in the investigation of thousands of relatively minor grievances. Thick files were being compiled on incidents which even the complainant did not regard as warranting exhaustive investigation, and the time taken to deal with them was creating dissatisfaction among police and public alike.

These problems, however, have always remained secondary to the fundamental criticism levelled against the system since the 1960s: the unacceptability of the practice of the police investigating themselves. The Royal Commission's complacency on this issue was soon called into question as new unsavoury incidents came to light in the early 1970s, particularly in London's Metropolitan Police District (MPD). As in the past, most of the officers concerned escaped prosecution or serious disciplinary action, and accusations of biased investigations began to fly. With public confidence at a low ebb, it was impossible for the police to persuade critics that they

---

[4] Royal Commission on Police Powers and Procedure 1929. This was set up largely as a result of the Savidge case of 1928, which raised questions about the honesty of the police in presenting evidence. A minority of the Commission suggested that the DPP should be empowered to conduct investigations into certain kinds of complaint—one of the first calls for an outside body to be responsible for investigation.

could keep their own house in order. Whatever the truth behind any individual incident, and however fairly or thoroughly the investigation may have been carried out, the exoneration of officers almost inevitably led to suspicion of a cover-up. Despite a determined 'clean-up' in the MPD when the new Commissioner, Robert Mark, required the resignation or early retirement of large numbers of detectives, the damage had been done. After a political battle between advocates of a totally independent system of investigation and the police lobby, who opposed *any* independent involvement, in 1976 the government set up a part-time lay body, the Police Complaints Board (PCB), to monitor police investigations retrospectively. Mark, incidentally, immediately resigned in protest.

Despite the granting to the PCB of one power which looked strong 'on paper'—the power to direct a disciplinary hearing—those who had argued that the compromise would satisfy no one were rapidly proved right. The new watchdog was revealed as virtually toothless. Inundated with case papers, the PCB simply added more bureaucracy and delay to an already unwieldy system, rarely doing any more than 'rubber-stamping' police reports. Between 1976 and 1985, members questioned chief officers' decisions in only 210 cases among more than 50,000 examined, in most instances eventually bowing to police advice. The Board had a low public profile and few defenders in the debates which followed.

With the PCB widely regarded as remote and ineffective, and with no reduction in public concern about police behaviour, the search for new solutions accelerated. A new Royal Commission was set up in 1979 to tackle the fundamental question of police powers, while between 1980 and 1984 no fewer than eight official committees and working parties reconsidered the specific issue of complaints (see Cohen 1985). Eventually, with effect from 1985, the Police and Criminal Evidence Act swept away the PCB, replacing it with the Police Complaints Authority. A full-time body with a new 'supervisory' role in investigations, the PCA has undoubtedly been provided with more teeth and higher status than its predecessor. On the other hand, it represents yet another compromise resolution of the argument between those demanding and those opposing a fully independent system of complaints investigation. As we shall see, discontent continues to rumble and many remain unconvinced of its true independence and its ability to ensure that complaints are properly dealt with.

2. PACE and the PCA

The central aim behind PACE was to define more clearly than ever before the powers possessed by individual police officers, both on the street and in the station. Powers were increased significantly in several areas, but attempts were made to balance this with more precise specifications of their limits and with new mechanisms (in particular, strict requirements for making written records) to make officers accountable for their use. Detailed Codes of Practice were subsequently drawn up to regulate behaviour, determining, for example, the length of time for which suspects could be held in custody. Any breach of these Codes now renders an officer liable to disciplinary action.

The handling of complaints was seen as an important part of this 'after-the-fact' accountability for actions taken. Sections 83–105 of PACE introduced a number of reforms intended to produce more effective scrutiny of investigations, which were still, however, to be conducted by senior officers. The main change was the establishment of the 'Independent'[5] Police Complaints Authority. At the time of our research in 1987–8, the PCA consisted of sixteen full-time members, all of whom had had fairly distinguished careers in other fields, assisted by civil service staff and two police advisers (since reduced to one part time). The Authority was divided into 'I' and 'D' Divisions, the first concerned with investigations and the second with discipline—although recently it has become more common for members to work part time on each function.

The most significant innovation was the involvement of this outside body at an early stage in inquiries into serious complaints. Under s. 87, a PCA member must 'supervise' the investigation, conducted by a senior officer, of any complaint in which it is alleged that the actions of a police officer led to the death of, or serious injury to, a member of the public. ('Serious injury' has been defined in practice as broken bones or wounds requiring three or more stitches.) Members may also choose to supervise other cases in defined categories if they consider it appropriate. Before an investigation is deemed to have been completed, a member must

---

[5] The Police Complaints Authority has adopted the unofficial prefix 'Independent' in most of its publications and public pronouncements. This step was taken on the PCA's own initiative in an attempt to distance itself from the image, partly created by its official title, of an organization closely associated with the police.

issue an 'Interim Statement', certifying that thorough inquiries have been carried out and a report compiled to his or her satisfaction.

The proportion of cases supervised in this way is low. In 1989, out of a total of 5,308 completed investigations in England and Wales, only 259 (5 per cent) had been supervised by an Authority member (PCA 1990: Table 4). It should also be noted that completions themselves represent a minority of all outcomes of complaints—well over 50 per cent are informally resolved, withdrawn, or otherwise not proceeded with. Prior to our study, little or no information was available about what 'supervision' actually means in practice, and whether it makes any difference to the shape or outcome of investigations. Our findings on these questions will be discussed presently.

Like their predecessors in the PCB, members of the PCA's 'D' Division have the responsibility of examining the files of all completed complaints investigations in England and Wales—an annual total of around 5,500 cases (which include over 11,000 individual complaints). It can be argued that this is the area in which members have the greatest opportunity to affect the outcome of complaints, as, although the police recommend what action should be taken, and in most cases set up and administer disciplinary proceedings themselves, in the last resort members have the power to direct the holding of a disciplinary tribunal. Moreover, when such a direction is made, the panel hearing the case consists of the Chief Constable and two members of the PCA (selected from those who have no previous knowledge of the case). In 1989, the Authority directed ten charges before tribunals, against the advice of deputy chief constables; a further forty-three charges were recommended by the PCA contrary to the original conclusions of the Deputy Chief Constable, these being accepted by the police without the need to resort to a direction.[6]

In addition to the new procedures for serious complaints, the architects of PACE attempted to ease the problem of excessive formality in the handling of minor cases. Noting that a complaint of

---

[6] If the Deputy Chief Constable accepts such a recommendation, a disciplinary hearing, rather than a tribunal, is held. PCA members do not sit on panels in this case, judgments being made by the Chief Constable sitting alone. It should also be noted that the statistics produced by the PCA are complicated by the use of 'complaints', 'charges', and 'cases' as the base figure at different times. The 53 charges referred to concerned 20 cases. On average, each case contains about 2.4 complaints. Thus e.g. in 1987 the PCA dealt with 5,596 cases containing 11,560 individual complaints.

rudeness could take as long to investigate, produce as much paperwork, and use as much of a senior officer's time as one of assault, they introduced a new system of 'informal resolution' to dispense with minor cases quickly, cheaply, and, it is hoped, to satisfaction of all parties. The key feature of informal resolution is that police officers face no risk of disciplinary action: they can admit misconduct and/or apologize to the complainant without their statements being admissible as evidence against them and without any stain on their record. This procedure effectively separates a proportion of complaints from the disciplinary system, thus, in theory at least, allowing more attention to be given to satisfying the complainant rather than the demands of the system.[7]

Before discussing the effect of these changes, one final important element of the system must be mentioned. The area in which decision-making power by outsiders is the clearest and the longest established is that of prosecution. It was first recommended by the Royal Commission of 1908–9 that decisions to lay criminal charges should be the prerogative of the Director of Public Prosecutions, whose office had been formally established in 1908. Although most forces soon co-operated fully with the DPP, it was not until 1964 that the referral of papers was put on a statutory footing. The current provision covering this is s. 90 of PACE 1984, whereby the senior officer responsible is obliged to forward to the DPP a copy of the investigation report, if he or she considers that 'a criminal offence may have been committed by a member of his force'. However, he retains the discretion to deal with the matter instead under the disciplinary code if he considers the alleged offence minor enough not to warrant prosecution.

Criticism of prosecution decisions has focused upon the apparent caution or conservatism of the DPP: the proportion of cases received by his office which are rejected for prosecution is considerably higher than average when police officers are the subject. In responding to allegations of pro-police bias, the DPP has pointed out first of all that many police cases, unlike ordinary cases, are referred to his office without even meeting the standard of prima facie evidence (because deputy chief constables are obliged to forward papers when they consider an offence *may* have been committed).

[7] More accurately, the new procedure *reintroduces* a separation between complaints and discipline. Similar procedures existed in the 19th c., to the extent of arranging meetings between some complainants and the officers concerned.

He has also spelled out the implications of the primary test which he has decided to apply to all cases submitted to his office, whoever is involved. Before bringing any prosecution, he wishes to be satisfied that there is a 'reasonable prospect' of conviction.[8] 'Reasonable prospect' is a much more stringent test than that of evidence amounting to a prima facie case, in that the question asked is not simply whether a jury *could* convict, or even whether a jury *should* convict on the available evidence, but *whether it is more likely than not that it will convict* (Peay and Mansfield 1986: 12). This element of prediction has particular significance for police cases, the DPP claims, because juries are traditionally more reluctant to convict police officers than other members of society. Thus he rejects many cases which, although apparently containing sufficient evidence, have in practice a poor chance of persuading a jury to bring in a guilty verdict. Indeed, he has taken the argument a step further, asserting that the high acquittal rate in police cases indicates that his office, far from favouring the police, may be prosecuting in too many cases. These arguments have brought vigorous responses from Williams (1985) and Lustgarten (1986), among others, who assert that the whole approach is untenable in principle. Lustgarten, indeed, describes it as 'a flagrant violation of the rule of law'.

THE EFFECTIVENESS OF THE CURRENT SYSTEM: SOME RESEARCH FINDINGS

As implied in earlier remarks, most complaints systems are intended to serve more than one purpose, although some of these may be in competition so that priority has to be given to one or more at the expense of others. Ideally, the police complaints system should meet all the following objectives:

1. The maintenance of 'discipline in the ranks'
2. The satisfaction of complainants
3. The maintenance of public confidence in the police
4. The provision of 'feedback from consumers' to police managers

In this section, we shall summarize research and other evidence on the effectiveness of the current system in achieving each of these goals. Particular attention will be paid to any impact made by the creation or activities of the PCA. We shall then take a closer look at

---

[8] He must also be satisfied that prosecution is 'in the public interest'.

the crucial issue of how the most serious complaints are handled, assessing the contribution of the new system of independent supervision.

1. Discipline

The first objective above, the maintenance of discipline in the ranks, has always been regarded by the police themselves (or at least by senior officers) as one of the main priorities. Complaints have traditionally been treated essentially as an adjunct to the internal disciplinary system, with its highly formal approach, adversarial procedures, and emphasis upon punishment and deterrence. A necessary condition for the system to work in this respect is that cases are dealt with fairly, consistently, and thoroughly, thus maximizing the chances that any officer who has breached police regulations will be 'brought to book' and others will consequently think twice before offending. One statistical indicator of whether this is occurring may be the substantiation rate for complaints, although it has to be recognized that an unknown proportion, made in error or in malice, should without question remain unsubstantiated, while many more are impossible to prove, however diligent the investigator. (This last point raises questions about the standard of evidence required, which will be referred to later.)

In fact, even taking the above provisos into account, the substantiation rate has always appeared to outsiders to be far too low to constitute a serious deterrent. Between 1979 and 1989, a total of 330,109 complaints were recorded, of which only 13,790 (4.2 per cent) were substantiated. The rate looks rather higher, though not impressively so, if one takes as a base only those complaints in which investigations were completed, that is, excluding those informally resolved, withdrawn or otherwise not proceeded with. Calculated this way, the annual substantiation rate ranged between 8 and 11 per cent over the same period.

It is also worthy of note that the advent of the PCA, like the PCB before it, has made no statistically significant difference to results overall. In 1989 there were only 765 substantiations among the 9,229 complaints fully investigated—a rate similar to earlier years.[9] There are, however, two claims the PCA can make regarding their

[9] The figures on substantiation are complicated by the advent of informal resolution, because some of the cases resolved in this way would have been investigated and substantiated under the old system. In 1989, 7,125 complaints were informally resolved. It seems reasonable to assume that under the previous

influence upon outcomes. First, in almost one in ten of those complaints in which some disciplinary action (in most cases, formal advice or admonishment) was taken, this followed a recommendation by the PCA, the Deputy Chief Constable having initially concluded that no action was warranted. And secondly—a possibility which will be discussed in the next section—there may be some effect where cases supervised by PCA members are concerned.

Probably a more reliable means of assessing the effectiveness of the system as a disciplinary tool is to examine the attitudes of junior officers towards it. In the course of the study, we interviewed fifty officers (mainly of constable rank) who had been the subject of a recent complaint. The majority told us that neither the existence of the complaints system, nor the fact of having received a complaint, had made any difference to how they behaved, largely because they did not consider that they engaged in misconduct anyway. About ten of these officers took a cavalier, even 'gung-ho' attitude to complaints, one asserting, for example, that they made 'good wallpaper'. Two in particular, who both admitted to us that they had handled people very roughly on arrest, seemed surprisingly sanguine. Both had received numerous (unsubstantiated) complaints over the years, mainly when serving in support units.[10] Although they conceded that there was an outside chance that some of their actions could be interpreted as 'going over the top', they remained confident that investigating officers understood the 'pressures on the street' and that, so long as any roughness was in response to aggression from the arrested person, there was little danger of a charge of assault being brought against them. What they had always used, they claimed, was 'reasonable force' in the circumstances. As one of them put it, 'When you're in a scrum of·fighting drunks, the last thing you worry about is complaints.'

However, at the other extreme, about one in five said that complaints had had quite a significant impact upon their style of

arrangements about half of these would have been fully investigated (i.e. not withdrawn). If 15% of the latter had then been substantiated (a very generous assumption) the overall substantiation rate for 1989 would have been about 10% i.e. very similar to the 'pre-PCA' average. For further discussion of outcomes, see Maguire and Corbett (1989).

[10] Support units are kinds of task force which patrol areas in which disorder is expected or respond to calls for assistance when situations seem to be getting out of hand. They often use heavily protected transit vans for transport and have a reputation for dealing with trouble in a strong, if not heavy-handed, fashion.

policing. This was generally put to us in a negative light. For example: 'You start to back away from situations when you should be taking action . . . If there's an obvious risk of a complaint you tend to pass the buck. Why should I risk my mortgage by giving some little yobbo the chance to have a go at me?' Of course, the line between 'backing away' wrongly when firm action is required, and taking a more cool-headed approach to potentially violent situations, is extremely narrow. It could be argued that those who said that they no longer 'went in so hard' when trouble loomed—although themselves regarding this as a weakness and poor policing—had actually been deterred from using an unnecessarily tough response to violence or disorder in the streets.

It should also be noted that complaints investigations were regarded by many of the officers as unpleasant, and sometimes stressful, experiences. This was partly because of the fear of a 'blot on the record' (a handicap to promotion) and partly because of the uncomfortable experience of being 'put under the spotlight' by a Superintendent. Several said they were less concerned about the complaint itself being substantiated than about the possibility of some other misdemeanour—a pocket-book error, breach of PACE regulations, etc.—being turned up in the course of inquiries. Certainly, too, in preparing for situations in which complaints were thought likely, for example, raids on houses, officers spoke of efforts to 'cover their arses' by ensuring that in any subsequent investigation they could not be found to have made technical breaches in the 'paperwork'.

In sum, while only a minority admitted to altering their behaviour significantly as a result of complaints, and a few treated them very lightly indeed, most agreed that complaints were unpleasant enough to be worth avoiding if there was a simple way of doing so. The possibility of a complaint definitely impinged upon their conscious-ness when handling certain kinds of situation (for example, arrests, 'domestics', traffic stops, and raids), and hence could have a marginal influence on their conduct. Quite simply, as one officer put it, 'they are always there in the back of your mind . . . they don't bother you, but obviously you avoid them if you can'.

2. Complainant Satisfaction

Evidence about the performance of the system in meeting the second of the four objectives listed above—that of satisfying complainants—

can be obtained from our interviews with 100 complainants in three police-force areas. Forty of these interviewees' cases had been fully investigated, thirty informally resolved, and thirty withdrawn by the complainant. When asked to rate their level of satisfaction with the outcome of their complaint, only 12 per cent declared themselves 'very satisfied' and 19 per cent 'fairly satisfied'. Almost half stated that they were 'very dissatisfied'.

As Table 1 shows, the bulk of the dissatisfaction was to be found among complainants whose cases had been fully investigated: only four of the forty were even fairly satisfied. It might be thought that these responses merely reflect people's disappointment at 'losing their case'. This may account for some of the reactions, but it was interesting to discover that satisfaction was not closely correlated with outcomes: even those whose complaints had been substantiated were generally unimpressed. The main reasons given for dissatisfaction were the length of time taken to deal with the complaint, the absence of any apology, and the inadequacy or lack of explanation for the decision. These findings are similar to those of Brown (1987), who conducted a survey of complainants' views shortly before the passing of the Police and Criminal Evidence Act 1984.[11] They suggest that neither the introduction of the PCA, nor 'D' Division's practice of drafting personal letters to all complainants when inquiries have been completed,[12] has had any significant impact upon complainant satisfaction, at least in 'run of the mill' cases (supervised cases will be dealt with below). Certainly, we found that few complainants had any clear idea about the source from which the final letter had come, and even fewer regarded the PCA as an effective or genuinely independent body. The general feeling was that the police made all the decisions and that these were biased in favour of their own officers.

[11] Brown found that about 20% of complainants were satisfied with their experience of the system, 20% had mixed feelings, and 60% were dissatisfied. He asked respondents to take account of all aspects of the handling of their case and not just the outcome (as we did in our postal questionnaire—see next section). He also found that an important factor in determining satisfaction was the way in which the investigating officer had treated the complainant.

[12] These usually consist of 1–2 pages in which the complainant is assured that a thorough investigation has been carried out, but that there is insufficient evidence to substantiate his complaint. Normally, a brief explanation is given: e.g. 'PC Smith denies that he struck you and this is supported by the other police officers present.' In addition, a standard enclosure explains the role of the PCA and the basics of the procedure.

TABLE 1. *Level of satisfaction by method used to handle case*

Level of satisfaction	Type of case						
	Investigated		Withdrawn		Informally resolved		All
	No.	%	No.	%	No.	%	%
Very satisfied	0	0	3	10	9	30	12
Fairly satisfied	4	10	7	23	8	27	19
A bit dissatisfied	9	22	7	23	5	17	21
Very dissatisfied	27	68	13	43	8	27	48
TOTAL	40	100	30	100	30	100	100

On the other hand, Table 1 shows a more positive response from complainants who had experienced another part of the new system introduced by PACE, the informal resolution procedure. Over half of these declared themselves broadly satisfied with the outcome. A further indication of the relative attraction of this procedure was that almost half of the forty whose cases had been fully investigated said that they would have preferred a less formal response to their complaint, most commonly a meeting with the officer and his or her superiors to discuss the incident in depth. This supports our conclusion from answers to other questions, as well as that of Brown (1987), that what complainants are seeking in most cases is not something akin to a trial and punishment of the officer concerned, but a full explanation, an apology, some pointed remarks to the officer from somebody in a senior position, and/or a clear assurance that steps will be taken to see that 'it does not happen again'. It also suggests that there is scope for wider use of informal resolution, which at present is employed in only about one in four of all cases, although, of course, judgements have to be made about the level of seriousness at which a 'justice'- or 'discipline'-oriented response becomes more appropriate than one geared primarily to the satisfaction of complainants.

3. Public Confidence

Past failures to achieve the third major objective—gaining the confidence of the general public—have already been described in the introductory section of this paper. Some evidence about the current situation can be obtained from the answers to questions we inserted in the 1988 British Crime Survey.

Respondents from a random sample of households were asked, 'If you were to make a complaint against the police, how thoroughly do you think it would be investigated?' A total of 46 per cent answered either 'very' or 'fairly' thoroughly, but there was a substantial minority (25 per cent) who thought the opposite, the remainder being unsure. Similarly, when asked how happy they were with the present system, only 36 per cent declared themselves 'very' or 'reasonably' happy. And to the question of who they thought *should* investigate complaints, under one in six replied that he or she was content to leave it to the police: the most frequent response was 'an independent lay body'. It is also important to note that all the above questions drew negative answers from significantly higher proportions of black and ethnic minority respondents than of white respondents.

In the absence of comparable data from the period before the creation of the PCA, it is impossible to tell how much difference, if any, this development has made to the level of public confidence. However, some of the survey responses may be relevant. Under 10 per cent of the full sample of householders said that they knew of 'an independent organization which supervises the way police investigate complaints', only one in five of these could name it correctly, and, even when the name was put to them, only 38 per cent of the full sample claimed to have heard of the PCA. It will also be remembered that many complainants were fairly hazy about the Authority's role. All of this suggests that the PCA has some way to go before it can claim to have made a major impact upon public perceptions of the fairness of the system.

4. Feedback and Change

Findings relevant to the last objective—the use of the complaints system as a provider of management information, leading to improvements in policy and practice—were again generally disappointing. It was rare for police forces to undertake any serious analysis of patterns of complaints or to make systematic efforts to learn from them. Nevertheless, there were some signs of change here. 'Numbers of complaints' is now used regularly by Inspectors of Constabulary as one indicator of each force's overall performance, and senior officers at headquarters were watching complaints rates in local divisions more closely than in the past, asking questions whenever these rose significantly. One force had also started a monthly bulletin to all divisions, produced by the Complaints and Discipline department, in which points arising from recent complaints were disseminated to local commanders. Even so, the rich potential of case-files, in which can be found, for example, detailed accounts of how police–public encounters 'went wrong', has as yet hardly been tapped at all. These could provide excellent training material, as well as information on which to base management reviews of policy and practice (for further discussion, see Maguire and Corbett 1989).

However, perhaps the most important development in this area has come from the PCA. Members have made several public statements about lessons which can be learnt from high profile cases. For example, following one major investigation, they recommended that individual officers should be more easily identifiable when wearing riot gear. They have also recommended changes in regulations covering the use of firearms and access to the national police computer. This appeared to us to be one of the most valuable spin-offs from the role of the PCA, and one which might be developed further. In addition to commenting upon individual cases, members could more often use their experience of large numbers of cases to make general comments on themes which recur frequently in lesser cases. For example, more than one member expressed to us concern about the frequency with which complainants referred to excessive tightening of handcuffs: by drawing attention to this, they could perhaps stimulate changes either in the design of the equipment or in guidelines for its use.

SERIOUS CASES: SUPERVISION BY THE PCA

The appropriate objectives of the complaints system are most clear-cut in the most serious cases. A primary goal here must be the conviction, punishment—and, if necessary, dismissal—of offending officers. Especially in the light of recent history, the other main priority must be the allaying of any suspicion of 'cover-ups'. The key mechanism designed to achieve both aims is supervision by the PCA, and it can be argued that, in the final analysis, the PACE reforms stand or fall by the Authority's performance in this area.

The essential task of supervising members, then, is to ensure that 'justice is not only done, but is seen to be done'. This entails not only seeing that a fair and thorough investigation is carried out (thus maximizing the chances that any seriously offending officer will be found guilty), but convincing the complainant and, perhaps more importantly, the general public of their own genuine independence and their ability to 'deliver the goods'. In this section, we shall attempt to make a broad assessment of the PCA's achievements in each of these respects.

1. Outsiders and Insiders: Modes of Supervision

There is quite an extensive literature on the problems of external agencies set up to regulate the activities of established professions (see, for example, Calvatia 1983; Lynxweiler *et al.* 1983; Hawkins 1984; Maguire, Vagg, and Morgan 1985; Hutter 1988). One of the main lessons from these studies seems to be that any outside body which hopes to play an effective part in the control of a complex and powerful organization like the police cannot hope to do so 'at arm's length'. The prerequisites include gaining some understanding of the organizational culture, learning how to extract key pieces of information, and establishing good relationships with—and gaining the respect of—internal investigators. Without making these inroads into the organization, members of the external body lack sufficient armoury to get to the heart of what is going on and equally lack credibility in the eyes of those on whom they rely for information. (They also have to guard against the opposite danger of becoming 'co-opted' through over-familiarity into police ways of thinking, and hence losing both their critical edge and their credibility; however, we saw few signs of this where the PCA was concerned.)

We begin our discussion of supervision with an account of the way it is actually practised by members of the PCA. As well as interviewing supervising members and observing them in action over a period of six months, we analysed the files of 100 supervised cases. In forty of these, the supervision had been mandatory, and in forty it had been discretionary, under s. 87 of PACE.[13] There were also twenty 'Section 88' cases—a special category which embraces inquiries into incidents which are not necessarily the subject of complaint, but which are referred by the police as matters of public importance.

Analysis of the above samples revealed considerable differences between cases in the degree of attention and intervention exercised by members. We identified two main modes of supervision, which we have called 'passive' and 'active', although the latter can take various forms. Passive, or 'routine', supervision describes the minimum level, in which the member simply reads through documents (witness statements, medical reports, copies of custody records, and so on) as they arrive from the investigating officer (IO), responding if necessary, but essentially carrying out a *post facto* monitoring task, rather than playing any active role in the investigation. In such cases, apart from, perhaps, an initial telephone call, member and IO tend to have little or no direct contact. Active supervision, by contrast, is characterized by frequent telephone calls, and occasionally meetings, between member and IO, the member keeping in fairly close touch with progress and throwing in comments or suggestions as the inquiry proceeds. At its extreme, active supervision may become quite intensive, or even, on occasion, 'participant', where the member spends time with the IO as he or she carries out the investigation, perhaps sitting in on interviews and meeting the complainant or other interested parties. A final possibility is that supervision, in whatever mode it was initially conducted, becomes at some point 'directive', IOs being formally requested to follow particular lines of inquiry.

We concluded that about half of all cases had been dealt with almost entirely in the 'passive' mode, and nearly all the remainder in a moderately active fashion. Intensive or participant styles of supervision were to be found in only a handful of cases. Members met IOs personally in only eighteen of the 100 cases sampled, and in

---

[13] Section 87 makes it mandatory for the PCA to supervise cases in which it is alleged that the actions of an officer caused 'death or serious injury'. Regulations drawn up under s. 87 also oblige the police to refer for possible supervision complaints in which it is alleged that an officer is guilty of conduct which, if proved, would constitute an offence of assault occasioning actual bodily harm, an offence under the Prevention of Corruption Act 1906, or any other serious arrestable offence under s. 116 of PACE.

most of these there was only one meeting. Meetings with complainants, witnesses, or other interested parties occurred only in
four. Finally, we could find only six cases in which members
directed the police to pursue a particular line in the investigation.[14]

It was somewhat ironic that the kinds of case most likely to be
dealt with in a routine, non-interventionist style were in the category
officially deemed to be the most serious: that is, complaints of
assault in which supervision was mandatory owing to the level of
injuries sustained (see 'PACE and the PCA' above and n. 13). Unless
there were special circumstances such as exceptionally grave injuries
(i.e. beyond the normal range of broken bones and deep cuts) or
significant media attention, such cases tended to be processed
without much close questioning or discussion. For example,
members had personal meetings with IOs in only 5 per cent of such
cases, compared with 27 per cent of others; and there were fifteen or
more letters and telephone calls exchanged between PCA and IO in
23 per cent, compared with 33 per cent of others.

The explanation for this paradox seems to lie in the circumstances
in which complaints of assault most often arise and the basic pattern
which their investigation tends to take. Allegations of assault are
almost always associated with the arrest of the complainant. The
relevant incidents often take place at night—in the street, in a police
vehicle, or in a police station—with no witnesses apart from other
police officers and, perhaps, the complainant's companions.[15] The
only evidence beyond the statements of those present tends to be
medical reports, which usually confirm only the extent of injuries,
not the way they were inflicted. In such circumstances, there is little
choice about the path the investigation will take. All the investigator
can normally do is to collect the medical evidence and to interview
the witnesses. If, as is regularly the case, the police adhere doggedly
to one story and the complainant and/or his companions to another
(e.g. 'He injured himself when struggling violently', as against 'They
hit me for no reason') the room for manœuvre is very limited. While,
on occasion, PCA members might ask the IO to search for new

[14] However, it should be noted that members saw the issuing of directions as a 'last
resort', indicative of a failure in their relationship with the IO. There were several
other cases in which they made suggestions which were readily accepted, so that no
direction was necessary, and others again in which the IO persuaded them that their
suggestions were not worth pursuing.

[15] For a more detailed analysis of 'complaint-producing incidents', see Maguire
and Corbett (1989).

witnesses, to explore any discrepancies they notice between the accounts given, or even, conceivably, to push certain officers 'harder' in interview, there is more often little they can usefully suggest as a way of producing more conclusive evidence.

The kinds of case in which members were most likely to take a highly active, even participatory, role were those in which there was intense media interest. This applied to a few complaints of serious assault on arrest, but was particularly likely in 'Section 88' cases, which include dramatic incidents such as shootings by police officers and apparent police violence at demonstrations. The police tend to refer such cases immediately without waiting for a complaint, and the PCA response is usually to make a prompt and publicly visible visit to the scene and to remain closely in touch with developments, at least in the early stages. For example, one member became so involved in a highly complex investigation of violence against picketing strikers that he regularly visited the police incident room over a period of months. He became familiar enough with the videotapes, photographs, and masses of statements to be able to discuss the progress of the investigation with the IO perceptively and in great detail. Another member, dealing with a death in custody, made his presence felt by setting up his own meetings with a Member of Parliament, the Home Office, the coroner, solicitors acting for both sides, and the bereaved family.

Section 88s tended to attract active, if not intensive, supervision for other reasons. The police are free to refer them with a wider than normal 'brief' for the scope of the investigation. Whereas, in ordinary complaints cases, the IO is concerned strictly with the question of whether individual officers have broken the law or breached a specific section of the disciplinary code, in Section 88s he may be asked to look critically at operational or policy decisions and standard police practices. For example, in cases arising out of public order policing, serious questions may be asked not just about alleged violence by named constables, but about the overall deployment of constables and their briefing by senior officers. Again, investigations of deaths in police chases have raised questions not only about the actions of the drivers, but about the guidelines they receive. In such cases, a supervising member clearly has more scope for suggesting or directing lines of inquiry.

Active attention was also more likely in complaints investigations which members had selected for supervision than in those they were obliged to take on. In 1987, they chose about 250 out of the 3,650 cases referred to them for possible supervision. Although nearly 95 per cent of these referrals were alleged assaults (which had produced lesser injuries than those referred for mandatory supervision), selection was weighted heavily towards the other 5 per cent: about half of those finally chosen contained allegations of dishonesty or corruption. The inquiries in the latter cases were often complex and wide ranging, which again gave members more scope for discussions about their shape and depth.

2. The Value of Supervision

The above account demonstrates that 'supervision' can mean anything from the routine monitoring of evidence to close involvement in the investigation as it progresses. What now needs to be asked is whether it has any real value, in any or all of its forms.

No definite conclusions can be drawn from statistics on outcomes, although they do provide some food for thought. According to the PCA report of 1987, 13 per cent of all cases passing through 'D' Division, but 22 per cent of those among them which had been supervised, resulted in some form of action against an officer (it should be noted that 'action' is a different measure to 'substantiation': it includes informal advice given to officers, even when the case against them has not been 'proved'). Similarly, among the sample of 382 cases we used for our postal questionnaire,[16] twice as many supervised as unsupervised cases had resulted in prosecution, discipline, or advice. However, impressive as such figures appear, account has to be taken both of the different types of complaint involved and of the element of selection in supervised cases. This is illustrated in Table 2.

It can be seen that cases in which supervision was discretionary were much more likely to result in prosecution or formal discipline than those in which it was mandatory. This suggests that members, consciously or unconsciously, tended to select for supervision cases with a better chance of a 'result'. If one compares only mandatorily supervised cases with unsupervised cases (thus excluding this element of choice), the difference is seen to be minimal—even when the comparison is restricted to assault cases only.

[16] These were selected randomly from 3 groups of cases completed over a 2-year period: cases supervised mandatorily, cases supervised at members' discretion, and cases rejected for supervision.

TABLE 2. *Outcomes of supervised and unsupervised cases (%)*

Type of case	Outcome				
	Prosecution or discipline	Advice	No action	All	(No.)
Mandatory supervision assault alleged	5	26	69	100	(152)
Discretionary supervision assault alleged	19	13	68	100	(37)
Discretionary supervision no assault alleged	13	33	54	100	(39)
All supervised cases	8	25	67	100	(232)
Unsupervised assault alleged	3	11	86	100	(140)
All unsupervised cases	4	13	83	100	(150)

On the other hand, there remains an interesting difference when one takes into account the outcome of 'advice' to officers. In cases where assault was alleged, this advice usually related either to a less serious ancillary complaint or simply to a technical breach of regulations which emerged during the investigation. It is striking that this outcome was much more common in supervised cases of all kinds than in unsupervised cases. It is quite likely that this is a real effect of supervision, arising from a closer attention to detail when evidence is being sifted regularly by members and their civil-servant assistants.

The question of whether the more active forms of supervision are more likely than passive supervision to 'produce results' is not answerable by means of the above type of evidence. Although more cases supervised in the former way ended with prosecution or discipline, this could simply reflect a tendency for members to take a closer interest in cases in which substantiation seemed likely at the outset.

However valid the evidence on outcomes, the effectiveness of supervision should not anyway be judged purely by this criterion. It is equally, if not more, important to look at the perceptions of those involved as well as of the wider audience among the general public.

First of all, we may consider the views of investigating officers. We interviewed nineteen superintendents and chief inspectors, twelve of whom had investigated cases under the supervision of the

PCA. Most of these had experienced only the more routine kind of supervision, whereby the PCA simply monitored evidence as it was produced, stipulating only that the IO should send a written report on progress every four weeks. Where this had been the case, the IOs all stated that supervision had impinged very little upon their work. One even confessed to a certain disappointment: 'I was quite pleased to have the opportunity of being supervised, to see what would happen. In fact, nothing did. It was another myth exploded.'

The few who had had personal contact with members were more favourably impressed. One said of a member that he was 'surprised how good he was' and another that a member had 'grasped amazingly quickly the essentials of investigations'. Even so, all were unanimous that supervision had made no difference at all to the shape or outcome of the investigation.

Speaking more generally, two-thirds of the IOs felt that supervision had some value—but only as a means of reassuring the public that investigations were fair, or, sometimes, of taking media pressure off the shoulders of the investigator. All doubted whether an outside presence was ever going to contribute anything more concrete to an investigation, beyond perhaps putting less diligent IOs more 'on their mettle' in matters of detail, by virtue of having somebody 'looking over their shoulder'.

The views of complainants about supervision can be gauged from responses to our postal questionnaire. Among the 186 respondents, 125 had made complaints investigated under PCA supervision, the remainder being investigated by the police in the normal way. We asked not only whether complainants were satisfied with the *outcome* of the investigation, but also whether, disregarding the result, they were satisfied with *the way the investigation had been conducted*. There were no differences between supervised and unsupervised cases in satisfaction with outcomes (only 4 per cent giving positive replies), but a slightly higher proportion (26 per cent) of those who had experienced supervision than of those who had not (17 per cent) were very or fairly satisfied with the general handling of their case. Moreover, higher proportions of the former group felt that the IO had treated their complaints seriously, that the investigation had been thorough, and that they had been kept well informed about what was happening. Even so, it has to be said that these differences were small and that, in any case, the great majority of reactions were negative.

The replies also indicated the importance of what might be called the 'disappointment factor'. We asked first whether, when they first heard that the PCA would be supervising the investigation, complainants had felt more confident that their case would be dealt with fairly. Those who stated that this news had made them 'much more' or 'a little more' confident accounted for 35 per cent. However, when then asked whether, having experienced it, they now had more or less faith in the complaints system than when they first complained, almost two-thirds of those whose expectations had been raised said that they had now had 'very much less faith'. In other words, the involvement of the PCA had elevated their hopes, only to dash them later.

A similarly bleak picture emerged from responses to questions about the general impressions complainants had received of the PCA. Only 9 per cent believed that the Authority was independent of the police, and 5 per cent that it was effective in its monitoring role. The vast majority were in favour of investigations being conducted by a totally independent body, rather than supervised as at present. This applied to those who had and had not experienced supervision alike.

We were unable to discover whether 'active' as opposed to 'passive' supervision resulted in higher levels of satisfaction, as we did not collect information about the investigation in the cases used for the questionnaire sample. However, we speculate that the level of involvement would have made little difference in most cases because complainants are generally unaware of what efforts are put into their case by the PCA: at the end of the day, all they receive is a letter informing them of the result and a brief account of the reasons behind it. The only exception might be found in the small number of cases in which the PCA play a 'participant' role, particularly when meeting the complainant in person.

Finally, there remains the question of the *symbolic* value of supervision: it could be that, even if it does not affect individual investigations, the announcement of the involvement of the PCA when serious allegations 'hit the press' provides some reassurance to the general public that remedial action will be taken. Certainly, the PCA has a higher public profile than its predecessor the PCB: most newspaper reports of serious allegations about police misconduct contain some reference to the Authority, and the results of major investigations are often announced through a press conference at which the chairman answers questions. On the other hand, two problems remain. First, despite the considerable efforts made by the chairman and other members to give it a higher profile in the media, knowledge about the PCA remains fairly hazy in the public consciousness. As stated earlier, even complainants who had received communications from the PCA tended to have little clear idea of its functions, and the 1988 British Crime Survey results indicate only patchy knowledge of its existence.

Secondly, there is the major problem that in many cases the PCA has to announce negative results. The vast majority of investigations eventually 'come to nothing' owing to lack of evidence, and the chairman or other members find themselves defending the lack of action. This is sometimes exacerbated by the fact that they are unable to give a full explanation of the reasons for the outcome: reports of investigations remain secret by law, and only general summaries are released. A good example of this was the 'Manchester students case', in which it was alleged that a group of protestors had been assaulted by uniformed officers and that one student had later been assaulted in retaliation for complaining. As this person fled abroad with charges outstanding against him, the matter remains *sub judice* and no public account has been given of the outcome of this part of the investigation. However thorough investigations may be, the absence of a full statement will always leave residual suspicions, causing the PCA to be seen by critics as, at best, ineffective, and even by some as part of a conspiracy to protect the police.[17] To date, there have been very few publicized examples of the opposite situation, where the outcome has clearly reflected credit upon police investigators or the PCA (one exception being the 'Holloway Road case', where the persistence of the Authority was given some credit in the media for helping to convict a group of officers for a particularly unpleasant assault).[18]

[17] Ironically, the PCA suffered when the contents of one report were revealed, not by themselves, but by the police (who are not covered by the restriction on disclosure of information contained in s. 98 of PACE). This was when, in order to defend the force against a pending civil action in a case where a woman had died, the police lawyer introduced into the coroner's court statements made by a witness during the complaint investigation, claiming that this showed discrepancies with the account currently being given by this witness. The PCA, who had supervised the investigation, were very concerned that this would deter other witnesses from making statements in complaints investigations, it previously having been understood that these were given in confidence.

[18] In this case, some boys were beaten up by police officers who could only have come from one of 3 vans, yet all 3 groups denied for a long time that they had been present. In the end, a public statement by the PCA Chairman, together with some other pressure, persuaded one of the officers involved to make a confession.

SUMMARY AND DISCUSSION

In this paper an account has been given of the main features of the complaints system in the form it now takes in England and Wales. The historical context has been emphasized, to show how it has reached its current hybrid status between internal and external control, and to outline the developments which have elevated it from a marginal to a conspicuously important position among the mechanisms designed to deal with the issue of police accountability. The past twenty-five years have seen several changes in the system, and it is likely that further change will occur before a situation of greater stability is reached.

Most of these changes, set against a background of long-term decline in trust of the police, reflect the attempts of a system which is historically rooted in the internal police disciplinary system to adapt to modern demands for openness, accountability, and the satisfaction of complainants. The results have been the introduction of an external element to oversee investigations and their outcomes (in the form of the PCA), more flexible procedures to meet complainants' wishes in minor cases (informal resolution), and improvements in the recording of complaints and the publication of statistics. What now exists is essentially a three-tiered system, in which investigations into the most serious complaints are supervised by outsiders, 'medium-range' complaints continue to be investigated in the traditional manner (with the addition of external scrutiny of the final report), and minor complaints are dealt with locally and informally. While these are welcome improvements, some fundamental problems and tensions remain, and few would claim that the adaptation has been entirely successful.

Doubts remain, first and foremost, about the system's capacity to play an effective part in the key problem of 'controlling the constable'. Junior officers, many of them quite inexperienced, have to deal regularly with difficult and violent situations in the street, for which they are necessarily equipped with considerable power and discretion. The complaints system carries more responsibility than ever before for preventing and redressing abuses of these powers: weaknesses in 'front-line supervision' (with sergeants and inspectors more often tied up in administrative work inside police stations) mean that deterrence in the form of disciplinary sanctions has to some extent replaced on-the-spot control by experienced officers. For such sanctions to be effective, they must be applied frequently and consistently enough to constitute a genuine deterrent. But as we have seen, the proportion of complaints which end in substantiation is extremely low, and most officers, although disliking the process of being investigated, know that there is little chance of a complaint of any but the most blatant misconduct leading to any action against them. Certainly, senior officers sometimes apply informal sanctions, such as 'sideways moves', after complaints which, though unsubstantiated, give them some cause for concern; and officers who accumulate numerous complaints over a short period are sometimes warned that their behaviour is being watched closely. However, such sanctions have their limitations, and are not backed up by the ultimate threat of dismissal. As the Chairman of the PCA pointed out in the Authority's 1988 report, once officers have completed their probationary period, it is extremely difficult to remove them from the force, however unsuitable they later turn out to be—even when it is suspected that they are frequently rude or violent. The problem is quite simply that the standard of evidence required to prove a disciplinary charge is higher than in any other professional organization: cases have to be proved, as in the courts, 'beyond reasonable doubt', not, as in disciplinary systems elsewhere, 'on the balance of probabilities'.[19]

While it may be defensible to demand the highest standard of proof when an officer's career is at stake, there is a much weaker case for this in less serious complaints, where the only sanction risked is a reprimand or formal advice. The difficulty in proving even minor cases undermines the effectiveness not only of the disciplinary system, but of the 'public relations' role of the complaints system. Complainants who are simply informed, many months later, that their complaint has been unsubstantiated through lack of evidence, feel that the exercise has been totally in vain. While some complaints are clearly trivial or malicious, we were generally impressed by the 'genuineness' of the complainants we interviewed—an impression confirmed by many of the IOs we spoke to. Most were making the first complaint against the police in their lives, and a large minority told us that it had taken some courage to do so: as one put it, 'It's

---

[19] e.g. in the Fire Brigade, which has a similar disciplinary code to the police, the standard used is the civil standard. This was established in law in the case of *R.* v. *Hampshire County Council* ex parte *Ellerton*, 1985. However, shortly after this case, new Police Regulations based on PACE went through Parliament 'on the nod', explicitly stating that a criminal standard of proof is required (see Lustgarten 1976).

like walking up to a six-foot man.' They were incensed by what had happened, and expected some form of redress, if only an apology, a full explanation, or an assurance that steps would be taken to prevent a recurrence. The 'black-and-white' nature of the outcome—the response to the complainant being totally dependent upon whether or not a breach of the disciplinary code can be proved against a named officer—meant that none of these wishes were met in the great majority of cases, and satisfaction was rare. (And even in some cases where advice was given to officers, this was either not communicated to complainants or it was not clearly enough explained that receiving advice was regarded in the police force as a significant penalty.)

Some of these problems have been ameliorated by the introduction of informal resolution, although the procedure is still not used as often as it could be. 'D' Division of the PCA, too, has made efforts to provide fuller explanations of the reasons behind decisions, but responses to our postal questionnaire indicate that few complainants consider these adequate. So long as the complaints system remains so closely interlinked with the disciplinary system, there is limited scope for making responses more akin to those provided by other, more 'consumer-oriented' organizations (in which satisfaction of the complainant has high priority). In sum, the position of the complainant against the police is rather like that of the victim of crime in relation to the criminal-justice system: he or she provides the initial input into a large impersonal system, which then takes over the case and processes it largely to meet organizational goals rather than the interests of the individual.

Perhaps the most important problem to be resolved, however, is that of winning general public confidence in the system. Inevitably, the key to this lies in the conspicuously thorough and unbiased investigation of serious complaints which attract media attention: it was such cases, not 'run-of-the-mill' complaints, which stirred up the controversy which led ultimately to the establishment of the PCA and the mechanism of supervision.

Whether or not supervision 'works' in the sense of making the conviction of guilty officers more likely, is impossible to answer with certainty, although we concluded that its very existence has probably had some 'sharpening-up' effect upon IOs, if only in matters of detail. However, one of the main problems we see with supervision is that, unless it is carried out—and seen to be carried out—in a sufficiently active style, it is unlikely either to influence the course of the investigation or to convince observers that it has any value. Passive supervision achieves little more than the *post hoc* monitoring of reports. Moreover, even very active supervision, although possibly influential (and certainly, in our experience, rigorous and conscientious), does not always appear to be so to outsiders. We read several files in which it was obvious that the member had put in an immense amount of work, yet none of this was known to the complainant or to anyone outside the police, PCA, and DPP. To achieve a higher public profile and to gain more credit for what it does, the Authority needs to find ways of 'blowing its own trumpet' harder.

The greatest hope for convincing a wider public of the Authority's effectiveness seems to lie in what we have called intensive, or 'participant' supervision. At its best, close involvement of this kind can develop into a fruitful 'partnership' between PCA member and police investigator. One member described such a relationship thus:

We discussed it all the time and knew what each other thought. We concluded mutually—I can't remember if it was him or me that suggested it—that we ought to appeal for any other witnesses to come forward. We decided to do a leaflet which we distributed by hand to neighbouring streets—I think I probably suggested it—that sort of thing . . . He and I got on well personally. I respected his expertise. He was more than willing to do everything that was requested. I didn't really have to 'direct' him. He became very sensitive to how the PCA should be seen by the outside world.

If this kind of relationship could be established in every supervised case, it might be argued that the new legislation had spawned a system with considerable promise, combining the advantages of the internal knowledge and 'clout' possessed by police superintendents (who can 'pull rank' to encourage officers to answer their questions) with the safeguard of well-informed outsiders being closely enough involved to constitute a genuine watchdog and occasionally to make a significant contribution. If, too, the supervising member were *conspicuously* involved in most investigations—by meeting complainants, making press statements, and so on—the problem of lack of public awareness of the PCA's contribution might become less acute. And finally, if more use were made of the practice of drawing general 'lessons' from complaints—either from individual cases or by identifying common patterns—and feeding these back to the police in the form of recommendations for changes in policy, practice, or training, something undeniably positive would be seen to emerge from the system.

Unfortunately, such an ideal is far from the present reality, where it is comparatively rare for members even to meet IOs in person. One of the main practical problems is that the level of PCA involvement is restricted by the size of case-loads. At the time of our research, each member was dealing on average with about 80 cases at any one time (although, admittedly, a fair number of these were *sub judice* and hence not yet 'live'). Moreover, the PCA has only one office, in London, so that meetings with IOs are made difficult by long travelling distances. These obstacles might eventually be overcome by expanding the membership of the Authority and opening regional offices. However, given the current restraints, the practical question is whether members should continue to 'spread themselves thinly' or should concentrate upon the intensive and publicly visible supervision of a much smaller number of carefully selected cases.

The latter course seems attractive from many angles, not least that of reducing the counter-productive effect of raising expectations among complainants (and, indeed, IOs), only to disappoint them. On the other hand, the issue of selection would cause difficulties. From the point of view of 'getting their teeth into' the investigation, many cases of alleged assault on arrest would have much less potential for members; yet assault complaints can be argued to be among the most serious of all, not only by dint of the extent of injuries caused, but because, if genuine, they represent an abuse of the crucial power which marks off the police from the rest of society—the right, where necessary, to use force to uphold the law. One would have to sacrifice the symbolic (and perhaps, on occasion, practical) importance of mandatory supervision in all such cases for the gains of a conspicuous presence in a few high-profile cases.

Ultimately, of course, pressure from critical responses to the weaknesses of the present system may grow to the extent that calls for the introduction of full-blown investigation by outsiders can no longer be resisted. However, while this step would have considerable support and has much to recommend it, it would be a mistake to assume that it would in itself provide a panacea for all the problems identified above. If outsiders were to investigate *all* complaints, the resource implications would be enormous, and one might simply be replacing one unwieldy bureaucratic system with another. If, as seems the most practical solution, outsiders were to investigate only the most serious cases, the question of selection would remain. Above all, experience in other countries suggests that independent investigation would fail to make any significant difference to the outcomes of cases (cf. McMahon 1988; Loveday 1989), so problems of credibility would still rear their head when only small proportions of complaints continued to be substantiated.

In conclusion, if satisfactory and lasting solutions are to be found, it is necessary to find an alternative to the reactive approach to reform which has prevailed in the past, whereby change has occurred largely in response to crisis. What is needed is a return to first principles: calm consideration of the fundamental aims and priorities on which a complaints system should be based, of the different kinds of cases it has to deal with, of the practical problems it faces, and of the interests and attitudes of those involved on all sides. Equally important, it has to be recognized that complaints are only one piece of the jigsaw: without improvements in training, supervision, police–public consultation, and other broader mechanisms of accountability, whatever way complaints are handled will make little difference to the fundamental problem of regaining full public confidence in the police.

REFERENCES

Brown, D. (1987) *The Police Complaints Procedure: A Survey of Complainants' Views*, Home Office Research Study No. 93 (London: HMSO).

Calvatia, K. (1983) 'The Demise of the Occupational Safety and Health Administration: A Study in Symbolic Action', *Social Problems* 30(4): 437–48.

Cohen, B. (1985) 'Police Complaints Procedure: Why and For Whom', in J. Baxter and L. Koffman (eds.) *Police: The Constitution and the Community* (London: Professional Books).

Critchley, T. (1978) *A History of Police in England and Wales* (London: Constable).

Hawkins, K. (1984) *Environment and Enforcement: Regulation and the Social Definition of Pollution* (Oxford: Oxford University Press).

Hobbs, D. (1988) *Doing the Business: Crime, Culture and Detective Work in East London* (Oxford: Oxford University Press).

Hutter, B. M. (1988) *The Reasonable Arm of the Law: The Law Enforcement Procedures of Environmental Health Officers* (Oxford: Clarendon).

Jefferson, T., and Grimshaw, R. (1984) *Controlling the Constable* (London: Frederic Muller).

Loveday, B. (1989) 'Recent Developments in Police Complaints Procedure: Britain and North America', *Local Government Studies*, May/June 1989: 25–57.

Lustgarten, L. (1986) *The Governance of Police* (London: Sweet and Maxwell).

Lynxweiler, J., Shover, N., and Clelland, D. (1983) 'The Organization and Impact of Inspector Discretion in a Regulatory Bureaucracy', *Social Problems* 30(4): 425–36.

Maguire, M., and Corbett, C. (1989) 'Patterns and Profiles of Complaints Against the Police', in R. Morgan and D. Smith (eds.), *Coming to Terms with Policing* (London: Routledge).

Maguire, M., Vagg, J., and Morgan, R. (1985) *Accountability and Prisons* (London: Tavistock).

McMahon, M. (1988) 'Police Accountability: The Situation of Complaints in Toronto', *Contemporary Crises* 12: 301–2).

PCA (1990) *Annual Report 1989* (London: HMSO).

Peay, J., and Mansfield, G. (1986) *The Director of Public Prosecutions* (London: Tavistock).

Reiner, R. (1985) *The Politics of the Police* (Brighton: Wheatsheaf Books).

Royal Commission (1908) *Report of the Royal Commission on the Powers and Duties of the Metropolitan Police* (London: HMSO Cd. 4156).

—— (1929) *Report of the Royal Commission on Police Powers and Procedures* (London: HMSO Cmd. 3297).

—— (1981) *Report of the Royal Commission on Criminal Procedure* (London: HMSO Cmnd. 8092).

Scarman, Lord (1981) *The Brixton Disorders* (London: HMSO Cmnd. 8427).

Select Committee (1834) *Select Committee on the Policing of the Metropolis* (London: HMSO).

West Midlands Police (1984) *Complaints Against the Police: Historical Perspective* (Birmingham: West Midlands Police Complaints and Discipline Department).

Williams, G. (1985) 'Letting Off the Guilty and Prosecuting the Innocent' *Criminal Law Review*, March 1985, pp. 115–23.

6

Multiple Realities, Divided Worlds:

Chief Constables' Perspectives on the Police Complaints System

ROBERT REINER

CRIMINOLOGY AND POLICE DEVIANCE

The received version of the history of criminological thought goes something like this (see, for example, Taylor, Walton, and Young 1973; Vold and Bernard 1986; Hagan 1987; Downes and Rock 1988; Rock 1988): first came the classical criminology of Beccaria; crime was rational action which needed deterrence by effective sanctions in order to overcome it. Then came the revelation that criminals were distinctive beings, whose behaviour needed special explanation so that the causes of it could be removed. At first these causes were seen as aspects of the individual peculiarities of offenders, later as lying in the special pressures of their particular social position. These varieties of positivism ruled the criminological roost until the 1960s when the epistemological break of 'labelling theory' and 'naturalism' occurred. Deviance was not a category that should be taken for granted. Its social construction required analysis. The perspective of deviants themselves had to be 'appreciated' rather than dismissed as obviously pathological. Labelling theory in its turn was fruitful and begat critical, radical, and Marxist criminology, involving an attempted synthesis of the labelling problematic with a structuralist political economy. (More recently, some of the pioneers of the 'critical criminology' perspective have broached a 'new-left realism' in criminology, the policy implications of which are more developed as yet than the theory (Lea and Young 1984; Kinsey, Lea, and Young 1986).

Systems for handling complaints against the police are concerned essentially with the processing of police deviance. The complaints system is usually perceived, in both official and academic discourse, as one of the main devices for controlling police misconduct (see for example Scarman 1981: 115; Home Office 1986: 18; Box 1983: 93–106; Lustgarten 1986 ch. 9; Uglow 1988: 132–6; W. Young 1986; McMahon and Ericson 1984).

Police deviance, and the arrangements for dealing with it, can be considered as a particular application of paradigms of explanation in criminology. For the most part, however, the issues raised by police deviance are approached at a concrete policy level, and theory is implicit not explicit.

Paradoxically the models of explanation implicit in accounts of police deviance by writers with different perspectives tend to be the reverse of those adopted for crime in general. Radical analyses, which are normally suspicious of classical deterrence theory, implicitly rediscover it in the case of police deviance. Their usual sensitivity to the phenomenon of moral panic does not preclude encouraging one when the folk devils wear blue uniforms. Presumed by many radical critiques of the police complaints procedure is the view that it is insufficiently rigorous in establishing charges against accused police officers, and applies sanctions which are inadequately severe in the minority of sustained complaints cases. Effective control of police malpractice would require sufficiently vigorous sanctioning to deter abuse (see, for example, Box 1983: 99; McMahon 1988: 322–5; Uglow 1988: 134–5). Box is explicit in seeing his stance on police complaints as 'a touchstone of deterrence theory' (ibid.), which is usually seen in criminology (and political debate) as a conservative approach.

Police officers by contrast favour a deterrent perspective when considering the control of crime in general. (For an account of the criminology of, for example, chief officers, see Reiner 1989a.) However, when considering police deviance they emphasize the complexity of the causal processes which renders problematic simple reliance on a rational deterrence model—precisely the usual arguments of critical criminologists. For example, the Association of Chief Police Officers argued in their evidence to the recent Home Affairs Committee Inquiry into the Police Complaints procedure: 'Complaints by the public are not the only, nor even the major, check on the behaviour of the police.' (Home Affairs Committee: *Minutes of Evidence* taken on 6 June 1989: Memorandum submitted by ACPO, para. 2. 4.)

All sides in the debate about police complaints procedures purport to be primarily concerned with matters of substance. Is the system the one best calculated to achieve the practical objective of minimizing police malpractice? However, it seems arguable that the debate is largely symbolic, that the arrangements favoured by different viewpoints are espoused for what they represent rather than what they are realistically capable of achieving.

This is particularly true with regard to the vexed question of independent handling (investigation and/or adjudication) of complaints against the police, which has been a source of controversy in most jurisdictions for many years. The complaints issue is the Achilles' heel of any organization, and in the police, who are charged with investigating everything else, is the quintessential *quis custodiet* problem. Experience of independent systems of policing complaints against the police seems to suggest they are unlikely to be more effective in sustaining complaints (Goldsmith and Farson 1987: 621–2; Goldsmith 1988; Loveday 1988; McMahon 1988). Support for this is usually based overtly on the belief that it would lead to more effective investigations, but may be better interpreted as concerned with appearance rather than substance. Yet it remains the crucial debating point in the politics of police complaints.

During the last twenty years the systems for handling complaints against the police have become controversial in many countries, usually in the context of scandals about alleged police abuses of power, corruption and/or discrimination (Reiner 1985). These controversies have generated much research, although most of it has been concerned with the legal mechanics of different systems (e.g. Cohen 1985; Brown 1983). There has also been empirical research of a statistical kind examining the nature of complaints, the characteristics of complaints, the correlates of substantiation, and the views of complainants and subject officers (Box and Russell 1975; Russell 1976; Stevens and Willis 1981; Brown 1987; Maguire and Corbett 1989). Complaints have thus been looked at from a variety of points of view, but primarily from one which takes the stand of the complainant, and tacitly assesses 'success' as substantiation of the complaint. Implicitly a form of deterrence theory is deployed: elimination of police deviance calls for enhanced certainty and severity of punishment. The problem with the police handling complaints against themselves is the likelihood of collegiate sympathy with the subject officer by the investigators and adjudicators. Hence the usual call for independent systems for handling complaints.

In this essay we will look at complaints from a different vantage point: that of the chief police officer. In the first place we will look 'appreciatively', presenting the perspective from the inside. We will then compare this perspective to others, and it will be suggested that progress is bedevilled because the different perspectives involved in the complaints process are fundamentally at odds.

THE COMPLAINTS SYSTEM: THE VIEW FROM THE TOP

In this section I will present and analyse the views which are offered by police officers on the system for handling complaints against the police. The account is based on a recently completed study in which nearly all chief constables in England and Wales were interviewed (that is, forty out of forty-three, amounting to a virtual census). The study was intended to probe the careers, backgrounds, and policing perspectives of chief officers in general, to supplement the numerous accounts of 'cop canteen' culture with a picture of 'top cop' culture. (The methods and preliminary results are discussed in detail in Reiner 1988; 1989*a* and *b*; 1990, and will be the basis of a forthcoming book). The study was not focused on the complaints system, but a section of the interview was devoted to discussing the complaints system specifically, and the issues of police management, discipline, and accountability more generally.

The views of chief constables on the complaints system are of particular interest, and offer a contrasting perspective to existing studies of complainants' perspectives (Brown 1987; Maguire and Corbett 1989) and of the views of rank-and-file officers (Maguire and Corbett 1989). Chief constables' perspectives are important in a number of ways. First, they perform a pivotal role in the adjudication of complaints. They decide guilt, innocence, and the appropriate sanction in most cases where disciplinary hearings take place, and sit alongside two Police Complaints Authority members in those rare instances where the PCA directs that a disciplinary tribunal be held. (Maguire's chapter in this volume sets out the formal system.) Second, deputy chief constables have the primary responsibility for complaints investigations, scrutinizing the reports of investigations and deciding on appropriate action (subject to oversight by the PCA). Almost all chief constables (87 per cent) have served as deputy chief constables, and have thus had the crucial experience of carrying the main responsibility for handling complaints within a force. Third, many chief constables have experience of conducting major complaints investigations when they were senior operational officers, and some will have been called on to investigate very serious complaints against other forces while they were chief constables (three were doing so at the time I interviewed them). Finally, chief constables as an organized body are an important pressure group. The Association of Chief Police Officers (ACPO) is a major influence on the politics of decision-making in the criminal justice field. In 1981 the Police Federation, the rank-and-file representative body, came out in support of a completely independent system for the investigation of complaints against the police. This was a remarkable *volte face* after years of opposing such a scheme, and found the Federation uniting with the Law Society and the National Council For Civil Liberties in the police equivalent of the Hitler–Stalin pact. Since then the Federation has been able to maintain the stance of support for completely independent investigation, while vigorously attacking the half-a-loaf of independence which exists in the shape of the PCA. (A unanimous vote of no confidence in the PCA was passed at the 1989 Federation Conference.) In this configuration of political forces, ACPO opposition to an independent system is crucial in maintaining the status quo by preventing independence from being the favoured policy of the major bodies of professional police opinion. The perspective of chief constables is thus of interest both because of their own experience of the complaints system from the top, and because they are pivotal in the politics of criminal justice reform.

In the interviews I raised two questions directly about the complaints process. The first was a general question asking the chief constables what were the main problems (if any) that they saw in the present system for handling complaints against the police. The second asked them specifically for their views on a completely independent system for investigating complaints.

With regard to the first question, most chief constables (70 per cent) did not see any problems in the present system, while the remaining 30 per cent did raise a variety of issues they saw as problematic. Despite this strong vote of confidence in existing arrangements, only a bare majority (52 per cent) rejected the idea of a completely independent system, the main plank of radical proposals for change. Nearly a third (30 per cent) supported a completely independent system, while 18 per cent were undecided, seeing strong arguments either way. Thus the ACPO position of rejecting a completely independent system, while expressing the majority viewpoint, is the subject of quite widespread internal dissent and debate amongst chief constables.

The characteristic chief constable perspective is the predictably Panglossian one: all is for the best in the best of all possible worlds. In this picture the existing system involves firm but fair investigation and adjudication of complaints against the police. Criticism of the system stems from villains and those with ideological axes to grind. It does not represent an anxiety which is shared by ordinary members of the public, but is the monopoly of unrepresentative yet noisy minorities. This is the view of 38 per cent of chief constables who both believe that there are no problems with the system, and reject the idea of independent investigation of complaints. It represents the modal view of chief constables, although not a majority.

The traditional view is summed up by the following quote from the chief constable of a large metropolitan force. He claims that the effectiveness and thoroughness of the present system of investigations is attested to on the basis of long personal experience. Independent investigators could not conceivably match the present standard.

Independent investigation sounds very attractive, but I think it will create more problems than it would solve. It would take a long time to set up a body with the necessary experience and wherewithal to deal with it, because I don't think the people that would staff that would understand the police culture or the police administration. In my experience, when I was at West End Central, and dealt with some pretty hairy discipline inquiries (post Kray and Richardsons) I was successful in preparing the papers on that because I know where to look. An outsider wouldn't know where to go, so anyway he'd be shielding those who were wanting shielding. And again, unless you're investigating historical nuances, you've got to run right quickly before anybody has an opportunity to destroy the traces. Policemen are human beings and there's a self-protect factor, but they couldn't pull the wool over *my* eyes. The bad guys will get away with it far easier than they appear to be doing at the moment, if it was an independent investigation. I remember making a point to the Home Secretary when we were talking about the new Complaints Authority. For God's sake we've got to get it right. We're never going to get it completely right, because there's always going to be a certain grouping of critics that are never going to be satisfied. But you've got to get it right, otherwise morale gets damaged and people's faith is lost. My custom here at the moment is so far right as it will ever be.

It's not without failures or problems—primarily the new Complaints Authority who are still in a learning process. On a personal level, I've made this point to Cecil Clothier [the first PCA Chairman] who I know pretty well: the people that make up the PCA at the moment are too military-minded. They can't understand that when you're dealing with a policeman you're not dealing with a lance-corporal or rating. They have rights that perhaps the services haven't got. That criticism could be levelled at some of our critics: policemen are entitled to the same precepts of natural justice as the next man. However I might have made up my mind an officer is as evil as hell, you've still got to go through the sort of process of justice.

This is the characteristic view of the more traditional chief constables. Their experience convinces them that only police officers themselves can successfully investigate other police. Criticism of the system comes mainly from those who will never be satisfied, so it is pointless to pay it much heed.

From this perspective, the recent support of the Police Federation for independent investigation is seen as a devious ruse. It is supported by the Federation precisely because it will be *less* effective in rooting out abuses. The present system has the twin virtues of effectively sanctioning the truly deviant police officer, while not applying irrelevant standards to minor peccadilloes. Senior police officers have a nose for the really corrupt copper, while having a more sympathetic understanding of the stresses and strains that generate minor misdemeanours. Outsiders would be defective on both counts, and end up being both ineffective and unjust. As another traditionalist (a county chief constable) expressed it:

You are never going to get a complaints system which will satisfy the minority complainers, so therefore you are trying to find something which doesn't exist. That's the starting point. However, you've got to give something that satisfies the vast majority of people. It's almost impossible to come up with a solution that will satisfy everybody. But when the Federation made their recommendation some years ago that it should be an entirely independent body, they knew and I knew that this was an extremely clever ruse. They knew that the chances of it working are very, very slight . . . I mean, so many complaints investigations are crime investigations. Now you know we are police officers with an original authority, not from the Government—we get our authority from the Queen. We are the people charged by the community with investigating crime. I am not quite sure how you can have people other than policemen investigating crime. The truth of it is you can't! So therefore do you have a split arrangement, where the police get on investigating crime, with somebody else investigating the system? The *causes célèbres* which cause all the concern are no more than about five or six a year throughout the country. OK, so there are probably another twenty or thirty that cause some concern locally. But you are really talking about taking a steam-roller to crack a nut. And at the end of the day you're not going to be successful, because unless the decision goes in favour of the complainer then that person isn't going to be satisfied . . .

The fact that the Federation are now asking for that independent system is evidence of the effectiveness of the present system. You ask any member of the other ranks what they feel like when they are being investigated, and the lengths that senior officers go to try and get to the truth. With one exception—it's no good being dishonest about it—that a practical police officer investigating a complaint, where he sees some degree of justification perhaps in a minor assault, human nature means there will be a tendency for him to more readily see the police officer's point of view. But in the more serious cases they are very, very effectively investigated. The problem is satisfying the public that those investigations are impartial and thorough . . . The Federation realizes the hopelessness of the situation of ever getting an adequate method of investigation, because at the end of the day the public do not believe police officers are entitled to the same protection as the ordinary member of the public. Even genuine complainers, when it comes down to it, it is their word against the police . . . To be perfectly honest, the Federation are very concerned with protecting their wrongdoers, as well as those that are only accused of wrongdoing, it seems at times, I wouldn't like to be too harsh on them, but if you speak to people in the Federation at a lower level than nationally you get a different picture. I know that the Chairman and Secretary of my own Federation realize the hopelessness of ever having a fully independent, effective complaints and investigation procedure.

It would be a mistake to conclude that satisfaction with the status quo and rejection of the idea of an independent system are the prerogative only of the more traditional chiefs. Some of the most progressive chiefs also reject the idea of further change because they positively support the innovations introduced by the Police and Criminal Evidence Act in 1984. The provision of facilities for informal resolution of minor complaints, and the mandatory supervision of the investigations of the most serious cases by the Police Complaints Authority, are welcomed by these chiefs as a system which achieves the optimal balance between effectiveness and legitimacy, justice being done and being seen to be done. This perspective is best expressed by one chief of a large metropolitan force with a reputation as one of the most progressive in the country:

I don't support any changes, because now we have got conciliation which is taking away a lot of, I use the word loosely, dross at the bottom. Not dross for the man who made the complaint I know, but we understand the term, you and I, perhaps. The low-level stuff, we are beginning to prune. In terms of independence, I was never unhappy with the policeman's left ball [the Complaints Board], and I am not unhappy with the new Authority. I am only bothered about the perception of it in the eyes of the public. Frankly I don't think the public give a toss. There is a vociferous pressure group that wants nothing short of independence, knowing they won't get it . . . With more serious allegations the PCA does introduce an element of independence . . . We had the shooting of——[a small boy] by PC——. It was about a week I think after the setting up of the PCA, we had that case investigation supervised. We saw it at close quarters, and I don't think the PCA could have done anything differently. I have no quarrel with the way it works at all. I think it is admirable. But we were still criticized for . . . investigating ourselves. I don't know the answer.

Full acceptance of the status quo is thus not necessarily the prerogative of the traditionalists who think independent investigation anathema. It may be a considered conclusion based on positive support for the attempt by PACE to solve the problems by introducing informal resolution of minor complaints and PCA supervision of the investigation of serious allegations. However, the modernist opponents of change share with the traditionalists the perception that this won't satisfy the 'vociferous minorities' of complainants and anti-police critics. There is also a shared perception of many complaints as 'dross'. In any event the problem of public confidence does not in this view warrant further changes in what is now an acceptable system in itself.

We have seen that the majority (70 per cent) of chief constables saw no problems in the present system. Of the 30 per cent who did, these divided evenly between those who saw the problems as being the failure to satisfy the public, and those seeing problems from a police perspective. The problems identified from a police viewpoint were the burden of complaints investigation for the police in terms of expense and manpower, as well as the damage to morale due to excessive bureaucracy and delays in the system.

Perceiving problems in the system usually but not invariably was associated with support for a fully independent structure. However, a few who perceived such problems did not support the change because they thought independence would make matters worse. Conversely, a few who supported change did so because of concern about public confidence but did not see this as based on any real defects in the present systems. In addition, there were a number who were undecided about the question of independence. While recognizing the problems of public confidence and the burden of investigations which were posed by the existing systems, they were unsure whether independence would improve or exacerbate matters. Altogether 30 per cent supported a fully independent system, almost but not entirely coinciding with the 30 per cent who felt there were problems in the present system. Another 18 per cent were undecided, but saw some potential advantages in independence.

The reasons for the view that lack of public confidence was a major concern, but would not be alleviated by independence, are indicated by the following quote:

I have been a deputy chief constable six years and have been responsible for complaints. One is always conscious of the fact that there is a public perception, at least in the minds of a minority, that you are judges in your own court. But I think any former deputy chief constable would say to you that we are probably harsher judges of our own organization. We don't want people in our organization who let the side down, tarnish their cap badge and tarnish mine. So we are probably more ruthless than any other organization. We weed people out who don't live up to standards. Where people misinterpret it is that people sometimes expect officers dealt with where there is no evidence to deal with them, particularly if matters have hit the national press . . . But police are entitled to the same degree of treatment in justice as anyone else. There is a sector of the public who don't believe that, for whatever reasons I don't know, it may be just to suit their own ends. Now, if you were to go as the Federation suggests to a totally independent system, that is the nub of it—how do you get a totally independent investigative body? I know it happens in some parts of the world, Australia for example. I am not so sure you would get the quality of investigation we get now. Because, like it or not, the Police Complaints Board before this, and the current Police Complaints Authority, will in almost every annual report comment on the quality and depth of police investigations. That is our bread and butter at the end of the day. Well, ok— I think there is another thing too. Police officers in trouble, in spite of the Federation advising 'don't say anything', by and large have a greater confidence in one of their own investigating, that they will get a fairer crack than they might from some faceless body. I like to speak from my own experience over a number of years—I can put my hand to my heart here and say to anybody I investigate, it is done in justice, and if he didn't deserve to stay in this force then they don't stay . . . An independent body wouldn't have the total confidence of the British police service, so they have got an uphill struggle in the first place . . . The Federation would say that the amount of criticism they're getting from sections of society saying the police are judge and jury in their own case, let's have a total change. Now I am not sure they are convinced in themselves that it would be better, but certainly it would take away that criticism. My apprehension would be that after two or three years we would still be getting the voices outside saying it is less than just because they are not finding policemen guilty of the offences we feel they are guilty of.

This view exemplifies the argument of those chief constables who, while recognizing that there is a problem of public confidence because police are perceived as judging themselves, reject the Federation solution of complete independence. They are convinced that independent investigators would be less successful at sustaining allegations, because of the blue curtain of silence which would be an even greater impediment to outsiders who are distrusted by the police in the first place. If this is so, an independent system would be a cosmetic change that would not even bolster public confidence in the long run, when it is seen to be unsuccessful in cracking cases where the public perceives complaints to be justified. The fundamental problem in this view lies not in the failure of the system of investigation, but the public's inability to accept the proper rights of police officers who are the subjects of complaints, and the limits this imposes on the prospects of complaints being sustained.

Those chief constables who support the idea of a move to a fully independent system (30 per cent), as well as those who were undecided (18 per cent), did not believe that such a system would be more effective. Like those who opposed change, they believed that the existing system did investigate and deal with complaints as effectively and fairly as possible (though there were mixed feelings about the Police Complaints Authority). Indeed, many of those who supported independence agreed with those opponents of the idea who argued that an independent system would encounter even more obstacles than did police investigators, and would therefore be less effective in practical terms. However, they supported fully independent investigation and adjudication on the grounds that it was necessary in order to achieve public confidence. In other words, it was an innovation with purely symbolic advantages in the battle for public opinion. Operationally it would if anything be less successful than the existing structure. Faith in the intrinsic soundness of the present handling of complaints was universal amongst chief constables.

Where there was deep disagreement was in judging the most effective strategy for securing public confidence. Supporters of independence believed in essence that the demands of legitimacy justified sacrificing a measure of effectiveness in dealing with complaints. Some believed that this was also the position of the Police Federation, while the more cynical felt that Federation support for independent investigation was precisely on the grounds of its lesser effectiveness. The following quotes encapsulate these arguments:

Yes, I would be happy to have the thing entirely independent. I think the principle is, is the scheme acceptable to the general public? If it isn't there's no good carrying on with it. But we've got to ensure that it's not just a small minority of left-wing councillors and odd-ball media and press criticizing, that the criticisms are founded on fact. I don't honestly think the great majority of the public know what the system is now against what it was before . . . The current criticism is emanating from a small group for political reasons, and not based on pure fact showing that the system isn't working, justice isn't being done, the truth isn't coming out. Having said that, my view is that the thing should go. I would be happy to accept a completely independent system. All I am saying is, the present system *is* working . . . I have been an investigating officer and would not risk my professional career to support some idiot who had done something wrong. I want him out. I was brought up in the police service and am proud of the police service. I go for policemen far harder than I would go for a criminal, if he is doing wrong I want him out and exposed. Now I may be a bit weak in that I think all investigating officers are like that. But I think most are, because most deputy chief constables who deal with it are my ilk. Our general view is we don't want wrong ones in the service, so we appoint as investigating officers people who we think share those ideals and are determined to get at the truth and who can investigate . . . If you are investigating a senior detective officer then your choice of investigators is reduced because you've got to have someone who is as sharp as he is . . . I am entirely of the opinion that the present system is honestly and properly done. Whether it is acceptable to the general public is entirely a different matter.

I still believe that we do our best to sort out a lot of rotten apples. We don't need them. There is evidence since I have been in this force that where an allegation was made that a police officer has assaulted someone whilst he was in custody, I can think of three cases where a constable has come forward and given evidence to that effect. So I think the level that is going on in police stations has reduced. Not eliminated—it never will for a number of reasons. Sometimes you might have to hit in response to an attack, it's very difficult to know who is the aggressor. As a rule if you look at our internal disciplinary inquiries it supports my argument that it's not just a whitewash. But I would favour independence in some ways, just to answer our critics. Because they then would say we've really nothing to hide. But quite honestly I don't think they would find out as much about what's happening in the organization as some of our experienced supervisors do, particularly somebody from an outside force. There's absolutely no cover-up or cock-up if you get somebody from an outside force.

All who supported independence were unconvinced of its merits, but felt it essential in public-relations terms. A few expressed great exasperation at the various piecemeal changes introduced over recent years. As they perceived an inexorable drive towards an independent system, they would prefer it to be introduced at once to clarify matters.

What I can't understand is why society, British society, jokes around with this issue. If you don't like the present form of investigation of complaints against policemen, for God's sake get rid of it, but don't wimp about it! I have been away from home, and away from my boss for the greater part of three years investigating complaints with great application, often in very unpleasant circumstances, doing something that I didn't really want to do, but I did it—perhaps even better because I didn't want to do it. I've never spared anybody and I've never spared myself. By all means get rid of it, and I welcome its release. But please do acknowledge that you cannot then introduce a counterfeit system. What I mean is if you intend to exchange a very professional approach with something which will not match it, get ready for the problems. Brace yourself for the substitute! Replace though if you are going to . . . Why the hell society and Parliament messes about with this I don't know! Get on with it! Who wants it? Great, do it, don't wimp about!

The shared view of chief constables, whatever they thought about the policy question of whether an independent structure should be established, was that it would not be able to surpass the effectiveness of internal police investigations. On the basis of their own experience almost all chiefs felt it was likely to be hopelessly ineffective in practical terms.

The system as it operates at the moment is no better than the one that was, and it won't get any better. You will never get it right, because at the end of the day you've still got the dissatisfied customer, no matter what you do . . . It is useful to have an independent element fitted in, but if you look at the Hong Kong system, the Independent Commission against Corruption, I had an enormous amount of dealings with them . . . My experience in Hong Kong was that it didn't work. The relationship between them and the Royal Hong Kong police was that they were head-on, physically came to blows, totally opposed to one another, and totally uncooperative . . . They didn't trust one another one inch, and the result was that the police officers were interviewed by them, and they said nothing, they said 'you prove it!' . . . Unless you change the rules and say police officers must answer or you can comment upon their lack of answering then if they're silent what can you do? If you did change our protection in law there would be great uproar. There is no doubt at all that the police service could destroy a new system overnight, by superintendents deciding when they're asked to investigate, saying 'what do you want me to do, you supervise it, you tell me what you want . . . I've taken a statement, what do you want me to do now?' The service won't do it because it's a pretty honourable organization, and unless they do it properly somebody is going to shout 'whitewash' . . . You end up asking: 'Do you trust us or don't you?' We're more ruthless than outsiders . . . I had an officer here who because he was removed from CID duties decided to take revenge on his detective sergeant. He did this by sending a series of obscene telephone calls to the officer's wife. That matter we detected, it was presented before the Magistrates, he went sick, it was heard in his absence, he was convicted. He then suddenly found he was fit again and appealed. He went before the Crown Court and was convicted on overwhelming evidence, and fined substantially. We had all the psychiatric evidence and all the rest of it and I sacked him, which I presume you would hope I would do. The Home Secretary reinstated him with a caution! I wrote to the Home Secretary and said it amazed me. What standards does he expect from the British police service when he allows people like that man who is a convicted criminal to remain? . . . We can be as tough as we like, but outsiders would let us down.

I honestly believe we are ruthless . . . My basic objection to independence is we will end up with more bad apples still within our barrel than we do now. You have got to get up very early in the morning to catch a corrupt, bent police officer. The old adage, it takes one to know one. Bearing in mind my background in A10 [the internal investigations unit set up at Scotland Yard by Robert Mark] and what have you, I know it's no good a solicitor ringing up saying, 'Detective Sergeant So-and-So, we are investigating a complaint. We will come and see you on Friday at 2, please have your pocket book, your CID diary, and your case-papers available for us.' By the time you get there they'll be gone! . . . Point number two: we are a conservative organization, small 'c'. We are a defensive organization. There will be extra bricks on the ramparts with outsiders, and with a closing of ranks it is going to take a sharp cookie to break through.

In the same way as chief constables' opinions were divided about an independent system, so too they were in two camps about whether the innovation of the Police Complaints Authority was welcome or not. One group of chief constables felt it got the difficult balance between effectiveness and legitimacy right:

The Police Complaints Authority have a very pervasive influence in the investigation of complaints now. I still think it is better for police officers to investigate them. But there is an improved perception of the investigation of complaints since the PCA have taken a higher profile. All chief officers don't approve of it, there are quarrels about demarcation, who is doing what. But I think they are seen to be more in control, and that is important. I've never eschewed the idea of an independent element, but what has concerned me has been the investigation. I don't think in practical terms you would get the sort of investigation police officers indulge in . . . They are the best trained investigators and interrogators and they get to the bottom of it . . . An outside body wouldn't do as well . . . They would say 'we are being blocked', and that would bring more discredit on the police.

An equal number however felt that the PCA was so anxious about establishing its credibility as an independent body that it acted in a heavy-handed way which damaged police morale and alienated the service:

I have had personal disagreements with the PCA when I was a deputy chief about my role in the maintenance of discipline and their role . . . At a most gentlemanly level, we didn't fall out as some of my colleagues have. But I do fall out with Cecil Clothier's pronunciation as head of the PCA when he said to me I don't think you as a chief constable sitting in discipline cases should demand the standard of proof that is required in criminal courts. I said hang on a minute, you are going away from Magna Carta! Let's not move the goal posts unless we do it democratically! We still agree to differ on that. But I shan't do anything! When a man stands in peril in front of me I want it proved beyond all reasonable doubt. Now a particular case where I was involved when I had to have a tribunal—much more good would have been achieved if that guy had stood in front of me with just the two of us and no attribution. He wouldn't ever have transgressed again! As it was I knew there wasn't a cat's chance in hell of ever getting him convicted of anything. He walked, and sort of did that [fingers up] to the whole system . . . We've been subject to so many changes in the complaints procedure in recent years that it's time to let the blokes at the bottom have a bit of a rest, a bit of stability, poor sods! I believe in rooting out wrongdoers ourselves. I have a philosophy as a chief constable that says that if you do your incompetent best I will support you to the end of the road. Even if I give you the biggest rollocking of your life, it will be with dignity and humanity, because I know with your hand on your heart you're not villainous in what you are doing. If you are middle down the road then I will decide in the circumstances how to deal with you, whether I touch your pocket, give you a good rollocking, or whatever. But if you have been utterly disregarding or villainous then I will sack you or demote you. My Federation know that, my force knows that. I am very uncomplicated—that's where I stand.

It was generally felt that the chief constables were and should remain responsible for police discipline. The PCA was resented for activities which threatened to dilute this with the purpose of demonstrating its strength as an independent watchdog:

I am not very pleased that my colleagues will not come out publicly and castigate the Annual Report of the Complaints Authority for the rubbish it is. They categorically claim that they are responsible for police discipline. They aren't at all! They have a responsibility for investigation of complaints against the police, a totally different thing. I mean, in the three and a half years I have been here I have had the unpleasant duty of sacking twenty-two officers. Only three of those cases arose from complaints by members of the public. The other nineteen were the result of internal disciplinary action. One of our problems is that we cannot demonstrate this to the public.

Thus chief constables were unanimously confident about their ability to deal effectively both with complaints and discipline, and to do so with justice to complainants and subordinates alike. The divisions which existed about the desirability of the PCA, or a fully independent system, arose over purely symbolic and strategic questions. What price in effectiveness was worth paying for greater public confidence and trust?

'YOU'RE RIGHT FROM YOUR SIDE, I'M RIGHT FROM MINE':
BARRIERS TO UNDERSTANDING IN THE COMPLAINTS
SYSTEM

There are five key parties relevant to the complaints process: the complainant, the subject officer, the general public as audience (itself internally variegated of course), the rank-and-file of the police force as another significant audience, and police management. All would probably subscribe to a similar general statement of what the system should achieve: justice to complainant and subject officers, by an impartial, thorough, accurate collection and assessment of the evidence indicating the facts in the case. However, operational indices of success for each are different. For the complainant it would be substantiation of the complaint, for the subject officer the reverse. The third-party audiences—the general public and the other police—can only assess the process aspects of the system, and thereby form judgements of its likelihood of reaching the 'right' outcome.

We know from other research (for example, Maguire in this volume) that the views of complainants, subject officers, and the public about the complaints system are generally negative. Complainants are unhappy not only about failure (which most feel, as less than 5 per cent of complaints are substantiated), but about the slowness, secrecy, and user-hostile process. Subject officers, by contrast, feel the experience is unpleasant, stressful, and something to be avoided—even if it won't deter them from their duty of policing as toughly as necessary. Surveys of the general public suggest that an overwhelming majority are unhappy about the police investigating themselves, and most are not confident that such investigations are adequately thorough.

By contrast on the evidence presented in the previous section the one significant party who is happy with the present system is the chief constable. Chief constables all feel ('know' on the basis of their own experience) that complaints are very thoroughly investigated. They are confident of their ability to judge cases, and assess the moral culpability of officers. If left to them, without problems of proof, they are sure that discipline could be maintained. However, in serious cases where proof has to be established (and they accept the justice of the criminal burden of proof for these cases) there are difficulties even for internal investigators. This must be even more true for outside investigators though, who would face tougher, perhaps insuperable problems, in penetrating police barriers of secrecy. So the system, with its imperfections, remains the best possible.

The only major problem they see is the apparent failure to command public confidence. Here there is a division in chief-constable ranks. They are split between those who feel public confidence must be won by an independent system, even at the price of some loss of effectiveness, and those who regard this as throwing the baby out to preserve the bath water. The latter tend to play down the significance of public dissatisfaction with the system by portraying active complainants as disreputable or 'dross'. (This is not borne out by the evidence, which suggests most complainants are 'first-timers' with previously positive perceptions of the police—though this varies with the type of complaint: Maguire and Corbett 1989: 182–92).

The chief constables' confidence that they usually 'know' the right outcome is ultimately as unfounded as the opposing view which 'knows' that many guilty officers escape sanction because of partial and inadequate investigation of police by police. Attempts to assess the effectiveness of complaints systems are necessarily bedevilled by not knowing the 'right' outcome against which to measure the results of cases.

However, if we approach the chief constables' perspective appreciatively and accept that internal investigations are usually as thorough as possible (and this is borne out by studies suggesting that independent review does not normally come to different conclusions: cf. Loveday 1988; McMahon 1988; Goldsmith 1988; Maguire in this volume) this raises an obvious problem. Studies of complainants (while obviously also not knowing the 'right' solution to cases) have been 'struck by the intensity of feelings expressed by complainants. Justifiably or not, many retain a lasting sense of grievance.' (Maguire and Corbett 1989; 189.) If investigations are thorough why do they so rarely result in sustaining allegations, leaving complainants with a sense of grievance?

There seem to be two main reasons why complaints usually fail to be sustained following an internal investigation, and these are indicated by the views of chief constables described above. First, many cases turn on straightforward conflicts of evidence between the complainant and the subject officer(s). In such cases the criminal burden of proof will almost certainly result in the complaint not being sustained. The realization of this, coupled with the intensification of public distrust of the police following a record number of scandals involving abuse of power (Reiner 1990*b*), has led the most progressive of chief officers (notably Sir Peter Imbert) to consider that the burden of proof might have to be changed, and to reconsider the maintenance of the right of silence in the face of disciplinary investigations (Imbert 1989). It is coming to be realized that the crucial issue is not who does the investigating, but the terms on which it is done.

However, a final problem is that many complaints cases are inherently intractable. They are incidents where two rights make a wrong. This was indicated to me by some chief constables who frankly admitted that one reason for opposing an independent system was that in some cases only a police officer could fairly assess the stress and provocations a subject officer experienced, which generated behaviour which outsiders might condemn but was understandable if not completely to be condoned. In other words, many complaints arise from conflicts involving escalating hostility in a mutually inspired vicious cycle which is understandable from both conflicting points of view. However, the actual experience of independent systems does not suggest that the sort of people who would be placed in positions of reviewing police behaviour turn out to be less sympathetic to the police (McMahon 1988). Again this implies that a barrier to greater substantiation of complaints is not the structure of the complaints system but the burden of proof. For where conflicts involve clashes between multiple plausible realities, if proof must be beyond reasonable doubt then the complaint cannot be sustained. All one can say is (in Bob Dylan's words) 'you're right from your side and I'm right from mine'. However, if this result was reached through a negotiated process incorporating the police rank-and-file, but which was more open to the general public gaze and which avoided the obvious taunts of 'whitewash' and 'cover-up' to which the present system lends itself, it could be that all sides would gain (Goldsmith 1990). But a divided world with multiple realities in conflict does not lend itself to happy solutions.

REFERENCES

Box, S. (1983) *Power, Crime and Mystification* (London: Tavistock).

—— and Russell, K. (1975) 'The Politics of Discreditability', *Sociological Review* 23: 2.

Brown, D. (1983) *Civilian Review of Complaints Against the Police: A Survey of the United States Literature*, HORPU Paper 19 (London: HMSO).

—— (1987) *The Complaints Procedure: A Survey of Complainants' Views*, HORPU Paper 93 (London: HMSO).

Cohen, B. (1985) 'Police Complaints Procedures: Why and For Whom?' in J. Baxter and L. Koffman (eds.), *Police: The Constitution and the Community* (Abingdon: Professional Books).

Downes, D., and Rock, P. (1988) *Understanding Deviance* (Oxford: Oxford University Press).

230   *Robert Reiner*

Goldsmith, A. (1988) 'New Directions in Police Complaints Procedures', *Police Studies* 11: 2.

—— (1990) 'Police Misconduct and the Limits of Law', *Policing and Society* (forthcoming).

Goldsmith, A., and Farson, S. (1987) 'Complaints Against the Police in Canada: A New Approach', *Criminal Law Review*, September.

Hagan, J. (1987) *Modern Criminology* (New York: McGraw Hill).

Home Office (1986) *Criminal Justice: A Working Paper* (London: HMSO).

Imbert, P. (1989) 'Glasnost at the Yard', *Police Review*, 1 December.

Kinsey, R., Lea, J., and Young, J. (1986) *Losing the Fight Against Crime* (Oxford: Blackwell).

Lea, J., and Young, J. (1984) *What is to be Done About Law and Order?* (Harmondsworth: Penguin).

Loveday, B. (1988) 'Police Complaints in the USA', *Policing* 4: 3.

Lustgarten, L. (1986) *The Governance of the Police* (London: Sweet and Maxwell).

McMahon, M. (1988) 'Police Accountability: The Situation of Complaints in Toronto', *Contemporary Crises* 12.

McMahon, M., and Ericson, R. (1984) *Policing Reform* (Toronto: University of Toronto Centre of Criminology).

Maguire, M., and Corbett, C. (1989) 'Patterns and Profiles of Complaints Against the Police' in R. Morgan and D. Smith (eds.), *Coming to Terms with Policing* (London: Routledge).

Reiner, R. (1985) *The Politics of the Police* (Brighton: Wheatsheaf).

—— (1988) 'In the Office of Chief Constable', *Current Legal Problems 1988* (London: Stevens).

—— (1989*a*) 'Thinking at the Top', *Policing* 5: 3.

—— (1989*b*) 'Where the Buck Stops: Chief Constables' Views on Police Accountability', in R. Morgan and D. Smith (eds.), *Coming to Terms with Policing* (London: Routledge).

—— (1990) 'Chief Constables: A Social Portrait of a Criminal Justice Élite' in R. Reiner and M. Cross (eds.), *Beyond Law and Order* (London: Macmillan; forthcoming).

Rock, P. (ed.) (1988) *A History of British Criminology* (Oxford: Oxford University Press), and *British Journal of Criminology* Special Issue 28: 2.

Russell, K. (1976) *Complaints Against the Police: A Sociological View* (Leicester: Milltak).

Scarman, Lord (1981) *The Brixton Disorders* (London: HMSO).

Stevens, O., and Willis, C. (1981) *Ethnic Minorities and Complaints Against the Police*, RPUP Papers 5 (London: Home Office Research and Planning Unit).

Taylor, I., Walton, P., and Young, J. (1973) *The New Criminology* (London: Routledge).

Uglow, S. (1988) *Policing Liberal Society* (Oxford: Oxford University Press).

Vold, G. B., and Bernard, T. J. (1986) *Theoretical Criminology* (New York: Oxford University Press).

Young, W. (1986) 'Investigating Police Misconduct', in J. Cameron and W. Young (eds.), *Policing At the Crossroads* (Wellington: Allen and Unwin).

7

The Police Complaints System in Northern Ireland

IVAN TOPPING

THE POLICING CONTEXT

Northern Ireland, or Ulster as it is otherwise known, is a small but sadly troubled region within the United Kingdom, comprising some 1.6 million citizens. Formed as an entity by the Government of Ireland Act 1920 (which was an Act of the British Parliament at Westminster) it was a largely self-governing province until 1972, when its local parliament was suspended and subsequently dissolved because of civil unrest and the inability of that parliament to cope with a worsening security situation. Since 1972 it has been ruled by a process known as Direct Rule, under which the Westminster Parliament has caused the Province to be governed by a Secretary of State, who is a member of Cabinet of the ruling governmental party. For all practical purposes the Secretary of State occupies the position once held by the Northern Ireland Parliament, and there is thus no elected forum in which to initiate legislation or discuss affairs. New legislation comes about largely (but not solely) by way of Order-in-Council under powers granted to the Secretary of State by Westminster. Day-to-day administrative control is exercised by the Northern Ireland Office (NIO) which is a department of the United Kingdom government operating under the control of the Secretary of State, assisted by a number of junior ministers, who have responsibility for particular government departments and functions, including one junior minister responsible for law and order matters (Bell 1987).

The law of Northern Ireland does bear many similarities to that in existence elsewhere in the United Kingdom, but is not in all respects identical. There are major differences in the security field, in that Northern Ireland has always had some form of emergency legislation designed to deal with civil unrest or terrorism. This has granted to the police substantial powers, particularly in regard to arrest and detention, which have no counterpart elsewhere in the United Kingdom.

Any work on Northern Ireland which has as its theme some aspect of policing, and not least complaints against the police, cannot meaningfully enter discussion without putting policing and its practices firmly in the context of 'The Troubles' as they are euphemistically known locally. The term refers to the civil unrest and terrorist violence in the Province, and these have had a substantial impact on both the organizational and functional aspects of policing, particularly in the past two decades.

Since its formation seventy years ago, the Province has experienced a number of periods of civil unrest and terrorism, although most of these were of fairly short duration and limited significance. The origin of these 'troubles' lies in the partition of the island of Ireland by the British government in 1920, and the formation of two separate states. The Republic of Ireland is an independent state, with a predominantly Catholic population, whereas Northern Ireland is an integral part of the United Kingdom, with strong British links and a predominantly Protestant population. Those Catholics remaining in Northern Ireland at the time of partition (who comprised about one-third of the population) resented the Protestant majority's dominance of local and provincial government. Serious disturbances occurred on several occasions with a 'familiar relationship between economic recession and inter-communal strife' (Darby 1983). There were also various bombing and shooting campaigns by the Irish Republican Army (IRA) which was the violent manifestation of extreme nationalism attempting to force the British out of Northern Ireland (Kelley 1988).

In 1968 matters came to a head, with widespread public disorder and sectarian strife arising from a nationalist civil-rights campaign. The police were unable to cope with the deteriorating situation and the British army was deployed in aid of the civil power in 1969. Eventually in 1972 the local parliament was suspended and direct rule from Westminster imposed, with the British army remaining in the Province.

Since 1968, the 'Troubles' in their present phase have attracted considerable international publicity, with security and policing matters receiving particular attention. During this period some 2,850 people have died in the violence, including almost 2,000 civilians and 280 police officers.

However, whilst violence and terrorism are of necessity dominant features in local life it must not be forgotten that large areas of the Province are stable, and to a considerable degree untouched by such events, with life proceeding more or less normally. As a corollary to this apparent normality, routinization of the management of terrorism has meant that during the years since 1968 incremental changes have caused restrictions on many activities. Thus, for example, the civilian population is accustomed to random police (and army) road-stops, and to being stopped and searched in public places. House searches and the cordoning of areas are likewise concomitants in the fight against terrorism, as are security restrictions on movement in connection with parades and gatherings. In short the population has come to expect and accept (with varying degrees of reluctance and animosity) restrictions which in other times and places would perhaps seem offensive.

The presence of the armed forces in Northern Ireland in relation to policing in general cannot be ignored. As already stated there is in Northern Ireland a large number of military personnel (at the time of writing around 11,000) whose presence is due to the continuing threat of terrorist violence. Initially the presence of the military, often in a policing role, caused considerable concern in relation to the constitutionality of their activities, as in certain matters the RUC played a role subordinate to that of the army. In short, it was in contradiction to the basic constitutional notion that the army was subordinate to government, whereas the RUC was independent of it, because for a time in the early 1970s the RUC was in fact subordinate to the direction of the army (Evelegh 1978). This feature undoubtedly caused friction between the police and army.

From 1974 there has been a move towards 'Ulsterization' of security policy, a term clearly explained by the then Secretary of State for Northern Ireland as an intention to restore 'the full responsibility of law and order to the police', a point reinforced on several occasions since. This has involved a decrease in the numbers of British army personnel and an increase in the numbers of police officers, coupled with a locally recruited army regiment, so that although the total number of security personnel has remained fairly constant, the Northern Ireland component has significantly increased. This feature has caused criticism for the reason that the police force draws heavily on the majority Protestant community for its recruits and thus the dominance of the majority community in security affairs and policy-making has been strengthened through Ulsterization of security matters (Hillyard 1983). The army thus now plays a support role to the police, with in some instances joint police and army patrols in difficult areas, and co-operation between the two is evident and acknowledged (Arthur and Jeffrey 1988). Nevertheless the very fact of the army presence does illustrate the difficulties involved in attempting to maintain normal policing roles and standards in certain areas.

THE RUC

Following the partition of Ireland, the Royal Ulster Constabulary was created by the Constabulary Act (NI) 1922 to serve Northern Ireland, with its membership and organization being taken largely from those of the previous all-Ireland force, the Royal Irish Constabulary. Although Northern Ireland remained part of the United Kingdom, the RUC was not entirely similar to forces on the United Kingdom mainland, differing in a number of respects. The force was an armed force, unlike forces elsewhere in the United Kingdom, or indeed in the Republic of Ireland. It had strong militaristic traditions, traceable to the nineteenth century when the Royal Irish Constabulary was responsible not just for dealing with routine policing matters, but also was required to contain civil unrest and political disturbances. And whilst such paramilitary policing would not have been acceptable on the United Kingdom mainland, it became a routine form of policing in the Province after 1922 (Arthur 1986).

In August 1969, as a result of the deteriorating situation, and a recognition that there were deficiencies in the structure of the RUC, an Advisory Committee on the Police in Northern Ireland (1969) was appointed by the then Northern Ireland government to investigate the problems. The Hunt Committee, as it was known, made a number of recommendations for the restructuring of the RUC along the lines of the mainland forces. Various concerns were expressed, including the need for the RUC to lose its militaristic image and security orientation, and for the force generally to be more accountable for its activities if it was to enjoy greater public support, seen as crucial for future stability. Also, as a result of the Hunt recommendations, the force was disarmed for a short time in the early 1970s. The Police Act (NI) 1970 swiftly followed the Hunt

Report and implemented many of its recommendations. Since the time of Hunt the RUC has undergone a radical transformation, increasing in size from 3,200 officers to a current level of around 11,250 full-time officers. In addition, it has moved from being a small paramilitary or colonial-style force to a modern police force supported by the most up-to-date technological and training resources with an annual budget of around £470 million sterling. By United Kingdom standards the force is large in comparison with the area which it serves—the ratio of officers to civilian population is approximately 1 : 142 as opposed to 1 : 411 in Great Britain.

In terms of its response to terrorism the RUC is perhaps best compared in European terms with forces in Spain or Italy. However, because of this response, RUC officers have one of the most dangerous policing jobs in the world, constantly operating in life-threatening conditions (Ryder 1989). Police officers live amongst the civilian population (unlike members of the British army) and face continual threats of bombing and shooting against themselves and their families. It must be borne in mind that the 'Troubles' have spawned terrorist groups on both sides of the community divide and so threats do not come solely from one community group.

The RUC has never, since its formation, enjoyed the full co-operation of all sections of the community (Hillyard 1983). In 1922 there was a recommendation in a Departmental Committee of Inquiry Report on the RUC (1922) that up to one-third of its numbers should be drawn from Roman Catholic recruits, in order to reflect the religious balance in the community, but in fact at the commencement of the present troubles in 1968 only 11 per cent of the force was Roman Catholic and that figure is not thought to have improved at the present time. A large section of the population thus saw the force at that time as closely associated with a government which had, since the setting up of Northern Ireland, been formed from the same party. There were, and still are, frequent accusations of partiality and bias, and in some quarters a feeling that the RUC regards itself as being above the law, and not subject to due process. This has been recently demonstrated by acute controversy surrounding the RUC's alleged 'shoot to kill' policy when arresting terrorist suspects (Stalker 1988).

However, the RUC has demonstrated its impartiality to a considerable degree in recent times, notably for example in 'facing down' Protestant community resentment of the signing and setting up of the Anglo-Irish Agreement in 1985. Consequently its members have become targets for loyalist frustrations in some areas, with officers being forced to leave their homes in areas previously regarded as safe.

In regard to the specific matter of complaints against the RUC, the Constabulary has its Complaints and Discipline Branch, just as do other forces. This was originally formed in 1970 (following the Police Act (NI) 1970) and was located at RUC Headquarters. Since that time it has expanded considerably and by 1981 had become a department headed by an assistant chief constable and divided into seven teams. It is mainly formed from middle-ranking officers, not least for the reason that under the relevant regulations investigation of complaints must be carried out by a person who is at least of inspector rank, or two ranks above the accused. At the present moment it comprises approximately sixty police officers and thirty civil servants.

INFLUENCES ON THE COMPLAINTS SYSTEM

Any change in structure, or in legislation affecting the police in Northern Ireland, is obviously subject to considerable comment and scrutiny, from sources within and without the Province. The local political culture has been described by Arthur as one of 'distrust and despair' (1986: 347) and involves predictable reactions from the different communities. Thus when the most recent changes in the system of police complaints were announced in 1986, they aroused adverse comment from all sides. They were seen, on the one hand, as going too far in the direction of liberality and accountability and as pandering to the minority community. On the other hand they were seen by some interests as being insufficient to tackle effectively a perceived lack of impartial investigation. The diversity of opinion was thus so great that all groups were dissatisfied to a greater or lesser extent.

Since 1985 the Anglo-Irish dimension in policing has been to the fore in an attempt to ensure public, and particularly minority community, confidence in the administration of justice. The result has been that many decisions have been subject to the scrutiny or approval of the government of the Republic of Ireland through the Anglo-Irish Inter-Governmental Conference, which meets periodically. Article 6 of the Anglo-Irish Agreement allows the Irish government to 'put forward views and proposals on the role and composition of bodies appointed by the Secretary of State for Northern Ireland', which clearly includes membership of the Independent Commission for Police Complaints. When this body was formed by the Police (NI) Order 1987, its membership was subject to the approval of the Republic's government, and a Code of Conduct has resulted from pressure issuing from the Conference. Thus London, Belfast, and Dublin are all involved in decisions in this sphere.

European and other similar influences on policy- and decision-making must also be taken into account. Since the beginning of the present phase of the 'Troubles' there has been intense scrutiny of the way in which events within Northern Ireland are conducted. The various interest groups have, for example, always been concerned with the effect of the European Convention on Human Rights on events in Northern Ireland. Thus the Northern Ireland Office will on the one hand seek to ensure (so far as is possible) compliance with the provisions of the Convention whilst those suffering some diminution in their rights will look to the Convention for redress. The government of the Republic of Ireland is in this connection an interested party and has been responsible for action against the government of the United Kingdom under the terms of the Convention. The first action in connection with breaches of the Convention which occurred in Northern Ireland during the present phase took place in 1972 when the government of the Republic of Ireland brought an action against the government of the United Kingdom alleging ill-treatment of terrorist subjects during interrogation. This resulted in a finding against the United Kingdom government of a breach of Article 3 of the Convention, amounting to 'inhuman and degrading treatment'. More recently in 1988 it was a defendant to allegations, again by the government of the Republic of Ireland, of excessive detention periods for terrorist suspects.

Amnesty International has also maintained an interest in events. In 1977 it made a formal Mission (or visit), and although, according to their Report, the delegates 'were impressed' by the machinery for handling complaints against the police, nevertheless they felt that aspects remained 'deficient in practice'. The International Committee of the Red Cross is also involved and its delegates have made many visits to Northern Ireland.

These external influences have had their effect. For example, following the Amnesty International Mission in 1977, a Committee of Inquiry into Police Interrogation Procedures in Northern Ireland was set up, known as the Bennett Committee, and made wide-ranging proposals to protect prisoners in custody, whilst at the same time seeking to prevent spurious allegations against officers. These procedures were in advance of those employed elsewhere in the United Kingdom, and the introduction in early 1990 of legislation for Northern Ireland along the lines of the Police and Criminal Evidence Act 1984 in Great Britain has caused no particular difficulty to the RUC in this respect, other than in terms of training. Most of the anticipated safeguards have already been built into the system.

ADMINISTRATION AND CONTROL OF THE RUC

Incidents such as complaints of ill-treatment or of excessive use of force, when dealing with crowds, through use of riot-guns (or 'rubber bullets' as their ammunition is popularly known) all generate much publicity and raise questions as to who is responsible for taking decisions leading to such events. For example, during the early 1980s there was, as previously mentioned, a series of incidents in which terrorist suspects were shot rather than taken into custody, thus raising the spectre of a 'shoot to kill' policy. This resulted in the infamous 'Stalker Inquiry' and once again raised the question of whether or not such a policy existed, and if it did, who had initiated it? Accordingly oversight and control of the RUC and its activities occupy much attention.

Within Northern Ireland there are three groups concerned with the administration and/or control of the RUC: the Police Authority for Northern Ireland; the RUC through its chief constable; and the Secretary of State for Northern Ireland. The relationship between these three is 'at once simple and complex, formal and informal, direct and indirect and single and multiple', and is difficult to describe adequately, as much of the relationship depends on practices which have evolved over the years and have no statutory basis (Oliver 1987). There are regular meetings between the three groups to provide a forum in which discussions on matters of common interest may take place, which is to be contrasted with the situation on the United Kingdom mainland, where such tripartite discussions are apparently a rarity.

There is prima facie a similarity between Northern Ireland and

Great Britain in the way in which the RUC is subject to constraint and oversight by a public body, as occurs with other police forces in the United Kingdom. Under both the Police Act 1964 (applying to Great Britain) and the Police Act (NI) 1970 (applying to Northern Ireland) the chief constable of the area has responsibility for the 'direction and control' of the police force, with the Police Authority for the area responsible for 'an adequate and efficient' police force. Clearly operational direction can be constrained by budget and from time to time budgetary considerations can dominate operational matters. For example in 1988 there were problems arising from overspending on operational budgets, resulting in reductions in RUC overtime payments and consequently in manpower. Budgetary considerations were also responsible for the closure of a number of small police stations, and substantial reductions in the strength of the RUC's traffic and community relations branches.

But in reality differences are greater than is apparent. The Police Authority for Northern Ireland is not composed of the same type of representation as elsewhere in the United Kingdom, but reflects instead the political and other realities of the region (Dickson 1988). The present Authority was created following the Hunt Report in 1970, and its membership is, as far as practicable, intended to be representative of the various community and other groups. These representatives are not however elected representatives but are appointed by the Secretary of State. Even this actual representation falls short of the proclaimed wish of the legislature with, for example, the Social Democratic and Labour Party (which is the main constitutional nationalist party) never having been willing to put forward a representative; and more recently the Northern Ireland Committee of the Irish Congress of Trade Unions, which is the Province's umbrella trade-union organization, has been unwilling to participate. Since 1970 two of the Authority's members have been murdered by terrorists and one resigned in 1986 as a result of threats to his life. Much of the work of the Authority takes place in comparative secrecy and little is made public other than basic decisions, which is in contrast to the work of Police Authorities in Great Britain.

Under Article 15 of the Police (NI) Order 1987, (which replaces s. 12(1) of the Police Act (NI) 1970) the Authority is required to keep itself informed of the complaints system amongst other matters. Although it has not ever taken a lead role in relation to the system it does have a Complaints and Public Relations Committee which periodically deals with such matters. Its investigatory role is confined to investigating complaints against 'senior officers' (i.e. those above the rank of chief superintendent).

Formerly under the Police Act (NI) 1970 it had the right to refer a public-interest matter to tribunal but this right was exercised only once between 1970 and 1987. In that case an allegation of police ill-treatment during an interrogation eventually, and after much public debate, became the subject of a tribunal of inquiry set up under the Act. Substantial technical problems on the compulsion of witnesses were encountered, and in this particular respect the legislation was found to be defective. The consequence was that the Police Authority was unable to play a meaningful role in dealing with complaints using this means, and the tribunal system under the Act was not tested again. There were calls for its reform both by the Police Authority and the previously mentioned Bennett Committee on Police Interrogation Procedures but it was not until the introduction of the 1987 Order that the system was in fact changed. Article 8 (2) of the 1987 Order empowers the Police Authority to submit to the Independent Commission for Police Complaints any matter which is itself not the subject of a complaint, providing that it is in the 'public interest'.

In addition there was, and still is under the 1970 Act, a provision whereby the Police Authority may require the Chief Constable to submit to the Authority a written report on such matters as may be specified. Whether this has been used in relation to complaints, and how frequently, is not known.

The Authority has been the subject of comment for its apparently passive role, particularly in relation to complaints, and the view has been expressed that it should have been more proactive in such matters, perhaps even by publicly expressing its concern (Walsh 1983). Such concern may have been expressed in private sessions or meetings but public information is restricted to reports that the Authority keeps itself informed of the workings of the complaints system through its Complaints and Public Relations Committee at its monthly meetings. It has been suggested that the Authority is responsible *inter alia* for the maintenance of police morale in a difficult situation, and that public airings of unease about the complaints system or police activity would serve no useful or positive purpose in this respect (Dickson 1988).

The Secretary of State for his part, has formal, but limited legal powers under the Police Act (NI) 1970, for example to approve the Police Authority's recommendations in respect of senior RUC appointments. Also he may require the chief constable to submit to him reports on any matter.

This relationship between the Secretary of State for Northern Ireland and the chief constable is simple to state in theoretical terms, but less easy to describe in practice. During the time of the former Northern Ireland Parliament when there was no Police Authority and the Minister of Home Affairs of the then Northern Ireland government was responsible for the RUC, there was considerable criticism of the relationship between the minister and the head of the RUC, on the basis that decisions were often taken purely for political reasons. Since the reorganization of the force in 1970 there has been a distancing of the RUC from political influence and most notably under the direction of Sir John Hermon, Chief Constable of the RUC from 1980 to 1989, contact with local politicians of all parties was kept to a minimum. In fact, between 1981 and 1984 Hermon had no contact with any local politicians in order to avoid claims of undue influence, particularly by politicians representing the majority Protestant community. Also in terms of dealing with demonstrations and public order problems, the RUC has taken positive steps to be seen as acting even-handedly.

But whilst the chief constable is responsible for all operational matters, the government, through the Secretary of State, has a role in the evolution and control of security policy, and it would be naïve to consider that policy and operations can be absolutely discrete. In theory the chief constable can conduct his activities in whatever manner he chooses, but if no account were to be taken of political realities, then even greater difficulties would be encountered. For example the use of baton rounds as a means of crowd control has led to considerable complaint from politicians and community leaders and it is obvious that continued or excessive use of this tactic would at some stage call for political intervention.

Another example occurred during the mid-1970s, when there were numerous allegations of RUC mistreatment of people being questioned in connection with terrorist incidents, in particular at one RUC holding centre at Castlereagh. The political significance of these allegations was such that eventually the Secretary of State found it necessary to appoint the Bennett Committee of Inquiry to look into police interrogation procedures, resulting in sweeping changes in the way in which suspects were dealt with. Whilst theorists may maintain that the method of dealing with suspects during questioning is a purely operational matter, there is nevertheless a wider political context to be considered, and when the established channels of dealing with such complaints are ineffective (that is, reports to the Police Complaints Commission, and the Director of Public Prosecutions, and internal inquiries), then the time may be appropriate for intervention by government politicians who are seeking a change in operational direction or tactics. As a final resort, politicians may of course seek to implement legislative change, in order to ensure conformity with a political wish.

THE COMPLAINTS SYSTEM

Following the partition of Ireland in 1920, separate police forces were established in the Republic of Ireland and Northern Ireland. The RUC in the north continued to operate under much of the pre-partition legislation, including those provisions relating to complaints against the police contained in the Constabulary (Ireland) Act 1836. Section 24 of that Act provided for an examination 'on oath into the truth of any charges or complaint preferred against any (constable) or any neglect or violation of duty in his office'. Terms used remained undefined and there was no accompanying Code of Practice. Investigation of complaints was not mandatory, but simply empowered the Inspector-General (as the head of the RUC was then styled) to investigate a complaint if he chose to do so.

These complaints provisions lasted until 1970, when the Hunt Report made sweeping recommendations for reform of the RUC, including changes in the complaints system, in order to bring the system in Northern Ireland into line with that which had operated in England and Wales since 1964. Hunt was critical of the system as it then existed, including the very small number of such complaints investigations which had taken place in preceding years, and hinted at suppression of complaints, and defective recording procedures.

The Hunt Report was not the only public manifestation of unease with the complaints system, and the Cameron Report, also issued in 1969, which enquired into the civil disturbances of the period and its causes, included in its findings a statement that part of the immediate cause of the disturbances was an ineffective complaints system. Cameron was concerned with the need for public confidence in the force, and 'that any inquiry should be wholly unbiased and that it should be in impartial hands'.

As a result of these findings and other pressures for reform, the Northern Ireland government incorporated many of the provisions found in the Police Act 1964 in England and Wales into the Police Act (NI) 1970. The Northern Ireland Minister of Home Affairs, Mr Robert Porter, was, however, prepared to suggest in respect of the provisions on complaints that the 'procedure proposed will be an advance on the rest of the United Kingdom since it incorporated the best features of the existing English and Northern Ireland procedures together with the gist of the recommendation of the Cameron Report'. Interestingly, his point was reinforced some five years later in the Gardiner Report on Civil Liberties and Human Rights in Northern Ireland (1975) which said: 'In fact the procedures for investigating complaints against members of the RUC are already more thorough than those at present in existence anywhere else in the United Kingdom.'

The 1970 Act placed a statutory requirement on the chief constable to cause the investigation of a complaint and, 'unless satisfied that no criminal offence has been committed', to send the report to the Attorney-General and in turn to the Director of Public Prosecutions (DPP).

In 1975 a working party on the handling of complaints against the police was set up in Northern Ireland. Curiously it had no specified terms of reference, but established its own on the basis of two relevant documents. The first was a government communiqué issued after tripartite talks amongst different interest groups at Sunningdale in December 1973, in which there was reference to the fact that an independent complaints procedure for dealing with complaints against the police would be set up. The second document was the government's 1973 White Paper on the future of government in Northern Ireland which referred to 'appropriate arrangements with an independent element for ex post facto reviews of the handling of complaints against the police to conform with those the Government is planning to introduce in Great Britain' (Northern Ireland Constitutional Proposals 1973). It is clear from the Working Party Report that in spite of the fact that members wished 'to consider possible innovations to take account of the distinctive features of the problem in Northern Ireland', nevertheless they were in effect totally constrained by the situation in Great Britain. In fact they were not prepared to present a report until the Home Secretary had announced a revised scheme for England and Wales. The Working Party was:

agreed at the outset that taking account of the guideline . . . and bearing in mind the links between the RUC and police forces in Great Britain . . . and the broadly similar statutory backgrounds, including provisions for mutual aid, the general principles of any new procedures to be introduced in Northern Ireland should as far as practicable conform with those introduced in Great Britain. (Black Report 1976.)

It therefore came as no surprise when in 1977 a Police Complaints Board was set up under the Police (NI) Order 1977, on lines similar to the English and Welsh system, which had existed since 1976. The Board provided an independent element in dealing with complaints against the police, with its main role being to consider the results of the investigation by the police of a complaint, and to decide if any subject police officer should be charged with a disciplinary offence, if the police themselves had not instituted such a charge. Thus the Board could if necessary direct the bringing of such charges, and might in some circumstances be involved in the subsequent hearing. It did not play any part in the bringing of criminal charges against officers, which was a matter for the DPP. Board Reports were at pains to emphasize that only in a small number of cases did they find it necessary to direct or recommend charges independently of the decision of the police investigation. The system was acknowledged as faulty in different respects. There was, for example, no system of informal resolution of complaints and a somewhat ponderous formal system was used for all complaints, no matter how trivial. The Police Complaints Board indicated its approval of informal disciplinary action, involving advice or warnings where this seemed appropriate, although such practices were clearly outside their remit.

During the late 1970s and early 1980s the government once again came under pressure to change the complaints system and various interest groups attempted to put forward their points of view. Some of these influences were external to Northern Ireland, but obviously shaped the government's thinking in relation to the police service, most notably Lord Scarman's Report on the Brixton disorders in 1981, which recommended the introduction of an independent element into the actual investigation of a complaint. There were also local pressures. For example, in October 1982 the Committee for the Administration of Justice, a locally based pressure group, made representations to the responsible Minister of State, in the knowledge that consideration was being given to possible changes in the system in England and Wales as a result of the Royal Commission on Criminal Procedure Report (1981). Similarly, the Northern Ireland Police Complaints Board submitted a memorandum to the Select Committee for Home Affairs (dealing with England and Wales), presumably in the belief that their suggestions might indirectly and ultimately affect the position in Northern Ireland.

In 1985 the government issued a Consultative Paper on Police Complaints and Discipline through the Northern Ireland Office which arose 'out of the Secretary of State's undertaking to consult with interested parties on whether and how changes might be made to the system for investigating police complaints in Northern Ireland, reflecting both the new procedures adopted for England and Wales, and the particular challenges of policing in Northern Ireland' (Northern Ireland Office 1985).

In 1986, the then Parliamentary Under-Secretary of State for Northern Ireland with responsibility for law and order matters, Mr Nicholas Scott, announced further reforms in the complaints system. This step was a consequence of changes introduced in the system in Great Britain through the Police and Criminal Evidence Act 1984 and in line with the government's commitment to legislative parity throughout the United Kingdom. In a later explanatory document accompanying the proposals for change in the legislation, the government pointed out that the system for handling police complaints in Northern Ireland was similar to that existing in England and Wales prior to early 1985 before the most recent legislative changes which had applied only to England and Wales. Since the system had been overhauled elsewhere it therefore seemed 'vital to maintain parity between the professional standards and procedures of the RUC and those of other United Kingdom police forces', and so 'the complaints system which applies to the RUC is being overhauled in a similar fashion'.

The result was the Police (NI) Order 1987, which is in general similar to the Police and Criminal Evidence Act 1984 in England and Wales, although it does contain important differences and has also taken account of changes suggested by interested parties during the consultation period prior to its implementation. It thus provided for the abolition of the Police Complaints Board and its replacement by an Independent Commission for Police Complaints. The Commission, comprising some eight members, formally came into operation in February 1988 and has extensive powers.

The new legislation attempts to right, amongst other matters, a major defect identified (in the NIO's 1985 Consultative Document on the system) as the lack of independent check on investigations. So although complaints under the new system are still investigated by a police officer (either from the RUC or some other United Kingdom force) there is now in most instances independent supervision of that investigation. Under the Order the Commission has extensive powers of supervision—in some cases, such as those involving death or serious injury, the requirement for the Commission to supervise is mandatory, whereas in other instances it possesses the right to supervise at its discretion. Police officers who are to conduct the investigation, whether from the RUC or another United Kingdom force, are subject to the approval of the Commission and so the Commission could, if it wished, insist on the appointment of an investigating officer from outside the RUC.

The Commission is not involved in dealing with complaints of a minor nature, which are those not justifying a criminal or disciplinary charge. In such cases, and providing the complainant agrees, a new informal resolution procedure is introduced where the matter is investigated and dealt with internally through warning or advice to the officer concerned. This procedure is in contrast to the involvement in all complaints of the former Police Complaints Board and in minor matters (which were not actually complaints) on a statutory basis.

Formerly, under the Police Act (NI) 1970, there was provision for matters affecting the police interest to be the subject of a tribunal. This particular provision owed its existence to the 1969 Cameron Report which had recommended, amongst other things, a tribunal to investigate complaints against the police, in the belief that this would support public confidence in a fair and impartial system. In point of fact, and as previously mentioned, between 1970 and 1987 only one such tribunal was constituted and it foundered in a welter of technicalities and complementary court actions arising from either lack of direction in the legislation, or poor drafting. The NIO's Consultative Document on the matter in 1985 was not in favour of increasing the powers of such tribunals, but in the end the new legislation now provides reserve powers to the Secretary of State and the Police Authority to refer to the Commission any matter which, though not the subject of a formal complaint, indicates the possibility of a criminal or disciplinary offence by an officer, and which affects the public interest. Thus major public interest cases, such as allegations of ill-treatment of prisoners, could be the subject of an investigation supervised by the Commission, although no formal complaint had actually been made.

Under the Order a complaint may be made by a member of the public, or on behalf of a member of the public without the written consent of the complainant. This provision did not form part of the NIO's original proposals but arose apparently as the result of representations. Its inclusion can be seen to an extent as an indicator of the level of distrust in which the RUC is held in some circles, in that many people will simply not have any contact with the police, personal or otherwise, and feel unhappy at the prospect of close encounter, particularly through visiting a police station to make a complaint.

As previously stated, the legislation is not identical to its mainland counterparts. The principal differences are as follows. There is nothing in England and Wales corresponding to the reserve power vested in the Police Authority or Secretary of State to refer public interest matters to the Commission for supervision of an investigation. In Northern Ireland all complaints which require a formal investigation must be referred to the Commission (unlike in England and Wales) but then the Commission has a discretion in some cases as to whether or not it should supervise such investigation. Thus all complaints are subject to the Commission's overview. And finally the Commission has the power of oversight of informal resolution of complaints, which must of course be referred to them.

It is worth noting one other change in complementary legislation, which was part of the total package of revision of the complaints system. Police disciplinary regulations are made under the Police Act (NI) 1970, and under this legislation new disciplinary regulations were enacted, providing for discriminatory practices by police officers on grounds of racial origin (as in England and Wales), religious belief, or political opinion to be a disciplinary offence. These provisions obviously exceed those contained in corresponding legislation in England and Wales and 'take account of the particular sensitivities of Northern Ireland'.

The 1987 Order has not enjoyed total support but has been the subject of criticism from politicians and other interest groups. Strong criticism has come from within the RUC, the group most obviously affected by the Order. This criticism has been voiced through the Police Federation for Northern Ireland, which is the RUC's representative body for all ranks below Superintendent level, or, in other words, the body which represents the majority of rank-and-file officers. The Federation has made clear the fact that it feels it was not properly consulted on the legislation arising from the government's 1985 Consultative Document, stating: 'The lack of meaningful consultation with the Federation at the formative stage of the present proposals, and their lack of proper discussion, does not inspire the necessary confidence of the Federation in the proposals.' For its part, the government, in a letter to the Federation, felt that it had 'taken [the Federation's] comments very seriously' but it is obvious that the government and Federation are at variance on many points.

The order, not unexpectedly, has failed to satisfy many interest groups, particularly and very importantly police officers, and only in the longer term is RUC distrust of the provisions in the legislation likely to be assuaged.

LAW AND PRACTICE

It thus seems that on the surface the legal provision for dealing with complaints against the police in Northern Ireland is much the same as elsewhere in the United Kingdom. However, the legislative provisions which apply cannot be viewed in isolation, and must be set against not only the day-to-day practice, but also the legal infrastructure in Northern Ireland, in order to establish if any hypothesis of similarity holds good.

Under the Police (NI) Order 1987 a complaint 'means any complaint about the conduct of a member of the police force which is submitted by, or on behalf of, a member of the public'. It does not extend to a complaint 'in so far as it relates to the direction or control of the police force by the Chief Constable', and so there is no recording of (or indeed requirement to record) any complaint in connection with the administration, efficiency, or procedures of the force, a point reinforced in the NIO guidance documentation on the handling of complaints. Thus only complaints of conduct are recorded.

As previously pointed out there are substantially more police officers per head of civil population in Northern Ireland than elsewhere in the United Kingdom—about three times as many in fact. Whether this fact alone accounts for the high level of complaints against the police is not altogether clear, but in 1987 complaints averaged approximately one per 600 head of population in Northern Ireland as opposed to one per 2,800 head of population in Great Britain.

The success-rate for complainants is low, and if the number of complaints substantiated in any one year is taken as a percentage of complaints dealt with in that year it can be seen as varying between 0.6 per cent in 1987 and 1.6 per cent in 1985. This very limited success-rate can be viewed either as reflecting a low rate of credibility in the complaints received for investigation, or, somewhat more cynically, as revealing the inadequacies and deficiencies of a system in which a police force investigates itself (Walsh 1983).

A substantial number of complaints in each year are incapable of receiving investigation. This occurs very simply because the complainant cannot be identified, or refuses or fails in some way to co-operate with the investigating officers, or to provide information necessary for the purpose of the investigation. Under the RUC (Complaints etc.) Regulations 1988, the Police Complaints Commission may grant dispensation not to proceed with the investigation in such circumstances. (A similar power existed for its predecessor, the Police Complaints Board.) As can be seen from Table 1, dispensation is granted in a substantial number of instances, representing a major proportion of cases.

The 'Troubles' have affected the complaints system, in that some complaints arise from matters related to them, rather than from more routine policing events, and the same system for complaints is applied equally to all complaints, irrespective of their origin. It is possible only to a limited extent to separate statistically the types of complaint into those which are Troubles-related and those which are not, due to available information being restricted to the most overt form of relationship. Complaints relating to the arrest, detention, and interrogation of suspects under emergency legislation were thus noted and monitored separately by the Police Complaints Board and currently by its successor, the Complaints Commission. The Commission deals with complaints notified to it by the RUC following investigation, and figures extracted from annual reports

TABLE 1. *Complaints against the RUC*

	1985	1986	1987	1988	1989
Cases of complaint received	2,254	2,785	2,396	2,291	2,484
Complaints dealt with	3,237	3,415	4,083	2,893	3,989
Number of complainants	1,781	1,837	2,217	1,967	2,534
Complaints withdrawn	1,349	1,474	1,381	1,068	2,404
Complaints fully investigated	1,270	1,120	1,793	899	1,384
Complaints incapable of investigation	618	821	909	870	1,115
Complaints substantiated	51	40	26	39	58
	(1.6%)	(1.2%)	(0.6%)	(1.3%)	(1.4%)

Notes: Under 'Cases of complaint received', it should be noted that more than one complaint may be involved in each case received.

All other headings refer to complaints which were dealt with etc. in that year, but which may have been initiated in that or an earlier year.

TABLE 2. *Proportion of complaints related to emergency legislation*

	1985	1986	1987	1988	1989
No. of cases	232	251	286	170	319
% of total cases	12.4	11.6	11.4	12.0	14.0

indicate that a fairly consistent proportion of the workload concerns complaints by those arrested under emergency legislation, as set out in Table 2. Within these figures, allegations of physical ill-treatment or assault constitute the largest single group (as they do for 'ordinary' complaints). Such allegations of assault or physical ill-treatment during interrogation have been a prominent feature of the present troubles since 1971 and in that year allegations of mal-treatment were particularly prevalent during widespread internment of terrorist suspects, resulting in two inquiries into the investigations of interrogation practices by the security forces. It also caused the United Kingdom government to appear as a defendant before the European Court of Human Rights in connection with these allegations. In 1976, in its evidence to the Black Committee (responsible for setting up the Police Complaints Board) the Northern Ireland Civil Rights Association vented its disquiet in the matter, saying: 'Complaints in the main do not arise from public settings . . . but in the interview rooms of police stations . . . where no question of force should ever arise.'

The Association of Forensic Medical Officers was also concerned at this time, and during 1977 made repeated representations to the Police Authority for Northern Ireland in connection with instances of such maltreatment.

On an international level Amnesty International, in its 1978 Report of a Mission to Northern Ireland made in the previous year, stated: 'The machinery for the handling of complaints against the police in Northern Ireland is elaborate. Although the delegates were impressed by this, they noted that, in respect of allegations of criminal misconduct by police officers—such as assault during interview—the machinery remains deficient in practice.' (Amnesty International 1978.) Bowing to these pressures, the government appointed a Committee of Inquiry into Police Interrogation Procedures, under Mr Justice Bennett, which investigated the matter thoroughly, and reported in 1979. Bennett was of the opinion that whilst throughout the United Kingdom there was an increasing propensity to complain against the police, there was also, particularly in Northern Ireland, evidence of a 'co-ordinated and extensive campaign' to discredit the police through a series of complaints. The Committee's proposals were twofold in nature—attempting to protect both persons in custody against harm, and police officers against false and exaggerated claims.

As a result of the recommendations, all persons in the custody of the RUC are now the subject of elaborate precautions to ensure their well-being. The chief constable of the day introduced a variety of measures including a code of conduct for officers dealing with those arrested on suspicion of having committed an offence under emergency legislation. Thus persons arrested under such legislation for serious offences (which are almost always but not invariably terrorist-related) are taken to one of a number of designated holding centres where their custody and interrogation are monitored by closed-circuit television; they have the right to frequent medical inspections and access to legal representation, as well as a number of other precautionary measures being taken. The Police Complaints Board as a matter of policy took a close interest in complaints emanating from such sources and, as previously indicated, has monitored these separately as has its successor.

A Police and Criminal Evidence (NI) Order 1989 has recently been enacted. It is based on, and similar to, the Police and Criminal Evidence Act 1984 in Great Britain, and contains a number of precautionary provisions dealing with those detained. When fully implemented early in 1990 its provisions are not likely to cause a requirement for change as extensive as occurred in Great Britain prior to the introduction of such legislation there, as many of the features of the 1984 legislation and its concurrent Detention Code already are in operation in Northern Ireland. In some respects the procedures currently in operation are more comprehensive, due simply to the nature of the situation in Northern Ireland.

There is close liaison within the complaints system between the investigating and supervising bodies and the Director of Public Prosecutions for Northern Ireland. Under the Police (NI) Order 1987 the chief constable, the Police Authority, and the Independent Commission for Police Complaints are all required or empowered to forward copies of their reports at various stages to the DPP. For his part the DPP already possesses powers under the Prosecution of Offenders (NI) Order 1972 (the legislation which originally created the office of DPP and granted powers) to require the Chief Constable to forward to him facts and information with respect to 'such other alleged offences as the Director may specify'. In line with these powers the DPP has requested the chief constable to send him details of all alleged criminal offences committed by RUC officers, which thus requires any allegation of criminality to be reported. The Black Committee was of the opinion that every allegation was subject to independent DPP scrutiny. In extreme cases this would mean DPP scrutiny for cases where the allegation was simply that and not an actual event, and even without any reasonable prospect of conviction in the courts.

CONCLUSION

Since the advent of Direct Rule in 1972 the RUC has operated as a separate force in much the same way as the other United Kingdom police forces. The differences, however, between the RUC and other forces lie in the context in which it must operate, and also in the indigenous body of law applicable to the Province which controls its actions.

Although the general law of Northern Ireland is in many respects similar to that elsewhere in the United Kingdom, there are nevertheless varying degrees of difference in that local law has not always replicated the law elsewhere. These differences are particularly acute in the security and policing areas and since the 1920s there has existed for the RUC, and continues to exist, a large body of legislation specifically designed to deal with terrorist violence. The legislation in some cases has given to the RUC a range of powers and, of course, obligations not always found elsewhere. Administrative and procedural arrangements also vary, and there are elaborate arrangements designed to ensure that complainants against the RUC are fairly treated. Recent reforms in the complaints system have been made against this background.

The present Conservative government's policy is to ensure parity of the systems in police complaints between Great Britain and Northern Ireland. This was stated recently in an open letter by the Minister of State then responsible for the RUC to the Chairman of the Police Federation, when he said: 'As often with Northern Ireland legislation, our policy on this matter has been one of broad parity with England and Wales, with some modifications to suit local circumstances.' There are, however, reservations in many sections of the community about slavish adherence to generalized political ideals which result in the transferring of legislation from one jurisdiction to another, without the full impact of such transfer having been fully explored. Reservations about this policy are not confined to questions regarding security-related legislation, but extend to many areas, including, for example, labour affairs. But in spite of such misgivings many pieces of legislation originating in Great Britain are being replicated in Northern Ireland.

The most recent changes have simply attempted to bring the police complaints system in Northern Ireland into line with that in Great Britain, but at some point the question must be raised as to the wisdom of this continued transplanting of legislation. To comparative lawyers the concept of transplantability is already familiar and its dangers are well recognized. There can be little argument with the proposition that an introverted legal system is in itself unhealthy and that an outward-looking system can lead to many better things—for example a clearer insight into the deficiencies and failings of one's own system, or again the promotion of social change and the formulation of identical national and international standards. But as has been pointed out by Kahn-Freund, 'we cannot take it for granted that rules or institutions are transplantable . . . any attempt to use a pattern of law outside the environment of its origin continues to entail the wish of rejection'. Or again, 'the effects of similar legislation may differ significantly as between the two differing settings' (Kahn-Freund 1974).

Whilst legal provision for complaints procedures in Northern Ireland therefore largely resembles that found elsewhere in the United Kingdom, such provisions cannot be viewed in isolation from their surroundings and must be read in conjunction with both day-to-day practice and their interaction with complementary legislation. Only then can any hypothesis of similarity bear scrutiny.

Northern Ireland is, and has been since 1968, subject to civil unrest and terrorist violence on a scale unprecedented elsewhere in the United Kingdom or indeed most of Europe. But in some respects the government of the United Kingdom in its approach to parity in policing matters, including police complaints, is operating under dual standards. There is on the one hand frequent complaint by the United Kingdom government that European and other attitudes to human rights are too liberal and not based on actual experience of a climate of terrorism. On the other hand the government is imposing policing standards upon Northern Ireland which have evolved in different circumstances. To equate, for example, the problems of the nationalist minority community in Northern Ireland with those of black minority communities in Great Britain is obviously a gross over-simplification.

Clearly there are high political stakes involved in the discussion and implementation of any change in policing standards and methods, particularly so in the context of the Anglo-Irish Agreement and the involvement of the Republic's government in Northern Ireland's affairs. But the wisdom of blind continuance down the road of parity without perhaps greater attempts to understand the full implications of change is open to question. In view of the fact that the social and political structures of the jurisdictions do vary considerably, there seems little point in imposing laws which, although prima facie bearing a resemblance to those elsewhere, operate differently because of differences in practice and adminis-tration, and the legal infra-structure.

REFERENCES

Amnesty International (1978) *Report of a Mission to Northern Ireland.* (London).

Arthur, P. (1986) 'Policing and Crisis Politics in Northern Ireland', *Parliamentary Affairs* 39(3): 341–53.

Arthur, P., and Jeffrey, K. (1988) *Northern Ireland Since 1968* (Oxford: Blackwell).

Bell, P. N. (1987) 'Direct Rule in Northern Ireland', in R. Rose (ed.), *Ministers and Ministries* (Oxford: Clarendon Press).

Darby, J. (1983) *Northern Ireland: The Background to the Conflict* (Belfast/New York: Appletree/Syracuse).

Dickson, B. (1988) 'The Police Authority for Northern Ireland', *Northern Ireland Legal Quarterly* 39(3): 277–83.

Evelegh, R. (1978) *Peacekeeping in a Democratic Society* (London: Hurst).

Hillyard, P. (1983) 'Law and Order', in J. Darby (ed.) *Northern Ireland: The Background to the Conflict* (Belfast and New York: Appletree and Syracuse).

Kahn-Freund, O. (1974) 'Uses and Misuses of Comparative Law', *MLR* 37: 1–27.

Kelley, K. J. (1988) *The Longest War: Northern Ireland and the IRA* (London: Zed Press).

Northern Ireland Government (1922) Departmental Committee of Inquiry, *Interim Report* Cmd. 1, and *Final Report* (June 1923) Cmd. 34.

Northern Ireland Government (1969) *Report of the Commission Appointed by the Governor of Northern Ireland* Cmd. 532 (Cameron Report).

Northern Ireland Government (1969) *Report of the Advisory Committee on the Police in Northern Ireland* Cmd. 535 (Hunt Report).

Northern Ireland Office (1985) *Police Complaints and Discipline: A Consultative Paper.*

Oliver, I. (1987) *Police, Government and Accountability* (London: Macmillan).

Ryder, C. (1989) *The RUC: A Force under Fire* (London: Methuen).

Stalker, J. (1988) *Stalker* (London: Harrap).

United Kingdom Government (1973) *Northern Ireland Constitutional Proposals*, Cmnd. 5259.

United Kingdom Government (1975) *Report of the Committee to Consider Measures to Deal with Terrorism in Northern Ireland*, Cmnd. 5847 (Gardiner Report).

United Kingdom Government (1976) *The Handling of Complaints Against the Police: Report of the Working Party for Northern Ireland* Cmnd. 6475 (Black Report).

United Kingdom Government (1979) *Report of the Committee of Inquiry into*

Police Interrogation Procedures in Northern Ireland, Cmnd. 7497 (Bennett Report).

United Kingdom Government (1981) *Royal Commission on Criminal Procedure*, Cmnd. 8092.

Walsh, D. P. J. (1983) *The Use and Abuse of Emergency Legislation in Northern Ireland* (London: Cobden Trust).

8

Police Accountability and Civilian Oversight of Policing:

An American Perspective

WERNER E. PETTERSON

You must first enable the government to control the governed;
and in the next place oblige it to control itself.

James Madison, *The Federalist Papers*

INTRODUCTION

Harvard University's John F. Kennedy School of Government periodically convenes meetings of police executives and criminal justice educators who debate issues of policing. A report regarding one of these issues, 'Police Accountability and Community Policing', begins:

> The accountability of individual police officers is a fundamental issue for police executives. This is fitting: police officers are the public officials society has authorized, even obliged, to use force. Ensuring that police officers use that warrant equitably, legally, and economically on behalf of citizens is at the core of police administration. The enduring concern of police executives to ensure accountability in American policing is a reflection of their professional commitment. (Kelling, Wasserman, and Williams 1988: 1.)

Professionalism and accountability are wedded in a matrix of police reform which has shaped thinking about policing in the United States of America for most of the twentieth century.

During this and the previous century, exposés of police corruption ignited public outcries denouncing the scandalous behaviour of police officers and demanding reforms. In the midst of the public clamour, a political axiom was employed: when an obviously popular solution is not available, appoint a commission. In 1931 President Herbert Hoover appointed the National Commission on Law Observance and Law Enforcement, better known as the Wickersham

Commission. The Commission examined several issues, including whether immigrants were more criminal than native-born Americans, and concluded by suggesting that the failure of police officers to perform their duties was primarily attributable to 'the insecure, short term of service of the chief or executive head of the police force and in his being subject while in office to the control of politicians in the discharge of his duties' (1968: 1). Exorcising this evil was to be accomplished, according to the Commission, by instituting a civil service system which would produce the best qualified police executives and select a better calibre of police officer. Training, of course, would be necessary in achieving a professional police force.

In tandem with these administrative reforms, the law was becoming a two-edged sword for police officers; they had become its enforcers and, at the same time, subject to its judgement. This ironic development has had insidious consequences in establishing means for police accountability.

Calls for professionalism and accountability were renewed in the 1950s and 1960s as police departments became embroiled in the civil rights movement. News media reports, especially the nightly television news programmes, portrayed police officers as oppressors of civil rights. Police were captured on film and in the public's eye as the 'Bull Connors' of the Alabama State Police, with dogs snarling at civil rights demonstrators, and then as participants in a 'police riot'[1] at the 1968 Democratic National Convention in Chicago. In both cases, as in the past, police and politicians were seen as cohorts in a demonic enterprise; also, then as before, citizens' complaints alleged police brutality and racial and ethnic discrimination.

Another presidential commission was appointed, the President's Commission on Law Enforcement and Administration of Justice; its 1967 report concluded that there were few easy answers to the problems of policing, but focused particular attention on the order-maintenance duties of police officers. It went so far as to suggest that necessary police–community relations efforts might 'interfere with other objectives and needs of the department . . . may mean that police officers will have somewhat less control over occurrences on

---

[1] Hon. Otto Kerner, Governor of the State of Illinois and Chairman of the National Advisory Commission on Civil Disorders issued a report which criticized the Chicago Police Department for its handling of street demonstrations during the National Democratic Party Convention. The report described the police response as a 'police riot'.

the street or even lead, in the short run, to apprehending fewer criminals' (1967: 206).

The works of James Q. Wilson (1968), William Ker Muir, jun. (1977), and Michael K. Brown (1981) call into question some of the underlying assumptions which inspired the police reform movements and help us better to understand the nature of police work. These scholars have proposed that an examination of the daily job of police officers and, in particular, the discretion they employ in carrying out their duties would be more constructive in identifying means for accountability.

In his book, *Working the Street*, Michael Brown points to two characteristics of the movement to professionalize American police departments: 'Autonomy from local politics and internal discipline are . . . the twin pillars of police professionalism'. (1981: 47.) Unfortunately, these distinguishing characteristics have fostered alienation from the community. In response to overcoming problems associated with the first pillar, police departments are returning to beat patrols and instituting 'community policing' whereby the police and community are collaborators in addressing crime and the maintenance of order. Kelling *et al.* suggest that community policing 'focuses on the substantive issues of problems, crimes, and quality of life in the neighborhoods' (1988: 4), and becomes the avenue through which the police are accountable to the community.

The purposes of this article will be to examine the dilemmas of police reform, to consider civilian oversight as a corrective response to the perceived and real inequities associated with the second characteristic of police professionalism, internal discipline, to compare the forms of civilian oversight in the United States of America, and to propose recommendations about civilian oversight and a model agency.

DILEMMAS OF POLICE REFORM

On 13 March 1972 Dr Herbert Odom, a black dentist, was stopped by Chicago police officers for not having a light over his rear licence plate. Later, Dr Odom complained that when he protested about being searched on the street the police used excessive force by throwing him against the car's bonnet and handcuffing him so tightly that his wrists were injured. There had been other stories of police abuse of black citizens; however, this complainant was a close friend of the Hon. Ralph H. Metcalfe, US Representative, of Chicago's first Congressional District. Mr Metcalfe, who was also black, came to his friend's aid by demanding that the officers be disciplined. Throughout his political career he had been an integral part of the Democratic political machine, headed by Richard J. Daley, Mayor of Chicago. This incident was to have two dramatic repercussions. First, Mr Metcalfe's harsh criticism of the police department and then of the city's political leadership for ignoring the black community's grievances would open the door for the rebellion of black politicians which eventually culminated in the 1983 racial schism of the Democratic Party and the election of Chicago's first black Mayor, Harold Washington. Second, the Chicago Police Department's internal complaints procedure was transformed so that civilian employees became the administrators and investigators of a citizens' complaints office within the Chicago Police Department, called the Office of Professional Standards.

Representative Metcalfe formed a panel of prominent community representatives to hear testimony about police misuse of authority. The black community responded with an outpouring of stories of abuse, including some told by black police officers. The panel invited the City's departmental executives, all of whom refused to appear or offered excuses; Police Superintendent James B. Conlisk, jun., was 'out of town'.

Following four days of hearings, the panel released a report which faulted the internal complaints system for being secretive and biased in favour of police officers; according to the panel's statistics, 1.4 per cent of investigated complaints were sustained (1,156 complaints were investigated and 16 were sustained). A Chicago Bar Association study was cited which found that the police department had no guidelines for judging the thoroughness of police investigations and that there were no written guidelines for evaluating the evidence, except for the general direction to 'find the truth'.

The panel recommended that 'an entirely new independent investigating agency reporting its factual findings to the Police Board for imposition of discipline by them should be created' (Metcalfe Report 1973: 12). Its proposal emphasized three elements: (*a*) the new agency should conduct independent investigations and determine facts and that the public have access to the investigations; (*b*) only certain complaints should be handled by this independent body—complaints of excessive force, other violations of civil rights, and corruption or criminal activity by police officers; (c) the imposition of discipline should remain the responsibility of the Police Board and the Police Superintendent.

One year later, a recently appointed police superintendent, James Rochford, announced that the Office of Professional Standards (OPS) had been organized through his executive order and would function as an extension of his office. The OPS would reflect the advice of the Metcalfe panel by limiting the types of complaints for investigation to those of excessive force and shots fired by police officers, and the imposition of discipline would remain the responsibility of the Superintendent and the Chicago Police Board. From its inception, the objectivity and integrity of the agency's staff were challenged; its critics pointed to those who were relatives of Chicago police officers, including the wife of former superintendent Conlisk. For the next ten years OPS was discredited in minority neighbourhoods because of its lack of independence and poor performance in pursuing complaints investigations.

During the 1983 mayoral campaign, Harold Washington, the only black candidate, promised to abolish OPS and replace it with an external complaints procedure. However, his police superintendent appointee, Fred Rice, convinced the newly elected Mayor not to fulfill that campaign promise but instead to grant him the opportunity to reform the existing internal mechanisms. As of 1990, the citizens' complaints process remains as originally implemented in 1973 with modifications in its administrative structure and more freedom from its past nepotism.

The above scenario has been and continues to be played out in major United States' cities, but not with the same script nor with the same outcome. Redressing citizens' grievances has gone through an evolution in most cities and the changes have been generally more substantial than in the case of Chicago. Police shooting incidents or violent confrontations, followed by the exoneration of police officers, has been a lightning-rod in police–community relations and the point at which the depth of alienation is revealed. It has been in the aftermath of these circumstances that new or revised complaints procedures have been instituted. Another set of circumstances bringing about similar reforms has been the exposure of police corruption and its cover-up.

These crisis periods are only one catalyst in the changing relationship between police officers and the citizens they serve.

Police–community relations have fluctuated over the years for various reasons. When the nation has become anxious about crime and social disorder citizens have reached out to their police for protection. In the 1970s, our preoccupation with 'law and order' prompted the infusion of millions of government dollars into police departments; it was also a period when the civil rights fervour was in retreat. Many of the initiatives commended in the 1967 presidential report, such as police–community relations units and affirmative action in police recruitment, were called into question. It was during these years that some civilian review boards, such as the ones in Philadelphia, and Washington DC, collapsed due to the benign neglect of political leadership and police opposition.

Wayne A. Kerstetter (1987) provides another perspective; he begins with a summary of research into the role of police officers which was prompted by Egon Bittner's definition of policing as 'the distribution of nonnegotiably coercive force employed in accordance with the dictates of an intuitive grasp of situational exigencies' (1970 36–47) and then expanded upon by Michael Brown, William K. Muir, jun., and Hubbard T. Buckner (1967). Kerstetter writes that 'the inappropriate use of coercive force is the central problem of police misconduct' (1987: 149). With this as background, he reviews the ways in which American society has attempted to control the misuse of this force: prosecutors, judges, news media, police administration, and external review agencies. Wayne Kerstetter's conclusion is that 'it is preferable to leave the work of complaint processing and decision making with the police department' (1987: 178). His justification is the following:

Why should the police department be given the authority to be the primary mechanism for complaint review? The departmental administrative structure has by far the greatest potential for efficient, effective action whether to prevent, to investigate, to adjudicate, or to punish police misconduct. Ultimately the major purpose of any system should be to prevent inappropriate conduct by police officers. The department has great capacities to contribute to this goal by the actions it takes in hiring, training, and supervising employees, and by the care it exercises in adopting policies and procedures which minimize the likelihood of misconduct. The first line supervisor is the person who can contribute the most—in informal but extremely effective ways—to discouraging inappropriate conduct. (1987: 178).

Although he argues against any external involvement in complaints processing because it would 'substantially reduce its [police department's] motivation to address problems and individuals before they get out of control' (ibid.), Kerstetter does advise that there be 'a meaningful external monitoring of the police review' (p. 180) which presumably means that civilians would be involved in examining and commenting upon the thoroughness and fairness of the internal complaints process.

One of the sources used by Dr Kerstetter in portraying the dimensions of police discretionary powers is Brown's *Working the Street* which never speaks to the question of who should discipline the police. It provides an explanation for developments in police–community estrangement and raises concerns as to whether internal control can, in fact, be efficient and effective. Brown states that the core argument of his book 'is built around the idea that police discretion is to be understood in terms of an enduring conflict between the uncertain requirements of police work and the demands of administration for control' (1981: 9).

This working environment of 'uncertainty' refers in part to the ambiguous nature of law which an officer is called upon to enforce and to the community's disparate interpretations of order which an officer is required to maintain. Both tasks are conditioned by the 'prevailing moral consensus of society' (p. 37) which defines and permits the enforcement of laws and the ordering of society. In addition, police work is further complicated, in the United States, by the ever-expanding heterogeneous quality of our communities, which is no longer confined to major urban areas.

In explaining police–community isolation, Dr Brown offers this analysis:

one might view the evolution of the American police as a moving away from a concept of 'personal authority', rooted in the character of a policeman's relationships with the community being policed, to a concept of 'impersonal authority', which is tied closely to the legitimacy of the state and based on a concept of the police as dispassionate servants of society. (p. 38.)

Brown attributes this shift to the professionalization of American police departments:

What the police actually do, though, depends on both their understanding of the community's expectations of the proper use of police authority and their own sense of what should be done. The link between what a community thinks should be done about crime and disorder and what the police actually do is always tenuous, but under police professionalism it has become even more so . . . A professional police force does not serve a community by responding to the unique and particular needs of its different segments; rather the police serve by controlling crime and enforcing law in the community as a whole. The police are more than servants, they are professional servants. They stand above the community and assume the responsibility for interpreting and judging what are the serious problems of crime and disorder that a community faces and what should be done about them. (p. 56.)

It should be acknowledged that what Brown described as a professional police department is not what is meant in today's description of professionalism as offered by the proponents of 'community policing'; in the latter case, the community is not a client, but a partner. Once again, to quote from the article by Kelling *et al.*:

It [accountability to the community] implies a new relationship to the community in which police departments establish an understanding with communities. This can take several forms. One form is for the community to be brought into policy-setting procedures—a practice pioneered during the 1960s by Chief Robert Igleburger of Dayton, Ohio. A second form of new relationship to the community, but not necessarily exclusive of the first, is for both police and citizens to nominate the problems with which police and citizens will deal, the tactics that each will use to address those problems, and the outcomes that are desired. (1988: 4.)

Although Brown briefly recognizes this new trend (1981: 12), his analysis rests on what he saw as professionalism in the 1970s.

As new initiatives surface which are designed to bridge police–community isolation in a systemic manner, rather than the superficial approaches of previous community-relations efforts, police and citizens will mutually participate in the community's politics; that is, they will be partners in guiding and influencing government policies on police-related matters. Since a common understanding would be reached, which would clarify each party's expectations of the other about the enforcement of laws and the maintenance of order, the conflicts associated with the uncertainties of police work could be significantly alleviated.

The second pillar of Brown's definition of police professionalism—internal discipline—and the subsequent conflict for police officers in coping with the 'demands of administration for control' remain troubling in coming to terms with police misuse of their discretionary powers. Brown's analysis is:

any assessment of the impact of administrative controls on the behaviour of patrolmen must set within the context of the ongoing tension between hierarchical and peer group controls within police departments. Due to the conflict between these two systems of control, police administrators have only marginal control over the discretionary choices of patrolmen (p. 97).

This 'bifurcation of internal control' has these consequences:

Police administrators and field supervisors have enormous influence and control over administrative matters, the enforcement of rules, the allocation of organizational resources, training standards, assignments, promotion requirements, and so forth. They have little influence or actual control over the routine decisions made by patrolmen. (1981: 99.)

The extent to which this bifurcation has become institutionalized can be seen in Pittsburg, Pennsylvania, where the internal control process of the Pittsburg Police Department has become a peer review. Police officers involved in disciplinary matters go before a trial board of three of their peers. When a complaint is filed, a new trial board is chosen from among the Fraternal Order of Police (FOP) membership and the board members do not rank higher than lieutenant; the board's decision, which does not involve police management and cannot be appealed, is final. A recent, controversial incident has renewed community efforts to change the complaints system. Its critics, including political leaders, say that the procedure predictably favours the accused police officers. One political leader, State Representative Thomas J. Murphy, jun., said: 'We need a balance in order to protect both rank and file and management. The present system doesn't encourage professionalism' (Philadelphia Inquirer, 30 June 1989: 1); he has introduced legislation to change the present system which was instituted by the State of Pennsylvania thirty years ago.

The conflict between rank-and-file and management over discipline can be seen in other ways. When management announces a new policy which police officers believe makes them more vulnerable to complaints, they will overtly or covertly challenge the police executives. An illustration of this occurred in the Dayton, Ohio, Police Department during the period referred to by the Harvard report (Kelling *et al.*, 1988). Chief Robert Igleburger issued a new firearms policy which set tighter restrictions on the use of deadly force and grew out of community involvement. The new policy came down the chain of command to the lieutenants and sergeants who sat on it until the day after a Dayton police officer was shot; on that day, the new firearms policy was read at roll call. The middle managers very effectively undercut the administration's efforts to control its officers' use of deadly force and demonstrate its accountability to the community.

Kerstetter's justification for internal complaints processing assumes that supervisors are able to discourage police misconduct. Brown, on the other hand, observes the limitations a supervisor faces in controlling his or her subordinates:

> The power that field supervisors possess is narrowly bureaucratic, and can only make life uncomfortable for patrolmen. They have no power to fire patrolmen; they cannot influence what a man is paid; and the rewards they convey are usually limited to minor pats on the back in the form of commendations. What field supervisors can do is to harass and coerce patrolmen by strictly enforcing rules . . . the chief problem in this regard . . . is that strict enforcement of rules can cut him off from the sources of information he vitally needs. (1981: 107.)

Police officers initially resist all forms of performance critique because it is seen as 'second-guessing' what he or she has done; nevertheless, officers will not openly refuse supervisory direction but can adroitly evade it.

The hesitancy of supervisors to second-guess a fellow officer taints administrative decisions about complaints. For instance, when adjudicating the merits of a complaint there are a number of options, one of which is 'unsustained', that is, there is insufficient evidence to validate the complaint or exonerate the officer. It can be a legitimate decision, particularly when one considers the one-to-one complaints where there are no witnesses. But it can become a convenient escape mechanism for administrators who are reluctant to pursue an investigation or find against a police officer.

Before moving on to the issue of civilian oversight, Brown's closing comment about the limits of police reform is worth considering because it poses the dilemmas of police reform and then recommends an approach for police accountability. For contextual purposes, he has just tendered four models for police reform: the police-making model, the professional model, the community control model, and the team policing model:

> Each of the proposals for reform we have examined is limited, for each finally comes up against the contradictions of police work and the

consequent police culture . . . If the limits to reform are to be found in the uncertainties of police work, part of the difficulty may rest with the interpretation the police have placed on their functions. Perhaps . . . change ought to begin with a reconstruction of police work. In particular, it is suggested that the crime fighting 'law and order' stance of the police ought to be replaced with the conception of the police as providers of human services . . . To talk of the police as 'social workers with guns' is not just a contradiction in terms, it is grossly misleading since it implicitly . . . obscures the coercive and political role of the police. An emphasis upon service delivery in police work only cloaks the coercive function of the police in humanistic shibboleths; it does not eliminate the coercive powers of the police and it will not control them; particularly for those subject to abuses of police power . . . What is needed is a system of institutions which will permit continued reflection on the ends of police work and encourage responsiveness, while forcing the policemen to re-examine continually the contradiction between the ends he serves and the means he uses to attain them. (1981: 303.)

CIVILIAN OVERSIGHT

I would suggest that civilian oversight should be a part of the 'system of institutions' for reflecting upon the ends of police work and for providing a structure in which a police officer can reflect upon the 'contradictions between the ends he serves and the means he uses to attain them'. An officer's reflection would be more than a philosophical exercise, it would be a participatory experience with citizens in ferreting out the contradictions that may exist in a specific incident where the officer has exercised his or her police powers and then has been accused of abusing those powers in the process.

Before going any further, I offer a definition of civilian oversight: In the management of citizens' complaints against police officers, a government entity is constituted through a legislative or administrative act which mandates citizens' participation in the processing of these complaints, from the initial filing of complaints through to the disposition of complaints.

This definition is particularly applicable to the United States of America where such agencies are created by acts of legislators or administrators; whereas, in other countries, the enabling authority is the purview of the legislature or parliament. Also, in the United States, civilian oversight agencies are primarily the creation of local government, either of city or county; there are a few exceptions[2] where local agencies have been instituted by state legislatures. The federal government has not established such an institution; policing is a local government function, with statutory and regulatory powers ascribed to the state government.

Traditionally, police executives and police associations have opposed civilian oversight. Police executives willingly establish police advisory committees which are meant to be forums for police–community dialogue; however, in too many cases, these committees are made up of persons who are already friendly, if not infatuated, with the police. Police associations have been aggressive in their opposition; if one wishes to observe how politically active police can be, the campaign surrounding a public referendum about civilian oversight is an exemplary arena. In this effort, they have had some successes, most notably the 1966 defeat of the New York City referendum. In the legal arena, the police-association challenges have met with few successes; in fact, their only successes have been in limiting the powers of civilian oversight, such as in the State of California.[3] However, those law suits which have sought to overturn the establishment of civilian oversight agencies have all failed; the basis of this litigation has been the allegation that such an agency violates a contractual agreement between the city and the police association. A typical scenario has been for a lower court to agree

---

[2] In the aftermath of exposés of police corruption, state legislatures have intervened and imposed commissions or boards as means of reforming local police departments. In the late 1800s, the State of Wisconsin established the Milwaukee Fire and Police Commission which controls most personnel decisions, including the selection of police chief. The legislation mandated that the police chief's position was to be a life-time appointment, the rationale was to eliminate political interference. Recently, the State rescinded the life-time appointment requirement. In the early 1900s, the State of Missouri passed legislation creating police commissions for the cities of Kansas City and St Louis; police corruption prompted the State's intervention.

[3] The State of California passed legislation, known as 'The Police Officers' Bill of Rights'. The statute prohibits the releasing of any information about police disciplinary decisions; therefore, a person is not to receive any information about the disposition of their complaint. In practice, there are California cities where such information is provided to complainants. However, when the San Francisco Police Officers' Association challenged the Office of Citizen Complaints for releasing aggregate statistics of complaint dispositions the Superior Court of California ruled that the statistics could not be released. The Court cited The Police Officers' Bill of Rights: *San Francisco Police Officers' Association* v. *Superior Court* (1988), 202 CA3d, pp. 191–2.

with the police association's allegations, but then for an appellate or supreme court to reverse the lower court decision.[4]

The police argument opposing civilian oversight is: 'If you have not been one of us, you cannot comprehend the "uncertain requirements" of our work; therefore, you are unqualified to judge our performance.' Superficially, and not so superficially, this contention has merit; on the other hand, our society does not adhere to such a standard when judging a person's behaviour. A 'jury of one's peers' has never been literally interpreted. It is also the height of cynicism to assume that a person from a different occupational or cultural background is incapable of making reasonable decisions about another's actions.

When discussing the issue of civilian oversight, I usually tell this story:

One early spring afternoon, a farmer went out to look at his fields to see how long it would be before he could begin to plough and plant. As he walked along a hedgerow, he heard the frantic cries of a young bird, which he discovered in the tall grass; it had fallen or been pushed from a tree. After picking up the injured bird, he decided to take it home, out of the cool night air, and nurse it back to health. But, as he headed back home, he realized that his wife would never permit him to bring it into the house. In the midst of fretting over what to do, the farmer stepped into a pile of cow manure. Then, an idea struck him. He bent down and placed the bird in the middle of the warm manure, hoping it would help the bird survive the cool night air. He headed on home. Half an hour later, a red fox entered the field in search of a meal and soon found the bird. In one swallow, it devoured the bird. The moral of this story is: the motives of the person who places us in what appears to be a stinking situation may be more in our interests than those of the one who wants to get us out.

This story is told so as to caution police officers not to assume that persons who serve as members of civilian oversight agencies are

---

[4] The Cleveland Police Patrolmen's Association (CPPA) filed suit against the Cuyahoga County Board of Elections so as to nullify a public referendum sanctioning the creation of a Police Review Board. The CPPA contended that the referendum's wording was misleading and confusing and that such a Board would violate the City's employment contract with the CPPA. A Court of Common Pleas in Cleveland upheld the CPPA's allegations and ordered the City to abandon its plans for a Police Review Board. The City of Cleveland appealed against the court's decision to the Ohio Court of Appeals which reversed the findings of the lower court. Subsequently, the Ohio Supreme Court agreed with the Court of Appeals' decision: *Paul Jurcisin et al.* v. *Cuyahoga Board of Elections et al.*, Appeal by the City of Cleveland, 2 Oct. 1986.

Machiavellian antagonists whose decisions will have catastrophic effects upon police authority and morale. Although, there is meagre research[5] into this police opinion, what is available indicates that civilian oversight has not caused such consequences. As cogent and persuasive as those points sound, they probably would not convince most police executives and officers.

The other side of this debate, of course, contends that an internal police disciplinary system is inherently partial and its results suspect because the 'blue code' will never permit the close scrutiny of an officer's behaviour. Proponents of civilian oversight argue that it would bring objectivity and credibility to the complaints process.

There has been enough evidence garnered through litigation and commissioned investigations to corroborate this contention. Even the most bizarre and tragic behaviour has been characterized as 'aggressive police work', which sanctions such activity and fails to recognize abnormal behaviour within the police department. Or consider those occasions when a chief executive has publicly announced, before his department has completed its internal investigation, that the officer's actions were 'apparently justified'. Such police responses have become the impetus for civilian oversight. A more telling caveat is that police officers may be willing to complain of another officer's misuse of police property, or laziness, or absence from duty, or receipt of preferential assignments, but rarely will they complain of another's brutality or corruption. When an officer does come forward with a complaint of brutality or corruption by a fellow officer, he or she is shunned and the entire police force closes ranks in silence and denial. This reticence is apparently attributable to their fear of civil liability, to their uncertainty as to whether they have acted similarly at one time or another, and to the 'bifurcation of internal control' where the administration's response is seen as punitive, rather than instructive. These may be valid explanations for the 'blue code'; however, for those who have not had their grievances redressed and for public officials who insist upon police accountability, civilian oversight becomes an alternative to internal discipline.

[5] The Perez (1978) research looked at police misconduct review systems in six jurisdictions and his interviews with police officers in Berkeley, California, revealed that a morale problem did not exist because of the City's Police Review Commission. Joseph Lohman and Gordon Misner (1966) reached the same conclusion after interviewing police officers in Philadelphia, Pennsylvania.

These dichotomous arguments may have their merits and may stand on their own; unfortunately, they do not afford an opening for conciliatory dialogue.

Since it often emerges in the midst of police–community confrontation and public accusations of police misconduct, civilian oversight can take on the image of an 'avenging angel', at least in the minds of police officers and some citizens. Its activities will certainly lead to the disciplining of some police officers, but such a restricted definition of its functions would be counter-productive and eventually disabling.

Another approach in defining the role of civilian oversight would be to broaden the frame of reference; its disciplinary responsibilities would not be diminished, but it would exist within a larger context. A possible approach can be inferred from a suggestion made by Michael Brown about the basis of police authority: 'The ability of the police to sustain their moral authority is problematic. The moral consensus upon which the legitimate authority of the police is based is rarely widespread as often presumed in an economically dynamic and socially heterogeneous society such as America.' (1981: 37.)

Although a community's moral consensus cannot be categorically declared and can be elusive, a crucible for clarifying the terms of this consensus could be civilian oversight, where citizens and police officers debate the ends and means of policing in relation to specific circumstances raised by a complaint. As individual complaints are examined, the acceptable limits of police practices in enforcing laws and maintaining order can be better delineated. Such an approach to civilian oversight would offer the opportunity for conciliating differences between police and citizens and for clarifying the community's moral consensus as to what is the appropriate police response to crime and disorder. The results would minimize the ambiguities faced by police officers as they are called upon to serve in our culturally diverse communities and would offer a complaints procedure for citizens which was free of the real and apparent inequities of the internal complaints procedure.

FORMS OF CIVILIAN OVERSIGHT

The multiplicity of civilian oversight mechanisms in the United States of America renders precise comparative analysis difficult. General categories have been developed by other scholars which are helpful in discerning patterns (Kerstetter 1987; Goldsmith 1988; West 1987). Therefore, what I am about to propose as forms of civilian oversight is, in part, unoriginal but also, in part, offers a new formulation of what has been previously known as the monitor style of civilian oversight.

Two ends of a theoretical spectrum depicting citizens' complaints procedures could be: the internal complaints procedure, with no civilian involvement, on one end, and the external complaints procedure, with no police involvement, on the other end. The former exists in numerous American cities but there are no examples in the latter. The existing external complaints agencies interrelate with police departments at different stages of the complaints process. A Police Executive Research Forum (PERF) survey of 101 United States' police departments, published in 1987, reported that 83.9 per cent considered their complaints procedures to be of the internal police variety. In between these two points, I would suggest that there are three other forms of citizens' complaints systems, each of which involves civilians.

The following is the PERF report's description of the *Internal Police Review*:

internal review of complaints may be undertaken either exclusively by an independent specific unit within the police department, on a local level by an officer's supervisor, or by a combined approach in which local supervisor investigation is supplemented by the involvement of an independent specific unit in those cases which are either more serious, potentially complicated or extremely time consuming (West 1987: 5).

Kerstetter cites a 1978 survey of American police departments which indicated that 80 per cent had special units (1987: 179).

I would add two nuances. First, the 'independent specific unit' should include those situations where a police executive has created an *ad hoc* body, made up of police officers from outside the local police department, to review a complaint. To 'muddy the waters' even further, there have been isolated cases where a police or criminal justice expert was a member of the *ad hoc* body and was a civilian. Second, other governmental and community agencies have been authorized to receive citizens' complaints and then forward them to the police department. In both cases, with the rare exception, civilians are not included in the complaint review; therefore, these variations would have to be considered internal procedures.

The *external review* form has three tiers: (*a*) the civilian oversight agency receives, investigates, adjudicates, and recommends discipline to the police executive; (*b*) these agencies carry out the same functions as the first tier, except for the investigative phase which is conducted by police departments; (*c*) agencies in this category have identical authorities as in one of the first two tiers, but the city's chief administrator acts as an arbitrator/mediator of disciplinary disputes between the oversight agency and the police executive.

(a) First-Tier Examples
The classical ombudsman, such as in Flint, Michigan, and Des Moines, Iowa, is an example of the first tier. Of course, the ombudsman's office handles complaints against all city employees, including police officers. Also, this agency is a staff operation; that is, there is no appointed civilian board or commission to whom they report. Rather, an ombudsman reports to the city's governing council.

Another example is the Office of Citizen Complaints (OCC) in San Francisco, California, where a staff conducts the full array of external review activities. The OCC and the San Francisco Police Department report to the San Francisco Police Commission.

(b) Second-Tier Example
In 1988 New York City's Civilian Complaint Review Board (CCRB) became an external review agency, although its autonomy remains not absolutely clear. As with most new oversight agencies, it is still testing the boundaries of its authority through disputes with the New York City Police Department. Prior to 1988, the CCRB was an arm of the police department; it was made up of sworn and non-sworn personnel who conducted investigations, adjudicated findings, and recommended discipline to the police commissioner. Presently, it functions as before, with the important distinction that the Board consists of six citizens who are appointed by the mayor and six representatives appointed by the police commissioner. The Board adjudicates the investigative findings and recommends discipline to the police commissioner; the investigators remain sworn and non-sworn police personnel.

(c) Third-Tier Examples
Cleveland, Ohio, has a system where the complainant chooses whether the police department or the Police Review Board (PRB) will handle the complaint. If the PRB is chosen, the complaint is

investigated by the Office of Professional Standards which is staffed with seconded Cleveland police officers and is a part of the PRB. The investigated complaints are reviewed by the PRB and a public hearing is held as another step in considering the complaint; the Board adjudicates the complaint and sends it to the police chief with disciplinary recommendations. If the PRB and the police chief cannot resolve their differences about the discipline, the city's public-safety director makes the final decision.

Cincinnati, Ohio's Office of Municipal Investigations (OMI) is an example of this third tier; it receives, investigates, adjudicates, and recommends discipline to the police chief. If there is a disciplinary dispute, the issue is referred to the city manager who, if necessary, will decide the discipline. The OMI is responsible for complaints against all city employees.

The Police Review Commission in Berkeley, California, has a civilian investigator, who reports his or her findings to the Commission which, in turn, holds a public hearing to review the complaint, adjudicates it, and recommends discipline. The Commission is chosen by the nine members of the city council; the arbitrator of discipline is the city manager.

The three other forms of citizens' complaints procedures are what I would call the *auditor* form, the *citizen inclusion form*, and the *monitor form*.

I have separated out particular agencies which perform an *auditor*'s function, rather than a *monitor*'s function. By this I mean that there are civilian oversight agencies which simply review complaints so as to comment upon the fairness and thoroughness of the internal complaints procedure. Their purpose is to improve the police complaints system, not to affect individual complaints. Such an agency, known as the Internal Affairs Unit Review Panel, has been operational in Minneapolis, Minnesota. Presently, the Minneapolis City Council is considering an external review proposal. The Police Internal Investigations Auditing Committee in Portland, Oregon, is of this variety.

In contrast to the auditing agencies, the *monitors* have the authority to intervene in the internal complaints procedure by recommending further police investigation of a complaint and debating the merits of a complaint with police officials; all these activities would occur before the police department issued its final decision. One interesting variation of this form of civilian oversight is the Police Services Committee of the Evanston City Council, Illinois. This Council committee of elected officials monitors the internal police process and, in addition, can hear from a complainant who wishes to appeal against the police department's decision.

The fifth form is where an internal complaints system has been modified to include civilian employees in the process; the Office of Professional Standards of the Chicago Police Department, which I described earlier, is an example of *civilian inclusion*.

ISSUES AND RECOMMENDATIONS FOR CIVILIAN OVERSIGHT

I have made general comments about civilian oversight which pose a framework in which citizens' complaints procedures might function, described the existing forms of complaints procedures in the United States, and outlined some of the operational problems faced by civilian oversight agencies. Now I will isolate issues raised by the introduction of civilian participation into the complaints process and then make recommendations regarding each issue that would improve the effectiveness of civilian oversight. In order to accomplish this task I will use the complaints process as a guide, concluding with a composite model citizen's complaint procedure.

Receipt of Complaints

A civilian oversight agency must woo and maintain the participation of citizens and police in its complaints process.

Often, there is a protracted time period between the initial call for civilian oversight and its eventual implementation due to the process of political compromise and the legal challenges. Therefore, when it does become operational the community and the police department will need to be educated about the authority and procedures of the civilian oversight agency.

Beyond overcoming this early inertia, who it is that receives complaints will be an important threshold issue in developing citizen participation. Complaints should normally be received by the civilian oversight agency, but this would not preclude the police department from being a recipient. However, one of the ongoing realities in the United States is that there are a significant number of potential complainants who never come forward because of their fear of police retaliation. This fear is especially prevalent in minority

278 Werner E. Petterson

neighbourhoods. As obvious as this has been, there remain numerous complaints systems where the police department is the sole recipient, such as in Minneapolis, Minnesota, or in other communities where the auditing or monitoring form handles complaints. Internal complaints systems are similarly handicapped.

If there are multiple recipients, a written policy and procedure to manage proper notification and forwarding of complaints will be necessary. Chicago's Office of Professional Standards and San Francisco's Office of Citizens' Complaints are exemplary, where all complaints are directed to the civilian agency which appraises who should handle the complaint. Those complaints outside its jurisdiction are referred to the internal police complaints system. In Chicago, a citizen has access to OPS twenty-four hours a day, seven days a week. Clearly, the expenses associated with such a time commitment would be excessive for most communities.

Assessment of Complaints

Certain civilian oversight agencies are legislatively mandated to investigate or hold hearings on all complaints. For some, this requirement becomes a time-consuming burden which produces unacceptable back-logs that undermine the confidence of both citizens and the police in the process. Assessing the merits of complaints should be a recognized function; a set of criteria should be established to determine the appropriate response to each complaint. Frivolous complaints would be quickly dismissed and the agency's attention would be proportionately focused on the seriousness of complaints and expediting their closure. San Francisco's OCC developed such an assessment procedure.

Conciliation of Complaints

One of the options available to a civilian oversight agency should be conciliation. It is surprising how few of them have this choice; see the chart in the Appendix. Conciliation of a complaint can be employed throughout the process. It permits the bringing together of the complainant and the subject officer to discuss what occurred during the encounter, or the civilian oversight agent can use shuttle diplomacy in achieving a resolution. One-to-one exchanges are preferable in resolving disputes, as such an arena respects confidentiality and offers the opportunity to mutually determine what took place. These exchanges will help assess the contradictions between the ends and means of policing and provide pieces to the 'moral consensus' puzzle.

Police co-operation is an issue throughout the complaints review process; civilian oversight agencies are often frustrated by police unresponsiveness. Some cities have resorted to mandatory requirements in compelling police officers to appear before civilian oversight agencies; Berkeley, California, has made it a condition of employment. However, one of conciliation's tenets is that it is a voluntary process. Somehow the leadership of the civilian oversight agency, the police administration, and the police association must find a way to ensure police participation. Again, conciliation skills will be necessary.

The bringing of civil and criminal charges against police officers, in both state and federal courts in the United States of America, will remain a constitutional right of citizens; nevertheless, our citizens' propensity to litigate their problems has created an environment where public servants, including police officers, are withholding their services and withdrawing into defensive postures, and our communities are suffering the consequences. This comment should not be taken as a rationalization for the 'blue code' which defends abusive and corrupt police officers. But it is offered for this purpose: a civilian oversight process which does not offer a conciliatory avenue for resolving complaints is subject to being seen as a part of a United States predilection to adversarial methods in redressing grievances.

Investigation of Complaints

Creating a balance of authority in reviewing citizens' complaints between civilian oversight agencies and police departments usually focuses on who should investigate the complaints and who should impose discipline. In the United States, when public pressure required a political decision about these two issues, the choice has been to grant the civilian oversight agency investigative responsibilities and to allow the imposition of discipline to remain the police chief's authority. This decision has not necessarily transferred the investigative authority from one agency to another; the police department, in most cases, continues to investigate the very same complaints being investigated by the civilian oversight agency. An unusual investigative approach was practised for some time in Miami, Florida, where civilian investigators of the Office of

Professional Compliance and Miami Police Department investigators joined together in conducting interviews of complainants and accused police officers; presently, this civilian oversight agency is undergoing substantial revisions following a police–community crisis.

Within the debate over investigating authority, the issue of subpoena power for the civilian oversight agency arises. Those who advocate subpoena power are concerned about compelling police officers to co-operate with civilian investigators or hearing boards; the reality is that if police co-operation is not achieved through political compromise as the review procedure is reformed, the use of subpoena power will not rectify this dilemma for civilian oversight agencies.

CIVILIAN OVERSIGHT MODEL

The following proposed model is not unique; in fact, it is a combination of the Office of the Public Complaint Commissioner in Toronto, Ontario, which is more adequately described in another chapter of this book, and Cleveland's Police Review Board. This model would use the inherent strengths of a professional staff of administrators and civilian investigators and a Board of community representatives.

This model is derived from my observations of and research into civilian oversight agencies which are very similar to those of Sidney Linden, Toronto's first Public Complaints Commissioner:

In designing the system, a threshold issue which had to be addressed was whether police, civilians or a combination of the two should conduct investigations into police complaints. My research into the structure and function of the police complaints system . . . had shown that a system has rarely, if ever, been successful if the opportunity to respond to complaints was completely removed from the police force . . . the facts as I found them indicated that jurisdictions which allowed for exclusive civilian investigation of police complaints were virtually non-existent. To be clear, several jurisdictions had injected a civilian component, but where there was civilian participation in initial investigations, there was always some effort made to balance the system in a number of ways . . . the model I recommended for injecting civilian participation into the complaints process in Metropolitan Toronto was essentially a balancing act. It consisted of a civilian review agency with broad powers to do initial investigation in some cases, and reinvestigation in others, coupled with a civilian adjudicative body which could impose discipline directly, and to which the review agency could refer cases for public hearings. (1987: 8.)

The citizens' complaints model I would propose would function in the following manner:

The *receipt* of complaints would be with the civilian oversight agency and with the police department. An information management system would record and track the complaints so that they were promptly referred from one to the other. If a complaint was informally resolved at the police station, a report detailing the complaint and its resolution would be sent to the civilian oversight agency which would periodically monitor this process.

Assessment of complaints would ensure that each complaint was evaluated by a set of criteria. Such evaluations would help govern case-entry decisions on the basis of priorities so that frivolous complaints and complaints with chronic information gaps would be immediately set aside and serious complaints with credible verification indicators could be quickly processed.

Conciliation of complaints would be a priority task and staff would be selected and trained to support such an effort. Extensive training resources in dispute resolution are available and could be designed to accommodate the specific demands of civilian oversight agencies.

Although Toronto's Office of the Public Complaints Commissioner provides for conciliation, only 3 per cent of their complaints are resolved in this manner. The past two years have been an especially contentious period between that Office and the Metropolitan Toronto Police Department which may explain why there were so few conciliated complaints. Based upon the use of conciliation in other arenas[6] of dispute resolution, a successful conciliation rate should be in the area of 50 per cent; such a success-rate is largely based on the willingness of the parties to accept this approach.

Investigation: by and large, the vast majority of complaints would be investigated initially by the police department. It should be anticipated that there will be sensitive complaints which will receive high visibility in the media and will be associated with severe tensions between community members and the police department;

---

[6] Dade County, Florida's Independent Review Panel emphasizes the conciliation of complaints and it resolves 50% of them. In USA courts, Alternative Dispute Resolution (ADR) is successful in a majority of cases.

these complaints should be investigated initially by investigators of the civilian oversight agency.

Civilian investigators will also be utilized when the complainant appeals against the police department's investigative findings to the civilian oversight agency, and its subsequent assessment determines that the appeal has sufficient merit. It is argued that a complainant who does not receive a sustained finding will appeal against the decision; again, this cynicism underestimates the goodwill of most people in redressing grievances. I have recommended three steps to be taken by police departments in improving citizens' acceptance of internal procedures: (a) the internal investigative unit should be representative of the community it serves; (b) the investigative steps taken and reasons for a particular finding should be included, with some detail, in the police report to the complainant; and (c) police officers who have a propensity for abusive behaviour should be dismissed from the police force.

Once the civilian investigation is completed, the civilian oversight board would hold a public hearing to adjudicate the complaint. This would not only be the time to hear both sides debate the disputed facts surrounding their encounter but also offer another occasion to discuss the ends and means of policing and to further delineate the community's 'moral consensus' regarding law enforcement and order maintenance. The board's adjudicated findings would be reported to the complainant, to the police department, and to the accused police officer. This report would include recommended actions for correcting police officers' behaviour through instruction, counselling, and supervision; it would also recommend punitive discipline where necessary.

In instances where the police executive and the civilian oversight agency disagree on the discipline, a panel of three mutually selected civilian arbitrators would hear the complaint and its decision would be binding.

The rationale for this model was to design a procedure that would balance two controversial functions of the citizens' complaints procedure, complaints investigation and disposition of discipline. It respects the police department's administrative authority by granting it the initial opportunity to investigate and resolve the complaint. On the other hand, when the entire complaints procedure has been completed and an accommodation in the disposition of discipline cannot be reached, a civilian panel of arbitrators will decide the discipline. This model was also designed to give priority to the conciliation of complaints so that civilian oversight can serve as a bridge between police and citizens in disputes. In addition, a civilian oversight process which includes a board of community representatives would offer an opportunity for citizens and police officers to struggle with the task of giving clarity to the community's 'moral consensus' which is the basis of police authority.

REFERENCES

Bittner, E. (1970) *The Functions of the Police in Modern Society* (Washington DC: US Government Printing Office).

Brown, M. K. (1981) *Working the Street* (New York: Russell Sage Foundation).

Buckner, H. T. (1967) 'The Police: The Culture of a Social Control Agency', unpublished Dissertation, University of California, Berkeley, CA.

Goldsmith, A. (1988) 'New Directions in Police Complaints Procedures: Some Conceptual and Comparative Departures', *Police Studies* 11: 60.

Kelling, G. L., Wasserman, R., and Williams, H. (1988) 'Police Accountability and Community Policing' (Washington DC: National Institute of Justice).

Kerstetter, W. A. (1987) *Police Leadership in America: Crisis and Opportunity* (Chicago: American Bar Foundation).

Linden, S. (1987) *Creation and Responsibility of Toronto's Public Complaint Commissioner* (Evanston IL; IACOLE).

Lohman, J. D., and Misner, G. E. (1966) *The Police and the Community: The Dynamics of their Relationship in a Changing Society*, ii. (Washington DC: Government Printing Office).

Metcalfe Panel (1973) 'The Metcalfe Report on the Misuse of Police Authority in Chicago', *Public Defender*, Chicago, IL.

Muir jun., W. K. (1977) *Police: Streetcorner Politicians* (Chicago: University of Chicago Press).

Perez, D. (1978) 'Police Accountability: A Question of Balance', Ph.D. Dissertation, University of California, Berkeley, CA.

US Kerner Commission (1968) *Report of the National Advisory Commission on Civil Disorders* (New York: Bantam Books).

US President's Commission on Law Enforcement and Administration of Justice (1967), *Task Force Report: The Police* (Washington DC: US Government Printing Office).

US Wickersham Commission (1968) *Report of the National Commission on Law Observance and Law Enforcement* 14, 'Police' (Montclair: Patterson Smith).

West, P. (1987) *PERF Investigation of Complaints Against the Police Survey*, (Washington DC: Police Executive Research Forum).

Wilson, J. Q. (1968) *Varieties of Police Behaviour*, (Cambridge, Mass.: Harvard University Press).

Appendix

CIVILIAN OVERSIGHT AGENCY CHART

City	Organization	Established	Enabling Authority	Members s.=staff	Appointment
Albuquerque, NM	Independent Counsel	2.23.87	Ordinance 4-1987	1	hired
	Police Advisory Board	1987	Ordinance 44-1978	11	mayor
	City Hearing Officer	1986	Ordinance	6-12-4	1
Baltimore, MD	Complaint Evaluation Board	7.1.77	General Order 48-77	7	ordinance-specific
Berkeley, CA	Office of Professional Standards	1974	Police General Order	police chief 80 s.	
Cincinnati, OH	Chicago Police Board	1961	IL Statute/Ordinance	9	mayor
	Office of Municipal Investigation	1984	Ordinance 101-1984	6 s.	hired
Cleveland, OH	Police Review Board	1984	Charter Amendment	5 9 s.	mayro hired
Detroit, MI	Board of Police Commissioners	1974	Charter Amendment	5	mayor
Dade County, FL	Independent Review Panel	1980	Ordinance	6	county manager
Dallas, Tex.	Police Review Board	1988	Ordinance	13	city manager
Flint, MI	Ombundsman		Charter Amendment		hired

Appendix (*cont.*)

CIVILIAN OVERSIGHT AGENCY CHART

City	Organization	Established	Enabling Authority	Members s.=staff	Appointment
Hartford, CT	Invest. Review Board	1982	Executive Order	7	police HRC
Indianapolis, IN	Citizen Complaint Review Board	proposed	City-County Ordinance		safety director
Los Angeles, CA	Police Commission		City Charter	5	mayor
New York City	Civilian Complaint Review Board	1988	Ordinance	12	6 by mayor 6 by police
New Orleans, LA	Office of Municipal Investigation	1981	Ordinance	6 s.	city manager
Milwaukee, WI	Fire and Police Comm.	1977	Wis. Law Ch. 62. 50	5	mayor
Minneapolis, MN	Police Review Panel	7. 83	Executive Order	4	mayor
Portland, Oreg.	Police Inter. Invest. Auditing Committee	4. 82	Ordinance 153076	3	city council
San Diego, CA	Citizen Review Board	1988	Ordinance	12	mayor
San Francisco, CA	Office of Citizen Complaints	1985	referendum/ Ordinance	3 s.	hired
Washington, DC	Civilian Complaint Review Board	10. 80	Ordinance Act 3–285	7	mayor and council

City	Conciliation	Investigation	Subpoena Power	Hearing	Disciplines	Mandated Authority
Albuquerque, NM	No	No	No	No	No	Police Advisory Board recommends policies and procedures to police chief
	No	Yes		No	No	Independent Council can initiate investigation
Baltimore, MD	No	Yes		No	No	Receives and investigates complaints alleging acts of discourtesy and excessive use of force
Berkeley, CA	Yes	Yes	Yes	Public	No	Receives, investigates, and recommends discipline: recommends police policies and procedures
Chicago, IL OPS	No	Yes		No	No	Receives and investigates complaints re excessive use of force and police shots fired
CPB	No	No	Yes	Public	Yes	Conducts administrative hearings re suspensions and dismissals
Cincinnati, OH	No	Yes	Yes	No	No	Receives, investigates, and recommends discipline
Cleveland, OH	No	Yes	Yes	Public	No	Receives, OPS investigation, Board hearing and recommends discipline
Detroit, MI	No	Yes	Yes	No	No	Receives and investigates complaints

Appendix (*cont.*)

City	Concili-ation	Investi-gation	Subpoena Power	Hearing	Disci-plines	Mandated Authority
Dade County, FL	Yes	No	Limited	Public	No	Conducts minimal investigations and conducts public hearings: heavy conciliation effort
Dallas, Tex.	No	Yes	Citizens'	Yes	No	Reviews shootings and citizens' complaints: may hire private investigator
Flint, MI	No	Yes	Yes	Public	No	Receives, investigates, hears complaints, and recommends discipline
Hartford, CN	No	No	No	No	No	Reviews complaints of excessive force, civil rights violations and racial slurs
Indianapolis, IN	No	No	No	No	No	Board only reviews complaints of excessive use of force and discourtesy and recommends discipline
Los Angeles, CA	No	No	No	Yes	No	Receives complaints, monitors police investigation, and recommends discipline
New York City	No	Yes	Yes	Yes	No	CCRB receives, investigates, and hears all citizens' complaints
New Orleans, LA	Yes	Yes	Yes	No	No	Receives, investigates and recommends discipline

City						Description
Milwaukee, WI	No	Yes	Yes	Yes	No	Receives, reviews, and makes decisions re excessive force and abusive language
Minneapolis, MN	No	No	No	No	No	Reviews internal complaints procedure and recommends improvement
Portland, OE	No	No	No	No	No	Reviews internal complaints procedure and recommends improvement
San Diego, CA	No	No	No	No	No	Board will review complaints and direct new investigation and comment on complaints procedure
San Francisco	No	Yes	Yes	No	No	OCC receives complaints, investigates, and recommends discipline
Washington, DC	No	Yes	Yes	Yes	No	Board hears citizens' complaints and recommends discipline

9

Civilian Oversight of the Police Complaints Process in the United States:

Concerns, Developments, and More Concerns

RICHARD J. TERRILL

Police misconduct in the United States has received national attention on several occasions during the century (see Gaynor 1903; Moss 1901; National Advisory Commission on Civil Disorders 1968; National Advisory Commission on Criminal Justice Standards and Goals 1973; National Commission on Law Observance 1931; Police Executive Research Forum 1981; President's Commission 1967; US Commission on Civil Rights 1961; US Commission on Civil Rights 1981). In the past the concern was directed at misconduct that was either clearly criminal in nature or would be categorized today as a procedural violation of a person's constitutional or civil rights. The criticisms often focused on the failure and at times even the unwillingness of the police, prosecutors, and courts to address the allegations.

Today the justice system has become much more sensitive to the problem. Prosecutors, grand juries, judges, and police often take a more proactive approach in handling such allegations. By acknowledging the existence of this problem and by accepting some degree of responsibility for it, various components of the justice system are practising a form of hierarchical accountability (Terrill 1988). This kind of accountability encourages the development of control mechanisms that are either completely internal to the organizational structure of the police or may be extended to include some of the other administrative components found within the justice system. To date, the procedures and administrative mechanisms designed to handle the typical allegations of misconduct have been completely internal to the police organization. The procedure usually consists of the department receiving the complaint, determining the authenticity of the charge, investigating the issue, and then imposing a sanction if the officer has not been exonerated. Over the course of the past twenty-five years these efforts have been encouraged and enhanced further by federal law expanding or clarifying what constitutes illegal or inappropriate behaviour on the part of law enforcement officers.[1]

In spite of this new sensitivity, efforts to frustrate the involvement of other components of the justice system in the oversight process remain an enduring concern. At least two factors contribute to the existence of this situation. One is systemic or organizational in nature, while the other relates directly to the individual human condition.

It is common knowledge that each component of the justice system must work with the others in order to achieve a modicum of success. The realization of individual objectives and collective goals is often marked by compromises among the components. The extensive use of plea bargaining in the judicial process is but one example of the need for such accommodation within the system. Attempts at compromise within the judicial process, however, could have an adverse effect on any proactive vigilance towards allegations of police misconduct. This concern is based on the opinion that established and legitimate forms of compromise could create a climate within the system that leads to one component co-opting another. In the context of police oversight co-optation could be accomplished by law enforcement either consciously or unconsciously creating a climate of opinion that might inadvertently encourage, permit, or even condone behaviour that might lead to illegal or

---

[1] In addition to the US Supreme Court handing down some significant case-law decisions in the 1960s, namely *Mapp* v. *Ohio* (1961), *Escobedo* v. *Illinois* (1964), and *Miranda* v. *Arizona* (1966), another controversial approach, utilized to control police abuse, was to bring suit in federal courts against a state or a local official under s. 1983 of title 42 of the United States Code. This section states: 'Every person who, under color of any statute, ordinance, regulation, custom, or usage, of any State or Territory, subjects, or causes to be subjected, any citizen of the United States or other person within the jurisdiction thereof to the deprivation of any rights, privileges, or immunities secured by the Constitution and laws, shall be liable to the party injured in an action at law, suit in equity, or other proper proceedings for redress.' For a useful discussion of s. 1983, see Anon. (1977). This law was originally enacted as part of the Civil Rights Act of 1871 in order to enforce fourteenth amendment guarantees, but it was not utilized until 1961 in *Monroe* v. *Pape*. In subsequent rulings on this matter, see in particular *Monell* v. *New York Department of Social Services* (1978).

inappropriate conduct. Presently, the most obvious situation where that could occur exists with the national campaign against drug abuse.

The other factor, which is closely related to the first, has to do with the fact that far too many people appear to show a greater deference to and trust in their peer group than they do towards any higher authority. The higher authority could be represented by either the upper echelons of an organization, the law, or a particular ethical position. The unfortunate result of people holding this attitude is that they are often willing to lie for their peers rather than support the long-term common good of either a specific organization or society at large. There is a significant body of literature that has discussed this tendency in people, irrespective of their occupation, and some of it relates to law enforcement (with regard to police, see Barker and Carter 1986; Bittner 1980; Chevigny 1969; Davis 1975; Knapp 1972; Lundman 1980; Manning and van Maanen 1978; Muir 1977; Niederhoffer 1969; Punch 1985, 1983; Shearing 1981; Sherman 1978; Ward *et al.* 1987; Williams 1984).

In the light of these systemic and human predispositions some people are of the opinion that there is a need to establish an oversight mechanism for law enforcement that is external to the existing method of hierarchical accountability. Such a scheme is characterized as democratic accountability (Terrill 1988). It is based on the premise that although the public has relinquished to the police the authority to enforce the law, the public retains the right to control the police bureaucracy externally, if the need arises (Yates, 1982). Law enforcement is singled out for such scrutiny because of the nature of its tasks, the powers deferred to the organization, and the significant discretion accorded to individual patrol officers. This last factor is particularly important, for in both private- and public-sector organizations, there are few, if any, who grant as much personal discretion to line employees as does law enforcement. The gravity of that authority is enhanced further by the fact that these line officers, at least in the United States, are mandated to carry lethal weapons.

As an aside, one should keep in mind that it has been suggested periodically that other occupations may also be in need of some type of external oversight. Doctors, lawyers, stockbrokers, and certain business enterprises come to mind, for, like law enforcement, they are invested with a significant amount of power and/or trust.[2] Although to include other occupations in this present discussion would be irrelevant, it is important to mention them, because police tend to think that proponents of oversight have singled them out as a pariah that alone should bear such scrutiny. That view is simply not true, at least when it is directed at all who support the concept of civilian oversight.

The success of hierarchical accountability in some jurisdictions over the course of the past twenty years has resulted in a narrowing of the concern for police misconduct or at least a refinement in the parameters of the problem. This could be perceived as a positive sign, for it implies that law enforcement is achieving some degree of success in monitoring itself with regard to criminal, constitutional, and civil rights forms of misconduct. More rigorous selection standards and improved and expanded recruit training are often cited as factors in this development. In these jurisdictions, the issue of oversight appears to focus more on misconduct of a non-criminal nature. This usually involves improper conduct as determined by the rules and procedures established by the police department.

Irrespective of the degree of concern, the oversight controversy has centred on the procedures, or the lack thereof, employed by law enforcement to assure accountability in the investigation of citizens' complaints and in the forthright resolution of such allegations of professional misconduct. This issue specifically raises questions about process: Who should receive the complaint; who should determine the authenticity of the charge; who should investigate the issue; who should adjudicate or mediate the case; and who should impose a sanction, if the officer has not been exonerated? These have been the recurring concerns of proponents of civilian oversight in the United States.

Finally, a caveat is in order. It is important to keep in mind that civilian oversight of police is intimately tied to the issue of civil rights for minorities. Racial discrimination or allegations of it are usually at

---

[2] Recently, it was suggested that another method exists to control police abuse, that is to revoke the officer's certification (Goldman and Puro 1987). In the USA all states with the exception of Hawaii have state boards usually called Peace Officer Standards and Training (POST) Boards. They are empowered to set training and selection standards for police officers, and they issue a certificate that enables a person to be employed as such. Although this idea should be explored, revoking one's professional licence is not always easy or effective. See e.g. the series 'Bad Doctors', *Detroit Free Press*, 1–8 April 1984.

the heart of most movements to introduce a civilian oversight mechanism. This is certainly the case in most jurisdictions in the United States, and it appears to be a leading factor in the development of such schemes elsewhere in the world.[3]

Having defined the nature of the problem in the context of the United States, the purpose of this essay is to explain the setbacks and advancements that have been made in the country with regard to civilian oversight. My approach is to examine this issue in the evolutionary context of three distinct climates of opinion. The first includes the period of the late 1950s and 1960s; the second essentially covers the 1970s; and the third considers the 1980s and beyond. Within each of these periods five factors are crucial to understanding the potential for success or failure of civilian oversight. They include: the nature of political support for the idea, the level of police opposition to the scheme, the degree of citizen interest for such a system, the legal standing accorded the oversight mechanism, and the extent to which the system is accorded an independent role in the complaints process.

THREE POLITICAL TENETS

Before the issue of oversight is examined, those readers who are unfamiliar with police organizations in the United States should be reminded of a few basic features found in the country's political philosophy. The historical evolution of law enforcement adminis-tration in any country is tied very closely to its political ideology, and the United States is no exception to this rule. There are three tenets within its political philosophy that have shaped the organization of police in a significant way.

One of the principal features of that ideology is reflected in how people view governmental authority. The primary reason for the American Revolution was to overthrow the centralized authority of the British Crown which the colonists found too arbitrary. After they gained their independence, the founding fathers had to grapple with the issue of what nature and form of government to establish. As a result, the drafters of the United States Constitution distinguished the authority of the executive, legislative, and judicial branches of government, so that power would be divided among the three. The

---

[3] e.g. with regard to Toronto, Canada, see Carter (1979) and Linden (1982). With regard to England, see e.g. Scarman (1981) and Terrill (1980, 1983).

inspiration for this idea came essentially from the French Enlighten-
ment philosopher, the Baron de Montesquieu.[4] In the United States
police powers are created by the legislative branch; those legal
powers are then interpreted from time to time by the judicial branch;
and law enforcement agencies are under the administrative control of
the executive branch.

The second feature deals with the federated nature of the country.
This was discussed in the *Federalist* and later given greater legal
clarity of expression in the Fourteenth Amendment to the US
Constitution (1868).[5] According to this amendment, each citizen of
the country is a citizen of the United States and subject to its federal
laws and governmental administration. The person is also a citizen of
the state in which he resides (of which there are fifty possibilities)
and subject to state laws and governmental administration. Thus, a
person holds a type of dual citizenship within the country.

The third tenet stresses the importance of local self-government.
This view basically suggests that each citizen should have the
opportunity to become actively involved in the conduct of government and that governmental authority and as many governmental
services as are reasonably possible should be based administratively
at the local level. Local means the municipal and county levels of
government. One of the original proponents of this position was
Thomas Jefferson, and the source for his inspiration came from
the political writings of the British philosopher, John Locke.[6] The
acceptance of this position has led to a long-standing tradition in
the United States of law enforcement being one of the principal
agencies administered at the local level.

Fear of centralized authority, the creation of a federal system of
government, and the importance placed on local self-government has
led to the development of more separately and publicly funded law
enforcement agencies than is found in any other country in the
world. The total number is approximately 40,000. Almost 20,000 of
these are viewed primarily as police agencies that have as their
principal responsibility the enforcement of law and the maintenance
of order in their respective local jurisdictions, while the others
possess only quasi-law-enforcement functions that often have either
a statewide or a federal jurisdiction. The roughly 20,000 law-

[4] See Montesquieu's *The Spirit of the Laws*.
[5] See *Federalist* 51 (1788), which is attributed to James Madison.
[6] See Locke's *Treatise of Civil Government*.

enforcement agencies are organized, administered, and accountable to either a federal, state, county, or municipal jurisdiction.

Thus, law enforcement in the United States is a fragmented system. It is not centralized or unified as is characteristic of most police organizations throughout the world. Admittedly, a few countries, namely Australia, Canada, and England, also have law enforcement systems that are somewhat fragmented, but the United States surpasses each of them in degree.

The long-standing significance of these three political tenets helps to indicate why civilian oversight of police has remained a recurring local issue in the United States. It also explains why there are so many administrative variations in the oversight schemes adopted in the country. And they demonstrate why a single oversight system for the country, such as that found with England's Police Complaints Authority, is simply not feasible at either the federal or state level of government.

THE FIRST CLIMATE OF OPINION: THE LATE 1950s AND 1960s

During this period Philadelphia was the only city in the country that implemented an oversight scheme that was operational for a number of years.[7] The manner in which the city approached the idea and the subsequent consequences of their method had and continues to have a profound impact on why some jurisdictions in the United States view the concept of civilian oversight in such an adverse light. As indicated earlier, five factors are crucial to understanding the potential success or failure of civilian oversight. They include: the nature of political support for the idea, the level of police opposition, the degree of citizens' interest, the legal standing granted to the oversight mechanism, and the extent to which the scheme is accorded an independent role in the complaints process. Each of these factors is critical to any objective evaluation and understanding of Philadelphia's early experiment with civilian oversight. Moreover, municipal policy-makers should heed the lessons of the Philadelphia experiment when contemplating an oversight scheme for their jurisdictions.

[7] The city of New York attempted to develop a civilian review board in 1966, but it was defeated in a referendum before it was really made operational, after police conducted a very effective propaganda campaign (Black 1968).

In 1957 the Philadelphia branch of the American Civil Liberties Union (ACLU) called for the creation of a civilian review board because strained relations had developed between citizens, especially blacks who alleged discriminatory practices, and the police department. It should be pointed out that the department did have an internal Board of Inquiry. Thus, there had been an attempt to implement some degree of hierarchical accountability. It has been suggested, however, that few complaints were filed with the Board and those that were usually resulted either in the officer being exonerated or in a judgment that the complaint was unsubstantiated (see Coxe 1961, 1965; Hudson 1968, 1971). This kind of information tends to lead to the supposition that an internal system of oversight is either ineffective or prone to covering up incidents of misconduct. While such generalizations are at times unfair, they none the less gain credence when it is revealed that the process does not handle citizens' complaints in a forthright manner.

Mayor Richardson Dilworth, who had received black support in the previous election because of his pledge to reduce racial tensions, introduced an ordinance to create a review board. The city council, however, did not support the measure and let the proposal die in committee. The following year Dilworth circumvented the city council and created the Police Review Board by an executive order.

The Board consisted of a blue-ribbon panel of five citizens who commenced operations on 1 October 1958. They were 'charged with the responsibility of considering citizens' complaints against the police where the charge involved brutality, false arrest, discrimination based upon race, religion, or national origin, or other wrongful conduct of police personnel toward citizens' (Police Advisory Board 1959: 1). The Board established procedures that essentially called for them to receive and hear citizens' complaints and to recommend to the Police Commissioner an appropriate sanction. The department was given the responsibility of investigating the charges, on the outcome of which the Board would then base its recommendation.

The mayor's initial decision to create the Board in this manner placed its future in jeopardy from the start. First, there was a lack of support within the political establishment for the idea as the efforts of the reform-minded mayor were at cross-purposes with the city council. Second, the Board was not granted any significant legal standing. An executive order which is signed into force by one mayor can just as easily be rescinded by the signature of another mayor. Third, the Board lacked any sense of permanency or independence with this kind of standing. Its existence was based totally on the decision of one person, the mayor.

Even Dilworth's commitment to the Board has been questioned (Terrill 1988). Following its creation, he apparently did not offer any recommendations pertaining to its internal regulation or to the establishment of co-operative procedures with the police department, and he did not provide it with a budget, office space, or administrative and clerical staffs. A budget was eventually appropriated in 1960, but when a request was made to increase it the following year, this was denied. With its 1960 budget the Board was able to hire an executive secretary, but it was a part-time position that did not become full-time until 1963. As indicated earlier, the Board relied on the police department to conduct the investigations into complaints. While this worked well during the initial years, the success has been attributed largely to the personal qualities of the single investigator assigned this responsibility. Upon his death officers from the department served in this capacity on a rotating basis (Coxe 1961; Hudson 1972).

In addition to these political and organizational factors there was a lack of citizen interest and support for civilian review. Admittedly, the ACLU and the NAACP (National Association for the Advancement of Colored People) supported the idea, but they did not speak for the majority of citizens. In fact there is some question as to whether there was any consensus among minority groups, for it has been suggested that some blacks were sceptical of the true intentions behind the creation of a board. They were apparently of the opinion that the concept was designed merely to placate the black community (Hudson 1968).

In order to appreciate this attitude one must keep in mind the climate of opinion during the late 1950s. In spite of the success with *Brown* v. *Board of Education* (1954) to desegregate the Topeka, Kansas, public school system, the civil rights movement, for the most part, was just beginning to emerge as a potential political force. Even then its attention was focused on the south. At that time blacks lacked significant political clout, not only in the south but also in the northern urban areas.

Moreover, the white community was essentially indifferent to the Board. At the time they were demanding more law and order, not less. Unfortunately, some people, both black and white, viewed the

Board as a vehicle that would in some way hinder the police from addressing that particular task. At least that was what they were being told by the police union in its campaign to discredit the Board. Finally, most citizens were not even aware of the Board's existence. This has been attributed to a lack of publicity coming from City Hall, which again illustrates Dilworth's possible indifference to the idea that he was initially instrumental in creating, and to a press that ignored the Board in spite of the fact that its hearings were open to the public (Coxe 1961, 1965).

Each of the aforementioned factors was sufficient in and of itself to facilitate the demise of this attempt at civilian oversight. What surely enhanced the inevitable, however, were the tactics employed by the Philadelphia police union, the Fraternal Order of Police (FOP). As one might expect, the FOP was the most ardent and vocal opponent of the Board, and it employed two strategies to ruin its already precarious standing. One was a propaganda campaign, designed for the public's consumption, that at times bordered on the irrational but was nevertheless quite effective. The other involved the FOP hindering the Board's efforts at conducting business by bringing suit in court. This strategy proved very instrumental in sealing the fate of the Board.

In their propaganda campaign the FOP made several illogical statements and unfounded allegations as to the true intentions of the Board. They alleged, for example, that civilians were incapable of judging the actions of police officers and that the true intentions of the Board would undermine the authority of the Police Commissioner. They also maintained that the Board's existence would have an adverse effect on the morale of the police force, implying that the city and its citizens would be placed in danger. But the *coup de théâtre* of the FOP's campaign was the charge that the movement to create civilian review boards throughout the country was a communist plot designed to debilitate law enforcement and ultimately to facilitate the overthrow of the government (Coxe 1965).

While this last allegation appears downright silly today, one must again keep in mind the climate of opinion at the time in which it was utilized. The cold war was very much in vogue, and the red scare had not been put to rest with the death of Senator Joseph McCarthy in 1957. The other allegations mentioned, along with several that are not stated here, proved quite popular among the opponents of civilian oversight throughout the 1960s. In spite of the fact that many were either illogical, incorrect, unsubstantiated, or over-simplistic, some are still used to this day by police administrators and line officers in their opposition to civilian oversight (Terrill 1982).

In October of 1960 the International Association of Chiefs of Police (IACP) joined in the debate over civilian oversight by offering their support to oppose civilian review boards. Their official views were at least a bit more reasonable than those previously advanced.[8] The IACP maintained that aggrieved citizens, especially those who believed their civil rights had been violated, had recourse to the criminal law through prosecutors and grand juries. They could also seek redress through civil claims.

Although this position appears sound, one must keep in mind that when the IACP initially offered this argument the United States Supreme Court had only just begun to scrutinize seriously the activities of law enforcement officers.[9] The criticisms that were alluded to at the beginning of this essay, regarding the unwillingness of prosecutors and courts to address allegations of misconduct that were at times clearly criminal in nature, were still very real. Thus, the proponents of civilian oversight were sceptical, and with good reason, about the proposition that the judicial institutions of the day were an effective source of redress.

The proponents were also sceptical of the IACP's suggestion that citizens could seek redress through a civil claim. The ineffectiveness of this approach had been cited frequently by legal scholars. The principal reasons mentioned included: (*a*) tort remedies are of limited availability; (*b*) the plaintiffs are unlikely to receive a sizeable recovery for damages; (*c*) the resolution of civil remedies is frequently slow; (*d*) the complainant is often unwilling to initiate a suit, because of a lack of personal funds; (*e*) the complainant usually is without witnesses to corroborate his statements; and (*f*) judges and juries are more apt to believe the officer than the complainant. While the first two objections are no longer completely valid, since

---

[8] The IACP's position was subsequently reprinted in *Police Chief*, Feb. 1964, p. 34.

[9] The now famous case of *Mapp* v. *Ohio*, which created the exclusionary rule against illegal searches and seizures, was not decided until 1961. Other landmark cases (such as *Gideon* v. *Wainwright* (1963), assistance of counsel for indigents accused of a criminal felony; *Escobedo* v. *Illinois* (1964), in-custody police interrogations and the right to counsel; and *Miranda* v. *Arizona* (1966), confessions and police interrogations) had not as yet been brought to the attention of the court.

the situation that applied to both has changed considerably since the early 1960s, the others remain significant concerns (Beral and Sisk 1963; Davis *et al.* 1978–9; Foote 1954–5; Lenzi 1974–5; Newman 1978; and Schmidt 1976). In spite of the arguments put forward by the IACP, the law and the judicial institutions of the day were not viewed as being terribly effective at checking allegations of police misconduct.

The other strategy employed by the Philadelphia FOP was to bring suit in court. In December of 1959 the FOP filed a petition for a preliminary injunction against the city and the Board to enjoin the Board from holding hearings. An agreement was reached in February 1960 that led to the Board altering some of its procedures.[10] This compromise illustrated the Board's willingness to accommodate some of the concerns of the FOP in the hope of assuring a more harmonious working relationship.

A second suit was filed in September 1965 that proved instrumental in the eventual demise of the Board. The other key factor at that time was the succession of James Tate as mayor, who had indicated his opposition to the Board at the outset of his administration (Coxe 1961; Hudson 1972). The FOP was able to enjoin the Board from hearing cases with this second suit. Although the injunction was lifted in February 1966, a cloud of uncertainty remained as the Board awaited the court's decision. Finally, on 29 March 1967, Judge Leo Weinrott of the Court of Common Pleas handed down his decision declaring 'that the executive order creating the Board, as carried out, violated the Philadelphia Home Rule Charter and the Board was enjoined from holding further hearings or from requesting investigations from the Police Department' (Police Advisory Board 1967: 1).

The city did not appeal against the decision immediately, and as a

---

[10] The agreement called for: (*a*) a change in the name of the 'Police Review Board' to 'Police Advisory Board'; (*b*) the Board's rules would be modified in that the Board would 'request' rather than 'order' a police investigation; (*c*) the Board would send its report to the Mayor rather than to the Police Commissioner; (*d*) members of the police department whose attendance was desired by the Board at its hearings would receive notice from the Commissioner rather than from the Board directly; (*e*) the Board would not hold hearings in connection with a complaint while related criminal proceedings were pending against an officer unless the officer requested that the hearings be held; (*f*) the fact that criminal proceedings were pending against the complainant would not be grounds to postpone the Board's hearings; and (*g*) an exact copy of the complaint would be transmitted to the officer or his counsel (Police Advisory Board 1960: 6).

result, the Board became inactive. Following the Board's threat to appeal on its own, Mayor Tate agreed to appeal. With this action the Supreme Court of Pennsylvania overturned Judge Weinrott's decision citing that it was 'eminently clear that the foregoing sections of the [Philadelphia Home Rule] Charter permit the mayor to appoint a board to advise the police department on community relations and police discipline' (*Harrington* v. *Tate*, 1969: 179). Tate, however, did not reactivate the Board, which was within his legal authority, since the Board had been created through an executive order in the first place.

In spite of the Board's political, organizational, and legal problems one should not be left with the view that they failed to achieve any of the goals that have long been associated with proponents of civilian oversight. Spencer Coxe, for example, pointed out that the Board 'was able to dispose of most of the complaints without a formal hearing through the cooperation of police inspectors and captains'. In addition the Board 'never recommended dismissal from the force, though it has recommended a psychiatric examination to determine an officer's fitness' (1965: 181). Finally, Coxe concluded that the Board was instrumental in vindicating officers unjustly accused of misconduct, in obtaining redress for legitimate civilian grievances, in educating citizens with regard to the extent of police authority, in clarifying for the police the limits of an officer's authority, and in helping to identify questionable practices and policies of the department (1965: 182). Therefore, although the manner in which the city approached the implementation of civilian oversight doomed it to failure from the start, the experiment was not without any redeeming value. For those who cared to examine the evidence object-ively, civilian oversight had the potential both of benefiting aggrieved citizens and of protecting officers falsely accused of misconduct.

THE SECOND CLIMATE OF OPINION: THE 1970S

In a recent study that explored the phenomenon of why and how political decision-makers focus their attention on a particular policy issue, it was suggested that a problem is not placed on the political agenda until people, both in and out of government, begin to pay some serious attention to it (Kingdon 1984). It was further argued that merely placing a problem on the political agenda was not enough. It would have to move to the decision agenda which consisted of those select items that were under active consideration by government officials.

Two kinds of factors influence the selection of problems for the decision agenda. One consists of participants. They are represented by significant government officials, the media, interest groups, political parties, and the public. The other factor involves processes. These are illustrated by the emergence of a problem through a crisis or a prominent event, the accumulation of knowledge and opinions in a policy area, and the inevitable changes in either the political climate through swings in national mood, election results, and public opinion polls, or shifts in party control and ideology, or in the transfer of power in the executive or the legislative branches. While it is not necessary for all these factors to be present in order to influence the identification of a problem or its placement on the decision agenda, the chances are enhanced considerably by a rich mix of participant and process variables.[11]

Kingdon's explanation of this decision-making process illustrates quite well how and why Philadelphia failed to implement a viable civilian oversight scheme. Although it had gained some recognition as a political problem, civilian oversight was clearly not ready for the decision agenda of that city, or for that matter, any other jurisdiction at that time. By the 1970s, however, the climate of opinion had changed considerably to one that had the potential of supporting civilian oversight.

Virtually every example that Kingdon associated with his participant and process variables was in place. For example, President Lyndon Johnson had established a commission to examine the administration of justice. In its report devoted to law enforcement, the issue of citizens' dissatisfaction with internal police complaints procedures was addressed (President's Commission on Law Enforcement and the Administration of Justice 1967: 200–2). Before the ink was dry on that report, several cities were engulfed in riots. This led to the creation of yet another commission and to its report on the causes of the urban unrest. Once again, concerns about the lack of effective methods by which citizens could voice complaints about police conduct were raised (National Advisory Commission on Civil Disorders 1968: 162–3).

[11] Although Kingdon's point of analysis was essentially the US federal government, his approach to the issue appears equally valid at the state and local levels of government.

By that time the civil rights movement had also emerged as a powerful political force. It demanded and received the attention of politicians at the federal, state, and local levels of government. As a result of blacks sensitizing whites to their plight, legislation was passed, policies were implemented, programmes were created, and court decisions were rendered to correct some of the past discriminatory practices. With all these changes there was a greater social awareness among white citizens, and a significant number of them became committed to redressing racial injustices. Finally, blacks were able to rise to influential political positions, particularly in municipal governments.

The climate of opinion was indeed ripe to try once again to implement forms of democratic accountability in the handling of complaints regarding police conduct. Proponents of civilian oversight were assured of at least a fair hearing in several jurisdictions as they attempted to move their idea from the political agenda to its placement on the decision agenda. In those jurisdictions that considered some form of oversight seriously, support from local politicians was usually forthcoming. The basis for this was related to the degree of citizen interest from both the black community and those whites who supported the objectives of the civil rights movements. Securing the blessings of influential local business leaders also enhanced such efforts considerably. This kind of support helped to restrict the effectiveness of local law enforcement's opposition to oversight. Nevertheless, it is important to keep in mind that the rank-and-file within the law enforcement community remained adamantly opposed to civilian oversight.

With this kind of broad-based support three of the factors or hurdles that had previously hindered attempts at oversight were curtailed or considerably reduced. These included the nature of political support for the idea, the degree of citizen interest, and the level of police opposition. Two of our original factors, however, remained potential problem areas for the viability of the idea. They were the legal standing accorded the oversight mechanism, and the extent to which the system would be accorded an independent role in the complaints process. Both emerged as particularly critical issues that had to be addressed in the civilian oversight debate of the 1970s. They are represented here by Detroit's Board of Police Commissioners, Chicago's Office of Professional Standards and its Police Board, and by the Metropolitan Dade County Independent Review Panel.

Detroit's Board of Police Commissioners

Detroit was one of the cities particularly hard-hit by the urban riots of 1967. The city's history of race relations had not been good, and the politicians were criticized not only for their handling of the civil unrest over that summer but also for their inattentiveness to the long-standing grievances of the black community.[12] In addition the police department was singled out for a good deal of blame.

Following a riot a group of civic leaders founded an organization called New Detroit that was designed to seek solutions to the racial discord that plagued the city. Two years later, and in a separate development, Mayor Jerome P. Cavanagh appointed a commission to study the possibility of revising the city charter that had been in force since 1918. While the Charter Revision Commission was examining the nature of city government, New Detroit conducted an opinion poll among city and suburban residents in which questions were asked about the direction the Commission should take. Nearly two-thirds of those questioned felt that a civilian review board should be established to monitor the actions and decisions made by the police department. As a result, civilian oversight became an important feature of the Commission's work. To heighten an already prominent situation, in 1971 the police department introduced a new tactical unit called STRESS which stood for Stop The Robberies, Enjoy Safe Streets. In a city already noted for its alarmingly high homicide rates, the unit's methods of operation only compounded this negative image. During the first year-and-a-half of operation, for example, it 'had caused more civilian deaths than the entire department had over the preceding decade (excluding deaths related to the 1967 riot). All except one of the victims were black.' (Littlejohn 1981: 209.)

With the November election of 1973 the citizens of Detroit selected their first black mayor, Coleman A. Young, who had served for several years as a senator in the Michigan legislature.[13] Young's opponent in that election was John F. Nichols, the former Police Commissioner who had authorized the creation of the STRESS unit. The voters were obviously sending a message to the police

[12] For a useful historical summary of the police department's relations with the city's black community, see Littlejohn (1981). For a balanced assessment of the Detroit riot of 1967, see Locke (1969).

[13] Young is still the mayor of Detroit having been re-elected in 1989 to a fifth term.

department that a change in tactics and procedures was in the offing. That message was made even clearer with the passage of a referendum on the new city charter.

The charter took effect on 1 July 1974, and one of its most prominent features was the administrative reorganization of the police department. The charter states that the department will be headed by a five-member board of civilian police commissioners. They are appointed by the mayor and serve at his pleasure following their approval by the city council. The Board is actually a blue-ribbon panel whose members serve in a part-time capacity; they appoint a full-time executive secretary who handles the day-to-day operations of the office. The duties of the Board include: establishing departmental policies and regulations in consultation with the chief of police, reviewing and approving the department's budget, resolving complaints concerning the department's operations, serving as the final arbiter in the discipline of department employees, and presenting an annual report on the department (City of Detroit Charter sect. 7–1103).

Throughout the Charter Revision Commission's hearings, the police were strongly opposed to the idea of civilian oversight. This attitude was expressed in particular by their powerful union. The department continued its uncooperative stance, even after the Board had achieved legal standing through its incorporation in the city charter. This impasse was not resolved until the mayor issued an executive order in 1978 directing the immediate implementation of the Board's mandate. Thus, although the charter provided the Board with legal standing, that did not dissuade the police department from attempting to stonewall its implementation.

To facilitate the Board's oversight responsibilities, it created the Office of Chief Investigator, which was also part of the charter mandate (City of Detroit Charter sect. 7–1104). This Office has a staff of trained investigators composed of both civilians and police officers. It co-ordinates the investigation of complaints and matters of discipline within the police department.

There are three kinds of complaints that the Board entertains: original complaints, inquiry reviews, and appeals. Original complaints can be filed with the Board, the Office of Chief Investigator, the police department, or any other government agency. All complaints are forwarded to the executive secretary of the Board. If the complaint cannot be resolved informally, the matter is turned over to the Office of Chief Investigator for an official investigation.

An inquiry review is a request for the Board to review a complaint investigation that has already been completed. A complainant's request for a review that is based solely on his dissatisfaction with the original outcome is not grounds for such a review. The reason must be a belief that an error or omission occurred in the original investigation. If there are sufficient reasons to reopen the case, the Office of Chief Investigator would conduct a new investigation to clarify the apparent discrepancies. An appeal is a complete reinvestigation of a citizen's complaint by the Office of Chief Investigator. This is only granted if the original investigation contained errors or omissions to warrant a full investigation.

Another type of appeal involves disciplinary actions taken against a member of the department. Once an investigation is completed, the case is turned over to a departmental trial board, composed of senior supervisory officers, who determine the officer's guilt or innocence. If the officer is found guilty of misconduct, he is then disciplined either by the trial board or by the chief of police. The Board of Police Commissioners has the right to review disciplinary actions through this appeal process. They can affirm the original decision of the trial board, set aside or reduce the penalty, remand to the trial board for additional testimony, or grant a new hearing before the trial board.

The Board of Police Commissioners, therefore, is empowered under the city charter to receive complaints, to monitor or conduct the investigation of a complaint, and to affirm or set aside any disciplinary action imposed by either a departmental trial board or the chief of police. What is obviously significant about the Detroit approach to civilian oversight is that it addressed the issue of the legal standing of the oversight scheme from the start by incorporating it into the city charter. Placing any form of civilian oversight on a firm legal footing is essential for its initial viability and for its long-term standing both in the community and with the police department. Moreover, the Detroit approach attempted to assure an independent role for the Board by providing it with a direct role in the reception and investigation of complaints and an indirect role in the ultimate determination of the sanction imposed on an officer found guilty of misconduct.

Chicago's Office of Professional Standards and Police Board

In the same year that Detroit introduced its Board of Police Commissioners, the Office of Professional Standards was established in Chicago. What prompted the creation of this office was the publication in 1973 of the *Metcalfe Report* on police abuse in the Chicago police department. A series of articles was subsequently published in the same year by the *Chicago Tribune* that reinforced the earlier allegations of police brutality (Letman 1980).

One of the interesting features of the Chicago experience is that the police department seized the initiative to create part of the oversight scheme, for it was Police Superintendent James Rochford who created the Office of Professional Standards through a general administrative order. The Chief Administrator of the Office, along with his staff, are all civilians who are administratively under the direction of the superintendent's office. Staff members of the Office of Professional Standards, who serve as investigators, have all had prior experience in that capacity either with the military or through some other agency of government.

The Office is involved in several of the procedural phases surrounding issues of police misconduct. It receives and records all complaints against departmental personnel. In terms of investigation, it handles all cases involving excessive force or other incidents specifically authorized by the superintendent, and it investigates all cases where a person has been shot by an officer irrespective of a complaint being filed. All the other allegations of misconduct are referred to the Internal Affairs Division of the department for investigation. In those cases where the Office substantiates a complaint, it also recommends a disciplinary action to the superintendent. Finally, it collects evidence for the Police Board when that body is involved in misconduct cases.

The Police Board is composed of nine civilians who serve staggered five-year terms. They are appointed by the mayor with the advice and consent of the city council. The legal authority for the Board is based on the Chicago Municipal Code (chapters 11–2 and 11–3) and the Illinois Revised Statutes (chapter 24–3–7–3.1). The Board has an executive director who handles the day-to-day operations of the office, since the Board members serve in a part-time capacity.

The Board has several responsibilities pertaining to the administration of the police department. For example, it recruits and interviews candidates for the position of superintendent and then submits the names of three finalists to the mayor. It adopts the rules and regulations governing the administration of the department. It also reviews and approves the department's budget. In terms of its oversight of police misconduct, the Board has two duties. It serves as an administrative trial board when the superintendent is seeking either to dismiss someone or to suspend him for more than thirty days. At the employee's request, the Board will also review the superintendent's action of suspension for periods of between six and thirty days.

The Board has been the subject of some criticism for the manner in which it has exercised this authority. It apparently has been willing to alter the original sanction imposed by the superintendent, and at times has made a considerable reduction (Fogel 1987: 14). Although this serves as but one example, it should put to rest the popular notion among police officers that civilians are apt to sanction officers more severely than if their fate was solely in the hands of an internal departmental review system.[14]

Thus, Chicago has developed two kinds of organization that are supervised and staffed by civilians and that are involved in the handling of complaints of police misconduct. On the one hand, the Office of Professional Standards is responsible for investigating the more serious charges of misconduct. It has also been authorized to recommend to the superintendent an appropriate sanction if allegations have been substantiated. The Office, however, is not an independent entity in the oversight process, rather it is an administrative unit within the office of the superintendent of police. It also lacks any sense of independence in terms of its legal standing, since it was created through an administrative directive of the superintendent. In spite of these apparent handicaps, the Office appears to be an effective feature in the overall complaints process.

The Police Board, on the other hand, is more in keeping with a civilian oversight scheme, at least as it has been defined in this essay. Its responsibilities are limited, however, because of the existence of

[14] For an earlier discussion on this point that reinforces the Chicago experience, see Niederhoffer (1967).

the Office of Professional Standards. For example, it does not receive complaints or participate in the investigative process. These duties have long been considered important and appropriate features of a civilian oversight scheme. None the less, it has a significant role to play in the complaints process, for it reviews and can ultimately overturn some of the more severe sanctions that are at the disposal of the superintendent when disciplining employees of the department. What is more, it is the truly independent feature in the Chicago oversight process. It is detached from the administrative hierarchy of the department, and its legal standing is based on state law and municipal ordinances.

Metropolitan Dade County Independent Review Panel

The emergence of a problem through a crisis or a prominent event was one of the variables mentioned by Kingdon in his explanation of how an issue moves from a community's political agenda to its decision agenda. The December 1979 death by beating of Arthur McDuffie, a black insurance salesman, at the hands of four white Dade County police officers following a high-speed chase in Miami, served as a significant catalyst for the community reviewing its method of handling allegations of police misconduct. The fact that all the police officers involved had a history of citizens' complaints levelled against them was particularly disturbing, and several of these were apparently serious enough to warrant a formal internal review. None of these cases, however, had led to the department taking any severe disciplinary action against the officers. As a result, there was a demand in some quarters for the introduction of a civilian oversight mechanism.

The creation in January 1980 of the Independent Review Panel through a county ordinance was Dade County's response to that request (Metropolitan Dade County Independent Review Panel 1983). What is unique about this Panel is that its jurisdiction is not limited to the police, rather it is mandated to consider complaints against any county employee or agency. Thus, law enforcement's long-standing belief that civilian oversight is designed to single them out for scrutiny is not always the case, at least not in Dade County. And, although the Panel's jurisdiction does not include the municipalities found within the county, on occasion the Panel has been asked by municipalities to conduct investigations into alleged cases of misconduct by their employees.

The composition of the Independent Review Panel is designed to ensure that the perspectives of the entire community are represented. The names of three candidates are submitted by each of the following community organizations: the Dade County Association of Chiefs of Police, the Dade County Bar Association, the Dade County League of Women Voters, the Dade County Community Relations Board, and the Dade County Community Action Agency. The Board of County Commissioners then selects one candidate from each community group for appointment to the Panel. The sixth member is selected by the County Manager, and that person is either a department director or a member of the County Manager's staff. Panel members serve on a part-time basis for a one-year term.

If the Panel decides by a majority vote that a case is so serious as to warrant a full investigation, three additional members are empanelled to consider the merits of that particular incident. These members are also appointed by the Board of County Commissioners. Two are selected from the community affected by the incident, while the third is a representative from the bargaining unit of the accused employee.

An executive director co-ordinates the work of the Independent Review Panel, and has a full-time position. Since the executive director plays such a key role in the daily operations of the Panel, it was felt that every effort should be made to remove local political influence from the selection of the director. As such, the appointment of the executive director is made by the Chief Judge of Dade County. While the Panel has the authority to hire its own private independent investigators, and does so from time to time, it also utilizes the investigative staffs of the Metro–Dade Police Department, other county investigators, or investigators from the State Attorney's Office. The only prohibition, regarding the exercise of one of these last three options, is that a person cannot be assigned a case in which he is investigating his own department or an employee of that department.

The procedures for handling complaints under this system are as follows: the Panel receives a complaint; if a complaint is being lodged against a department or employee that has an internal review process, the Panel will turn the matter over to that unit for a preliminary investigation. If the department does not have an internal investigative unit, the Panel would undertake the preliminary review. The Panel then reviews the preliminary findings to determine if additional investigations are necessary or if a major investigation is appropriate given the gravity of the charges.

The Panel selects the investigator for all major cases. Once the investigation is completed, the Panel holds an open public hearing to consider the merits of the complaint. It would then produce a formal report in which it could recommend either, to the department head, a disciplinary action, or, to the State Attorney's Office, the initiation of criminal proceedings. Since the Panel is authorized to review county policies and procedures that may have been the initial sources of conflict or misunderstanding between members of the public and county departments, it is also empowered to recommend appropriate changes to mitigate such occurrences in the future.

Therefore, the legal standing of the Metropolitan Dade County Independent Review Panel is based on a county ordinance. Its independence as an oversight system is reflected at several stages in the complaints process where it has a direct role in the reception, investigation, and deliberation of the merits of cases. While the Panel is actively involved in the complaints process, it ultimately serves an advisory role in recommending to the department both an appropriate method of discipline for those employees found guilty of misconduct and in suggesting alterations in policies or procedures that may have been the actual basis for the complaint. This method of oversight is strikingly similar to the ombudsman concept as adopted in Scandinavian countries, and the people involved in the design of the system acknowledge this.

The climate of opinion had indeed changed significantly during the 1970s to the extent that the concept of civilian oversight was accorded a fair hearing in several jurisdictions throughout the United States. Detroit's Board of Police Commissioners, Chicago's Office of Professional Standards and its Police Board, and the Metropolitan Dade County Independent Review Panel represent the diversity with which oversight schemes have been implemented in the United States. One must keep in mind, however, that these are only three examples. Other municipalities, such as Berkeley (California), Cincinnati, Kansas City, and New York City, were also actively establishing civilian oversight mechanisms. The diversity of this experimentation clearly indicates that there are viable alternatives to hierarchical accountability and that democratic accountability can work if sufficient support is forthcoming from local politicians, if a significant degree of interest and commitment is expressed by the citizenry, if the oversight scheme is placed on a sound legal footing, and if civilian involvement is accorded an independent role in the complaints process.

THE THIRD CLIMATE OF OPINION: THE 1980S AND BEYOND

The political climate of the 1980s has been characterized as conservative. One of the more prominent features of that conservative expression has been the renewed interest in and support for law and order. What prompted this attitude by citizens and politicians alike has been the emergence of the national concern over illicit drug use. It is important to point out that support for greater efforts in the area of law enforcement and order maintenance were neither limited to nor the sole interest of the white community. Black citizens and politicians, especially those located in large urban areas that had been hard hit by the drugs problem, became quite vocal about the need to curtail this kind of activity.

In spite of this conservative climate, interest in civilian oversight continued throughout the 1980s. The creation of the San Francisco Office of Citizen Complaints, the San Diego Police Review Commission, and the Dallas Citizens' Police Review Board are three examples of the viability of the oversight concept during the decade. What prompted each community to action were allegations or proved cases of police misconduct. Of particular concern were instances of physical abuse perpetrated on members of a minority group. Like the oversight schemes created in the 1970s, those that have emerged in the 1980s are diverse in organizational structure, in legal standing, in both direct and indirect involvement in the actual complaints process, and in the administrative relationship to the police department that they are asked to scrutinize.

The law enforcement community remains essentially opposed to the implementation of such oversight schemes. While the rank-and-file often continue to use some of the old unfounded reasons for rejecting the concept, police executives have attempted to improve the effectiveness and veracity of their internal review systems (Police Executive Research Forum 1981). And reasoned debate over the advantages and disadvantages of hierarchical accountability as against democratic accountability occasionally appears in reputable literature on policing (Geller 1985: 147–98).

The most pressing issue in the oversight debate of the 1980s and beyond remains the question of independence. The fact that independence is such a nebulous term in this context explains in part why it is the source of so much controversy. Two methods of considering this term are utilized here. One focuses on independence as a function of the complaints process, while the other assesses the form that it should ultimately strive to achieve (Terrill, 1990).

Over the course of the past two decades the oversight systems that have been established have for the most part been assured a degree of independence in function. Functional independence is reflected in two ways, and both are equally important to the future of the oversight concept. First, the oversight scheme must gain approval through a formal legal process. The passage of the new city charter in Detroit and the changes in municipal and county ordinances in Chicago and Dade County respectively illustrate this feature well. Without legal standing the efficacy and long-term stability of these oversight schemes would have been placed in doubt at the outset.

Second, the oversight scheme must be assured a functional role in the actual process of handling citizens' complaints. This includes direct or indirect responsibility for such phases in the process as: receiving complaints, determining the authenticity of charges, investigating incidents, adjudicating or mediating issues, and imposing a sanction if officers are not exonerated in the cases. The acceptance of one of these roles but in most instances multiple roles varies with each scheme. This is to be expected as each community takes into consideration the unique political features of their municipality and the state of the political climate when the oversight scheme was proposed and eventually adopted.

Irrespective of the particular scheme, all the oversight methods that have been adopted have subscribed to the basic political tenet that their purpose is independently to help check and balance governmental power in an effort to arrest or curtail possible abuses. As alluded to earlier, this has been a long-standing feature in the democratic process of the country and was prevalent since its inception. That is what democratic accountability is all about, and civilian oversight of law enforcement is simply a variation of that theme employed in a specific context.

Acceptance of the checks and balances tenet, however, has been placed in jeopardy in recent years. The administrative efficiency school of public administration, for example, raises a significant theoretical consideration. This school subscribes to the view that public-sector organizations should strive to adopt the administrative features that are found in the private sector. This would include attempts at enhancing the degree of autonomy, centralized authority, rationality, and professionalism. Attaining these characteristics are worthy goals, but the means of achieving them can and often do suggest a change in who should control the direction of public organizations. With administrative efficiency it is suggested that there is a rise in the ascendancy of the experts and bureaucrats over those of the politicians and citizenry (Yates 1982).

A particularly troubling belief with this theory is that most of the problems associated with an organization, if not all, are technical in nature. Organizations, therefore, need only look inwards for solutions to their problems. What is totally dismissed or overlooked with this perspective is the recognition that some management problems are of a non-technical nature and that such issues might best be resolved by looking outwards to the community for possible solutions.

Some of the more recent critics of civilian oversight have adopted, either consciously or unconsciously, the position of the administrative efficiency school. They contend that police misconduct is essentially a technical flaw in the organization and that it should be addressed internally, for that is the most efficient method of resolving the problem. The endorsement and acceptance of this theory by influential political figures in municipal government could place the concept of democratic accountability at risk. Such a development would not bode well either for existing systems of civilian oversight or for the expansion of the idea to other jurisdictions.

Long before the emergence of this administrative efficiency theory, social scientists had questioned the checks-and-balances view of government, but for a different reason. They argued simply that too much emphasis and confidence had been placed in it (Dahl 1956, 1982; Lindblom 1965; Truman 1971). Their principal concern centred on the fact that the formal process of checks and balances omitted from any serious consideration the significance of the informal process of government decision-making. Acknowledging the existence of powerful interest groups in recent years has encouraged a greater recognition and awareness of this informal process. The ascendancy of experts and bureaucrats, who are proponents of the administrative efficiency theory, represent one of these more recent and important interest groups. The checks-and-balances philosophy, therefore, is not a terribly accurate portrayal of the actual distribution of political power.

The civilian oversight movement should consider this fact in the light of its current position. While one might assume by the very nature of the movement's mission that oversight schemes have achieved the status of interest groups, they have not in either their collective or individual forms established themselves as a powerful political interest group.[15] In order to attain that status, they must secure for themselves independence in form, which is significantly different from independence in function.

It has already been suggested that many civilian oversight schemes have gained functional independence in their respective communities because of their legal standing and the nature of the work that they perform. Retaining that functional independence is tied to several variables that the oversight scheme has little or no control over. They essentially include the goodwill of the mayor and city council, the support of the citizenry, and the grudging co-operation of the police department. This places oversight on rather tenuous ground if the support of the political power-brokers wanes and if the interest of citizens is diverted to other issues.

Gaining independence in form is designed to mitigate this problem. Independence in form means achieving a level of political strength within and across the various groups that make up the total community. To date this has not been explored, let alone attempted, as the principal goal within most local civilian oversight movements is still to secure the survival of the idea.

Although civilian oversight has had the general support and goodwill of those who look after the interests of the politically disenfranchised, the intensity of that support can and has waned throughout the decade of the 1980s. For some the civil rights movement appears to be in a state of retreat, or it has at least directed its efforts elsewhere. Mayors and city council members appear uninterested, or more appropriately, distracted from issues of police misconduct when drug abuse is ravaging their cities. And in

---

[15] See e.g. David Truman's definition of an interest group as: 'A shared-attitude group that makes certain claims upon other groups in society. If and when it makes its claims through or upon any of the institutions of government, it becomes a political interest group.' (Truman 1971: 37.)

this particular context citizens are often sceptical of scrutinizing the tactics of police too closely when they consider the heightened dangers of the tasks they are expected to perform.

By building a broader constituency, civilian oversight could shed its dependency on the goodwill of this small group of political players for its survival. To achieve that goal, the leadership of oversight systems must plan a proactive strategy of educating the politically enfranchised to the merits of civilian oversight. Independence in form does not mean abandoning the co-operative efforts that were such an important feature in the initial development of oversight schemes. That kind of co-operation must continue of course, particularly with the police department, for that is essential to the total oversight mission of enhancing and assuring the integrity of the law enforcement agency. But without a concerted effort to assure a degree of independence in form, civilian oversight will remain on tenuous ground and subject to the whims of a small group for its survival. That would indeed prove unfortunate for the viability of democratic accountability in general and the experiments with civilian oversight in particular.

SUMMARY

This essay attempted to explain the setbacks and advancements in the development of civilian oversight mechanisms in the United States. The approach examined the issue in the evolutionary context of three distinct climates of opinion. The first included the period of the late 1950s and 1960s, when the city of Philadelphia attempted but failed to implement a civilian review board. The second period essentially covered the 1970s, when several attempts at oversight were successful at achieving a degree of legitimacy and permanency in the complaints process. The success of those efforts was made possible by establishing each oversight scheme on a sound legal footing and by providing it with some functional degree of independence in the handling of citizens' complaints. The third period covered the 1980s and beyond. While it recognizes the continued success of establishing oversight schemes, it warns that the idea of civilian oversight could be placed at risk unless proponents of the concept take a more proactive approach in ensuring that the oversight schemes achieve a degree of independence in form. It was suggested that this be accomplished by building a broader constituency for the idea of civilian oversight, since the intensity of the earlier support appears to have waned with the emergence of new issues on the political agenda.

REFERENCES

Anon. (1977) 'Developments in the Law Section 1983 and Federalism', *Harvard Law Review* 90: 1133–361.
Barker, T., and Carter, D. (eds.) (1986) *Police Deviance* (Cincinnati: Anderson Publishing Company).
Beral, H., and Sisk, M. (1963) 'The Administration of Complaints By Civilians Against The Police', *Harvard Law Review* 77: 499–519.
Bittner, E. (1980) *The Functions Of The Police In Modern Society* (Cambridge, Mass.: Oelgeschlager, Gunn, and Hain).
Black, A. D. (1968) *The People and the Police* (New York: McGraw-Hill).
Carter, G. E., Cardinal (1979) *Report to the Civic Authorities of Metropolitan Toronto and Its Citizens* (Toronto: Office of the Cardinal).
Chevigny, P. (1969) *Police Power* (New York: Vintage Books).
City of Detroit Charter (1974).
Coxe, S. (1961) 'Police Advisory Board: The Philadelphia Story', *Connecticut Bar Journal* 35: 138–55.
—— (1965) 'The Philadelphia Police Advisory Board', *Law in Transition Quarterly* 2: 179–85.
Dahl, R. A. (1956) *A Preface to Democratic Theory* (Chicago: University of Chicago Press).
—— (1982) *Dilemmas of Pluralist Democracy: Autonomy v. Control* (New Haven: Yale University Press).
Davis, K. C. (1975) *Police Discretion* (St Paul: West Publishing Company).
Davis, L. B. *et al.* (1978–9) 'Suing the Police in Federal Court', *Yale Law Journal* 88: 781–824.
Escobedo v. *Illinois* (1964) 378 US 478.
Fogel, D. (1987) 'The Investigation and Disciplining of Police Misconduct: A Comparative View—London, Paris, Chicago', *Police Studies* 10: 1–15.
Foote, C. (1954–5) 'Tort Remedies For Police Violations of Individual Rights', *Minnesota Law Review* 39: 493–516.
Gaynor, W. J. (1903) 'Lawlessness of the Police in New York', *North American Review* 176: 10–26.
Geller, W. A. (ed.) (1985) *Police Leadership in America* (New York: Praeger).
Gideon v. *Wainwright* (1963) 372 US 335.
Goldman, R. and Puro, S. (1987) 'Decertification of Police: An Alternative to Traditional Remedies for Police Misconduct', *Hastings Constitutional Law Quarterly* 15: 45–80.

Harrington v. *Tate* (1969) 435 Pa. 176.

Hudson, J. R. (1968) 'The Civilian Review Board Issues as Illuminated by the Philadelphia Experience', *Criminologica* 6: 16–29.

—— (1971) 'Police Review Boards and Police Accountability', *Law and Contemporary Problems* 36: 515–38.

—— (1972) 'Organizational Aspects of Internal and External Review of the Police', *Journal of Criminal Law, Criminolgy, and Police Science* 63: 427–32.

Kingdon, J. W. (1984) *Agendas, Alternatives, and Public Policies* (Boston: Little, Brown, and Company).

Knapp, W. (1972) *The Knapp Commission Report on Police Corruption* (New York: George Braziller).

Lenzi, M. A. (1974–5) 'Reviewing Civilian Complaints Of Police Misconduct', *Temple Law Quarterly* 48: 89–125.

Letman, S. T. (Jan. 1980) 'Chicago's Answer to Police Brutality: The Office of Professional Standards', *The Police Chief* 16–17.

Lindblom, C. E. (1965) *The Intelligence of Democracy Decision Making Through Mutual Adjustment* (New York: The Free Press).

Linden, S. B. (1982) *Interim Report on the Activities of the Office of the Public Complaints Commissioner from July 23, 1981 to December 20, 1981* (Toronto: Office of Public Complaints Commissioner).

Littlejohn, E. J. (1981) 'The Cries of the Wounded: A History of Police Misconduct in Detroit', *The University of Detroit Journal of Urban Law* 58: 177–219.

Locke, H. G. (1969) *The Detroit Riot of 1967* (Detroit: Wayne State University).

Lundman, R. J. (ed.) (1980) *Police Behavior: A Sociological Perspective* (New York: Oxford University Press).

Manning, P. K., and van Maanen, J. (eds.) (1978) *Policing: A View from the Street* (Santa Monica: Goodyear Publishing Company).

Mapp v. *Ohio* (1961) 367 US 643.

Metcalfe Panel (1973) 'The Metcalfe Report on the Misuse of Police Authority in Chicago', *Public Defender*, Chicago, IL.

Metropolitan Dade County Independent Review Panel (1983) *The First Three Years* (Miami: Metropolitan Dade County Independent Review Board).

Miranda v. *Arizona* (1966) 384 US 436.

Monell v. *New York Department of Social Services* (1978) 436 US 658.

Monroe v. *Pape* (1961) 365 US 167.

Moss, F. (1901) 'National Danger from Police Corruption', *North American Review* 173: 470–80.

Muir, W. K., jun. (1977) *Police: Streetcorner Politicians* (Chicago: University of Chicago Press).

National Advisory Commission on Civil Disorders (1968) (Washington DC: GPO).

National Advisory Commission on Criminal Justice Standards and Goals (1973) *Police* (Washington DC: GPO).

National Commission on Law Observance and Enforcement (1931) *Report on Lawlessness in Law Enforcement* (Washington DC: GPO).

Newman, J. O. (1978) 'Suing the Lawbreakers: Proposals to Strengthen the Section 1983 Damage Remedy for Law Enforcers' Misconduct', *Yale Law Journal* 87: 447–67.

Niederhoffer, A. (1967) *Behind the Shield: The Police in Urban Society* (Garden City: Anchor Books).

Police Advisory Board (1959) *First Annual Report of the Police Advisory Board of the City of Philadelphia.*

—— (1960) *Second Annual Report of the Police Advisory Board of the City of Philadelphia.*

—— (1967) *Ninth Annual Report of the Police Advisory Board of the City of Philadelphia.*

Police Chief (Feb. 1964, p. 34).

Police Executive Research Forum (1981) *Police Agency Handling of Citizen Complaints: A Model Policy Statement* (Washington DC).

President's Commission on Law Enforcement and the Administration of Justice (1967) *Task Force Report: The Police* (Washington DC: GPO).

Punch, M. (1985) *Conduct Unbecoming* (London: Tavistock Publications).

—— (ed.) (1983) *Control in the Police Organization* (Cambridge: MIT Press).

Scarman, Lord (1981) *The Brixton Disorders 10–12 April 1981*, Cmnd. 8427 (London: HMSO).

Schmidt, W. W. (1976) 'Recent Developments in Police Civil Liability', *Journal of Police Science and Administration* 4: 197–202.

Shearing, C. D. (ed.) (1981) *Organizational Police Deviance* (Toronto: Butterworths).

Sherman, L. W. (1978) *Scandal and Reform Controlling Police Corruption* (Berkeley: University of California Press).

Terrill, R. J. (1980) 'Complaint Procedures Against Police: The Movement for Change in England, Canada, and Australia', *Police Studies* 3: 37–46.

—— (1982) 'Complaint Procedures: Variations on the Theme of Civilian Participation', *Journal of Police Science and Administration* 10: 398–406.

—— (1983) 'Complaints Against Police in England', *American Journal of Comparative Law* 31: 599–626.

—— (1988) 'Police Accountability in Philadelphia: Retrospects and Prospects', *American Journal of Police* 7: 79–99.

—— (1990) 'Alternative Perceptions of Independence in Civilian Oversight', *Journal of Police Science and Administration* 17: 77–83.

Truman, D. B. (1971) *The Governmental Process: Political Interests and Public Opinion*, 2nd edn. (New York: Knopf).

United States Commission on Civil Rights (1961) *The 50 States Report* (Washington DC: GPO).

—— (1981) *Who is Guarding the Guardians? A Report on Police Practices* (Washington DC: GPO).

Ward, R., McCormack, R., and Bracey, D. (eds.) (1987) *Managing Police Corruption: International Perspectives* (Chicago: Office of International Criminal Justice).

Williams, G. H. (1984) *The Law and Politics of Police Discretion* (Westport: Greenwood Press).

Yates, D. (1982) *Bureaucratic Democracy* (Cambridge, Mass.: Harvard University Press).

Index

Abel, R. 18, 20, 31
Aborigines, deaths in custody 85
'Age Tapes' 139
A/G NSW v. Perpetual Trustee Co.
  Ltd. (1955) 126 n.
Aickin, J. 138
Alderson, John 121 n.
Arthur, P. 238
Association of Chief Police Officers
  (UK) 212, 215
Australia:
  'Age Tapes' 90
  Aborigines, deaths in custody 85
  Australian Law Reform Commis-
    sion Reports (1975, 1978) 39–41,
    65, 116, 119, 132, 134, 137, 143,
    144–6
  Australian, The 90
  judiciary, role of 135–9
  law reform 8, 78–81, 96–7, 115–48;
    accountability of police, and
    143–7; failure of legislature
    133–5; judicial reform 135–9;
    new principle reform 140–4;
    and randomness of 118–20, 141,
    142; and social change 132–9;
    and society specific 118, 140
  Liberal Party 68
  Melbourne Age, The 22, 77, 85, 88,
    90, 106–7
  Missen Report (1979) 134
  National Crime Authority 79, 147
  New South Wales Ombudsman 27,
    42–5, 66, 144–5
  Queensland: Criminal Justice
    Commission 48–50, 51; Fitz-
    gerald Commission 1, 19–27, 30,
    31, 37, 48–50, 66, 73, 94, 98, 100,
    105–6, 109, 119, 124; Internal
    Investigations Sector 1; Police
    Complaints Tribunal 37, 146–7
  Royal Commission on Drug-
    Trafficking (Stewart, 1983) 25,
    27, 41, 42
  South Australia 45, 116, 143;

  Grieve Committee (1983) 45,
    46, 116, 143; Mitchell Committee
    143; Police Complaints Authority
    45–8; Report of Royal Commis-
    sion into September Moratorium
    Demonstration (1970) 121
  Sydney Morning Herald 66
  Victoria 22, 26–32 passim; Beach
    Board of Inquiry (1978) 22, 23,
    119, 145; Council for Civil
    Liberties 89, 107; Federation of
    Community Legal Centres 85,
    90; Freedom of Information Act
    (1984) 89; Inquiry into Police
    Misconduct (1978) 21; Law
    Reform Commission 89; Legal
    Aid Commission 89; Minister for
    Police and Emergency Services
    81–2, 89, 90; Police (Powers of
    Investigation Bill) 1987 69; Police
    Regulation Act 1958 69 n; Police
    Regulation (Allegations of Mis-
    conduct) Act 1987 144; Police
    Regulation (Amendment) Act
    1985 69, 78, 103 n; Society of
    Labor Lawyers 90; Supporters
    of Law and Order 89
  see also Victoria Police Complaints
    Authority

Barnhill, E. A. 99
Barton, P. 34
Bayley, D. 48, 54
Beach Board of Inquiry (Victoria,
  1978) 22, 23, 119, 145
Beccaria 211
Best, A. 16 n.
Bittner, E. 122–3, 128, 132–3, 264
Booth v. Dillon (1976) 145
Boyd v. Ombudsman and Others (1983)
  144
British Crime Survey (1988) 179, 192,
  202
Brixton Riots (London, 1981) 17
  see also Scarman

Brown, D. 25 n, 190
Brown, M. K. 261, 264–8, 273
Brown v. *Board of Education* (1954)
　299
Buckner, H. T. 264
Bunning v. *Cross* (1978) 137–8

Caiden, G. 38
Cain, Premier 67
Canada:
　Bar Association 168
　British Columbia 170
　Charter of Rights and Freedom 165
　Council on Race Relations and
　　Policing 168
　Criminal Lawyers Association 168
　Maloney Inquiry (1975) 20, 31, 154
　Manitoba 169
　Metropolitan Toronto Police Force
　　Complaints Act (1984) 154, 165
　Ontario 1, 155, 173–4
　Public Complaints Commissioner
　　(Metropolitan Toronto), *see*
　　Public Complaints Commis-
　　sioner (Metropolitan Toronto)
　Quebec 169
　Royal Canadian Mounted Police
　　169
　Toronto Complaints Authority
　　8–9, 280–1
　Urban Alliance on Race Relations
　　168
Castan, R. 103
Castles, A. 136, 140, 142
Cavanagh, Jerome P. 306
Chesshyre, R. 75, 93, 94, 101 n.,
　102 n.
Chicago Office of Professional
　Standards 36–7, 156, 262, 263,
　278, 309–11, 313
chief constables 9, 180, 211–29
　belief in internal investigation
　　221–6
　opposition to independent system
　　216–17, 219–23
　Police Complaints Authority, and
　　214–15, 217, 219, 225–6
　Police Federation, and 215, 217,
　　222
　public confidence, attitude to, and
　　219–23, 227–8

　role in complaints adjudication
　　214–15
　support for independent system
　　219–23
Christianson, S. 110
Ciocarelli, B. 102
citizen review boards 33–8, 68 n.,
　101n., 264, 275, 300, 304
Chicago Office of Professional
　Standards 36–7, 156, 262, 263,
　278, 309–11, 313
Detroit Board of Police Commis-
　sioners 36–7, 156, 306–8, 313
Metropolitan Dade County
　Independent Review Panel 311–
　14
Philadelphia Police Review Board
　34, 156, 297–303, 304, 318
police opposition to 33–5
civilianization of complaints
　procedures 8–9, 153, 169, 171
Cleveland Police Patrolmen's
　Assocation 271
Clothier, C. 217, 225
Coe, R. M. 99
community policing 54, 128, 261,
　266
complaints against police:
　characteristics of 16–19, 84–6, 172,
　228
　civilianization of mechanisms 8–9,
　　153, 169, 171
　complainants: rights of 162–3;
　　satisfaction of 189–91, 200–1,
　　226–7; vexatious 94–6
　conciliation of 278, 281
　desirability of 52
　failure to complain 20–1
　mechanisms and public confidence
　　2–4, 9, 19, 21, 24, 31, 35–6
　police deterrence of 21–3, 74
　processing of 28–31, 160–2, 183–5,
　　278–80, 281
　substantiation rates 25–6, 29, 73,
　　187, 204, 251
　under-recording of 21–4, 181
　see also external review, police, self-
　　regulation
conflict theory 123–9
Conlisk, J. B. 262
Constabulary Act (NI) (1922) 236

Constabulary (Ireland) Act (1836) 244
Corbett, C. 179
County and Borough Police Force Act
1859 (UK) 179
Coxe, S. 303
Cunningham, Andrew 48 n.

Daley, Richard J. 262
Detroit Board of Police Commis-
sioners 36–7, 156, 306–8, 313
Dilworth, Richardson 298–9, 300
disputes, anthropology of 21, 23
Doig, J. 55
Duncan, R. 99, 100

Enderby, K. 143
Enever (1906) 126 n.
English Law Commission 141
Escobedo v. *Illinois* (1964) 292 n.,
301 n.
Eskridge, W. 135
European Convention on Human
Rights 239, 252
evidence in police disciplinary charges
186, 204
exclusionary rule of evidence 117,
137–9, 301 n.
external agencies 7–9
see also citizen review boards;
external review; Public
Complaints Commissioner
(Metropolitan Toronto); Victoria
Police Complaints Authority
external review:
demands for 14, 291–5
educative role of 55–6, 192–3
effect on internal systems 14–16,
28, 30–1, 54
'interpolable balance' 51, 54–6
modes of supervision 194–8
ombudsman model of 38–50, 109,
147, 275; Australian Law
Reform Commission model
39–42, 43, 65; definition of 38;
ex post v. *ex ante* issues 49–50;
New South Wales Ombudsman
42–5; Queensland Criminal
Justice Commission, and 48;
South Australia Police
Complaints Authority, and 45–8
see also citizen review boards;

police; Public Complaints
Commissioner (Metropolitan
Toronto); Victorian Police
Complaints Authority

Felstiner, W. 18, 20, 21, 31
Findlay, M. 28
Fisher v. *Oldman Corporation* 126 n.
Fitzgerald Commission (Queensland,
1989) 19, 20, 22–3, 25–7, 30, 31,
48, 66, 73, 94, 98, 100, 105–6,
109, 119, 124
Fitzgerald, Commissioner 1, 3
Fraternal Order of Police 33, 300, 302
Freckelton, I. 7, 8, 11, 14 n., 20,
40 n., 57

Gelhorn, W. 23, 33, 35, 39
Gideon v. *Wainwright* (1963) 301 n.
Goldsmith, A. 65, 130, 162, 169, 170
Goldstein, H. 26, 30
Goode, M. 7, 8, 14, 46
Gould, S. J. 119
Government of Ireland Act 1920 235
Grabosky, P. 77
Gray, J. 24, 25 n.
Graziano, A. M. 72
Grieve Committee (South Australia,
1983) 45, 46, 116, 143

Hall, R. 100 n.
Harrington v. *Tate* (1969) 303
Hart, H. L. A. 16
Hay, Trevor, 106
Hazlehurst, K. 86
Hermon, Sir John 243
Hill, L. 38
Hirschman, A. 18, 19, 20
Hodgson, D. 141
Hodgson, J. 33–4
Hogg, R. 28
Home Affairs Committee Inquiry into
Police Complaints Procedure
(UK) 212
Hong Kong Police 223–4
Hood, C. 51
Hoover, Herbert 259

Igleburger, Chief R. 266–7
Imbert, Sir Peter 228
Ingber, S. 120 n.

internal investigation, *see* self-
regulation by police
International Association for Civilian
Oversight of Law Enforcement
(IACOLE) 10, 174
International Association of Chiefs of
Police 301–2
International Bar Association 38
International Commission of Red
Cross 239

Jefferson, Thomas 296
Johnson, J. M. 67 n.
Johnson, Lyndon 304
judiciary, role of 135–9

Kahn-Freund, O. 256
Kamenka, E. 136
Kelling, G. L. 259, 266, 267
Kennison v *Daire* (1986) 131
Kerner, Hon. Ott. 260 n.
Kerstetter, W. A. 264, 265, 268, 274
Kessler, R. 132
Kirby, M. 24, 139, 143
Klein, D. 100 n.
Knapp Commission (New York) 41

labelling theory 211
Lackersteen v. *Jones and Others* (1988)
126 n.
Law Enforcement Review Act (1982)
(Canada) 169
law reform 4–5, 8, 78–81, 96–7, 115–
48
conflict theory 124–9
failure of legislation 133–5
exclusionary rule of evidence 117
judicial reform, and 135–9
new principle reform 140–4, 148
overcriminalization argument
129–32
police accountability, and 143–7
randomness 118–20, 141, 142
social change, and 132–9
society specific reform 118, 140
vicarious liability 117
Law Society (UK) 215
Levine, J. 136
Lewis, C. 8–9
Linden, S. 155, 157, 280
Lippitt, R. 100 n.

Littlejohn, E. 36, 67 n., 73 n.
Locke, John 296
London Policing Strategy Unit 20
Lustgarten, L. 25, 32 n., 73, 126 n.,
186

McCarthy, Senator Joseph 300
MacDermot, N. 38
McDuffie, A. 311
Machiavelli, N. 99
Maguire, M. 7, 9, 51
Maloney, Arthur, QC 154
Maloney Inquiry (Canada, 1975) 20,
31, 154
Mapp v. *Ohio* (1961) 292 n., 301 n.
Mark, Robert 182
Masterman, George, QC 45
media, the 14, 25 n., 76–7, 84–5, 91,
93, 104–8
Metcalfe Report (Chicago, 1973)
262–3, 309
Metropolitan Dade County Independ-
ent Review Panel 311–14
see also citizen review boards
Metropolitan Police Force Complaints
Project Act (Ontario, 1981) 154
*Metropolitan Toronto Police Complaints
Board and Weller, Re* (1987) 165
Metropolitan Toronto Police Force
Complaints Act 1984 154, 165
Miranda v. *Arizona* (1966) 292 n.,
301 n.
Missen Report (Australia, 1979) 134
Mitchell Committee (South Australia,
1974) 143
Mitchell, Dame Roma 143 n.
Monell v. *New York Department of
Social Services* (1978) 292
Monroe v. *Pape* (1961) 292 n.
Montesquieu, Baron de 296
Morris, N   128
Muir, W. K. 261, 264
Murphy, Thomas, J. 267

Nader, L. 20, 21, 23, 31
National Council for Civil Liberties
(UK) 215
National Crime Authority (Australia)
79, 147
National Crime Authority Act (1984)
(Cth) (Australia) 79 n.

neighbourhood watch schemes 54, 126
Nelson, P. 27, 71 n.
New York 297
  Knapp Commission 41
  Police Department 275
  Referendum (1966) 270
Nichols, John F. 306
Nonet, P. 15
Northern Ireland 9–10, 233–56
  Advisory Committee on Police in NI (1969) 236, 244
  Amnesty International reports 239, 240, 253
  Anglo-Irish Agreement (1985) 238, 256
  armed forces, presence of 235
  Association of Forensic Medical Officers 253
  Bennett Committee 240, 242–4, 253
  Black Committee 252, 254
  Cameron Report (1969) 244, 248
  Committee for Administration of Justice 247
  Complaints and Discipline Branch (RUC) 238
  Director of Public Prosecutions 254
  emergency legislation 235
  European Convention on Human Rights, and 239, 252
  Gardiner Report (1975) 245
  Independent Commission for Police Complaints 248, 251, 254
  legislative provisions 250–4
  Northern Ireland Constitutional Proposals (1973) 245
  Police Authority 241–3
  Police Complaints Board 246, 251, 253
  police complaints system 238, 244–50, 255
  Police Federation 250
  Republic of Ireland, and 238–9
  Royal Ulster Constabulary 235–8, 240–4, 251, 253–6
  Secretary of State for NI 243
  'shoot to kill' policy 237
  Stalker Inquiry 240
  substantiation rates 251
  Troubles, the 234–5, 237, 239, 251

Ulsterization of security matters 235–6

Odom, Dr H. 261
ombudsman model of review, *see* external review
Ombudsman v. *Moroney* (1983) 144
Ontario Race Relations and Policing Task Force 1, 173, 174
overcriminalization argument 123, 129–32

Packer, H. 16
Paul Jurcisin et al. v. *Cuyahoga Board of Elections et al.* (1986) 271 n.
Peelers, the 125
Petersen, Sir Joh Bjelke-63
Petterson, W. E. 6, 7, 10
Philadelphia Police Review Board 34, 156, 297–303, 304, 318
Pittsburgh Police Department 267
police:
  and civilian review boards 33–5
  community relations 3–4, 17, 23–4, 54, 120–3
  conservatism of 98, 100, 122 n.
  discipline 28–31, 187–9
  'constabulary independence' 2–3
  discretion 16, 178, 293
  group loyalty 22, 24, 100–3, 293
  legitimacy of institution 3–4, 9, 125, 132
  misconduct 24–5, 29, 83; deterrence approach to 212–14; and legal controls 116, 137; organizationally located 14, 125, 131, 170, 292, 316; rotten apple theory 9, 41, 222; sanctions against 29–30, 159; vicarious liability for 117
  negative stereotyping 17
  obstruction of reporting complaints 21–3, 74
  opposition to external review 32–5, 51–4, 69–72, 81–2, 86, 98–103, 155, 161, 164–72, 192, 300, 305
  politicization of 67–9, 92–3, 99, 101
  public confidence in 2–4, 9, 19, 21, 24, 31, 35–6, 177, 178, 219–23, 227–8
  street-level officers 14, 16–17, 48

police (*cont.*):
support for independent review
219–23
see also chief constables; complaints;
external review; policing; self-
regulation
Police Act (1964) (UK) 177, 241
Police Act (NI) 1970 236, 241–9
passim
Police Act RSQ 1988 (Canada) 169 n.
Police Complaints Authority (UK) 9,
179, 182, 187, 192–202 *passim*,
214–15, 217, 219
Police Complaints Authority
(Victoria) 8
Police (Complaints) (Mandatory
Referrals, etc.) Regulations 1985
(UK) 71 n.
Police and Criminal Evidence Act
1985 (UK) 9, 71 n., 178, 179,
183–6, 218, 219, 247
Police and Criminal Evidence Act (NI)
Order 1989 254
Police Federation (UK) 215, 217,
220, 222
Police (NI) Order 1987 239, 241, 247,
248, 250
Police (Powers of Investigation) Bill
1987 (Victoria) 69
Police Regulation Act 1958 (Victoria)
69 n.
Police Regulation (Allegations of Misconduct) Act 1978 (Victoria) 144
Police Regulation (Amendment) Act
1985 (Victoria) 69, 78, 103 n.
Police Services Act 1989 (Canada) 168
policing:
community policing 54, 128, 261,
266
history of 124–9
order-maintenance 16
of public protests 120–3
Porter, R. 245
precedent, doctrine of 137
Public Complaints Commissioner
(Metropolitan Toronto) 153–74
accountability of police, and 153–4
characteristics of complaints 172
civilian boards of inquiry 162,
163–4
fairness of 172

legislative background 154–7
penalties 159
Police Association 161, 165, 166
police challenges 164–9
police, initial investigation by
159–60
Public Complaints Investigation
Bureau 158–9
race relations, and 172
structure of 157–64

Queensland, *see* Australia

R v. *Hampshire County Council ex parte
Ellerton* (1985) 204
Radelet, L. 53
Ramsay v. *The Chief of Police for
Metropolitan Toronto et al.* (1988)
170
Reiner, R. 3, 7, 9, 48
Rice, F. 263
Richardson, J. 73, 82, 107
Richardson Report, *see* Victorian
Police Complaints Authority
Rochester Citizen Review Board 34
Rochford, James 263
Royal Commission of Inquiry into
Drug-Trafficking (Australia,
1983) 25, 27, 41, 42
Royal Commission on Criminal
Procedure Report (UK, 1981)
247
Royal Commission on the Police (UK,
1962), 177, 180, 181
Rumbaut, R. 122–3, 128, 132–3

Sackville, R. 140
Salisbury, Harold 116
Sallman, P. 120
Sandler, A. 38
San Francisco Office of Citizens'
Complaints 275, 278
*San Francisco Police Officers' Associa-
tion* v. *Superior Court* (1988) 270
Sarat, A. 18, 20, 31
Scarman, Lord 1, 3, 13
Scarman Report: The Brixton Dis-
orders (UK, 1982) 1, 17, 20, 21,
30, 31, 246
Schuck, P. 16
Scott, Nicholas 247

Selby, Hugh 27, 29, 96, 104 n.
Selby v. *McCrohan* (1988) 70, 146
Select Committee (1834) (UK) 179
self-regulation by police:
    disciplinary sytems, and 29–30
    failure of 19–31
    investigative techniques 74–5
    lack of investigative zeal 26–7, 73–4
    public support for 24, 221–6
    public dissatisfaction with 19–20,
        181–2, 192, 219–23, 227–8
    sanctions against misconduct
        29–30, 159
    uncertainty of objectives 29
Skolnick, J. 14
Smith, D. 24, 25 n.
South Australia, *see* Australia
Stephen, J. 138
Stewart, Mr J. 25
St Johnston, Sir Eric 22. 65
stop and search powers 20
Storch, R. 128 n.
street-level officers 14, 16–17, 48
Sumner, C. 118, 124–5, 131 n.
support units 188 n.
Sydney Morning Herald 66

Task Force Inquiry (USA, 1967) 20
Tate, James 302
Tay, A. 136
Taylor, I. 120
Terrill, R. 7, 10, 28
Topping, I. 7, 9
Toronto, *see* Metropolitan Toronto
Truman, D. 317

United Kingdom 9, 120, 125–7,
        177–208
    Association of Chief Police Officers
        212, 215
    British Crime Survey (1988) 179,
        192, 202
    Brixton Riots (1981) 17; *see also*
        Scarman, Lord
    Chief Constables, *see* Chief
        Constables
    complaints against police: difficulty
        proving cases 186, 204; handling
        procedures 183–5; informal
        resolution procedure 191, 205

complainant satisfaction 189–91,
        200–1
Director of Public Prosecutions
        180, 185–6
English Law Commission 141
history of complaints system
        179–86
Home Affairs Committee Inquiry
        into Police Complaints Procedure
        212
Law Society 215
London 20, 24, 177
Metropolitan Police 25
National Council for Civil Liberties
        215
Police Complaints Authority 9,
        179, 182–208 *passim*, 214–15,
        217, 219, 225–6; complainant
        satisfaction 189–90; effectiveness
        of supervision 198–202; modes of
        supervision 194–8; Police and
        Criminal Evidence Act 1985
        183–6; public confidence 192–3;
        recommendations of 192–3;
        substantiation rates 187–8
Police Complaints Board 182, 186,
        187
Police (Complaints) (Mandatory
        Referrals, etc.) Regulations 1985
        71 n.
Police and Criminal Evidence Act
        1985 9, 71 n., 178, 179, 183–6,
        218, 219, 247
police discipline, maintenance of
        186–9
Police Federation 215, 217, 220, 222
public confidence in police 195,
        205, 219–23, 227–8
Royal Commission on the Police
        (1962) 177, 180, 181
Royal Commission on Police Powers
        and Procedures (1929) 181
Scarman Report: The Brixton Dis-
        orders (1982) 1, 17, 20, 21, 30,
        31, 246
section 88 cases 195, 197
see also Northern Ireland
United States 10–11, 33, 35, 121–3,
        125, 156, 259–83, 291–319
    American Civil Liberties Union
        298, 299

United Kingdom (*cont.*):
 background to reform 261–9, 291–5
California 270
cannabis, criminalization of 129 n.
civil rights movement 294–5, 299, 305, 317
Chicago Bar Association 262
civilian oversight in 259–83;
 arguments in favour 269–73; and civil rights 294–5, 299, 305, 317; forms of 273–7; handling of complaints 278–80, 294; independence of 315–18; ombudsman model of 275; police opposition to 270–2, 305, 307; police review boards 275–6; *see also* citizen review boards
Cleveland, City of 271, 275–7, 280
Constitution 296
Dallas Citizens Police Review Board 314
Dayton, Ohio, Police Department 267
Democratic Party 267
Fraternal Order of Police 33, 300, 302
local self-government, importance of 296
Metcalfe Report (Chicago, 1973) 309
National Association for Advancement of Colored Peoples 299
New York 297; Knapp Commission 41; Police Department 275; Referendum (1966) 270
Philadelphia Police Review Board 34, 156, 297–303, 318
Pittsburgh 267
police-community relations 264–7
Police Executive Research Forum 274, 291, 314
political ideology 295–7
President's Commission on Law Enforcement and Administration of Justice 260, 291, 304
professionalization of police 260, 265–6
race relations 262–3, 299–300, 306
San Diego Police Review Commission 314

San Francisco Office of Citizens' Complaints 275, 278, 314
Task Force Inquiry (1967) 20
Wickersham Commission 259–60
Wisconsin 270 n.

vagrancy 128 n.
vicarious liability for police misconduct 117
victimless crimes 130–1
Victorian Council for Civil Liberties 89, 107
Victorian Inquiry into Police Misconduct (1978) 21
Victorian Police Complaints Authority 8, 29, 40, 63–110, 145–6
 anti-bureaucratism 97–8
 background to formation 65–7
 characteristics of complaints 84–6
 independence of 92–4, 103–4
 Internal Investigation Department, Victoria Police, and 72, 81–2, 90, 106
 legislative problems 69, 78–81, 86, 91, 96–7
 length of inquiries 75
 media, and 76–7, 84–5, 91, 93, 104–5, 106–8
 Ombudsman, and 88, 145
 police and: attitude to complainants 73–4; obstruction of 84–5, 86–7, 101; politicization 67–9; resistance to reform 98–103
 reformist approach 86–7
 Richardson Report (1987) 82–3, 89, 104
 termination of 86, 87–91
 vexatious complainants 94–6
 Victoria Government, and 87–91, 103, 104
 Victoria Police, and 81–2, 83, 87, 98–103; Sexual Offences Squad 84–5
 Victoria Police Assocation, and 68, 70, 81, 92–3, 99
Voumard, S. 64

Walker, S. 14 n.
Walsh-Buckley, W. 28
Walton, P. 119, 120
Washington, Harold 262, 263

Wasserman, R. 259
Watson, A. 4, 118 n.
Watson, G. 100
Weinrott, Judge Leo 302–3
Wesley, B. 100
Wilenski, P. 69 n., 93, 97
Williams, G. 14 n.
Williams, H. 259
Wilson, G. 5
Wilson, P. 64

Wisconsin, State of 270 n.
Wright v. *McQualter* (1970) 121 n.

Yalden, Maxwell 174
Young, Coleman A. 306
Young, J. 119, 120

Zaltman, G. 99
Zander, M. 142 n.